LITERARY CRITICISM AND SOCIOLOGY

YEARBOOK OF
COMPARATIVE CRITICISM

VOLUME V

Literary

Criticism and

Sociology

Edited by

Joseph P. Strelka

THE PENNSYLVANIA STATE
UNIVERSITY PRESS
University Park and London

Library of Congress Cataloging in Publication Data

Strelka, Joseph, 1927–
    Literary criticism and sociology.

    (Yearbook of comparative criticism, v. 5)
        1. Criticism—Addresses, essays, lectures.
2. Literature and society. I. Title. II. Series.
PN98.S6S8   801'.95   72–136963
ISBN 0–271–01152–1

Library of Congress Catalog Card Number 72–136963
International Standard Book Number 0–271–01152–1
    Printed in the United States of America
    by Heritage Printers, Inc.

    Designed by Marilyn Shobaken

CONTENTS

PREFACE

ACCORDING TO RENÉ WELLEK, "A LARGE MAJORITY OF THE QUESTIONS raised by literary study are at least ultimately or by implication, social questions."[1] Wellek then proceeds to demonstrate all the major possibilities of the sociological approach to literary criticism. These possibilities are so numerous that only a selection of the most important ones can be included in a book of this scope. However, within the broad range of relations between literature and sociology there are many possible perspectives which lead to valid conclusions, although there are some which lead to methodological error from the viewpoint of literary criticism. The most common fallacy from this viewpoint is the perversion of the literary work from a subject having its own ontological value to mere material for sociological investigation. The latter approach is perfectly legitimate for the sociologist, whereas for the literary critic it leads perforce to the heinous crime of sociologism. Nevertheless, some studies of literature on the part of sociologists can be most helpful in providing the literary critic with important and interesting insights and suggestions, and such studies can be utilized by literary criticism as material. Currently, one of the most fashionable types of specific errors resulting from literary critics' use of sociological methods is the axiological or judicial criticism, which is based on prejudices stemming from the application of political or ideological criteria. The proponents of this method are "not only students of literature and society but prophets of the future, monitors, propagandists; and they have difficulty in keeping these two functions separate"[2]—their studies are without merit as literary criticism.

I once attempted a systematic and comprehensive cross-section of the possibilities and limitations of sociological methods as applied to literary criticism.[3] A comparison of this methodological scheme with the topics of the contributions contained herein shows that, although these essays do not by any means exhaust the broad spectrum of possibilities, they do comprise a certain unity. They are highly valuable as a collection because they cover some of the most important perspectives of the problem from different angles, either by presenting model cases or by synthesizing basic results and summarizing the present state of the study of the problems.

The four literary scholars who have contributed the basic comprehensive essays dealing with the general problems of theory apparently could easily find a common ground of understanding, even though they sometimes differ in their placement of emphasis. The differences increase as we proceed from the first part and its general theoretical contiguity to the more practical and historical contributions of the second part. The divergence becomes more visible here not only because of the greater variety of the topics, but also because the contributing literary critics, sociologists, and cultural anthropologist hold differing points of view. Yet beyond all the differences are common interest in the subject matter and, to some extent, concurrence in conclusions.

In regard to the third part, I regret particularly that the essay dealing with France's contribution did not arrive in time to be included. I also very much regret that the untimely death of Hugh Dalziel Duncan deprived us of one of the most fundamental contributions, which was to have dealt with the key role played by a particular kind of symbolism in the sociological patterns that characterize the interrelationship of life and letters. This symbolism is embedded within the complicated and complex structure of language which constitutes the literary work; it is a symbolism that corresponds to the cluster of symbolic roles which every institution represents. Duncan had started to analyze it as he saw it: "If symbolic expression is so much a part of culture and if we accept literature as a social institution which is concerned with the conservation, efficiency, and invention of symbols not simply as means of 'knowing' or 'believing' but as means for acting, sociologists must reflect on the social organization of those who are so skilled in the creation of new, and the refinement of old, systems of verbal expression."[4]

Finally I should like to express my thanks to the Awards Committee of the State University of New York at Albany and especially to Vice President Louis R. Salkever for a Grand-in-Aid for the purpose of editing this volume of the Yearbook.

JOSEPH P. STRELKA

Notes

1. René Wellek and Austin Warren, *Theory of Literature* (New York, 1956),
   p. 94.
2. Wellek and Austin Warren, p. 95.
3. Joseph Strelka, *Die gelenkten Musen* (Wien-Frankfurt-Zuerich, 1971).
4. Hugh Dalziel Duncan, *Language and Literature in Society* (New York, 1961),
   p. 74.

BASIC THEORETICAL PROBLEMS

Walter H. Bruford

LITERARY CRITICISM AND SOCIOLOGY

VARIOUS TYPES OF INQUIRY, MOST OF THEM FAIRLY RECENT AND NOT
yet clearly defined in their aims and methods, have been called "sociology of literature." Sociology itself is of course a somewhat elastic
term. It *may* be understood in this connection as what Umberto Eco
calls "sociometry": "A team of researchers chooses a sample of the
public and, using exact methods, measures the reactions of its sample
to certain prearranged stimuli. . . . Research has been done into the
number of people who buy a certain type of book, into what is read
by French soldiers, etc."[1] In East Germany a similar opinion poll has
been carried out by students of Erfurt to discover how certain living
"socialist" authors compare with each other in popularity, with a view
to improving the official propaganda for approved literature.[2] The
English or American literary scholar, however, will probably not
usually have market research of this kind in view when he speaks of
sociology of literature, but something less exact and of greater human
interest.

For the understanding of foreign literatures, information about
their social and cultural background has long been considered most
helpful, if not essential. Sociology of literature may be said to have
begun in this way with Mme. de Staël. In *De l'Allemagne* (London,
1810) she developed, with new material from her German travels,
ideas which she had already outlined in *De la littérature considérée
dans ses rapports avec les institutions sociales* (Paris, 1800). Her main
point is the contrast she sees between the *esprit de conversation*,
which originated in the salons of Paris and pervaded the whole of
French literature, and German individualism, which resulted from
solitary habits and the lack of lively social intercourse. Consequently,
a Frenchman tends to sacrifice the substance of his thought to the

form, and a German the form to the substance. The French, she says, feel a social need to think like everyone else, draw on a reservoir common to all, and above all else fear to be boring. The Germans value only the bold independence of thought that comes from solitary brooding and feel they have a claim on the hearers' time. Frenchmen study men and society, with a practical aim in view. Germans study books, for the life around them is too uneventful to be interesting, and the nature of their government prevents intellectuals from having any influence on the course of events. These ideas became a commonplace of French criticism. Half a century later, Taine, further influenced by the scientific atmosphere of his time, developed a deterministic theory of literature in which literary works are seen as the "results" of a process of "psychological mechanics" involving the forces, *la race, le milieu, et le moment.* Taine also stresses the importance of the salons in the shaping of classical French literature. Brunetière, in his turn, while avoiding the excesses of Positivism, repeatedly insists on the eminently social character of French literature, and especially on the importance of the social inheritance on which all writers draw. A classical literature can only arise when the language and the chief literary forms, through long cultivation, have achieved a certain ripeness.[3]

Another French scholar, Alexandre Beljame, in 1881 initiated research on the topic that has claimed most attention from the sociologists of literature, the relations between author and public. The theme of his book, *Le public et les hommes de lettres en Angleterre au 18ᵉ siècle*, was not pursued further until 1904, when Leslie Stephen's *English Literature and Society in the Eighteenth Century* appeared. Two or three more studies, mostly by medievalists, emerged before 1914, as did Levin L. Schücking's first of a series of essays on the history of literary taste published in 1913. In the sixty-four–page bibliography he compiled with Walther Ebisch just before the Second World War (which appeared in *Anglia* in 1939 as "Bibliographie zur Geschichte des literarischen Geschmacks in England") one can follow almost the whole history of research in the sociology of literature up to that time. A list of sixteen theoretical works is followed by five main sections under the following headings: 1. The sociological conditions of literary creation and influence, subdivided into: (a) The poet and his social standing, (b) The reading public, and (c) The agencies mediating between author and public (that is, patronage, publishing, lending libraries, state influence, anthologies; and hostile forces). 2. The history of fame and influence. 3. Tendencies

and fashions in taste. 4. Literary criticism and its effect on the public. 5. The literary taste of particular individuals. Schücking's own
chief works were: *Die Soziologie der literarischen Geschmacksbildung* (München, 1923; English translation, 2d ed. rev., London,
1966) and *Die Familie im Puritanismus* (Leipzig, 1929). Other
Anglisten who did good sociological studies of English literature
were, for instance, Herbert Schöffler with his *Protestantismus und
Literatur* (Leipzig, 1922) and Walter F. Schirmer with *Der englische
Frühhumanismus* (Leipzig, 1931). A series *Literatur und Leben* was
started by Georg Keferstein in 1933 which included amongst other
things his own *Bürgertum und Bürgerlichkeit bei Goethe* (Weimar,
1933) and Victor Lange's *Die Lyrik und ihr Publikum im England
des 18. Jahrhunderts* (Weimar, 1935).

It is clear that a good deal was published in Germany in the inter-
war period on the sociology of English literature, and there were also
similar studies for French, notably Erich Auerbach's *Das französische
Publikum des 17. Jahrhunderts* (München, 1933), followed in 1946
by his brilliant *Mimesis*, and a number of essays by Ernst Curtius.
But on German literature there was little relief from the fashionable
Geistesgeschichte except for Arnold Hirsch's *Bürgertum und Barock
im deutschen Roman* (2d ed., Köln, Graz, 1957) and, written in exile,
E. Kohn-Bramstedt's *Aristocracy and the Middle Classes in Germany
—Social Types in German Literature, 1830–1900* (London, 1937)—
apart from purely Marxist work, such as A. Kleinberg's *Die deutsche
Dichtung in ihren sozialen, zeit- und geistesgeschichtlichen Bedin-
gungen* (Berlin, 1927) and L. Balet's *Die Verbürgerlichung der
deutschen Kunst, Literatur und Musik in 18. Jahrhundert* (Strass-
burg, 1936). Much more subtle and learned than the last two were
the studies of the German classics written by the Hungarian Georg
Lukács in the nineteen-thirties and published as *Goethe und seine
Zeit* in 1947 (Bern). These are essentially concerned with the expression of political and social thought in literature and refer only in the
most general terms to the life of the time. Lukács examines works like
Wilhelm Meisters Lehrjahre to see where Goethe stands in the struggle for new forms of society, and he finds him, surprisingly, on the side
of the angels. A paragraph in the preface explains his point of view:
"Mehring has explained in his book on Lessing that there is only one
right point of view if one is considering German literature of the
late eighteenth and early nineteenth centuries: this literature is the
ideological preparation for the bourgeois-democratic revolution in
Germany. It is only if we look at the whole period from Lessing to

Heine from this standpoint that we can see where the truly progressive and where the truly reactionary tendencies are to be found."

Literary values hardly count for this kind of critic, but he has a sharp eye for any hint of hostility to the established powers of the time, using every text as a sociopolitical document in the ideological conflicts of the present. Ever since the early correspondence of Marx and Engels there has been much discussion of literature as part of the cultural superstructure erected, according to the materialist conception of history, on a particular economic and social basis and never free from its influence. However, an East German professor of German literature, Thomas Höhle, admitted a few years ago that although more attention had been paid for some time in the German Democratic Republic to empirical social research, there had been a long period when this neglected subject was left to bourgeois scholars in capitalist countries.[4] I myself had been told in Weimar in 1958 that at the Goethe Bicentenary nine years before, the organizers of the Weimar exhibition on Goethe and his age had had to draw extensively on my *Germany in the Eighteenth Century*, which had appeared in a German translation before the war, because there was so little else available in German to help them, and on some surviving exhibits in the City Museum I still found labels quoting, without acknowledgment, phrases from the book. Höhle says that Marxist literary sociology has occupied itself so far almost entirely with the effects on literature of the class struggle. He would like to see the sociology of literature established on an equal footing with literary theory and literary history as a branch of literary scholarship, but chiefly in the form of what I have called "market research." There should be a great extension of research, he thinks, into the effect, that is, the reception, of literature, not in the past, for there the evidence is indirect and scanty, but in the present, and in relation to contemporary "socialist" (i.e., Marxist) literature. "In this way the results of literary-sociological research can most readily be brought into the service of socialist cultural policy and Marxist literary theory." Will the public accept "tragic" endings to novels, for instance? An opinion poll could find out, and save critics from guessing. He does not think that "at present" there is any danger that authors will be deterred by such findings from exploring new questions and techniques.[5] Dietrich Sommer makes rather similar suggestions in an informative article on the development of "bourgeois" sociology of literature, adding: "It goes without saying that in all this our sociology of literature will be guided by the principles of dialectical and historical materialism, and

that it must serve the practical requirements of socialist reconstruction and the extension of socialist culture," that is, we shall of course
keep strictly to the party line. It is by no means easy to do this and, as
Peter Demetz has shown in his *Marx, Engels und die Dichter*, the
founding fathers of Marxism had far more liberal and sensitive ideas
about literature than their modern disciples. "What was in Marx and
Engels an impromptu remark in a letter and an interesting *bon mot*
has become an article of faith, which says to the intellectuals, critics,
and scholars concerned: 'Thus far shalt thou go and no further!'"

   Non-Marxists will find in sociology of literature pursued on these
lines, and probably in the whole market-research approach, hardly
anything which has the remotest bearing on literary scholarship as
they conceive it. Höhle is aware of this and quotes H. N. Fügen,
whose book *Die Hauptrichtungen der Literatursoziologie und ihre
Methoden. Ein Beitrag zur literatursoziologischen Theorie* (Bonn,
1964) I have not seen, as saying that the sociology of literature considers works of literature not as an artistic, but as a social phenomenon, and consequently has nothing to say in the matter of aesthetic
valuation. "It is obvious," Höhle continues, "that this sharp distinction between literary scholarship and the sociology of literature, making the latter a branch of sociology, is based on the view which has
prevailed for decades in the bourgeois countries, that a work of literature, as an aesthetic phenomenon, is an autonomous entity and
stands, in respect of its aesthetic nature, in no connection with social
reality, so that the aesthetic criteria of literary scholarship are taken
solely from the aesthetic sphere, regarded as isolated."[6]

   It is not surprising that when Stanley Hyman surveyed Marxist
criticism of English literature in *The Armed Vision*, he found its outstanding characteristic to be a marked blindness to literary values.
"Marxism seems to be for these critics," he says, "a weapon with
which to kill poetry." It does not follow that Marxism may not sometimes have a favorable effect on critics who pass beyond it. George
Watson writes in *The Literary Critics:*

> The Marxist tradition in modern English has been overwhelmingly
> American, for the flirtation of the British intelligentsia with Marxism in
> the era of the Spanish Civil War was too transient, and too stubbornly
> English and moralistic, to create a genuine Marxist school of letters.
> The American outcome, though no doubt heretical too by strictly po-
> litical standards, bears the evidence of Marxist influence more deeply
> etched upon its character. Much of it, paradoxically, is ex-Marxist and
> even anti-Marxist; but we feel the weight and seriousness of social
> concern even in the later writings of such critics as Edmund Wilson

and Lionel Trilling, whereas the post-war criticism of British ex-
Marxists like W. H. Auden and Stephen Spender bears little or no
scar of past political wars.[7]

The idea referred to by Höhle of the autonomy of a pure work of
art, of its special order of existence as a structure of words or other
symbols, has become familiar to us through the New Criticism of the
nineteen-thirties, and it underlies the preference expressed for instance by Wellek and Warren in their *Theory of Literature* (1949)
of the "intrinsic" to the "extrinsic" approach to literature. The point
is well made by E. M. Forster in one of his lively essays in criticism
("Anonymity," in *Two Cheers for Democracy*, London, 1951). He too
believes that pure poetry is to be appreciated and judged entirely
from within, by an effort of the imagination. In reading poetry, he
says, "we have entered a universe that only answers its own laws,
supports itself, internally coheres, and has a new standard of truth.
Information is true if it is accurate. A poem is true if it hangs together.
Information points to something else. A poem points to nothing but
itself. Information is relative. A poem is absolute."[8]

It is a great gain to have seen through the excessive claims of the
positivistic, would-be scientific literary scholarship of the later nineteenth century, but it would be foolish to deny its real achievements,
or the usefulness of biographical and psychological literary research
and the comparative study of motifs, forms, ideas, and so forth that
continue on the foundations it laid. It is misleading too to take pure
poetry as the norm for literature. As Mr. Forster insisted, it is a rather
rare form of literary composition, and we are more often concerned
with forms which are in varying degrees linked up with everyday
life, and appeal less exclusively to the imagination. He suggests that
we think of these various kinds of verbal composition as forming a
series, poetry, drama, the novel, works of science and scholarship,
newspaper articles, advertisements and finally a piece of merely useful information in words, like "bus stop." At each stage the activity
of the writer is less freely creative, more conditioned by the world
around him, by facts. It is for these genres lower down the scale that
social comment may be most useful, just because they are not "autonomous." Yet in them too the specifically literary element speaks to us
directly, often defying rational explanation, as do music and painting; but some minds respond little, or not at all. Literary sensitivity,
if not inborn, seems to be more readily acquired by a kind of infec-
tion from those who have it than by learning facts about literature.
It is perhaps from awareness of a certain tone-deafness in regard to

literary values, even in some of their learned colleagues, that the New Critics rejected "information" so firmly, but even the sensitive have their blind spots. One must be capable of spontaneous enjoyment of *some* kinds of literature to set up as a literary scholar, but there are always highly praised works which fail to appeal to us directly, but for which it is possible that our eyes might be opened by others more sensitive in this range or possessing some clue, some essential piece of information.

I have discussed the necessity for information in the interpretation of literature at some length in an earlier article, from which I quote: "For aesthetic enjoyment and for the purposes of a humane education, information about literature, whether biographical, psychological, sociological or whatever it may be, is not an end in itself, but a means towards a fuller understanding and appreciation of individual works and authors. A certain measure of external information, however, it may be more or less, according to the nature of the work of art in question, can greatly deepen the internal impression on the reader's mind which is the ultimate goal."[9] I supported this view philosophically by an appeal to Nicolai Hartmann's modernized version of Hegel's "objective idealism" in *Das Problem des geistigen Seins* and elsewhere:

> The indispensable material vehicle by which meaning is conveyed from mind to mind, the patches of paint on canvas, the letters printed on paper, or at an earlier stage, the sounds of speech, possess meaning only for living minds and cannot truly be said to "exist" at all, as works of art and so on, except when perceived. "The meaning is not present as 'a thing in itself' in the shaped material," Hartmann says, "but only 'for us,' the readers (viewers, spectators, hearers)." The sleeping symbols have to be awakened each time to new life, the work of art has to be as it were resurrected by contact with a living mind. It is the word "resurrection" that is used by Goethe in a letter to Zelter (24.8.1824), who had just read *Iphigenie* again, and in this way called it forth "from word and letter into the life of the mind and heart."[10]
>
> It follows from such a conception of art that ... all works of art, being created *by* living men *for* living men, depend for their effect on the existence around them of a continuous culture, that links up author and reader, those who create and those who enjoy works of art, through a common language and common artistic conventions; or at least on a measure of understanding consciously acquired by the reader.[11]
>
> A further consequence ... is that the "resurrected Iphigenias" and so forth are in no two instances exactly the same, and cannot possibly be identical with what was present to the author's imagination as he

wrote. . . . The same words have different resonances in different minds. A further complication is that in presenting his material, to a public generally thought of as consisting of fellow-countrymen and contemporaries, a writer always takes certain things for granted and does not trouble to state them. He would be found tiresomely prolix if he did not rely a good deal on the apperceptive habits of his readers, and leave it to their imagination to supply a great deal from a mere hint. When a novelist writing about London or Berlin brings in the name of a world-famous street or square, he usually assumes a knowledge of its associations, and so it is also with all sorts of concepts which, to be understood as he means them, require some knowledge of the political, social and cultural traditions of the country in question.[12]

As Hartmann says: "The arts cannot cut themselves off from life. What they are in their essence they can only be in the framework of the historical reality which gave them birth, and not in some shadow realm outside it."[13]

The historical and social background studies to German literature which I began immediately after the First World War had not yet any of these theoretical foundations, nor were they due to either Marxist or German influence. They were meant as an approach to what would now be called a better integrated study of modern languages. Until long after this, it was only in the classics that British students of foreign languages and literatures were expected to take a whole civilization as the field of their studies, but partly as a result of the war, and of the bewildered ignorance of the country's nearest neighbors which had come home to so many since its outbreak, a reform of the university teaching of modern languages was initiated, mainly by some Cambridge dons, about 1916. This led to a thorough revision of the regulations for the Cambridge Tripos in English and modern languages, to a remarkably broad-minded and challenging government report on *Modern Studies,* and to a corresponding overhaul of the competitive examination for posts in the higher civil service. The aim was to make modern language and English studies acceptable as an equivalent training in literacy to that so long provided by the classics. Already a good tradition had been established in the scholarly reading and writing of some modern foreign languages. Their history and philology had if anything been overemphasized by some, mainly German, teachers. It was hoped that this new approach would enlarge and deepen the student's appreciation of the content of what he read, by encouraging him to view the language and literature of a foreign country always in close relation to its history, institutions and thought. Such an approach, roughly parallel to that envisaged by the German advocates of *Kulturkunde* in Weimar Republic days, would tend, it was thought, to make the young graduate a better citizen, in his awareness of foreign countries and their ways, as well as a better humanist.[14] The main question in my own mind soon came to be: had Germany ever really been the "nation of poets and thinkers" which early Victorian England had learned to admire through Carlyle? If we understood the earlier Germany better, might we not be less puzzled by later developments there and also perhaps better understand the intentions of the classical German writers, and the effect they produced on contemporaries?

In practice, most British universities have been slow in following up the government committee's recommendations, at least as far as the neglect of history is concerned, chiefly no doubt because few undergraduates have time to learn much about a foreign country's history and general civilization while studying its language and literature in any depth. Modern history and culture are so enormously complex and controversial compared with those of the ancients, and the sources are so much more abundant. It is difficult to find teachers with the right kind of knowledge and interests, and well justified claims are made on all sides in staff meetings for more time for this or that particular period or aspect of language or literature, as well as for philosophy, general linguistics and comparative literature. But at any rate it has come to be recognized as an ideal that the student of a foreign literature should be as widely aware as possible of the general life and civilization of the country concerned, and various compromise solutions of the problem have been attempted. Further, a small number of research students and mature scholars have ventured into the ill-defined socioliterary border country.

Perhaps a short description of some of this work will serve to illustrate the concrete and practical nature of the English type of sociology of literature, if indeed a study of the social background of literature, not consciously guided by any ideology or by the theories of any sociological school, deserves to be dignified by that name. Three-quarters of my *Germany in the Eighteenth Century* (Cambridge, 1935) was straightforward social history, illustrated where possible from the writings of contemporary travelers, and arranged under the following headings: Political structure and system of government; The old order of society—nobility and peasantry; The new order of society—the middle class. In the selection of material for these chapters the interests of the literary student were always kept in mind.

(The fact that this can only be attempted by a writer who is, however uneasily, astride of the two very different disciplines of history proper and literary history is one reason why good university teachers of history for modern language students are hard to find.) Certain towns are of particular interest to the student of literature—Leipzig, Hamburg, Frankfurt, Weimar, as well as Berlin and Vienna, and many details are of special relevance to the understanding of particular works. The last quarter was wholly concerned with "Reactions on literature," dealing first with the "Profession of letters"—patronage, publishing, literary earnings, the reading public, and so on—and finally with "The influence of political, economic and social factors on literature." The summary of this final chapter reads as follows:

> Influence of "Kleinstaaterei." Lack of a national style—contrast with France. Gradual evolution of pride in German language and literature, but lack of national subjects and of patriotism. Goethe's analysis of the difficulties of a German classic. German literature unsocial—contrast with France. Some positive effects—individualism, originality, speculative freedom, lyrical sincerity, openness to foreign ideas. Cosmopolitanism of the educated and worship of Greece, an escape from the provincialism of the masses. Picturesque variety of provincial life little appreciated. Influence of social structure. Domination of aristocracy in seventeenth century, gradual disappearance of patronage and court ideals under "Aufklärung." Importance of the larger towns. Influence of the middle class on literature illustrated from the drama. "Sturm und Drang" and its criticism of society. Hostility to courts outgrown, middle-class and court influences fused by the Classics. Their enlightened conservatism. The nature of Weimar classicism. Divorced from much of the life of the time. Incompleteness of its synthesis makes it in a wider sense "Romantic." Its influence on the nineteenth century.

In later books, parts of this field have been examined in greater detail. *Theatre, Drama and Audience in Goethe's Germany* (London, 1950) dealt with one genre, the drama, in both its passive and active relations with the life of the time and contemporary conditions in the theatre, while *Culture and Society in Classical Weimar, 1775–1806* (Cambridge, 1962) pursued further the topic of personal cultivation, *Bildung*, so important an aim for the book-drama of that age. Connections were traced between the idea of culture as a supreme good and the particular conditions of life in Weimar, as well as the individual tastes and talents of the literary men attracted to the court. The broadening of the field, from society and literature to society and culture in general, was continued in the broad sketch of the age

Deutsche Kultur der Goethezeit (Konstanz, 1965). In between times, a special fondness for Chekhov had led to an attempt to apply the method to him, "to see Russia through Chekhov's eyes and to see Chekhov as the product of a particular age and country," in *Chekhov and his Russia* (London, 1948).

Other Cambridge Germanists who have worked at least in part on similar lines are, for instance, Roy Pascal, with work on the background of the Reformation, *Sturm und Drang* and the German novel; C. P. Magill, on the German author and his public in the mid-nineteenth century; R. Hinton Thomas, on expressionism; Siegbert Prawer, on Mörike's reception in Germany; and W. A. Coupe, on the illustrated broadsheet in the seventeenth century. John Lough has written introductions to seventeenth- and eighteenth-century France and detailed studies of eighteenth-century theatre audiences and of the *Encyclopédie*. The initiative in all these cases came from the literary scholars, not the sociologists, and always from those interested in modern foreign languages, though for English Mrs. Q. D. Leavis was early in the field with *Fiction and the Reading Public* (London, 1932). Sociology established itself very late as a university subject in Great Britain, in most universities only after the Second World War, and though socioliterary problems have no doubt been encountered and discussed by sociologists and anthropologists, I am not attempting to include such material here, any more than to consider the use, which has been made since time immemorial, of literary works as historical documents or illustrations. The question here is simply what relevance sociohistorical studies have for literary scholarship, whether for literary theory, history or criticism. Having touched on the development of the sociology of literature as a distinct field of inquiry in France, Germany and Great Britain and defended it against the New Critics, I wish finally to suggest some more general reasons for extending the scope of the study of literature to include as wide an awareness as possible of the sociocultural background, as a reaction against the post-romantic neglect of the idea of communication in the theory of literature, and over-emphasis on expression. A glance at the conditions which prevailed before the invention of printing will serve as introduction to this section.

The intimate involvement of literature and all the arts in the social life of the community seems to be beyond question for the early stages of civilization, to judge, for instance, from what we know of the survival in modern times of old practices in the composition and oral transmission of folk tales, songs, and drama. That monumental work, *The Growth of Literature,* by H. Munro Chadwick and N. Kershaw Chadwick, is full of instances, such as:

> The extempore composition of popular poetry by non-professional people was very widely practised by the Russian peasants in the eighteenth and nineteenth centuries, and no doubt continues to be so still in remote districts. In 1824 the German traveler Erman found that in the neighbourhood of Tobolsk the Russian groom accompanied the alternate bounding and rattling of the carriage "with ever-varying, apposite addresses to the horses separately, always in rhyme, partly with songs of considerable length." He tells that the horses are adjured, in heroic fashion, "not to flag on the road which constantly grows shorter, but to bound without delay from hill to hill." [15]

Occupational songs like the one referred to here are found of course almost everywhere, though they are seldom extempore compositions. The Chadwicks also quote the English traveler Coxe as saying, late in the eighteenth century, that the Russian peasants used to compose extempore songs relating to their past experiences and their present situation, among other subjects, even chanting, in dialogue with one another, their ordinary conversation. The most interesting body of poetry in this category was always associated with social rituals, and in Russia as elsewhere, there was a close association of the art of telling tales with certain occupations, such as that of the traveling tailor or shoemaker. Chapter XI of the second volume of *The Growth of Literature* gives fascinating details about the narrators and singers of folk tales, *bylini,* encountered by the great folklorist Rybnikov.

The experiences of the Irish collector of traditional lore, J. H. Delargy, are a close parallel to Rybnikov's. He considers the Irish storytellers he found early in the present century to be the nearest European counterpart to the *bylini* singers and narrators.[16] The traditional tales and songs were for centuries the chief form of entertainment known to the peasantry scattered over the countryside and to the fishermen on its coasts. In the fifteenth and sixteenth centuries earlier versions of many stories collected since from oral tradition had been told or read aloud in the homes of the Irish-speaking aristocracy of mixed Norman and Irish descent, as can be proved from manuscripts of the so-called romantic tales still existing from that time. Earlier still, down to the eleventh or twelfth century, there had been similar performances in princes' halls, and motifs and whole stories, like that of the Sons of Uisneach, the Deirdre story, can be traced right back to the Old Irish epics. The variations in parallel versions are innumerable, and it is an interesting point for the critic to note that aesthetically preferable forms of motifs, sometimes apparently original creations, may occur in quite late recordings. It is a superstition to believe that everything good must necessarily be old.[17] Connections are clearly established, the sociologist of literature learns, between certain types of story and particular social groups, and between storytelling in general and recurrent social occasions. Delargy writes, for instance: "the stories were told as a rule by night around the winter fire from the end of harvest until the middle of May. . . . The recital of Ossianic hero-tales was almost without exception restricted to men. . . . *Seanchas* (socio-historical narratives), genealogical lore, music, folk-prayers were as a rule associated with women, or at any rate they excelled the men in these branches of tradition."[18]

There were two institutions above all which preserved oral literature, the *Céilidhe*, or festive evening of song and story in a private house, still a familiar happening in the Scottish Highlands; and, in the Aran Islands especially, the *Áirneán*, something very like the *Spinnstube* of southwest Germany in preindustrial times. A number of women, with perhaps an odd man or two, used to meet at a certain house in the evening to spin or card wool, often by the light of the fire, while someone entertained them with stories, readings or songs. The Irish word came to mean just a session of storytelling.[19]

W. J. Entwistle has given us, in Book I of his *European Balladry* (Oxford, 1939), a whole array of parallels to these gatherings, where "the audience, drawn without abstentions from the whole community, conditions the minstrel's performance as reciter and creator. The matter belongs to them all, and any one who knows a better version may produce it. After a song has been sung, the audience falls into a discussion, and mention may be made of variants. There is no professional wall separating the performer from his hearers; he is no more than *primus inter pares*. If he composes a new song, he must meet the people's expectations; the course of the tale must have the prescribed order and formulas. The art is greater than the artist, who must not show his hand if he is to be believed."[20]

There is of course an enormous literature on this subject of *Volkspoesie*, from Herder onwards, but enough has been said to draw attention to the fact that very much has been lost, as well as gained, through the revolution in communication, the change from hearing stories or poems read aloud in a small company to private reading from the printed works of professional writers, which began in the leading countries of Europe at the Renaissance, but was delayed at the circumference of modern culture perhaps for centuries, and in many parts of the world has not yet taken place. It has been one of the chief tasks of the sociologists of literature to describe and analyze the ever increasing complexity of the media which developed between author and reader following this change, which destroyed old but created new forms of social interdependence in the sphere of literature, new attitudes and aspirations in writers and readers and an immense increase in the number of both. The summary given above of Schücking's bibliography has indicated the chief headings, for a typical advanced country down to the last war, in the history of this research.

A new theory of literature and of criticism might well result from a systematic comparison of the literary situation in an age of oral literature with that which gradually ensues through the multiplication of books, the loss of direct contact between storytellers and coherent social groups, and the growth of a public of solitary readers. It would be a theory not, like most modern theories, of expression, but of dialogue and communication. It would be unlike any of those, for example, so lucidly surveyed by M. H. Abrams in the introduction to *The Mirror and the Lamp*. There, as is clear from the diagram, the artist is represented as connected with the audience only through the work, but in fact artist, audience, and "universe" (the relevant part of which is the society, large or small, surrounding both artist and audience) are connected by a whole web of other links as well. The diagram shows the state of things familiar to us now, when author and audience normally have no contacts. At this stage, but only then, poetry may seem to be wholly expressive, "feeling, confessing itself to itself in moments of solitude" (J. S. Mill), when, as Abrams says, the poet's audience is reduced to a single member, the poet himself. If he even thinks of the impression he will make on another mind, his poetry becomes "eloquence," according to Mill. "There is something singularly fatal to the audience in the romantic point of view," Abrams comments. "Or, in terms of historical causes, it might be conjectured that the disappearance of a homogeneous and discriminating reading public fostered a criticism which on principle diminished the importance of the audience as a determinant of poetry and poetic value."[21] It is different of course with the drama, so far as it resists the tendency to become book drama, and Alewyn reminds us that "down to the time of the young Goethe the great mass of what we call 'the lyric' was not something

read but something sung, and usually sung in company (poetry for
a social purpose) and only written down by chance." "In our attitude
to art to-day," he points out, "we assume its emancipation from
society (and at the same time its autonomy—and dispensability), as
it came about in the eighteenth century. It can hardly have been an
accident that it was accompanied by the dissolution of the literary
topos and genre, and the replacement of poetry of convention by
other possibilities—poetry of human experience (*Erlebnis*), realism,
symbolism. Art loses its social basis because its psychological function changes, through changes within man himself."[22]

Broadcasting and television have added a new chapter to this history, in some ways restoring the importance of the spoken word and
bringing the theatre into every home, but essentially to individuals
not to natural groups, except for a certain amount of family listening
and viewing, and in any case only to dumb listeners, unable to answer back. These services have come to require so vast an organization, subject to social and political pressures in so many ways, that
one is bound to speak of a second revolution as important as the first,
from listening to reading. Much of the discussion these new wonders
have evoked is germane to our theme, but there is room only for one
early voice, that of George Orwell in 1943, after his war-time experience of broadcasting with T. S. Eliot and Herbert Read. He talks
about some of the implications for literature in his essay "Poetry and
the Microphone," from which the following is a typical passage:

> That grisly thing, a "poetry reading," is what it is because there
> will always be some among the audience who are bored or all but
> frankly hostile and who can't remove themselves by the simple act
> of turning a knob. And it is at bottom the same difficulty—the fact
> that a theatre audience is not a selected one—that makes it impossible
> to get a decent performance of Shakespeare in England. On the air
> these conditions do not exist. The poet *feels* that he is addressing
> people to whom poetry means something, and it is a fact that poets
> who are used to broadcasting can read into the microphone with
> a virtuosity they would not equal if they had a visible audience in
> front of them.[23]

The effect on any chosen writer of the very general kinds of social
influence which we have been discussing is of course difficult or
impossible to demonstrate, but none the less important for that. As
I realized very early, the interest of such studies is apt to be in inverse
proportion to the degree of accuracy attainable in the result. Philip
Bagby has put very persuasively his hope "that historical researchers

will give up their futile attempts to establish the exact truth as to individual actions in the past, and seek more and more to investigate, as far as possible, every aspect of the culture of every period," culture being, in his view, "the intelligible aspect of history." Much in the following paragraph has its obvious applications to literary history of the social-cultural type:

> Even individual actions, it should be noted, are scarcely intelligible without reference to their cultural background. A man's most intimate desires and beliefs are very largely moulded by what he has been taught and what he has unconsciously absorbed from his fellows, while the situation with which he is confronted at any given time is also largely the product of prior actions by members of the same or different societies. The very language which he speaks imposes on him certain well-defined modes of thinking about the situation. He cannot possibly escape from these influences since he is largely unaware of them. The most original of geniuses is invariably seen, after enough time has elapsed, to be very much a man of his period and country, to share more with his contemporaries than he or his contemporaries realized. When we discuss the behaviour of a member of our own society with our friends, we take this cultural background for granted, since it is the same for all; it is the man's personal idiosyncrasies which leap to the eye and call for explanation. But as we look back in time or out across national boundaries, individual differences sink into insignificance; it is the broad differences in behaviour between different times and places which must first be explained. Only when we know and understand this thoroughly shall we be able to isolate and identify what is peculiar to particular individuals.[24]

What has come to be known as sociology of literature may perhaps best be regarded then as an extension of literary history to include an account of as many as possible of the innumerable connections which can be discovered between literature and social life. By such an extension literary history is brought nearer to being a history of culture in general, of culture defined, as it was by T. S. Eliot, as "the way of life of a particular people living together in one place. That culture," he continued, "is made visible in their arts, in their social system, in their habits and customs, in their religion. . . . These things all act upon each other, and fully to understand one you have to understand all."[25] Goethe, reading French poetry in 1829, had already come to a similar conclusion. "French poetry, and French literature generally, is always inseparably connected with the life and passions of the whole nation. . . . Let us remind ourselves therefore that a nation's literature cannot be known or appreciated unless we bear in mind along with it the whole complex condition of that nation."[26]

Notes

For the theatre-audience relationship, with a full bibliography of recent work, see:
Heinz Kindermann, "Die Funktion des Publikums im Theater," *Sitzungsberichte der österreichischen Akademie der Wissenschaften*, philosophisch-historische Klasse, vol. 273, Vienna, 1971.

1. Umberto Eco, "Sociology and the Novel," *The Times Literary Supplement*, 28 September 1967, p. 875.
2. Ernst-Ludwig Zacharias, "Zwischenbilanz eines Vorversuches zur Wirkungsforschung," *Wissenschaftliche Zeitung der Universität Halle*, vol. 15 (1966), pp. 511–17.
3. Ferdinand Brunetière "Sur le caractère essentiel de la littérature française," *Etudes critiques*, vol. 5 (Paris, 1892).
4. Thomas Höhle, "Probleme einer marxistischen Literatursoziologie," *Wissenschaftliche Zeitung der Universität Halle*, vol. 15 (1966), p. 477.
5. Ibid., pp. 482, 485.
6. Ibid., p. 482.
7. George Watson, *The Literary Critics* (London, 1962), p. 225.
8. Edward Morgan Forster, *Two Cheers for Democracy* (London, 1951).
9. Walter H. Bruford, "Interpretation and Information," *Orbis literarum*, vol. 19 (Copenhagen, 1964), p. 6.
10. Ibid., p. 7.
11. Ibid.
12. Ibid., p. 8.
13. Nicolai Hartmann, *Aesthetik* (Berlin, 1953), p. 40.
14. For these reforms, see Walter H. Bruford, "First Steps in German Fifty Years Ago," Presidential Address of the Modern Humanities Research Association (1965), pp. 24–28.
15. H. Munro Chadwick and N. Kershaw Chadwick, *The Growth of Literature*, vol. 2 (Cambridge, 1936), p. 284.
16. John H. Delargy, "The Gaelic Story-Teller," Sir John Rhys Memorial Lecture, *Proceedings of the British Academy* (1945), p. 180.
17. Alan Bruford, *Gaelic Folk-Tales and Medieval Romances* (Dublin, 1969), p. 2 and Chapter 18.
18. Delargy, "The Gaelic Story-Teller," p. 193.
19. Ibid., pp. 191f.
20. William J. Entwistle, *European Balladry* (Oxford, 1939), p. 12.
21. M. H. Abrams, *The Mirror and the Lamp* (Oxford, 1953; reprint ed., Norton Library, New York, 1958), p. 25.

22. Richard Alewyn, "Aufgaben der deutschen Literaturwissenschaft," *Aufgaben deutscher Forschung*, ed. Leo Brandt (Köln and Opladen, 1953), pp. 188, 190. Reprinted in *Jahrbuch für internationale Germanistik*, Yearbook 2, vol. 1 (1971).
23. George Orwell, *Collected Essays, Journalism and Letters*, vol. 2 (London, 1968), p. 56.
24. Philip Bagby, *Culture and History. Prolegomena to the comparative study of civilization* (Berkeley and Los Angeles, 1963), pp. 128f.
25. Thomas Stearns Eliot, *Notes towards the Definition of Culture* (London, 1948), p. 120.
26. Johann Wolfgang von Goethe, *Werke*, vol. 38 Jubiläumsausgabe, p. 140.

Paul Ramsey

LITERARY CRITICISM AND SOCIOLOGY

THE PURPOSE OF THIS ESSAY IS TO EXPRESS AND SUPPORT SOME CLOSELY related ideas:

1. that literary and social judgments—involving value—can be genuine knowledge
2. that there can be genuine evidence for such judgments
3. that such judgments are a major end of other literary and social studies
4. that such judgments are not philosophically, temporally, or procedurally posterior to analysis, interpretation, or "fact" gathering
5. that such knowledge does not necessarily or automatically improve literature and society
6. that literary and social studies have distinct and central methods; respectively, the careful observation and comparison of deeply experienced literary texts and the careful observation and comparison of deeply experienced human activities
7. that each has many and overlapping subsidiary methods and there is no adequate or exhaustive way to limit or delimit those methods in advance
8. that consequently good literary and social criticism should be humane studies, guided by wisdom, thoughtful and varied in method, rooted in sound metaphysics, expressed in good language.

Since literature is largely about society, and since the men who write it are under various social influences, the study of literature necessarily and extensively overlaps the study of society, a truism that hardly needs urging. It is an offense verging on the criminal for a teacher of literature to use literature only as a means of understanding society (which often in practice means reducing literature to "social issues," with a tacit intent of ideological conversion). Yet one cannot teach the *Odyssey* well without discussing the virtue of hospitality and its importance to the Greeks or the Homeric sense of the intimate presence of the divine in, over, and against society.

Literature offers to the student of society a vast field of study, inevitably misstudied unless the student of society is also a good literary critic who can see structures, qualifications, reserves, distancing, qualities, contextual and rhetorical surprises. Still, with cautions, literature can be of considerable benefit to the student of society, just as studies of society can be to the literary critic; to speak of the possible relations in specific would be to redo many books and add others. I shall turn to a more special kind of comparing.

"By what theory of method shall we undertake the job?" is not really the first (or later) question to ask in getting a job done. One does any job by gathering the tools that one hopes will work and starting out. Or, if it's a new job, by taking a look first and then deciding what tools to use. The theory of making tools is not necessary to selecting the right tools to use or using the tools well. If the requisite tools are not available or are not invented, one improvises as one can, but that is not done by theory either.

I doubt that there is a *theory* of making tools. Makers of tools have their private and subtle professional differences of opinion, but they do not write books breeding books about the developing theory. They just go ahead, well or badly, and make tools. Some tools are nonetheless better than others. We all know this, can give reasons, and are not worried about exceptions: a good knife should be very sharp, but not an electrician's knife, which, if too sharp, cuts the wire as well as the insulation. Such an analogy reaches only so far, but it does reach some distance.

Suppose that physicists had really heeded Bacon: no hypotheses, no mathematics. Suppose on the other hand they had had no notions of new methods—either way, no modern physics. Yes, there are methods and principles, but not advance, systematic, elaborated theories of methods. Methods are adumbrated, put to work.

Suppose we were stubborn about method and tried to study literature or society strictly by the methods of physics and chemistry. We would, if we succeeded, produce (reproduce) truths about gases, valences, gravitational attractions, litmus paper, nuclear reactors, and the rest. We would then be doing, precisely, physics and chemistry.

Suppose the chemist had decided to work "strictly" by the methods of chemistry and the biologist "strictly" by the methods of biology— no biochemistry.

Good literary critics observe carefully and relate thoughtfully; so do good biologists. Biologists need microscopes more often, literary

critics less often. (I have never used a microscope in studying literature, but I do have a 10-power magnifier, an old and trusted friend.)
Biologists and literary critics have emotional responses to their object
of study; the biologists' responses are largely irrelevant, the literary
critics' highly relevant. Methods overlap and diverge; their purpose
is to help men find truths.

Society exists, has good and evil, beauty and ugliness in it. It can
be studied, in part understood, and (perhaps) improved by study.
Literature exists, has good and evil, beauty and ugliness in it. It can
be studied, in part understood, and (perhaps) improved by study.
Study is an end in itself. Put hedonistically and psychologically, it is
gratifying to have a question answered, a puzzle solved. Put theologically and metaphysically, the mind fulfills its nature by the discovery
of truths. To know truth is the good of the mind. All truth involves
or implies value; some truths are about value; some truths are more
important, intrinsically or practically, than other truths.

The student of society and the student of literature share a three-
fold motive: (1) they seek truths as such; (2) they seek truths of
value, truth-in-value; (3) they wish to do good, to improve society
and literature. As I have already suggested, truths as such and truths
of value are not neatly distinct. One can, provisionally and usefully,
separate interpretation and analysis from judgment and belief. Thus
a fair-minded reader of Shakespeare's sonnets may decide whether
some obscure references in Sonnet 124 are to Catholic martyrs whether the reader is a Catholic or not, or whether he is sympathetic, hostile,
or indifferent to religious martyrs. Likewise, an anthropologist may
accurately describe the marital and religious customs of the Skitta-
getan Indians whether he approves, disapproves, or is indifferent.

But, even on that provisional level, belief and judgment have not
really vanished. One has to enter at least imaginatively into the spirit
of what is described or one does not understand it. It is now a truism
of anthropology that the anthropologist who sees only as an outsider
does not see, that the observer who thinks a religious ritual is merely
inefficient technology does not understand and hence cannot accurately describe or interpret that ritual. What is true of at least some
sociology and anthropology is true of every literary work: not to
enter it imaginatively and responsively is not to understand it. Nor
is interpretation temporally prior to judgment or response. We do
not begin to respond to a poem and to say, "Ah, this is beautiful,"
only after we have clarified all the obscurities of meaning. That is
simply not what happens.

Literary works and many social customs, rituals, laws are evaluations and to interpret truly is to grasp the evaluation. The ideal social or literary critic should be able both to grasp (imaginatively share) such an evaluation and also to evaluate it justly. The tension is real, and unavoidable; and the procedural ideal itself raises a serious question: how far should we even imaginatively sympathize with evil? The very requirement that one be open, fair-minded, and accurate is evaluative and based on a view of reality: that truth can be in some part known, that powers of discrimination, analysis, and observation can be improved, that some methods are useful. That view is largely true, and deeply involved with value. At no point are the questions of value really put aside (not even in physics, but that's a different discussion), nor are the crucial questions for literary criticism and sociology. The entanglement of the strands of the problems is one of the chief problems, a difficulty which supports a thesis I have advanced. Since the relations of truth and value in our studies are entangled, and since students disagree widely and confusedly about those relations, only pure audacity could claim that our studies are necessarily and lucidly beneficial.

The relation between knowledge and improving society or literature is stunningly problematical, a matter largely of hope and guesswork. Urban Renewal (to take an example where wide agreement reaches across political lines) has put the poor in worse economic plight than before; and reviewers sometimes say with justified contempt that a novel written by a critic reads exactly like what it is. Knowledge is not automatically power, nor is power automatic for good. Even in the presumably more manageable realm of achieving sound knowledge, the problems are considerable.

Sociology suffers typically or at least frequently from positivism, determinism, relativism, and zealousness, from confused admixtures of those four inconsistent ingredients, and from jargon. The positivism is built into the names "social science" and "sociology," and into the inception of sociology via Auguste Comte. Roughly stated (and since positivism is a spirit and a confusion, not a lucid position, one can only roughly state it), positivism is the view that there is scientific method and language which deals with facts and that there is no other knowledge. The chief objection to positivism is that it is antireligious and, in spite of itself, antimoral; the chief procedural objection is that it is false: there is no one method and language. There are methods and languages, overlapping and varied, in the varied disciplines of knowledge; and there are no facts, only truths.

Positivism is further inconsistent with any form of moral zeal; if there are no moral truths, it is senseless to go around urging them. It is also inconsistent with relativism; according to a strict positivism, all moral systems are simply false, not "relative." One can object that positivism is no longer that reductive, but (1) reductive forms exist in much sociology at least as a prejudice and pressure, and (2) nonreductive positivism is not positivism any more. The essence of positivism is the insistence on the exclusive validity of scientific knowledge (narrow and undefined), and to surrender the position is to surrender it and the superior epistemological sanction it was imagined to confer. The spirit of narrow positivism does lurk in much sociology, and confuses it.

Positivism and determinism are often enthusiastic companions, but are inconsistent. If men can by effort achieve more scientific knowledge and apply it, men are not merely determined but determiners. If men cause things (and if we don't know that we do, we know nothing whatever), they are not merely "products" of heredity and environment. The metaphor "product" begs the whole question between men and boxes. If men choose between alternatives, then total prediction of their action is theoretically very unlikely and perhaps impossible.

The positivist has the zeal to apply firm scientific knowledge to the obediently predictable in order to benefit mankind (not to mention any zeal for power), but the contradictions are insuperable. If only facts are true, the idea of benefiting mankind is nonsense. If society can be completely controlled, no man can control it (since the controller would be an uncontrolled part of society). If men can control some of nature and society, society cannot be neatly controlled. Men can resist, despair, disobey, at least for an important while. If men have freedom, to overcome that freedom by scientific manipulation is a grave evil; if men lack freedom, controllers cannot control. If there is no value, control cannot be beneficial. If there is value, controllers must submit to moral truth or do evil. Sociology, then, cannot be at once utterly "scientific" and beneficial, nor can it consistently be relativistic and impose its values on society.

The differences between the subject matter of physics and sociology are much discussed and real, though not (if one modestly wants knowledge and help rather than an obedient beehive) insuperable. Men are fallible, active, deciding; they obey and disobey rules; they have views why they do things. If rocks have such views they are blessedly silent about it. Men also are moral beings. If a man does not believe rules to be genuinely right, one may get him to obey the rules as convenient, rational, or the like (therefore in some sense *right*—another complication), but it is surely irrational of him not to break any rules when he judges it to be to his own convenience to break them, unless he really believes he owes a duty to other people. The dilemma may be fudged or clouded in various ways, but can only be solved by a belief in the reality and intelligibility of value.

Relativism is a thicket in a marsh. Men do not follow different systems of rules; they hold and act on different (and greatly overlapping) moral beliefs. If all the beliefs are false, they are all false. If some are true and others contradict them, the latter are false. If some beliefs are true for certain circumstances, then they don't conflict with beliefs which are true for different circumstances, and there is no problem. And so on. Either value exists and is knowable, or not. The moral *anomie* (Durkheim's word appropriate here) of many young people is surely in real part a consequence of the academic teaching of relativism. A serious charge, seriously intended. Nor can one rationally use relativism to argue for tolerance or to insist that absolutism is objectionable because it occasions disastrous zeal. The relativist who is consistent should applaud Odysseus's lie in Book Fourteen of the *Odyssey* since it manages to combine determinism and relativism of sorts: "Carnage suited me; heaven put these things in me somehow. Each to his own pleasure!" (Relativism, being inconsistent in its foundations, cannot be consistent on all points, a truth of some polemical advantage to relativists.) Relativists are often zealots, not purely by accident and paradox. To persuade the members of an audience that the views they hold are merely socially conditioned, ethnocentric rules is to persuade them to disbelieve their beliefs and may prepare the way for the beliefs the persuader wishes to impose. Some converts are made; some listeners are briefly or at more length confused; some are drawn towards or into *anomie*, the logical result of the teaching.

The struggle between scientific objectivity and commitment certainly bothers many thoughtful sociologists, largely because of the tendency of positivism and relativism to undermine all moral and social beliefs, in conflict with the demands on sociologists and psychologists to act as a lay priesthood of high moral authority. The problem is real and not resolvable in positivistic and relativistic terms.

Good sociology takes intellect, professional training and discipline in methods (and criticism: the bases are visibly shakier than those of physics or chemistry, the problems more personally complicating), and humane and rooted ethical understanding. Good sociologists should be humanists, *as* sociologists. The pain of serious reflection on the human good is always professionally relevant, and they cannot solve the problem by being stern scientists in investigation and sentimental, confused partisans when the data is in. Insofar as they attempt to do so, they are part of the confusion. Jargon could well take a separate and long essay, the first target of which might be the word *sociology* itself, shackled historically to the wrong metaphysics. The student of society or literature needs to distinguish special language that is especially appropriate and accurate, from language that sounds more precise than it is, that sounds professional and hence "respectable," that is wordily confused, that parades pompous tautologies or sneaks in unexamined value judgments, that is sterile, ugly, and self-defeating. The rule is that language should be appropriate to subject, intent, and audience, a rule not to be applied by computers or by imitating bad current styles. Social and literary studies should be at times written with exacting technical precision (mathematics can be a beautiful language), at times with an aliveness of nuance which is also exact. Much sociology and literary criticism is very badly written, although it need not be.

Literary criticism suffers, like sociology, from the impact of positivism and relativism and from jargon; it suffers, probably more than sociology, from self-doubt. The self-doubt is in good part occasioned by the positivism and relativism of our culture as well as by the great variety of critical views being expressed. If positivism is true, there is no aesthetic knowledge and consequently no literary criticism, dodge as we may. If relativism is true, all literary criticism is equally true, and hence equally false since it claims to discriminate. Often writers say that the critic's true job is to analyze, not evaluate, but that does not solve the problem since, on those grounds, analysis is of no value either. One could cheerfully turn the argument about and say that, since sometimes students certainly do learn to understand literature better, positivism and relativism are necessarily false, but that sort of confidence is rare enough to sound more like bravado rather than quiet certitude.

The divisions between literary scholarship and criticism in the past few decades is surely partly caused by positivism. Historical scholars' attempts to be resolutely factual and nonevaluative have been positivistic in bent; and much labor of literary critics has been spent trying to find a place and justification for literature in what they felt to be a positivistic climate. Writers have often turned away from, or just ignored, both camps so that we have the curious division between scholarship, criticism, and literature: that is, knowledge versus judgment versus doing! The division is of course preposterous, but shows that the benefits of learning are not automatic and that something is amiss in our civilization.

Every teacher of literature knows that some interpretations and criticisms are better than others and can give true reasons why. I once had a student who thought, until corrected, that Keats's "On First Looking into Chapman's Homer" was a baseball poem, about Chapman's four-base hit. If he was wrong, some interpretations are better than others; if some interpretations are *better* than others, then positivism in the narrow sense and relativism in many of its vapor-quick senses (that is, positivism and relativism in the damaging senses) are false. It is not probable, but certain, that he was wrong, and the readers of this essay know that he was. Further, a criticism of the poem using that interpretation would be inferior *as* criticism to criticism which used the right interpretation of the title. Critical judgments of literature, then, can be right on certain evidence, evidence with a probability of one, even judgments a great deal more complex than my sample. The statement "Many of Shakespeare's sonnets display an extraordinary talent for rhythm and imagery" is true, certain, and quite complicated to arrive at.

Literary interpretations and judgments (as other judgments-involving-value) are typically thought of as ambiguous, problematic, uncertain because *it is the hard examples not the easy ones* which are chosen to discuss. Many judgments of "fact" are exceedingly problematical; many judgments of value are straightforward and sure. Some interpretations and judgments are certain, some highly likely, some dubious, some extremely eccentric. Interpretations and judgments are better or worse; to support them one can offer better or worse evidence, better or worse arguments. What is more, students of literature (when not arguing theoretical positions) know these truths. What methods are of use? Since literary criticism requires interpretation and knowledge, any knowledge may prove of value: literary students relevantly use computers, laboratory recording devices, collating machines, copying machines, microfilm readers, airplanes, parish registers, old maps; but mostly they use books, books of many descriptions from many places. Since any book may become relevant, any method which achieved the truth or falsity in a book may be relevant. How and what should be excluded?

The essential evidence for the literary critic is literary texts and performances, observed in close relation to context, to convention, and to other relevant literary texts and performances. The most essential "instruments" are a well trained and responsive ear, eye, and mind. Judgments are made by human beings; no methodology can take the place of the act of judgment. It is an act, not an inference or an epistemological erector set or sandpile. Since response is fundamental and corrigible, fairness requires not "objectivity" (the whole subjective-objective scramble of dilemmas is best just ignored) but concern; yet fairness also requires a clear-headed recognition of one's tendencies and oddities and a thoughtful comparison of one's own with other judgments. Some critics are better than others; all have something to learn.

These observations apply also, changing not very much, to sociologists. Many literary and social studies can go by many and special ways to knowledge of value; but the human and moral act of judgment is nonetheless required. Truth can be known, intelligibly if imperfectly. It matters how we speak of it.

I shall let T. S. Eliot have the last word: "For the question of questions, which no political philosophy can escape, and by the right answer to which all political [and literary and social] thinking must in the end be judged, is simply this: What is Man? what are his limitations; what is his misery and what his greatness? and what, finally, his destiny?" (*The Literature of Politics* [London: Conservative Political Center, 1955], p. 22).

Jeffrey L. Sammons

THE THREAT OF LITERARY SOCIOLOGY AND WHAT TO DO ABOUT IT

THE RELATIONSHIP BETWEEN THE DISCIPLES OF CRITICISM AND LITERARY sociology is not exactly what one would call collegial. Until recently, these pursuits have been rather aloof, with only an occasional wince directed from one to the other, impelled usually by the humanist's fear of quantifying sciences and the scientist's scorn of impressionism. Lately, however, mutual disdain has escalated into hostility and in some quarters to a degree of fury that suggests an issue located somewhere between them of sufficient gravity to arouse the affects and emotions of scholarly, intellectual persons. It is disturbing for academic disciplines to be in rude conflict with one another. The Germans in particular have a recurring tendency to conduct the intellectual life as though it were a kind of War in Heaven, and many young German literary scholars are opening up a new theater of belligerency that has been spreading into this country. For the good of education and scholarship, it is worth asking where this highly abrasive front really lies.

In reading the polemics, especially the misrepresentations of each side by the other, one gets the impression that the issue between them concerns the phylogeny of literature. The critics often pretend that literary sociologists believe works are "caused" or "explained" by environmental and class determinants, while the new academic guerrillas accuse the traditional *Literaturwissenschaftler* of isolating literature in a hovering realm of eternal verities and denying its connection to society and the historical life of man. What is remarkable about these statements of the problem is that they have the characteristic earmarks of mutual bigotry. They take extreme and minority phenomena from each side of the dispute and use them as caricatures of the whole, and they neglect, as a rule, to sift the premises and follow the logic of the opposing side, but rely primarily upon the quotation out of context.

The fact is that these misrepresentations are serious distortions. Modern criticism, by and large, has not denied that literature is a social phenomenon and that it has a history that is intertwined with the objective history of mankind; even in René Wellek's *History of Modern Criticism*, which is consistently hostile to any suggestion of external determinants for literature or criticism, there are repeated adversions to social and political considerations. Rather, criticism has tended to argue that its proper task and obligation is to regard literature intrinsically as such, rather than as something else or a reflex of something else; and even if this view is ultimately untenable, as I believe it is, it has a rationale and a usefulness that can be appreciated by a fair-minded observer. On the other hand, literary sociology has regularly been respectful of criticism's special province. One thinks of E. K. Bramsted's admission, in his classic *Aristocracy and the Middle-Classes in Germany*, that a novel "has its own laws of composition" and that "the social content of a work of art is . . . wrapped up in a texture of aesthetic elements,"[1] or of Norbert Fügen's unwillingness to involve sociology in the critical enterprise and his view that the sociologist must go to the critic for interpretation.[2] It is really only Marxism, with its pretensions to a total comprehension of reality and consciousness, that is exceptional, and even Marxists differ widely in this respect. One need only recall the highly refined aesthetic sensitivity of Ernst Fischer, or the curious range between obtuseness and delicacy of perception in Theodor W. Adorno. Furthermore, it is doubtless fair to say that the great body of academic literary interpretation and teaching has never aspired to the extremes of the New Criticism and the Staiger school, or, even in Eastern Europe, to the rigors of a consistent Marxism, but has tended to be methodologically eclectic or synthetic and moderately pluralistic. One could imagine, therefore, that the differing theoretical positions could come to be mutually respectful and supportive, and the reason they have not, on the whole, is perhaps to be sought at a more fundamental level.

I will leave out of consideration for the present what I believe to be the most basic cause of the conflict: the dismay and disorder in society and especially in intellectual society that has been brought about by the lamentable political record of the Western democracies in the last two decades. That this is what has brought universities and much academic intercourse into a state of intermittent civil war can hardly be reasonably doubted. The question remains: why is so much of the conflict focused on the literary enterprise and why does the sociology of literature appear to pose such a threat to literary criticism and education? I should like to suggest that a large part of the reason lies less in differing views on the genetic or ontological status of literature than in the potential of sociology for challenging the very importance of the literary tradition we regard as worthwhile.

Two things have been obvious to observers of modern society at all times: that the overwhelming proportion of what is produced as imaginative writing is ephemeral, and that the residue is of interest to a quite small proportion of the population. One can, if one likes, ascribe this to the progressive degeneration of modern society and, like Q. D. Leavis, postulate a time in the past when the population and its writers were in harmonious communication with one another.[3] Even if true, however, this does not help us very much, for it leads only to ineffectual railing against our fellow man. Moreover, there are some developments in literary sociology that suggest the situation may be even worse than Mrs. Leavis thought. There is a body of sociological evidence tending toward the point that all literature, even that we canonize as great, is ultimately ephemeral, that it vanishes from the cultural memory once the social context to which it is related has passed away. The most prominent proponent of this view has been Robert Escarpit. He has observed that people of any given time generally know about as many contemporary books as books of the past, which suggests a continuous recession of literary works in the cultural memory into oblivion. He has computed that, within one year, ninety per cent of the new books on the market have become unsaleable, and, in the course of time, another ninety per cent of the remainder disappears: "If we count the names of all the writers retained by the historical memory of a given nation—that is, the writers mentioned in the histories of literature, the encyclopedias, the school or university curricula, the academic theses, the erudite articles published in specialized reviews, the papers read in symposia and congresses—we find that they represent about 1 per cent of the number who actually wrote and published literary books."[4] Since Escarpit believes that a work of literature remains alive only as long as it speaks to the experiential world of the literary (and ruling) class, it follows logically that even a Molière will vanish eventually from the cultural memory. This view has been sharply challenged by another literary sociologist, Hans Robert Jauss,[5] and it is one that literary critics would be inclined to reject angrily.

But what are the facts? Several years ago a Swede, Karl Erik Rosengren, undertook to find out. The implications of his remarkable *Sociological Aspects of the Literary System* have not, I think, been sufficiently pondered. Although Rosengren presents his work as a technical investigation in sociology, it is, in fact, an inquiry into the cultural memory of literature. His ingenious method was to take reviews of new books and count the mentions in them of authors other than the one under review. In other words, it is an investigation of the consciousness of past literature in the minds of a literate although nonacademic segment of the population. Rosengren's study is complicated and cannot be treated in detail here, but what he found was this: "the mentions tend to concern writers that are some 60 or 70 years old, that is, in most cases, they are the writers who were leading the development some 30 or 40 years ago. . . . The reviewers, who might choose among writers for a huge time period, some 3000 or 4000 years, prefer to move within a span of some 50 or 60 years."[6] Moreover, this result was the same for reviews taken from two widely differing periods: the 1880s and the 1950s and 1960s. Rosengren concludes from his analysis of the data that all classics, ancient and modern "are less and less remembered. . . . At last they will be dropped for good into that basement storey of the literary system inhabited by the historians of literature."[7] The process described by Escarpit has a vanishing point; all authors eventually die.

Even Homer? Even Shakespeare? Well, I know from my own boyhood environment that an appreciation of Shakespeare is far from a natural instinct. Where I went to school, Shakespeare was generally regarded by my peers as hopelessly highfalutin, fustian, and pointless, one more absurdity in the incomprehensible hazing process that schooling meant to most of them. I doubt if the great majority of my schoolmates have read or heard a line of Shakespeare since, and sometimes I think that the only counterbalance to such an attitude on my own part at the time was the sight of my not excessively intellectual father silently reading his Shakespeare year upon year. The genteel are likely to ascribe this difficulty to the Boeotian taste of the petty bourgeoisie and working class, but in fact the character and sensibility of many of our teachers did not inspire confidence in the culture they professed to propagate, and it was hard to invest credibility in a system that regarded Thomas Hardy as appropriate required reading for adolescents in a midwestern industrial city. The taste for Shakespeare is a cultivated one in the literal sense of the word. Of course, we have all known this for a long time, but we have protected ourselves against the knowledge by implicit value judgments on cultural levels. The threat of sociology lies in the implication that, from the point of view of society as a whole, Shakespeare is not important or is an ornamental possession of a minority culture.

Objections can easily be raised to Rosengren's results. One critic of his book complained that a study of reviewers was distortive because they would have a natural bias for the moderns.[8] Presumably a reviewer confronted with a new work of Ibsen would not normally think of adducing Horace or Chaucer for comparison. But there is something to be said for the selection of book reviewers as representatives of the most cultivated and literarily sensitive nonacademic part of the population that one is likely to find apart from writers themselves, despite the bad reputation reviewers have in academic theory. One might also object that under certain circumstances literature of the distant past can be propelled into commanding relevance. The Renaissance is the paradigmatic example in Western culture; on a smaller scale, the orientation of a self-educated neo-Romantic like Hermann Hesse on a century-old literary culture is similar. But whether the tendency toward the vanishing point is absolute or not, there is enough plausibility in Rosengren's codification of the peripheral status of literature in modern society to give one pause. In another place, Rosengren determined that not even students of literature read poetry voluntarily,[9] a result that has not surprised any of my colleagues to whom I have mentioned it.

The point of all this is surely not that the intrinsic value we know in literary culture is not in itself important and real. A society without a conserving culture would presumably forget all its experience apart from the technological knowledge needed for its material support and a body of myth necessary to its continuing self-regard. No one, except perhaps some extremists on the farthest Left, is proposing that the cultural memory should be allowed to work this way. But the implications might well cause us to take the student slogan of "relevance" more seriously or to be a little more cautious about denouncing it as "presentism." For it would seem that the preservation and transmission of past literature in the educational process is unnatural from a sociological viewpoint, and this may cause some concern when we consider the remarkable hold that the study of literature strives to maintain upon university education. In higher education in the West, literature is pursued more consistently and universally than any other subject, certainly more than any other art. Is it really true, as Herbert Singer has recently asked, that literature is so much more sublime than, say, visual art or music?[10] Furthermore, it is often a particular kind of literature, and the kind of criticism generated by it, that maintains this monopoly. When I went to college, it would have been the wily undergraduate who could have got a bachelor's degree without studying Wordsworth, but now a number of rather hard questions about this kind of exclusiveness are forcing themselves upon the agenda. Nor does it seem that confidence is intact within the academic profession itself. Frederick Crews was able to write in *PMLA*, without much fear of contradiction, that "it is widely known that most academic criticism is practiced without enthusiasm and even with a certain disbelief,"[11] and we have been recently treated to an account of a progress from student of literature to academic prominence in scholarly work, textbook-writing, and grant-holding so shamelessly cynical that the author in decency found it appropriate to hide behind a pseudonym.[12]

For these reasons, the challenge of literary sociology is not exhausted as a conflict in the realm of hermeneutics, as strenuous and vexing as that part of the debate may be. It raises questions about the status and importance of literature in the whole human experience that are threatening for those who believe that education is primarily or in very substantial part literary education, and it confronts us inescapably with the long-observed fact that literary culture is an elite possession and that efforts to make it more catholic and disseminate it more broadly have not succeeded. Contemporary academic criticism has reached such a level of esoteric refinement and abstraction that it requires an effort to remember that the New Criticism, as Helge Hultberg[10] and Geoffrey Hartman[14] have had occasion to point out recently, was born in a desire to democratize access to literature. The challenge of literary sociology, its range and seriousness, as well as the experiences of recent years, make it probable that our response will have to be something more substantial than contemptuous remarks about "sociologism," insistence upon the specialized purity of the interpretive endeavor, or incantations about the autonomy of art and its timeless values.

One possible response is to mount a broad attack upon the transmission of traditional literary culture and academic criticism as irrelevant, elitist, supportive of the status quo, and as a diversionary anodyne to critical opposition. It is no accident that some of the bitterest rebelliousness in the German university has come from students of *Germanistik* or in the Modern Language Association from the English contingent, for these are, in both cases, the literary disciplines that are in closest touch with primary and secondary education and thus have the widest social implications. The imperious willingness of the most outspoken of these activists to cut the link with the whole literary tradition as it has accumulated canonically is supported by and inspired by the results of literary sociology. The determination and dedication of these dissidents has resulted in the installation as president of the Modern Language Association a man who could write: "Force-feeding people on a rich diet of Western masterpieces will only make them more sick," or, "The obsessive concern for the self—perhaps best exemplified by the academic popularity of Camus during the McCarthy years—internalizes all aspects of reality and immobilizes the will; it effectively disables the capacity for action," or, "I doubt that I shall teach Proust again, though I hope to read him on the barricades—if it comes to that."[15] This is our native version of the confident fanaticism of the German student who requires of the literary discipline "die Zerschlagung kultureller Privilegien."[16]

Academic literary scholars of a less radical bent have had few means of coping with this sort of thing other than an unvarying insistence upon the purity of aesthetic experience or a retreat into a posture of injured and often surly innocence. The reason is, I think, an unwillingness to listen to and assimilate those principles of literary sociology that actuate the radicals and that are irrefutable or at least plausible. Among them are the kind of perspective that is put upon the issue of "presentism" by studies such as those of Escarpit and Rosengren, which require us to regard the kind of literary education we have been pursuing as unnatural and therefore modifiable under compelling circumstances, without denying its value and justification in a properly defined universe of discourse. Such a willingness seems to me especially necessary in the area of public school education— the failure of which is so evident that it can no longer be ignored— and must be found also in higher education if we are to reach the forlorn self-seekers that make up a substantial portion of our university population. Even more urgent than the sociology of literature may be some admission of a sociology of criticism. The fact that much of the New Criticism developed from an analytical, rational, and democratic purpose into a neo-Romanticism, often ecstatic and sometimes obscurantist, which elevates literature to a redemptive universalism that sociological results flatly contradict,[17] cannot be separated from the fact that many New Critics were conservative or reactionary in their views generally and susceptible to religious orthodoxies. Until the moderates and the radicals begin talking about roughly the same thing, the discipline of criticism will continue to be lacerated by controversies without partners.

Another possible response is to recognize that the academic literary enterprise has probably become overextended. Voices suggesting this are heard from time to time. Leonard Forster has remarked: "It seems to me that we are now, in universities all over the Western world, virtually compelling students to exercise a talent [of critical appreciation] which very few of them possess."[18] Such an admission is painful, for it implies the bankruptcy of a universalistic endeavor of many decades. But literary sociology can help us to cope with it. Whether the students possess the talent or not is not altogether on the point. For reasons that sociology makes plausible and natural and that have become exacerbated by the circumstances of the contemporary world, it is not possible effectively to hold the attention of all students upon the kind of literary study that the mainstream of academic criticism has come to represent. Therefore, some contraction is inevitable and proper, and experiments in opening different kinds of doors and windows upon literature, as ill-founded as some of them may seem at the outset, are also inevitable and proper. The danger in Forster's response is that it can slip into an intensified form of the kind of elitism that is part of the dilemma in the first place. When a critic can argue that the proper study of literature will be of meaning only to a few, and that even these few will have to "take on trust the value of the activity,"[19] then he is giving his hand to the most thoughtless of the radicals in a common effort to bury humane letters in unreason and irrelevance.

A third set of options is offered by Jost Hermand in his resourceful book, *Synthetisches Interpretieren*. Fundamental to this approach is the desire to demystify literature (thus continuing the original, unachieved purposes of the New Criticism), to abandon efforts to treat it as a religious surrogate or as an esoteric intimation of the mystic oneness of things:

> Let us limit ourselves to seeking our values elsewhere; neither in beauty nor in eternity, but in the framework of the so-called developmental and historical forces. But that is perhaps only possible if we thus giving it a value in itself. It is, after all—like all things human— were finally to cease regarding art as a special modality of being and only an interesting, if imperfect instrument in the framework of the

larger connections of life, the importance of which stands or falls according to whether we ascribe meaning to these connections of life or not. Art can neither bring about an "aesthetic education" of man-kind, nor can it transcend the historical and concrete into the ex-istential or the generally human. Strictly speaking, even the greatest works of art are only stepping-stones on the enigmatic paths to hu-manity, whose course is often so meandering that one could almost despair of them.[20]

Hermand, in his energetic role as apostle of the Enlightenment to modern times, has a tendency to hyperbole, which derives from his impatience with Heideggerian excesses in German criticism. But his appeal for some modesty in our endeavors is very needful now, and "synthetic interpretation" requires of us at the very least that we cease refusing admission to knowledge and understanding drawn from other disciplines. Would a botanist argue that one must study a plant without regard to the soil, the sun, and the rain, the diurnal and sea-sonal cycle, the conditions and purposes of its cultivation, the whole web of life and reality in which it is involved? The refusal to admit pertinent knowledge and thought is a peculiarity of modern literary scholarship that it shares only with obsolete forms of theology, and the comparison itself suggests something about what happened to criticism a generation ago.

It should not be forgotten that one of the important impulses of modern criticism was I. A. Richards' discovery that university stu-dents could not read poems. Education is the most substantial aspect of literary scholarship, and it may be doubted whether this purpose has been advanced appreciably in recent times by the interior mono-logues of critical savants or analytic techniques refined beyond the reach and reasonable interest of most students and educated people. If the purpose of education is neither to produce functionaries for the status quo, nor to pursue the self-centered version of *Bildung* that sometimes has gone under the heading of "liberal education," but to civilize human beings, expand their horizons, increase their sensitivity to the potential of imagination and reality, emancipate them from superstition and the unreflected life, in the hope that human society can thereby be made less barbaric, the study of literature ought prop-erly to be conjoined to these ends by maintaining an awareness of all the lines of interaction with human experience. The paradoxical atti-tude of some literary scholars that they are the guardians of a holy place to which there is only one entrance and that everyone must pass through that entrance willy nilly is not conducive to this end. The way to meet the threat of literary sociology is to cease regarding it as a threat. If the literary scholar regards himself as among the chiefest of the humanists, as he generally does, then nothing human should be alien to him.

Notes

1. Ernest K. Bramsted, *Aristocracy and the Middle-Classes in Germany. Social Types in German Literature 1830–1900*, rev. ed. (Chicago and London: University of Chicago Press, 1964), pp. 3–4.
2. Norbert Fügen, *Wege der Literatursoziologie* (Neuwied am Rhein: Luchterhand, 1968), p. 33.
3. Q. D. Leavis, *Fiction and the Reading Public* (London: Chatto & Windus, 1932).
4. Robert Escarpit, "The Sociology of Literature," *International Encyclopedia of the Social Sciences* (New York; The Macmillan Company and The Free Press, 1968), 9:420.
5. Hans Robert Jauss, *Literaturgeschichte als Provokation* (Frankfurt: Suhrkamp, 1970), pp. 179–80.
6. Karl Erik Rosengren, *Sociological Aspects of the Literary System* (Stockholm: Natur och Kultur, 1968), p. 85. Cf. studies tending to the same point by other means, cited by Joseph Strelka, *Die gelenkten Musen. Dichtung und Gesellschaft* (Vienna, Frankfurt, and Zurich: Europa Verlag, 1971), p. 294.
7. Rosengren, *Sociological Aspects of the Literary System*, p. 83.
8. Lars Lönnroth in *Scandinavian Studies* 41 (1969): 79–81.
9. Rosengren, "Litterära attityder och litterärt beteende," *Litteratursociologi*, ed. Karl Erik Rosengren and Jan Thavenius (Stockholm: Natur och Kultur, 1970), p. 174.
10. Herbert Singer, "Literatur, Wissenschaft, Bildung," *Ansichten einer künftigen Germanistik*, ed. Jürgen Kolbe (Munich: Hanser, 1969), p. 59.
11. Frederick Crews, "Objectivity in Scholarship," *PMLA* 86 (1971): 281.
12. Simon O'Toole [pseud.], *Confessions of an American Scholar* (Minneapolis: University of Minnesota Press, 1970).
13. Helge Hultberg, *Semantisk Litteraturbetragtning*, 2d ed. (Copenhagen: Munksgaard, 1969), p. 7.
14. Geoffrey H. Hartman, *Beyond Formalism. Literary Essays 1958–1970* (New Haven: Yale University Press, 1970), p. xii.
15. Louis Kampf, "The Trouble with Literature," *Change in Higher Education* 2, no. 3 (May–June, 1970): 30, 33.
16. Michael Pehlke, "Aufstieg und Fall der Germanistik—von der Agonie einer bürgerlichen Wissenschaft," *Ansichten einer künftigen Germanistik*, p. 44.
17. Richard Foster, *The New Romantics. A Reappraisal of the New Criticism* (Bloomington: Indiana University Press, 1962).
18. Leonard Forster, "Literary History as an Academic Discipline: Is It Re-

spectable?" *Western Canadian Studies in Modern Languages and Literature* 1 (1969): 21.
19. Wesley Trimpi, "The Definition and Practice of Literary Studies," *New Literary History* 2 (1970): 191.
20. Jost Hermand, *Synthetisches Interpretieren. Zur Methodik der Literaturwissenschaft* (Munich: Nymphenburger, 1968), p. 234.

Karl Tober

POETRY, HISTORY, AND SOCIETY?
REFLECTIONS ON METHOD

THE FORMAL TITLE OF THIS ESSAY PLACES POETRY IN A FRAMEWORK OF relationships as if these were self-evident. Yet, within this title are concealed all the possibilities of German literary criticism, from anti-lyrical positivism to antihistorical close reading and sociological analysis of literature that is alienated from poetry. A critical study and evaluation of the topic in terms of a history of criticism certainly cannot be attempted here;[1] however, such a study would draw attention to the danger of arbitrary and quick-and-easy critical solutions. It would also be an invitation to a more liberal and unprejudiced, though not unconditional, contemplation of poetry that would be preferable to a progressive critical violation of German studies by means of one-sided doctrinaire manifestos. Here I take the somewhat conservative view that there does exist a difference in the intention, in the structure and in the communicative value of an advertisement and a poem. In doing so I purposely refrain from justifying this viewpoint. Unhewn blocks of marble and Michelangelo's David both exist.

Having thus established terra firma, however, the terms appearing in the title must be clarified, at least with reference to our topic, before we can discuss their highly debatable interrelation. To begin, there is no kind of agreement as to what is a poem, and it is very doubtful that this question can be answered at all in the sense of the concept "lyric." The "lyrical"[2] would admit rather more easily of a definition, but even this would call for such limitations and reservations as appear, for instance, in the qualification of Staiger's concept put forward by Henel.[3] Thereby, however, we would in fact be limiting our considerations to the *Lied* and we would be excluding the

ode and the hymn, the sonnet, the epigram and the elegy, philosophical and didactic poems, to name but a few. And yet the lyric,
this "enthusiastisch aufgeregte Naturform der Poesie,"[4] embraces all
these genres and forms.

They are distinguishable from one another by the degree of structure and the consciousness of form, by universal content and the self-
awareness of the poet. One may, like Günther Müller, consider the
song and the ode as the two basic and ultimate forms of poetry: the
former as the expression of a hermetic self, the latter as the inner
response to a "richtendes Gegenüber,"[5] an external and objective
stimulus or idea. In them, and in allied forms, history and society
will assert their influence in different degrees through the person of
the poet, through the nature of the publication and the readers,
through criticism and manipulation, either directly or indirectly.

Definitions of the lyric in the sense of Aristotle, of Horace, yes even
of Benn, or in the sense of all other principles of normative poetics,
from the very outset would offer neither a basis for nor an approach
to a historical or sociological enquiry, quite apart from the fact that
poetics as a theory of literature has never been concerned with the
lyric and the lyrical to such a degree as it has with the epic and
the drama. Doubtless this is in part caused by the nature of lyrics
as "unmittelbare dichterische Gestaltung gemüthafter Weltbegeg-
nung ohne das Dazwischentreten eines Geschehens . . ."[6] Thus in
a certain sense it is understandable if some of the more recent studies
of poetry also aim at literary theories based only on close reading
of individual poets, especially when from the beginning one must
decipher the genesis of cryptographic images and motives, as in the
case of Clemens Brentano or Conrad Ferdinand Meyer. On the
other hand, an interpretation based solely upon the notion of epochs
or periods in poetry would lead to an isolation of the problem within
historical phases and would virtually prevent any literary judgement
from transcending epochs.

However, this means that we cannot really do justice to the problem which we have set ourselves—neither on the basis of a normative
ars poetica, nor yet by means of the poetics of periods. A more modest
starting point would be the poetics of genres and of forms transcending periods. Thus in the terms of our topic there cannot even be any
question of the poem per se, that vague, ageless and delicate structure of poetical imagination, which, be it in regular or irregular
rhythm, could be distinguished from the epic and dramatic forms
through structure and length, through origin and function, or through

lack of events and intention. With reference to our topic, one cannot even speak of the Middle High German *Spruch,* or of Hölderlin's *Hymne;* one can only speak of them as changing forms which transcend the epochs, as they have been examined as song or elegy, sonnet or ballad, ode or epigram.[7]

But if we return to the "lyrical," then it soon appears that the continually changing relationship to it is visible not only in the manifold and contradictory views, but also in the preponderance of single forms of the "lyric" in specific epochs, and in the dominant position of epic or dramatic genres. One can take as an example the dominance of the "lyrical" in symbolism which deeply permeates the other genres, as in the "lyrical drama," or in the structure of the *Novelle* which is determined by the interrelation of symbolical images and gestures.

When we attempt to understand the poem within the sphere produced by the tension between history and society, we are actually dealing with something which in this sense does not exist: we are dealing with a normative factor, or with a historical category of an abstract genre. Yet our theme demands a most concrete kind of treatment, for history is after all the sum of very real and individual facts and events, even though these can be related to each other. However, corresponding to this very general conception we have a highly personal element in the lyric, as a poetical reality, a literary experience of deep intimacy. It is against the theoretical discussion of this that opposition arises, particularly in the very sphere which makes us attempt to understand poetry: in our love for the fashioned word. We hesitate in subjecting this most immediate of all verbal manifestations, borne upon rhythmical impulses as a formative principle, to the process of rational decoding and diminution.

Neither the function nor the structure of the same traditional form, for example of the sonnet, is constant from epoch to epoch; indeed they are not constant even when found within the same literary period. We need only think of the sonnet during the Baroque period, of Weckherlin's[8] varied moods: a manner à la *Landsknecht* and gallantry displayed with a natural talent in odes and songs, grossness or delicacy often leading to surprising lyrical success. We may consider his metaphysical sonnet "Traum,"[9] in which he stumbles through the alexandrines, quite unaware of the antithetical possibilities of the alexandrine's dual structure and not using it as an instrument of expression or as a mold for contrasting images; he is unable to achieve unity of structure in sound and meaning.

Opitz is quite different: purposely emphasizing the formal principle by calling his poem "Sonnet," he develops the dualistic theme
of mind and matter, spirit and flesh, from the caesura of the alexandrine in the first line onwards, unfolding it in the two quartets of the
opening and supporting the vertical sequence of the syntactical line
upwards by images through the movement of the syntax. In the opening stanza, imprisonment of the body and freedom of the spirit are
antithetic themes bound to the mythological and allegorical fiery
death of Heracles, and, in the closing stanza, reflected in the light
from the eyes of the beloved. These are the opposite poles from which
the triumph of the beauty of the beloved as a reflection of eternal
beauty is postulated, academically phrased, rhythmically controlled
and rhetorically shaped.

But where do such considerations lead us before our theme has
even developed into one of the notorious, what may be called double
"and-" themes, in which everything and nothing can be said? A
poem is not a poem, a sonnet is not a sonnet, a Baroque sonnet is
not a Baroque sonnet. The line could be extended at will beyond
Opitz to the stoically disciplined and dialectically elaborate verses
of Fleming; to the somberly speculative pictorial splendor of Andreas
Gryphius, who completely masters the alexandrine; to the nominally
determined religious panegyrics with circular motion by Catharina
Regina von Greiffenberg; and finally to the rationally metaphysical
structures, over-elaborate mannerisms and emblematic conglomera-
tions of Lohenstein and Hoffmannswaldau.

Already this sketchy and casual outline, which singles out some
features of the Baroque from the broad stream of the developments
and changes of the baroque sonnet in superficial codewords, implies a
historical process and suggests a specific position for each of these
poets within the period. This survey of the development of the sonnet
in the Baroque becomes clearer if we consider also the connection
with certain *Sprachgesellschaften,* the impact of the biographical
and social formative powers, and the differing principles of poetics
to which the authors subscribe. Not only does the sonnet form then
become enriched with different universal content by the phasic evolution of the seventeenth-century lyric, but its variability is further
determined by the development of the poetical language in the
Baroque period. Whether we interpret a single poem, study the complete lyrical works of an author, or study a specific lyrical form, an
emblem or a topos of the Baroque, we shall always (of necessity to
a different degree and with varying emphasis) bring historical and

social factors, principles of poetics and elements of interpretation dialectically into critical opposition.

When viewed in epochs the questions keep multiplying, and increase further when the history of genres is also taken into consideration. Goethe's poem "Das Sonett," [10] for instance, shows the middle-class concept of classicism to be questionable, while in "Natur und Kunst . . ." this is reaffirmed in the manner of an exemplary belief. On the other hand, Eichendorff's third sonnet [11] is a poetical transcription and a cryptography of the subjective echo situation, far removed from society, made communicable through the romantic consciousness of being a poet. His historical and sociological characteristics are not to be deduced from his lyrics, which tend inwards, but from his prose and novel, political thought, philology and literary criticism.

The poems of Conrad Ferdinand Meyer do not become understandable through the revelation of their biographical basis or of their content, but only by means of an insight into the genesis of a few complex and interwoven circles of motives. Like his other poems, Conrad Ferdinand Meyer's sonnets are subject to those laws peculiar to himself: laws demanding a slow ripening and a widely ramified relationship of a small number of images and motifs which change or unify, as a hidden and static reflex of his inner self. This is not applicable only to "Die Waffen des Achill," [12] for instance, but also to those long poems in which the form of the sonnet remains hidden, as "Im Spätbot" or "Chor der Toten." The "Neue Gedichte" with over forty sonnets is not only Rilke's real breakthrough in the purely symbolist poetry—in which the most fleeting thing, the coming of inspiration, assumes form in the most substantial, in the thing—it is first and foremost, as can be seen in the contrapuntally dominant introductory sonnet "Früher Apollo," the culminating point of a movement which begins with the young Goethe and reaches into the lyric of the present, of the "Moderne": the poet's self-awareness and self-expression as the leitmotiv in a work of art. Yet this historical insight, which goes beyond the concept of epochs, is a result of structural and textual analysis and of a knowledge of poetics. Their interaction and conflict, their interplay, reveals that the problem is one of method.

Up to this point we have brought elements into relationship with the poem as if they were constant, and as if the poem in all its forms and types on the other hand were something which cannot be ascertained as either "the lyric" or "the lyrical." But is this so? Let us turn first to the most obvious: when we say "history," what "history" do we mean? History as Christian revelation underlying the Old High German and Middle High German literature; as a historical reflex of the present from humanism to the early eighteenth century; as a radical equation devoid of value judgement of every historical moment in the sense of positivism; as the teleological doctrines of a messianic nationalism or communism, or as the "Antihistorismus des gegenwärtigen Zeitalters"?[13] And history in which sense? Poetry as history or history as poetry, as object, as cause or as concept? As that which was valid, or that which is valid?

Above all every poem of the past and of the present is history as an embodiment of language, and by this I do not refer only to the main phases in the history of language, for instance Old High German, Middle High German and New High German, but to the factual existence at a given time of a colloquial idiom with its provincial, social and functional differentiations, upon which every poem is built. We do not need philological or linguistic examples to establish this. The fundamental existence of words as text and information cannot be separated from the element of time affecting the being of the word and the change in meaning and in form: *Herz* as used by Walther von der Vogelweide, Goethe and Celan semantically denotes something entirely different. The poem is always of the past, it becomes real and problematic and of the present by means of reading or hearing.

Not only the words in the poem, but firstly their existence in form and genres have a historical nature. The alexandrine sonnet of the Baroque, the free rhythms of Goethe in the early seventies, the amphibrachic verse of Celan are not specific structural phenomena by chance, but organic expressions of a changing consciousness of art and time; metaphysically based antithesis, the shaping of experience in the free association of nature, of art, and of love, a passing from the vegetative and organic to the inorganic and petrified, from the speaking with God to the poetic soliloquy even to the answerless silence: these are lyrical attitudes which become decisive in the selection of words, in rhythm and syntactic movement, in melos, strophic form and imagery, but each in a very different way.

It is precisely the analysis of epoch-transcending constants in the lyric, like that of the forms, which opens one's eyes to the historical nature of these most immediate and intimate works of literature. This is also true of research into the topos. Its results should not stress the unifying factor as much: on the contrary, they should lay emphasis on the uniqueness of related phenomena. Thus the topos of the *Schiff*[14] as employed by Sebastian Brant is a vehicle for moral and didactic thought steeped in traditional rhetoric and middle-class humanism, varied by allegorical allusions which are justified juridically and biblically. In the poems of Andreas Gryphius the ship expresses the stormy voyage of human life between time and eternity. Eichendorff[15] uses it as a means of showing the poetical journey through the world between the demonology of nature and the service of the poet, ordained by God. For Conrad Ferdinand Meyer[16] it is a poetical hieroglyph of the *rätselhafte Flammenschrift* of his own work. For Hofmannsthal[17] it is the *Erlebnis* of the poet between preexistence and existence; for Weinheber,[18] a magical figure for a world-wide journey *Im Grase*; for Paul Celan[19] it is a *Schuttkahn*.

The outlines of development are no different if we select a few from amongst those poems in which history is the subject. Rist's[20] sonnet on the death of Wallenstein becomes an example of the universal drama, which seeks to *erweisen* the subjection of all mankind to *vanitas* and *fortuna* by the sudden downfall of a great man. Goethe's occasional verses[21] prior to his stay in Weimar, those concerned with the Weimar society, its persons and its events all bear the authentic stamp of the style of his epochs, from the storm and stress to classicism and his late poems, all attempt to perpetuate the moment of inspiration by rendering it tangible. The historical phenomenon of the style of an epoch is also important in understanding poetry. How much history as a theme is always only an incentive to lyrical representation is shown particularly by the poems of Conrad Ferdinand Meyer. In his works the artistic and historical motifs have no other function than that derived from nature and from love; they offer possibilities to render concrete inner visions—the "Traumwelt" of Meyer which rests upon few symbols—and to make visible the inspiration itself. It is illuminating that it is in the nature of historical facts to offer greater resistance to the complete transformation into symbolical images than do the symbols derived from nature and from love; the historical seems to make that parallelism between the interior and the exterior more difficult. For this Meyer finds an epochal poetic technique, the static poem. Its structure is not determined by the matter or by the idea, but by the poet's intention. Meyer's poems speak of themselves. In the poem the poet aims at making visible the moment of inspiration in a state of timeless suspension.

For this reason the historical material withstands the imprint of a truly static structure. Meyer is least successful where he attempts to transform history into this kind of lyric. Even in the later poems, he has to grasp at dynamic structures, a form not suited to either him or his poetical intentions. When for example he imitates Goethe and the Romantics in his first attempts, he does so clumsily. Such considerations may offer a basis for a value judgement. Despite all Meyer's efforts, poems such as "Cäsar Borgias Ohnmacht," "Der sterbende Fechter," or "Vercingetorix" do not belong to his best. The ballad is the appropriate lyrical form for the representation of historical matter: it allows by narrative means the presentation of time-bound themes. Where the historical becomes part of the lyrical program in the sense of everyday events, as with the "Jugenddeutschen," the poem degenerates into trivial literature; where it appears as a poem of praise and admiration, it hides its triviality under the cloak of heroic verse. This is true of tendentious literature in all epochs, no matter if the poem is addressed to Prince Eugene, Hitler, or Mao. History as the content of the poem has, therefore, in the phases of literary development necessarily a different significance in the various categories of the lyric. Yet again the poem is history by virtue of the person of the author, of the moment and of the manner in which it has been written down, and further through its origin, printing, distribution and impact. Language, author and reception make the poem a product of time.

We have reduced the abstractions "poetry" and "history" to many nuances of meaning, for what would be the sense of interpreting the general, if it did not also serve to aid us in the recognition of the specific? If we consider the relationship of poetry and society, then similar questions arise, as in the interplay of poetry and history, because society after all is a decisive manifestation of the historical.

The poem already has a "social" existence in so far as it is language. Language wishes to communicate and to mediate and even as a poetical instrument it still has this desire, whether we agree with the differentiations made by Wladimir Weidlé, who distinguishes between a language of communication (l) and a second one, an actual language with fictional (f) and poetical (p) elements, or whether we accept F. W. Bateson's definition of style as an aesthetic cycle. In the poem, language is also communication, by means of the "I–you" relationship between text and reader existing beyond the author as the creator, although the making and intention of the poem may be very much in the character of a soliloquy. On the other hand this does not mean that poems are only understandable in sociolinguistic terms. On the contrary, the sociology of language aims at the "linguistic cycle" and precisely for this reason it has offered no useful results to the critic or to the historian of literature up to the present. This has lately been shown by Strelka with great clarity.[22]

In addition, the obvious and manifold relationships between language and society have not been productively enough explored in the understanding, interpretation, and evaluation of poetry, except in the very limited field of biography. The role of the ministeriales in *Minnesang*, of the guilds in *Meistergesang*, of the *Sprachgesellschaften* in the Baroque and of the sons of parsons in eighteenth-century German literature is sufficiently known. However, one should not imagine that in accepting these facts one has exhausted the whole range of critical questions. This is not so even in the case of poems which may contain direct references to the author's position within a changing society, such as Walther's "Sprüche," Logau's epigrams, some of the *Xenien*, the political lyrics of the Napoleonic wars of liberation, or Brecht's songs.

The Christian social hierarchy of the Middle Ages, the eighteenth century concept of man as a citizen of the world, the Marxist utopia of classless society all leave their mark on the poetry of these eras. By acknowledging this fact, however, we certainly haven't "done with" poetry, neither in respect of its making nor of its continued existence. Social forces have at different times various effects on the many forms of poetry. They will determine the poem as an entire whole in its stylistic formation, viewed both individually and as representing a genre, and will appear on the one side as a national style and on the other as a period style. One should not think of this as a series of causal connections, but rather as a richly shaded interplay of forces shaping the creation of a poem.

It may be worth while to apply the five methodological models, which I suggested in a different context, to the relationship between society and poetry, particularly as up to now literary-sociological and sociological-literary attempts have with few exceptions been studies in drama and the novel. Whether one can thereby reach a tabular "sociology of imagination"[23] in the sense of Kavolis, or whether we should rather seek sociological parallels to literary structures according to the example of Heselhaus,[24] would depend upon methodological premises.

The two extreme positions are easily described. (1) Literary criticism and sociology have the same object. Principles of sociology are to be transferred directly and exclusively to literature and history.

While we do not wish to limit the Marxist theory of literature to Georg Lukács, he may still serve as an example thereof. His significantly few contributions to the understanding of poetry are for him at best "Schlüssel zur Dechiffrierung der Epik und Dramatik dieser Periode,"[25] namely the time of Wilhelm II. Here the subjectivity of Rilke and George is derived from "der objektiv falschen gesellschaftlichen Lage der deutschen Schriftsteller"[26] and is understood as compensatory achievement of the discontent of the artist caused by his surroundings in the age of security: "In der 'Klage' gewinne—oft ungewollt, fast immer unbewusst—das wirkliche Objekt des Jammers, die unerkannte Struktur der Gesellschaft, eine dichterische Gegenständlichkeit."[27] Lukács also quotes from the "Neue Gedichte" and the "Duineser Elegein" as if, for instance, the meaning of "Der Panther" could be restricted to this sociological formula. Even in literary sociology the text of poems should still be of importance and not only a digit in the history of society. If we compare the assertions of Lukács concerning "Der Panther" with the interpretations by Berendt[28] or Bradley,[29] then the critical weakness of an arrogant, nonliterary methodological dogmatism stands out, just as much as that of a purely textual analysis with occasional references to biography.

(2) The studies of literature and sociology have neither the same object nor the same method. When attempting to understand poetry, one is not concerned with the question of human relationships in the typological sense. We are concerned, however, with the changes wrought by time upon the form of the poem (the general history of literature and literary genres), literary tradition (rhetoric, topos, the history of the mind), and the more exact determination of the "other" reality of the poem, fashioned in "fictional" language (the theory of interpretation).

The last-mentioned possibility was represented in its purest form by Wolfgang Kayser. This is at the opposite pole to the position taken by Lukács, and denies the interchange between imagination and reality in the poem. The fact that literary sociology has its primary roots in the drama and the novel, whereas those of the theory of interpretation are found mainly in the lyric, is a significant methodological viewpoint.

The five possibilities are: to relate criticism and sociology, instead of declaring them identical (1), or to confront them as irreconcilable (2), have hardly been attempted to this day in discussing poetry. One need only to glance at the important collection of essays edited by Reinhold Grimm. At least, one could by means of an individualizing or typifying process pursue the sociological questions in the lyric by *analogy* to the phenomena within literature (3), or one might develop a particular form of the sociology of the poem *within* a more comprehensive theory of literature (4), or, finally, one might try to bring about a unification between the aesthetic and the social in the sense of a dialectical synthesis between formalism and realism (5).

Such a "synthetic" interpretation of a cautiously used dialectical *Kombinatorik*, which must not be confused with a cheap methodological "pluralism," already exists as a theoretical outline, but has led to hardly any practical applications. Such attempts do not extend beyond casual observations, as in Werner Günther's hint about the elimination of the social problems and the fear of the historical in "absolute" poetry, which presupposes a "neues perspektivisches Verhältnis zur Umwelt."[30]

An unsatisfactory and merely partial inclusion in this manner of the historical and social in a more comprehensive approach to interpretation may also have its advantages. For Staiger's warning is to be taken particularly to heart with regard to literary-sociological thinking: "Man kann die poetischen Grundbegriffe nicht schlimmer missbrauchen, als indem man mit ihnen die Interpretation einzelner Werke bestreiten zu können glaubt."[31] For the considerations and systems of literary theory can be nothing but abstractions, which verify suggestions for critical procedures, but which can never replace these. They are—as are also, in a modest manner, the five methodological positions mentioned above concerning the possible relationship between poetry and society—nothing else than models and certainly not secret recipes by which every slovenly cook can be turned into a culinary grand-master.

So the unavoidable result of a blind acceptance of our first position, of the equating, in content and method, of literature and society would be an empty, irrelevant and dangerous schematism to which popularised sociology is particularly susceptible. In 1953 Hugo Kuhn[32] prophetically recognised the need to integrate sociological thought with interpretation as a presupposition of a sociology of art which alone can steer us clear of the domination of "politisch-doktrinären Soziologien." We cannot hope to understand poetry by regarding it simply as documentation of history or a product of society. The limitations of the first have been shown up by positivism, the other is demonstrated by certain trends in the criticism of our day. The poem is primarily a text; its own specific historical nature is shown in its *Sageweisen*,[33] which reflect and represent the moment of inspiration.

The continuous change of the *Sageweisen* is brought about by "die fortschreitende Veränderung des Wirklichkeitssinnes,"[34] a fact which is not peculiar to contemporary literature but which can be gathered from the development and transformation of the *Minnesang*, from the early verses of Kürenberg and Dietmar to the blossom-time of Reimar, Walther, Morungen and to the late *Minnesang* from Neidhart to Wolkenstein, just as it can be gathered from the allegorical character of reality in the Baroque and from the theory of imitation underlying the poem in the age of enlightenment.

Perhaps sociological studies in literature should initially be based on considerations concerning the changing consciousness of reality, for instance on the dual aspect of *Einstellungswelt* and *Vorstellungswelt*; for Heinz Otto Burger this renders Goethe's pictures of *Exorbitanz* as "zur unbefangen von eigener Einstellung angeschauten Wirklichkeit, in der das Leben sich offenbart."[35] The "modern" lyric, on the other hand, accomplishes the "Rückverwandlung der verfremdeten Wirklichkeit in eine neue Welt des Schönen,"[36] which may be interpreted as "Verlust der Wirklichkeit,"[37] or as an attempt "hinter die Oberfläche der Wirklichkeit zu kommen."[38]

Not all the historical and sociological questions concerning poetry can be detached from the wider question concerning the relationship between literature and reality. Here neither the definitions of political realism nor those of hermetic symbolism will suffice. These are fences which cannot be used to confine even a valuable contemporary poem.[39] This is what Goethe[40] had in mind when he wrote in the *Xenien* on "Poetische Erdichtung und Wahrheit":

> Wozu nützt die ganze Erdichtung?—Ich will es dir sagen,
> Leser, sagst du mir, wozu die Wirklichkeit nützt.

History is only part of this "reality" which, even in the era of "imitation poetics," is subject to becoming real by means of the word. In its effect on the making of poetry, its nature and continued existence, society is also a part of this part of reality. Talk about poems flourishing poorly under the omnipotent glare of the sociological basilisk. It would be regrettable if political hysteria and methodological neuroses were to paralyze sociological analysis, which has always been neglected in the study of German literature, before it can take up the insight of Hofmannsthal, "dass das Material der

Poesie die Worte sind," and also that "von der Poesie kein direkter Weg ins Leben, aus dem Leben keiner in die Poesie führt."[41]

A poem by Goethe[42] may serve as a postscript to this tentative line of thought:

> Gedichte sind gemalte Fensterscheiben!
> Sieht man vom Markt in die Kirche hinein,
> Da ist alles dunkel und düster;
> Und so sieht's auch der Herr Philister:
> Der mag denn wohl verdriesslich sein
> Und lebenslang verdriesslich bleiben.
>
> Kommt aber nur einmal herein!
> Begrüsst die heilige Kapelle;
> Da ist's auf einmal farbig helle,
> Geschicht' und Zierat glänzt in Schnelle,
> Bedeutend wirkt ein edler Schein;
> Dies wird euch Kindern Gottes taugen,
> Erbaut euch und ergetzt die Augen!

Notes

1. Karl Tober, *Urteile und Vorurteile über Literatur*, Sprache und Literatur, vol. 60 (Stuttgart, 1970).
2. Emil Staiger, "Lyrik und lyrisch," *Deutschunterricht*, part 2 (1952), pp. 7–12. Reprint in *Zur Lyrik-Diskussion*, ed. Reinhold Grimm, Wege der Forschung, vol. 111 (Darmstadt, 1966), pp. 75–82.
3. Heinrich Henel, *The Poetry of Conrad Ferdinand Meyer* (Madison, 1954); idem, *Gedichte Conrad Ferdinand Meyers, Wege ihrer Vollendung*, ed. Heinrich Henel, *Deutsche Texte*, vol. 8 (Tübingen, 1962); idem, "Erlebnisdichtung und Symbolismus," reprinted in *Zur Lyrik-Diskussion*, pp. 218–254.
4. Johann Wolfgang Goethe, *Goethes Werke*, ed. Erich Trunz, 3d ed. (Hamburg, 1956), 2: 187.
5. Günther Müller, "Grundformen der deutschen Lyrik" in *Von deutscher Art in Sprache und Dichtung*, ed. Gerhard Fricke, F. Koch and C. Ingowski, vol. 5 (1941): 95 ff.
6. Herbert Seidler, "Lyrik," *Kleines literarisches Lexikon*, 3d ed. (Bern and Munich, 1963), pp. 149–51.
7. The studies by Günther Müller, Friedrich Beissner, Karl Viëtor, Wolfgang Kayser and others are adequately known.
8. Cf. the sonnet "Traum" in *Deutsche Dichtung des Barock*, ed. Edgar Hederer (Munich, n.d.), p. 7.
9. Ibid.
10. Johann Wolfgang Goethe, *Werke*, ed. Erich Trunz, 6th ed. (Hamburg: 1962), 1:245.

11. Joseph von Eichendorff, "Sonnet 3: Wer einmal tief und durstig hat getrunken" in *Neue Gesamtausgabe der Werke und Schriften,* ed. Gerhard Baumann with Siegfried Grosse, 4 vols. (Stuttgart, 1957), 1: 69.
12. Cf. works cited in n. 3.
13. Kurt Sontheimer, "Der Antihistorismus des gegenwärtigen Zeitalters," *Neue Rundschau,* 75 (1964): 611–31. I have already drawn attention to the significance of this work in my inaugural lecture at the University of the Witwatersrand: "The Meaning and Purpose of Literary Criticism" (Johannesburg: Witwatersrand University Press, 1965). Reprinted in *Colloquia Germanica* 2 (1967): 121–41.
14. Cf. Rainer Gruenter, "Das Schiff: ein Beitrag zur historischen Metaphorik," *Tradition und Ursprünglichkeit,* Proceedings of the 3d congress of the IVG (Amsterdam, 1965), ed. Werner Kohlschmidt and Herman Meyer (Bern and Munich, 1966), pp. 86–101.
15. Eichendorff, "Der Einsiedler" in *Neue Gesamtausgabe,* p. 299 f.
16. Conrad Ferdinand Meyer, "Schwarzschattende Kastanie," *Sämtliche Werke,* historical and critical edition prepared by Hans Zeller and Alfred Zäch, vol. 2, no. 6 (Bern, 1964), pp. 135–39.
17. Hugo von Hofmannsthal, "Erlebnis," *Gedichte und lyrische Dramen, gesammelte Werke in Einzelbänden* (Stockholm, 1946), pp. 8–9.
18. Cf. Nadler, Josef, *Josef Weinheber. Geschichte seines Lebens und seiner Dichtung* (Salzburg, 1952), p. 242 f.
19. Paul Celan, *Sprachgitter* (Frankfurt a.M., 1961), p. 34.
20. The baroque concept of history not only permeates the novel and the tragedy, but has also a strong influence on the lyric.
21. Cf. Goethe, *Werke,* 1: 86 ff., 106 ff., 256 ff.
22. Cf. Joseph Strelka's exact survey, *Die gelenkten Musen: Dichtung und Gesellschaft* (Vienna, Frankfurt, Zürich, 1971), p. 225 ff.
23. Ibid., p. 238 ff.
24. Clemens Heselhaus, *Deutsche Lyrik der Moderne, von Nietzsche bis Yvan Goll; Die Rückkehr zur Bildlichkeit der Sprache* (Düsseldorf, 1961).
25. Georg Lukács, "Repräsentative Lyrik der wilhelminischen Zeit," *Schriften zur Literatursoziologie,* selected and introduced by Peter Ludz, Soziologische Texte, ed. Heinz Maus and Friedrich Fürstenberg, 2d ed., vol. 9 (Neuwied a.R., Berlin-Spandau, 1963), pp. 469–75, 470.
26. Ibid., p. 470.
27. Ibid., p. 469.
28. Hans Berendt, *Rainer Maria Rilkes Neue Gedichte; Versuch einer Deutung* (Bonn, 1957).
29. Brigitte L. Bradley, *R.M. Rilkes neue Gedichte; ihr zyklisches Gefüge* (Bern, 1967), pp. 73–75.
30. Werner Günther, "Über die absolute Poesie. Zur geistigen Struktur neuerer Dichtung," in *Weltinnenraum: die Dichtung Rainer Maria Rilkes,* 2d ed. revised and enlarged (Berlin, Bielefeld, 1952), pp. 255–84. Reprint in *Zur Lyrik-Diskussion,* pp. 1–45, 29, 37.
31. Staiger, "Lyrik und lyrisch," p. 79.
32. Hugo Kuhn, "Eine Sozialgeschichte der Kunst und Literatur," *Text und Theorie* (Stuttgart: 1969), pp. 59–79, 79.
33. Paul Böckmann, "Die Sageweisen der modernen Lyrik," *Zur Lyrik-Diskussion,* pp. 83–114.
34. Claude Vigée, "Metamorphosen der modernen Lyrik," translated from the English by Josefa Nünning, *Comparative Literature* 8 (1955): 97–99; idem, "Métamorphoses de la Poésie Moderne," *Claude Vigée Révolte et Louanges, Essais sur la Poésie Moderne* (Paris: 1962), pp. 9–43. Translated from the French by Ronald Weber in *Zur Lyrik-Diskussion,* pp. 128–72, 131.

35. Heinz Otto Burger, "Von der Struktureinheit klassischer und moderner deutscher Lyrik," *Festschrift für Franz Rolf Schröder* (Heidelberg: 1959), pp. 229–40. Reprinted in *Evokation und Montage* (Göttingen: 1961), pp. 7–27 and in *Zur Lyrik-Diskussion*, pp. 255–70, 256, 259.

36. Hans Robert Jauss, "Zur Frage der 'Struktureinheit' älterer und moderner Lyrik," *Germanisch-romanische Monatsshrift*, n.s. 10 (1960): 231–66. Reprinted in *Zur Lyrik-Diskussion*, pp. 314–67, 359.

37. Edgar Lohner, "Wege zum modernen Gedicht," *Etudes Germaniques* 15 (1960): 321–37. Reprinted in *Zur Lyrik-Diskussion*, pp. 368–89, 389.

38. Karl Otto Conrady, "Moderne Lyrik und die Tradition" in *Germanisch-romanische Monatsschrift* 41 (1960): 287–304. Reprinted in *Zur Lyrik-Diskussion*, pp. 411–35, 432.

39. Walter Höllerer, "Nach der Menschheitsdämmerung, Notizen zur zeitgenössischen Lyrik," *Akzente* 1(1954): 423–35. Reprinted in *Zur Lyrik-Diskussion*, pp. 115–27.

40. Goethe, *Werke*, 1: 231.

41. Hugo von Hofmannsthal, "Es führt . . . in die Poesie" in the essay "Poesie und Leben" from a lecture in *Gesammelte Werke in Einzelausgaben*, Prose 1, ed. Herbert Steiner (Frankfurt/Main, 1950), pp. 303–12, 307.

42. Ibid., p. 326.

SPECIAL HISTORICAL PROBLEMS

Maxwell H. Goldberg

THE RETICULUM AS EPOCHAL IMAGE
FOR THE TECHNETRONIC AGE

TO ESTABLISH THE SOCIOCULTURAL CONTEXT FOR THIS STUDY, THERE HAS been a deliberate attempt to draw on a wide range of illustrative and implicative materials. In drawing on the extraliterary arts, especially music and visual arts, we have a number of precedents—including the McLuhan-Parker volume *Through the Vanishing Point* (New York: Random House, 1968), which carries the subtitle *Space in Poetry and Painting*, and Wylie Sypher's *Literature and Technology* (New York: Harper & Row, 1968), subtitled *The Alien Vision*, with its extensive treatment of parallels and interrelationships between literature and the other arts.

Most important for the present volume is the premise that the literary mind is bathed in the total sociocultural sea in which the writer is immersed; and that characteristics and phenomena in this sea are likely to become involved, one way or another, with the workings of his imagination, the expressions of his sensibility, and his reactions to the psychosocial sea around him. This holds, particularly, for the reticulum imagery which, like kelp, so variously floats upon or in that sea, and which both influences and is influenced by that sea. History, declared Thomas Carlyle, is philosophy teaching by experience. Similarly, though in no dogmatic sense, this study elucidates by numerous specifics the interconnections between sociology and literary criticism.

I have drawn illustrative contemporary materials largely from American sources. Robert Redfield described the specific questions in Socratic dialogue as being asked with universal intent. The instances, the examples, the illustrations, the cases are here given, if not with universal intent, then certainly with general intent transcending the national boundaries and the geographic limits of given cultures. Thanks to the accelerating exponential increase of those changes that give us the epithet "Technetronic Age," thanks to the totalistic drive of that change which Jacques Ellul has so vividly treated under the term *la technique*, and thanks to those electronic networks of communication and control that help make *reticulum* a key image for the age in which these powerful changes are taking place, what we now experience in one national or cultural locale almost instantaneously makes its mark globally. Indeed, as a result, we may well predict the worldwide acceptance of what Albert Guerard (Senior) insisted upon: literary study is nothing if not comparative. Bergson once observed: "The more one heeds the invitations to analyze urged on by contemporary thought and science, the more one feels imprisoned in the cosmic net of relationships." This leads us to the observation that the more one studies our contemporary and impending sociocultural milieu and matrix, the more vividly one becomes aware that all of us are enmeshed in the same technetronic networks. This brings up to date the definition of society as "a network of nervous systems," which S. I. Hayakawa set forth three decades ago in his best seller *Language in Action* and which he reiterates in the third edition, *Language and Thought in Action*.

Taking our cue from Thomas Kuhn,[1] we may describe the present paper as reflections on what might well emerge as a key paradigm for the Technetronic Age, and hence for the sociology, the literature and the literary criticism of that age. In C. H. Waddington's terse definition, *paradigm* denotes, "simultaneously an apparatus of perception (which brings into focus certain aspects of our existence) and a framework by which the many facets of the universe can be related to each other."[2] The imaging here treated is advanced as likely to replace what Floyd W. Matson has designated the image for the "scientific world view which has been identified for three centuries with the names of Galileo and Newton." This has been derived from the cosmology of classical mechanics, "which has looked upon an infinite universe of perfect symmetry and absolute precision." It has been "in fact, nothing less than the image of the Great Machine." According to Professor Matson, this master image has been broken.[3] It is my thesis that, by way of replacement, another image— or mode of imaging—is asserting itself. To this imaging, I apply the term *reticulum*.[4] By this I wish to suggest not only those containers that are called *reticules*, but also such related images as weavings, webs, meshes, weirs, nets, networks, lattices, cables, ropes, tapes, grids, and systems, as well as tools and processes associated with these: knotting, spinning, weaving, knitting; shuttles, reels, spools, bobbins, distaffs; strands, strings, twine, rope, chains, cables, vines, trellises.

While, on its more formal levels, *paradigm* may be used, with considerable strictness, to describe some of the functions being attributed to *reticulum*, other appropriate usages call for less severe indicative terms. *Paradigm* suggests concentrative foci, interrelational exchanges, and containing frameworks achieved dominantly by what F.C.S. Northrop has called the "Theoretic component,"[5] and what Henry Margenau calls "constructs." It suggests, chiefly, systematic and discursive intellection. True, as may be seen in Alan Jewell Chaffee's "The Triple Eye: Paradigms of Time in Shakespeare's Plays,"[6] it may be applied to analyses in dominantly esthetic studies. Yet for our present purposes, *paradigm* may prove too formalistic. We will therefore feel free to resort to terms that, while possessing a firm core or nucleus of definition, will suggest comparative latitude and open ranges for intuition, imaginative suggestiveness, penumbras of connotation and of perceptive-emotive complexes, bursts, clusters, or constellations.

Taking our cue from José Ortega y Gasset's observation[7] that "perhaps one of man's most fruitful potentialities is metaphor," we might use such terms as *root metaphor, key metaphor, dominant metaphor, controlling metaphor, ruling metaphor*. Where the metaphor is a synecdoche or a metonymy, we may use the term: *partial metaphor. Image, imagery, imaging* may be used comprehensively, generically. These terms may include both literal and figurative components; and may be used when, as Justice Cardozo said of the language of legal opinion and decisions, further distinctions would be needless refinement; or when the attempt at such distinction might prove awkward, even confusing.

It might be said that, in considering the possible use of *paradigm* and *metaphor*, the effort is being made to take care of both the dominantly rationalistic and the dominantly imaginative-intuitive; both the artifactual and the mythopoetic. The latter, Levi-Strauss and the structuralists would maintain, has to do with the parabolic weavings and shapings of the collective unconscious. In this study, *archetype* will be avoided. While recognizing the appropriateness and utility of Jungian (or Platonic) concepts elsewhere, the intent, in the present study, is to waive the ontological issues so often connected with the Platonic *archetype* (or prototype) and to leave at one side the Jungian associations so often made with this term, and also the some-times mystical phylogeneticism so often implied by it.

As is readily recognized, the delimiting lines of *paradigm, metaphor, image* do not run straight; nor are they hard and fast. Actually, there are overlappings—the one shading off into the other. This occurs more frequently nowadays when students of artificial intelligence and of the creation of artificial organisms are challenging traditional notions as to the alleged differences in kind between the so-called literal and the so-called figurative.[8] (These students include those following Turing as well as Marvin Minsky, Charles Rosen, Nils Nils-son, and Bert Raphael of M.I.T.) Yet—to stay within less experimental and tentative bounds—this lack of definitive lines of demarcation is noticeable, particularly, when *paradigm* is used in extended, derivative fashion, or even as outright metaphor. Indeed, one can readily call to mind Frost's observation that "ultimately, all science is metaphor."[9] Nor would one willingly forget the unintentional irony that occurred when, in his history of the Royal Society (1667), Thomas Sprat reported that resolutions adopted by the society ex-acted from all the members "a close and naked way of speaking"[10] in their papers.

Numerous names have been proposed for the age with which this study deals—among them, *post-civilization* (Kenneth Boulding), *megatechnical* (Lewis Mumford); *post-industrial* (Kenneth Galbraith), the *Age of Technopolis* (Nigel Calder); *The Age of Aquarius* (William Braden and *Hair*), and *The Electronic Age* (Marshall McLuhan). Such names for generations, decades, eras, epochs, or ages are themselves likely to designate more or less selective paradigms, more or less comprehensive, suggestive metaphors. I realize, therefore, that any of the names given above is likely, in a given context, to have its appropriateness. My own preference, nevertheless, has been for another epithet: *The Technetronic Age*.

In choosing this new coinage, I risk the purist's charge of jargoneering and of verbal mutilation, of being a linguistic barbarian. Yet I have chosen this neologism because it effectively signals un-precedented features of the impacts and implications, for literature, the literary mind, and literary criticism of exponentially accelerating and—as Jacques Ellul has so variously set forth—totalistic technological change. Professor Zbigniew Brzezinski's hybridizing of *technological* and *electronic* into *technetronic*[11] provides a very useful distinctive demarcation for the present age.

Already in the Spring 1970 issue of the *American Scholar, technetronic*, though differently spelled, appears. Herbert Russcol uses it in an article on "Music Since Hiroshima: The Electronic Age Begins." Linking the concept with Marshall McLuhan's "global village," Russcol declares that the "kids have new ears," and that "they groove with electronic music, the true voice of our 'technotronic [sic] age.'"[12] In another periodical appearing later in the same year, the quotation marks have vanished. In the publisher's column of *Time* magazine, *technetronic* appears without italics and without quotation marks, as a word in general usage.

In this new coinage, the *techne*—from *technology*—suggests effectively building structures, first for shelter, later for other purposes. Then it suggests efficiently constructing tools, instruments, machines to get results faster or otherwise better; then, by analogy, the efficient construction of other sorts of machines, including organized groups of men.[13] As seen in *technique*—especially as the term was used in ancient Greece—*techne* suggests the skill, the craftsmanship, the art demanded for the efficient production of effective instrumentalities for efficacious processes.

The *-tronic*, a linguistic torso derived from *electronic*, suggests the distinctive features of the latest and impending technological developments. This is a heavy reliance on electricity that goes beyond its conventional uses to run the set machines and assembly lines carried over from the earlier epochs of technology. It likewise goes beyond the much more complex and sophisticated noncybernational machinery more recently developed. It goes beyond such usage of electricity as is suggested in the relatively simple, gross and palpable electric imagery seen in Jasper John's *Light Bulb*, of 1966. This is the reduced copy of a lithograph ($19'' \times 24''$) which depicts, on a flat base, the following (from left to right): a twisted tag-end of electric cord with the covering and the wires frayed as though the piece had been ripped from its original connections; the switch-fixture into which one end of the cord had apparently once been inserted and fastened, and then the bulb itself.[14] Indeed, with its stress on the broken and on breakdown, this lithograph might seem to memorialize the end of the classical or Edisonian electric period.

The *-tronic* of *technetronic* also suggests the line of modern development, of achieving visible ends through an invisible means. It is a line of development, moreover, that shows one main branch moving, via the new science of cybernetics, through the modern computer—the first one was built in the same period (1944) that gave us the beginnings of electronic music. The line runs through the computer both in itself, and, as connected into systems, with other computers; with industrial machinery (numeric control), with the "wireless";[15] and more or less symbiotically with organisms, especially man—as seen in *cyborg: cybe*rnetic *org*anism. Used by an eighteenth-century Polish savant and by Ampère and revived in our century by Norbert Wiener, the term *cybernetics* in its root meaning goes back to the Greek for *helmsman* or *steersman*. Hence it comes to mean *controller* (cf. *governor*). This Wiener emphasized when he provided one of his most widely read books, *Cybernetics*, with the subtitle, *Or Control and Communication in the Animal and the Machine*.[16]

The term *technetronic* describes a new variation of consciousness—at least (to use the term that T. S. Eliot helped make current), a new variation of sensibility—a new psychosomatic rhythm of life. Herbert Russcol suggests this when he declares that the "kids have new ears," and that they "groove with electric music." This is seen in such a popular phenomenon as "Electric Rock" and particularly in the "Rock Opera" *Jesus Christ Superstar*, composed by two young Englishmen, Andrew Lloyd Webber and Tim Rice. This was recorded on sixteen-track tape; and, included among the instruments used, were the electric guitar, the electric piano, the positive organ and the Moog synthesizer.[17] As *Life* reported it, only seven months after its release the expensive two-record album of *Jesus Christ Superstar* had already sold over two million copies in the United States alone, and had become "a hit in such far-flung places as Thailand and Brazil." The article went on to observe that, because this rock opera "treats Jesus as a modern man and because the music and lyrics please a variety of tastes, it has bridged the generation gap"; and that because "it is both secular and reverent, it has been embraced by many of the clergy as a way to reach youth." It has been played on Radio Vatican. In their services, churches of various faiths and denominations all over the United States have used segments of the opera. Before an injunction was brought against them by the copyright holders, the American Rock Opera Company produced a choral version and booked 177 dates.[18] The front cover page of the *Life* issue which runs the story about *Jesus Christ Superstar*, carries the banner "Worldwide Success of Jesus Christ Superstar."

The new variation of sensibility or consciousness marked by *technetronic* not only cuts across generational, class, national, and cultural boundaries, it extends, also to those who ostensibly reject the whole technetronic "Establishment." This is seen in the very title of Tom Wolfe's account of the hippies: *The Electric Kool-Aid Acid Test.* It is seen, also, in the *Newsweek* review of this book, where Wolfe is described as a genuine poet. The reason given is "his ability to get inside, to not merely describe (although he is a superb reporter) but to get under the skin of the phenomenon and transmit its metabolic rhythm."[19] This psychosomatic rhythm is—in the term that T. S. Eliot took over from Remy de Gourmont—the objective correlative for a pervasive new variation of collective consciousness. It is not unlike the Consciousness III, which Charles A. Reich sees in the treatment of Ken Kesey in *The Electric Kool-Aid Acid Test* by Tom Wolfe, as a process of continuing growth in new experiences.[20] It is this new variation of consciousness or sensibility which has been so arrestingly articulated in *Jesus Christ Superstar.* This, as *Life* puts it, translates the ancient story of Christ's Passion in "wrenchingly modern idiom." It is the wrenching idiom and rhythms of the Technetronic Age.

Often, as Whitehead and others—among them Carlyle and Coleridge before him—have pointed out, the symbols of a given epoch cease to be vital or viable for later epochs. They may suffer debilitating or devitalizing drain or entropy which, either through desiccation or through atrophy, renders them useless. Or they may default through being a mismatch or a misfit—through no longer being adaptively synchronic with change in the outer world; or with changes in the inner world of the personal consciousness or of the collective unconscious. When this happens, then either freshly adapted and invigorated or altogether new symbols, charged with nascent energy and thrust, have to be elicited or engendered. As Carlyle has so definitively put it: *each generation has to rewrite history in its own idiom.* It must similarly recast its symbols. *Jesus Christ Superstar* strikingly demonstrates both the need and a spectacular response to this need. In terms of Gerard Manley Hopkins' theologically freighted image—what we here witness are shifts of external landscape resonating with symptomatic and radical changes of *inscape.*[21]

Various explanations are being offered both as to the causes of this new variation of consciousness and as to its nature. William Irwin Thompson's *New York Times* articles "Beyond Contemporary Consciousness" constitute one such effort. Under strong influence of Levi-Strauss and the "European Structuralists," Professor Thompson regards this new mode of consciousness as consisting in the shaping of a new cosmic *Gestalt*, which has to be seen through the intuitive and holistic vision of a new "collective unconscious." This new *Ges-*

talt, he claims, will be a function of the psychological process of "spiraling backward" for reunion with the intuitive holistic insights of pristine man and of pristine cultures. It will function in the "relativistic space-time of the unconscious where the past and the future mysteriously interpenetrate in exactly the way the ancient Maya understood in their fantastic calendar of millions of years of cycling, spiraling time."

Already, with varying degrees of talent, art, and insight, there are writers, not necessarily known to one another, or influenced by one another, who are providing visions—albeit of reduced-dimension and but partial outlines—of the structure of this new planetary model for the new planetary consciousness[22] for us sojourners on "Spaceship Earth."

Goethe declared that Nature reveals herself in her wholeness in every part. Robert Frost—like Goethe, exposed in his youth to Swedenborgian analogizing—declared himself to be a synecdochist: "I always put the part for the whole." Ralph Waldo Emerson observed: "The world globes itself in a drop of dew." We may similarly say: an epoch globes itself in its characteristic images, which may be synecdoche, symbolizing the totality through the part; or metonymy, symbolizing, for example, through the container, that which is contained.

The Technetronic Age into which we are so abruptly being catapulted may be said to globe itself in such imaging, particularly that of the reticulum. In reticulum imaging, we have at once an effect and a symbol of our Technetronic Era. We have, also, an agency of unification and synthesis—to trap and bind together the myriad disparates of our age of kaleidoscopic change and of cosmic and parabolic expansiveness. To change the figure, we have, in the reticulum, a master matrix or, better, an armature (as in electric generators and motors, or in certain types of contemporary sculpture), around which to cluster, to organize, and to integrate these myriad disparates into some sort of pattern, however fleeting and transient. Both as social or cultural barometric indicator and as vehicle for personal and social expression, integration and unification, reticulum imaging is worth our study. This imagery might well serve as an index of the capacity of a culture creatively to contain the technetronic expansions and proliferations. The index would be a function of the increased incidence, range, variety and subtlety of the integrative, unifying, reticulum imagery. It may serve as objective correlative for characteristic states of sensibility or consciousness—personal or collective, and for characteristic states of personal and collective internal ecology.

Reticulum-related words are today ubiquitous. On television, a participant in a "talk program" seeks to describe an unexpectedly favorable development in human relations among 800 passengers impatient to disembark, yet kept aboard a cruise ship by a long delay in docking: "They got beautifully enmeshed with one another" (2 May 1971, David Susskind Show, Station WNYC). Notice that the "enmeshed" here shows the characteristic paradoxic ambivalence of reticulum imaging: entrapment, and enfranchisement. Akin to *mesh* is *web*. Explaining why he started to write, Eldridge Cleaver declared: "To save myself." He added that he "had to seek out the truth and unravel the snarled web of [his] motivations."[23] Here *web* is connected with the negative. At other times it is used positively— as in "the seamless web of society."

In *The Chronicle for Higher Education* (5, no. 27, 12 April 1971), a front-page feature article is captioned: "Colleges Trying New Ways to Teach Science." A picture six inches by nine inches accompanies it. It shows about twenty students seated in a classroom. A large spool of twine, about four and a half inches at the base, is held above the center of the group by the instructor. Spokes emanate from that spool of twine—as from the center of a spider's web—out to different terminals. These terminals are either the backs of chairs or students' outstretched hands. Some of the lengths of twine, intersecting en route, form nodes or knots. The text that accompanies the picture tells us that, in a growing number of innovative science courses dealing with the "Human Environment," "University of North Dakota students learn about the 'web of life.'"[24]

Ralph Waldo Emerson is among famous American writers who have utilized reticulum imagery in ways significant for the present study. Sometimes the usage is quite operational. Thus, in his 1844 lecture on "The Young American," he speaks of the "new roads, steamboats, and railroads, especially the railroads," which "annihilate distance," and, referring to Leonardo da Vinci's seminal invention, "like enormous shuttles . . . pattern the various threads of American life into one vast web."

Elsewhere, Emerson's use of reticulum imagery is more philosophic, transcendentalist, mystical. (In this, it anticipates Teilhard de Chardin's concept of the *noosphere*.) Later, Walt Whitman, William Carlos Williams, and Hart Crane were to be among those American writers who insisted that poetry must come to terms with industrialism and technology and assimilate it, humanize it. Thus, almost a hundred years later than Emerson, Hart Crane was to declare that

"unless poetry can absorb the machine—i.e., *acclimatize* it as naturally and casually as trees, cattle, galleons, castles . . . [it] has failed
of its contemporary function." In his essays of the 1840s, Emerson
had made similar pronouncements. He saw, as one of the offices of
the poet and the artist in an industrial age, to render poetic the arti-
facts of the new technology by "re-attaching" them to "nature and
the Whole." Echoing such English transcendentalists as Coleridge
and Carlyle, Emerson declared, "Blessed with high perception," the
poet-artist sees the factory town and the machinery "fall within the
great Order no less than the beehive or the spider's geometric web."
In so doing, the poet-artist is true to nature, who fast adopts, into her
"vital circles," "the gliding train of cars she loves like her own."

The web image appears, too, in Peter Marin's 1970 "Children of
the Apocalypse." In this article, the author voices his aspirations
toward strength, sanity and wholeness. He sees these qualities as "a
function of culture, part of its intricate web of approved connecting
and experience, a network of persons and moments that simultaneously offer us release and bind us to the lives of others."[25] In this
passage, we have two reticulum-related words—*web* and *network*.
We also have a characteristic reticulum paradox: *release—bind*.

Network, indeed, is perhaps the widest and most variously used
of the reticulum-related terms. Of the program for an experimental
production of Ann Jellicoe's *The Sport of My Mad Mother*, the director, Professor Kelly Yeaton of The Pennsylvania State University,
writes: "Sound, light, and movement are tightly locked together in
this production method, as some of the modulations of the light are
caused by the sounds, which are caused by the actors and musicians,
who are responding to the effects of the light. In short, light, sound,
and motion are tied together in a resonant network . . . like mirrors
that all reflect each other." The light, it might be added, is electronically controlled; and much of the sound is of electronic music.

In an educational TV lecture, a professor of business management
explained PERT—that is, Program Evaluation and Review—using a
diagram not unlike that used for organizational charts. It looked
like an organizational grid or flow chart. The lecturer described it
as an "event layout." It depicted, on a time schedule, a series of
events some of which are critically dependent upon others. Some of
them cannot take place until others have taken place before them.
These interrelated critical events were joined by arrows indicating
the contingent cause-effect relationships, thus graphically providing
benchmarks of progress made toward the end-objectives. The lec-

turer described this systematic pattern as a "network of events leading to an end-objective."

In management theory, teaching, and practice, a variation of the
network reticulum imagery is that of the arboreal lattice-analogy—for
instance, "the decision tree," reminiscent of Georgio Tagliococci's
Systems Tree of Universal Knowledge, suggested, possibly, by his
favorite—Vico. Thus, in the *Harvard Business Review* for May-June
1970 (pp. 80–81), the example is given of a New York broker who
may have the option of delaying his decision while he gathers more
information. If so, "the additional options and the consequences of
every set of act-event sequences could be shown on the decision tree,
and an optimum strategy determined in essentially the same way."

Very often, nowadays, *network* is used when reference is made to
communication—especially when associated with such technetronic
instrumentalities and processes as are involved in defense systems,
news gathering, and disseminating combinations (for example, UPI,
AP, Reuters) as well as stock market recordings, exchanges, and
other transactions; radio and television combinations—special cases
being Telstars. The network image, moreover, is suggested in the
very title of the journal *EDUNET*,[26] published by an organization
called EDUCOM, the purpose of which is to make cybernational
systems of information storage, retrieval, and communication as
widespread and as deeply penetrating as possible in American institutions of higher education. There is a wry sort of humor in the circumstance that so-called spy networks increasingly resort to various cybernational and other technetronic instrumentalities and processes in
their farflung and penetrative machinations, as do the fast-spawning
agencies, legal and illegal, of surveillance.

True, as Professor Ernest F. Hayden and others have insisted, for
the man in the street, *network*, as with so many potential image-
words, remains a sheer verbalism, devoid of explicit imagistic content, and foisted upon him by such image-makers as those Professor
Boorstein has depicted in *The Image*—that is, Madison Avenue and
mass media publicists. Yet, in varying degrees of awareness and
vividness, *network* is indeed used with imagist specification.

In all of these instances, the networks may involve major threads,
strands or filaments that are invisible, known only by their effects. If
such networks were to be represented diagramatically, they would
appear as initiatory, nodal, and terminal points punctuating stretches
of open space. Visualized thus, and especially when the diagram
marks a full circuit—from point of origin to point of origin—we thus

see the familiar relationship between such networks and our generic reticulum image.

The technetronically related network imaging, however, is not limited to the prose of practical men of enterprise. It becomes ruling metaphor for the poet, too, as shown by Palmer Bovie in "The Daniads":

> (1) *The electronic network of the telephone*
> Proust heard Our Ladies of the Switchboard
> connecting one soul
> With another, cutting them off, siphoning love
> From one liquid heart to another, eternally still
> Carriers of incomplete messages . . . .
> (2) *The Archaic spinning image*
> Anonymous ancients conferred completeness in life,
> Swelling the spindles with wool when the bread
> was done.
> (3) *The Electronic network image again*
> With the broken rhythm sounds of electronic
> circuitry
> . . .   . let me not fail to mention
> Our daughters of today . . .
> . . .   . sometimes quite thrilled
> To type out evaporative words or answer the phone,
> Connecting one thing with another in adult adoration:
> Listening for the definite ring. First, dial tone,
> Then seven digitary clicks, then the ring your finger
> Fashioned. Now some passion. Is this Our Lady of
> the Perforation?
> I wanted to talk to you. I think it's about my
> salvation.[27]

In this poem, for purposes of satiric irony, the writer juxtaposes, by flashback, the traditional, agrarian reticulum-related imaging with the modern, technetronic reticulum-related imaging. Although not necessarily for ironic purposes, this sort of drawing the reticulum imaging of the past into the present and uniting it with imaging of the present is a frequent practice. Positively, one thus takes advantage of the accumulated freight of association traditionally linked with the imagery drawn from the past.

In celebrating that memorable suspension structure—the Brooklyn Bridge—orators, reporters and poets used the whole stockpile of reticulum-related words—the spinning of the cables, the networks of the support cables, and the harplike nature of these strands when viewed as an ensemble. One of the paintings of the Bridge shows a person on the bridge itself, playing a harp. Indeed, in Henry Miller's violent dreams, the Brooklyn Bridge, he says, became "incorporated in his consciousness as a symbol, a means of reinstating himself in the universal stream." The symbol was "a harp of death." The picture of the Brooklyn Bridge in which the harp appears is an oil by O. Louis Gugliehemi (1938), entitled "Mental Geography." The tower top looks as though a giant had taken a great bite out of it. The major cables are twisted, buckled—both concavely and convexly. Struts are correspondingly strained, dislocated, distorted. Some have snapped like broken harp strings.

Thus, both in Henry Miller's dreams and in O. Louis Gugliehemi's painting, we have two time-differentiated complexes of reticulum-imaging: the harp, from earliest times associated with esthetic beauty and harmony; the suspension bridge, with its associations of the patterning and integrating of the weaving process, and the rational and functional symmetry of technological structuring (John Roebling, designer of the bridge and former student of Hegel, described this process in Hegelian terms: bringing reason into matter). In both instances, the telescoping of time and the juxtapositions of space in the two sets of imagings produce an ironic effect. In the picture the harp is intact and supposedly producing harmony; whereas the bridge is grotesquely mutilated. In Miller's dream, correspondingly, the bridge becomes a harp, not a harp of life however, but a harp of death.[28]

We get another sort of double increment of time in a *Look* item furnished by Louis Botta for his "In the Know." Botta tells of a New Yorker, Helen Dunn, who used to be an actress, and who has turned to creating highly unusual art works. These she calls "3-Dimensional Designs." Her medium itself, related to traditional reticulum imaging, is thread. One of the subjects for which she uses it is Brooklyn Bridge, which, too, is associated with reticulum imaging. Its "threads," however, are associated with the modern megatechnological rather than with personal handicraft experience of what MacLeish has called "the ancient wisdom of the hand." In Helen Dunn's finished representation, we have a composite reticulum imaging, in which the ancient and the modern unite to form a new composite. The literal threads imitate figurative threads (the bridge supports) to produce another imitation of a great reticulum patterning. Here is double (or is it triple?) irony engendered within the *reticulum* mode of envisionment.[29]

In the 1971 catalogue of a publisher of college textbooks (Prentice-

Hall) we have abundant illustrations of how the reticulum imagery of the technological nineteenth century has been carried over into the latter third of the twentieth century—into the technetronic period itself. All in all, this catalogue of thirty-five pages contains eleven bridge-related pictures. They vary all the way from the protobridge formed by stones irregularly placed across a brook to a wooden footbridge, to a concrete and metal overpass footbridge, to elaborately constructed bridges that contain quarters for living and doing business, to the Tower Bridge of London.

By far the larger number of these pictures—either in whole or in part—show suspension bridges. The outside front cover picture shows a tower and span of one of these. It exhibits a double reticulum motif: the lattice, or harp-string, motif of the lateral suspension cables and the loosely lattice-work effect of the trunks and branches of the leafless trees below. The emphasis here, albeit implicit, is already on the combination of the natural reticulum with the man-made reticulum; this combination suggests a twofold pattern of educational experience that is twofold in more than one view. In addition to the man-nature twoness-in-oneness, there is also the art-utility tandem later explicitly stressed. "The intricate design of a bridge formed from steel through the skill of craftsmen; the practical becomes the esthetic" (opposite p. 5). The nature-art or man-made-nature-made duality—twoness that becomes one, a whole—is rendered explicit (on p. 11) by a picture depicting "The contemporary approach—a new way of looking at life. Seen through trees, the bridge becomes a new and interesting pattern against the sky."

Later, the reticulum imagery of the suspension bridge becomes even more explicitly identified with characteristic modes of technetronic envisaging in a very small picture on a black background, which fills the rest of the page. The picture, which suggests one frame on a cinematic film, shows a longitudinal view of a suspension bridge that looks like a thin ribbon. The arcs of suspension suggest waves marching off into the distance. The lateral suspension cables suggest the reticulum. All is in motion; all is kinetic. This is the picture facing a page that features the book *It's Only a Movie*, by Clarke McKowen and William Sparks. That is, it features a textbook on an art which so vividly stresses and demonstrates the kinetic master-impulses of our technetronic era. The film itself—with its reels—is a reticulum metonymy.

What is held up as an ideal unattainable by human beings is the utter and aerial mobility of the gull: "The gull needs no bridge—he needs nothing but the power of his own wings to carry him across the river." This is the condition, according to Jack Burnham, toward which sculptural art, too, is moving. Short of this total divestment of body, the reticulum provides, along with a pattern, a maximal combination of mobility and openness.[30]

Elsewhere we have that kind of reticulum imaging in which the leafless branches of trees, either in themselves or by the alternating images they cast of light and shadow, form a reticulum. In *Life,* 19 March 1971, there was a full-page advertisement for De Beers diamonds. A half-page photo by Jack Ward gives a side-view of the beautiful face of a woman apparently lying on her back and looking up to the sky. We see this face through a lattice of tree branches. The caption is: "A time when mind and heart and all the beauty in the world beat as one."

Such crosshatching, so often superimposed upon drawings, paintings and sculptures of our time, may well be linked with the contemporary predilection for the paradoxic brought out through reticulum-imaging. The dialectic ambivalence—of the antinomic arms of paradox held in dynamic tension—matches a similar ambivalence in the technetronic mentality.[31]

As reticular, the lattice spines that so often crosshatch drawings, paintings, and sculpture favorably responded to nowadays, suggest both a negative—partial obstruction of vision and confinement—and a positive—namely, containment for coherence, for creative constraint. At Davidson College, there has been prominently on display a painting, over the signature of "Jim McCormick," which is entitled *Urban Temple* (1969). Along the bottom of the picture is the word *mecca.* Down the right-hand portion of the picture are various lines—some curved, some oblique rather than actually vertical. But, at the left, reminiscent of the reticular screenings seen everywhere in the Middle East, are crosshatchings that suggest the finely meshed wire used for low garden fences. The total effect here of the reticulum-related imaging is paradoxic: confinement and constraint versus opening up and the freedom of inner space.

In 1971 in the lobby of the Arts Library in Pattee Library at The Pennsylvania State University there was a display by Michel Merle, whose sculptures were made up largely of pieces of machines and junked tools. Some of them were electrically equipped for intermittent light and motion. Covering most of these sculptures from top to bottom, like barnacles, were metal-grid pieces of varying sizes that looked like miniaturized vegetable graters. "Like barnacles" suggests that the works so covered were encased and hence pinned down, rendered immobile. What does this mean? To help us understand, we turn to a mimeographed statement of a "non-interview" with the sculptor, which supposedly is for our edification. From this remarkable contribution to the broadside literature of the absurd, we do seem to extract Merle's basic artistic intention to create iron creatures that are alive, that have basic urges—including the erotic—that have, each of them, his essence, his guiding faith, his basic convictions. Is it stretching the imagination too far to see in the myriad metallic reticula, with which the sculptor has clothed his iron creatures, an expression of the reticulum paradox that is at once an agency of confinement and an agency of constructive or creative containment?

One of the paradoxes that reticulum imaging may suggest has to do with the essential or characteristic epochal rhythms of the Technetronic Age. It is an affair of rhythms that are broken, that nearly break down or nearly break up; yet that are often retrieved in the nick of time by sudden assertions, impositions, or elicitings of pattern. John Marin, in his life style and in his paintings, provides illustrations. Paul Richard has pointed out that, in contrast to the customary associations of gentleness and slowness with *water landscape*, Marin's treatment produces quite the opposite effect of "darting swiftness, of staccato modern speed." This is in keeping with Marin's own methods. With a fat shaving brush in one hand and a paint brush in the other, he "dashed to the finish." His writings, too, says Richard, have something of that go-go-go." For, continues this reviewer, "Marin saw the airplane and the motor car accelerate the tempo of his world, and his pictures seem to crackle with sudden forceful movement." In this he was like that fellow artist associated with Rutherford, New Jersey, William Carlos Williams, whose writing, Walter Schott has declared, "snaps pictures like a marvelous image machine." He "snatched poetry from the instant"; his technique was "swift, fragmentary, compressed." Yet for all this emphasis upon the abrupt, the staccato, the punctiliar rhythms of the snapping camera shutter, Marin himself declared that it was his desire "to paint disorder under the big order."[32] He was seeking to paint a paradox. The reticulum imagery provides a versatile and vivid means for such portrayal of paradox.

We have to exercise tact and flexibility in treating of reticulum imaging as hallmark of the Technetronic Age. We should, for example, distinguish between such imaging when it seeks to be all-encompassing and all-suggesting and when it is only partial. A good instance of the latter is seen in the graphic-arts treatments of Mc-Luhanite books and periodicals. McLuhan's *War and Peace in the Global Village*, with Quentin Fiore as designer, is one such instance. Buckminster Fuller's *I Seem to Be a Verb*, with the same designer, is another.[33] Some issues of *Media and Methods*[34] provide further instances. As a result of the graphic artist's efforts to achieve effects of the multisensory, multilinear, discrete simultaneity attributed to the Technetronic Age, the impression gained from a page in these publications is of a number of different pieces set into a mosaic. The white spaces that serve to separate the pieces, when viewed in a different aspect, form the connective network.

This is seen in an eighteenth century reference to a structure consisting of "small pieces of baked earth cut lozengwise . . . and . . . called reticular from its resemblance to fishing nets." It is likewise seen in another eighteenth century reference to remains, in Salino, of "some walls, evidently, of Roman origin [judging] from the reticulum." *Reticulum* here refers to the netlike effect produced by the raised fillers and binders of mortar inserted in the interstices of the separate stones making up the wall. This is seen also in Home's *Armoury* (1688), where he refers to a "Reticulate or Net Worke walk made Net-wayes or Loseng-wise (III, 45:1).[35]

Let us imagine these "lozenges" dissolved. Then the network would become all the more immediately apparent. This double vision of the reticulate mosaic or the reticulate wall anticipates op art. With op art vision, the reticulum becomes vividly explicit. Something similar occurs when we view a McLuhanesque page; or when we consider a wireless circuit (radio, television) as a network, a technetronic reticulum. Indeed, the McLuhanesque page or the wireless reticulum would be quite appropriate as symbolic of the Technetronic Age. Both of these reticula would be quite appropriate as resonating to a distinctive mode of collective consciousness, and as objective correlatives for personal sensibility characteristic of the age. In reticulum imaging that articulates such distinctive modes of emergent sensibility in the Technetronic Age, the electronic factor as such, may be quite submerged or altogether lacking. What is explicit and imagistically significant is the reticulum imaging—more or less direct, which is so congenial to the age.

In a seminar, one member tried to convey his idea of the relationship between the individual and society. He likened individuals to the strands often embedded in fiberglass used as panels to cover the insides of commercial aircraft. According to this imaging, just as the fiberglass fixes the overall shape of the individual strands and fixes the pattern they form, so society fixes the overall shape of the individual and fixes the pattern the individuals collectively form. Another member of the seminar preferred a different imaging. He said that the relationship between the individual and society is best represented by a semipermeable membrane—allowing for mutually enriching osmotic exchanges. Both analogies are reticulum-related. The fiberglass-strand combination produces a network effect; and a semipermeable membrane is a kind of network—very fine-meshed, to be sure—yet after all, reticulate.

Often the present technetronic reticulum-related imaging represents a cumulative process—the taking over, from the past, of association-laden reticular imagings and then combining them into a freshly fused technetronic amalgam or alloy stronger than any of the components alone. The nervous system as network provides varied illustration. With reference to the human organism, reticulum imagery has a long history. Thus, writing in the period of the late sixteenth or early seventeenth centuries, when both biological and intellectual anatomizing was the vogue, John Donne memorably gives us such imagery. In his "The Funeral," he psychosomatically—or neurophysiologically—declares that it is "The sinewie thread" his "braine lets fall/Through every part" of his body which "Can tye those parts" and make him "one of all."[36]

The linkages between (1) the imaging of the nervous system as network and (2) the reticulum as generic metaphor for the Technetronic Age have been made more intimate by the increasingly frequent association of the electrical and electromagnetic with the traditional imagery of the neural network. This has been occurring in at least two ways. First, as with other bodily systems, there has been the increasing use of electronic devices in connection with experimental and diagnostic treatments of the nervous system. Second, there have been the progressive discoveries and refinements showing how pervasive and subtle the electronic phenomena associated with the neural network are. Thus, there are the references to the synaptic electronic discharges, to neural oscillations to electromagnetic fields. There is the comprehensive imaging of the neural processes as those of electronic circuitry.

Recently, the electronic phenomena related to the neural network have been given two kinds of public dramatization likely to make their mark on the literary imagination. The first has to do with scientific corroborations of what the masters of yoga have known and exemplified for centuries: we can learn to control body functions commonly regarded as involuntary (and stressed as such, for example, by Dr. Cannon in his *Wisdom of the Body*; and following him, by the literary scholar-critic Stanley Burnshaw). We can learn to sweat more, salivate less, control heartbeat and blood pressure, and above all—for our present emphasis—change the rhythm of brain waves. Further, with greater sophistication and subtlety, these waves are differentiated as electronic excitements and patternings. Thus, in his "Brain Waves, The Wave of the Future," Dr. Rovik writes: "psychedelic drugs may soon give way" to a "new brain-wave mastery over mind and body . . . the electronic high."[37] A perusal of the reports of the experiments warranting this prediction shows, moreover, that electronic instrumentalities have been pervasively involved. We thus get a double dose of fresh electronic associations related to the neural network, hence to the reticulum image. Such associations, however, are not linked to the neural network alone. They are associated, as well, with the spectacular achievements in molecular biology. This, moreover, liberally utilizes cybernational conceptualization, idiom, and imagery—including "genetic code," "information storage, retrieval, overload, and breakdown," and "information network."

On the front-cover picture for the 2 April 1965 issue, *Time* celebrated that extraordinarily versatile technetronic instrumentality, the computer, depicted by Boris Artzybasheff as domineeringly hominoidal, and as being serviced by a swarm of *homunculi*. Five years later (issue of 18 April 1971) with the caption: "The New Genetics: Man Into Superman," *Time* gave the same prominent position to a celebration of one of the most dramatic biological achievements. This was done largely with technetronic instrumentalities and processes (electronic microscopes, and so on). It was the identification of the double helix that carries the genetic code and the deciphering of that code itself. The terms used to describe the nature and functioning of the "double helix"[38] are in the cybernetic idiom linked with information theory and general systems science and technology. The double helix, moreover, forms a type of reticulum-related imaging. In the sense of enmeshment, too, the helixes are here depicted as reticula. For, running down the left-hand side of the page, there is a double helix, made up of two criss-crossing strips with horizontal latticing across one of the four oval segments made by the crisscross. This is superimposed upon the image of a male, with arms uplifted and hands criss-crossed, and with legs similarly criss-crossed, hands and legs thus coalescing with corresponding oval segments of the double helix. Along the right-hand side of the picture is a corresponding treatment of a female figure. The total effect is that of the two human beings enmeshed in their genetic codes and under its domination. The article itself that treats of these biological wonders and promises, or threats, is generously illustrated with diagrams that provide examples of practically the whole range of reticulum-related imagings. When we recall the emphasis now being given to the electromagnetic impulses or discharges associated with molecular phenomena, with macrobiological phenomena, the relevance of this *Time* issue to the present theme becomes all the more specifically spelled out.[39]

Experimentation having to do with the internal economy of the neural and other psychosomatic networks leads to that pertaining to the modification of this economy. Reports on this are heavily freighted with electronic imagings and associations. Both in his experimentations, now so widely publicized via the technetronic media, and in his writings, Jose M. R. Delgado furnishes numerous instances. In his "Brain Technology and Psycho-civilization," he writes that a new technology is being developed for the exploration of cerebral mechanisms in behaving subjects. He goes on to report that "movements, sensations, emotions, desires, ideas, and a variety of psychological phenomena may be induced, inhibited, or modified by electrical stimulations of specific areas of the brain." Hundreds of thousands have now witnessed some of Professor Delgado's more spectacular demonstrations of the success of these methodologies. These include the external control of particularized cerebral nerve centers through radio terminal implants, which in turn consist of the very characteristic technetronic reticulum—the wireless circuit.[40]

In *Through the Vanishing Point*, McLuhan and Parker make much of the sensory effects of the advent of electric circuitry in the early nineteenth century and of its subsequent development. According to them, the intrinsic invisibility of electronic phenomena threatened men with sensory deprivation. As they interpret what happened, electronic invisibility caused an attrition of stimuli for the exercise of that sense which for some centuries had been dominant in western culture, namely, the sense of sight. To offset this deprivation, other senses, either singly or in concert, were resorted to as avenues of human experience, of the hidden dimensions of energies which are ultimately cosmic.[41]

In addition to such compensatory resort to non-visual senses functioning simultaneously, there is at least one other mode of creative accommodation to the electronic devaluation of the sense of sight. This is intermediation through that flexible, versatile, and protean agency—reticulum imaging. You can see through it; yet it is visible. It is visible; yet it proves an apt metonymic embodiment for that which is invisible—such as a wireless circuit, whether one of some hundreds of yards, or one that stretches to the moon and back, or a radar beam, or a computer's internal electronic processes, or the laser beam. Just as reticulum imaging mediates the fixed and the flux, the solid and the fluid, so it mediates the visible and the non-visible—including, for many, non-visible cosmic energies themselves. It is this Janus-like capability of reticulum imaging that helps make for its congeniality to the technetronic mentality or sensibility, and as characteristic epochal image for the Technetronic Era. It makes telling contributions to what has been suggested as the major function of art in times of drastic change—it helps make tangible and subject to scrutiny the nameless psychic dimensions of new experiences. Just as it is likely to prove increasingly useful in the creation, explication, and evaluation of literature, so freshly adapted, pervasively societal reticulum imaging is likely to put its stamp generically upon the literary mind in an age of pervasive and exponentially accelerating technetronic change.

The terms "electronic revolution" and "technetronic revolution" are often used. They are used by many who have made of electronic and technetronic change an apocalyptic, millennial mythos with electricity as the new messiah. I concur in the efforts of James W. Carey and John J. Quirk to defuse, so to speak, this mythos, which they rightly regard as a cosmic will o' the wisp. Yet I cannot go along with them in dismissing as illusion, the idea, in itself, of "the electronic revolution"—and, by implication, of the technetronic revolution. I believe that both of these, for better or worse, are matters of fact—present or impending.

I cannot accept, in S. Handel's *The Electronic Revolution*, the strain of what Leo Marx in *The Machine in the Garden* and Professors Carey and Quirk after him have called, because of its sentimental grandioseness and its extravagant optimism, "the Technological Sublime." Yet I go along with him in his stress on electronics development as having revolutionary dimensions. This revolutionary character may be seen when we realize that the word *electronic* will not be found in any English dictionary published before 1940. This may be seen, also, even in Handel's quite narrow definition of the term *electronics*. "Electronics may be defined as the technique of marshalling free electrons for the transmission of images, the recording and reproduction of sound, the storing and treatment of information, and the automatic control of industrial process."

In what he then asserts, Handel resorts to reticulum imagery. Electronics, he declares, "has become the nerve system of modern power and the brain of modern society." In thus resorting to the reticulum-related imagery of the brain and nervous system—in the very process of defining the electronic revolution, Handel provides compelling evidence of the movement toward ascendancy of the reticulum as characteristic figure for the Technetronic Age.[42] Both for its paradigmatic and for its generally metaphoric potency, it merits central attention of all concerned with the affairs of the literary mind in this Technetronic Age, and with the relationships between sociology and literary criticism.[43]

Notes

1. Thomas Kuhn, *The Structure of Scientific Revolutions* (Chicago and London: University of Chicago Press, Phoenix Books, 1962).
2. C. H. Waddington, *Behind Appearance: A Study of the Relations between Painting and the Natural Sciences in This Century* (Cambridge, Massachusetts: The M.I.T. Press, 1970). First published by the University of Edinburgh Press, 1969.
3. Floyd W. Matson, *The Broken Image: Man, Science and Society* (Garden City, New York: Doubleday & Company, Anchor Books, 1966), p. 3. Originally published by George Braziller, New York in 1964. Cf. in Thomas Carlyle's *Sartor Resartus*, Professor Teufelsdröckh's description of his personal experience of "The Eternal Nay": "To me the Universe was void of Life, of Purpose, of Volition, even of Hostility: it was one huge, dead, immeasurable steam-engine, rolling on in its dead indifference, to grind me limb from limb. O, the vast, gloomy, solitary, Golgotha, and Mill of Death" (*Sartor Resartus: The Life and Opinions of Herr Teufelsdröckh* [London: Chapman and Hall, Ltd., 1893], p. 115).
4. The term *reticulum* is a diminutive of *rete, a net*. The related term *reticule* is applied to a netlike handbag or basket. Thus, we have Jane Welsh Carlyle writing, in 1857: "You came tripping in with a reticule basket, and gave me little cakes." Carlyle himself (1852) used the adjective *reticulary* in a more extended sense: "The Rine, of a vile reddish drab colour, and all cut into a reticulary work of branches, was far from beautiful about Rotterdam." Byron, to whose writings both Carlyles were strongly attracted before Car-

lyle turned to Goethe, wrote (1822): "Yet many have a method more reticular— 'Fishers for men,' like sirens with soft lutes" (*Don Juan*, 1822). Here, in addition to the more obvious associations with the word *reticulum*, we have resemblance to a net in intricacy or entanglement. This is seen, too, in Thomas Love Peacock's 1818 reference to "cutting the Gordian knot of his reticular development" (*Nightmare Abbey*). It is seen, also, in the following statements: "The law is blind, crooked, and perverse . . . its administration is in the practice of by-gone ages, slow, reticular, complicated" (*Century Magazine*, 1883); "Penetrating with the fine reticulation of its common Christian sentiment into recesses of the German Forest" (*Puritan Review*, 1878); "The minute reticulations of tyranny which we had already begun to spin around a whole people" (John Lothrop Motley, *Dutch Republic*, 1855). (These citations are from *The New English Dictionary*.)

5. F. C. S. Northrop, *The Logic of the Sciences and the Humanities* (New York: Meridian Books, 1960).

6. Doctoral dissertation, The Pennsylvania State University, University Park, Pa., 1970.

7. *The Dehumanization of Art*, trans. Heline Weyle (Princeton, N. J.: Princeton University Press, 1948), p. 34.

8. These students include those following Turing. See A. M. Turing, "Computing Machinery and Intelligence" in *Computers and Thought*, ed. Edward A. Feigenbaum and Julian Feldman (New York: McGraw Hill, 1963), pp. 11–35; and Brad Darrach, "Meet Shaky, the first electronic person," *Life* 69, no. 21 (20 November 1970): 58c–58d, 61, 63, 64, 65, 66, 68. See also M. H. Goldberg, "The Structures and Problems of Human Values," *Symposium II: Technology and Education in the 21st Century*, ed. Donald Strel (Daly City, California: Center for Technological Education, San Francisco State College, 1967), distributed by Communication Service Corp., 1629 K Street, N.W., Washington, D.C., 20006. "Technological Mythmaking and Humanities Teaching," *School and Society* 96, no. 2303 (17 February 1968): 98–99; "Socrates, the Computer, and Ivied Walls," *School and Society* 97, no. 2320 (November 1969): 424–26. See also Michael J. Apter, *The Computer Simulation of Behavior* (New York, Evanston, San Francisco, London: Harper & Row, Colophon Books, 1971), p. 10: "It is hoped that this book about computers will be of interest to students of psychology and philosophy, the general reader and, who knows, perhaps also one day computers." Here we catch the analogetic-figurative poised for metamorphosis into the literal. For certain of the charnel-house effects of the metaphysical poets of the School of Donne, we already have the name "Metaphysical Shudder." Perhaps, nowadays, in connection with these *who knows?* futuristics about the computer, we need to provide another term: "Cybernational Shudder," or more comprehensively, the "Technetronic Shudder." This last would be counterpart to the "Technetronic Aha!" or the "Technetronic Gloria!" *Life* for 6 November 1970, (vol. 69, no. 19, pp. 80-83) carries an article "Love That Computer," which graphically illustrates how youngsters personalize the computer, and, in so doing, blur the distinctions between what has traditionally been regarded as human and what has been regarded as nonhuman and inanimate. The examples that *Life* cites are from the pictures and models of computers submitted by 650 school children in a contest sponsored by the Data General Corporation of Massachusetts. To these youngsters, according to the *Life* report, computers "are friendly helpmates—often with hands, feet and beaming smiles—who will read *Lassie* aloud, help with homework and clear up pollution. 'Love makes the world go round,' wrote one optimistic young competitor, 'but a computer can help.' " The article shows how technetronic companies are deliberately encouraging the favorable internaliza-

tion of technetronic reticulum-related imagery among youngsters. Of interest in connection with what I have called the "cybernetic figurative-literal flip," is the following item in the *Faculty Bulletin* of The Pennsylvania State University: "*Mother as Machine*—a colloquium talk by Dr. Michael Lewis, Center for Psychological Studies, Educational Testing Service, will be concerned with "Mother as Machine: Infant-Environment Interactions' " (February 1971).

9. Robert Frost, *Poems*, with an Introductory Essay, "The Constant Symbol" (New York: Random House, The Modern Library, 1946), p. xvi: "Poetry is simply made of metaphor. So also is philosophy—and science, too, for that matter, if it will take the soft impeachment from a friend."

10. Cited by Max Eastman, *The Literary Mind: Its Place in an Age of Science* (New York and London: Charles Scribner's Sons, 1931), p. 131. The full projective significance of this book has not yet been adequately appreciated. In his Messenger Lectures at Cornell University—later published as *The Idiom of Poetry*, 2d ed. rev. (Bloomington, Indiana: Indiana University Press, 1963), Frederick A. Pottle favorably drew on *The Literary Mind*. In their *Through the Vanishing Point: Space in Poetry and Painting*, Marshall McLuhan and Harley Parker cite the same passage from Bishop Sprat's history of the Royal Society (New York, Evanston and London: Harper & Row, 1968), p. 11.

11. Zbigniew Brzezinski, *Between Two Ages: America's Role in the Technetronic Era* (New York: The Viking Press, 1970). Before the publication of this book, *technetronic* was in fairly wide circulation. Professor Brzezinski had used the term in widely publicized lectures, in interviews published in periodicals and television interviews. For detailed treatment of *technetronic*, see M. H. Goldberg, *Design in Liberal Learning* (San Francisco, California: Jossey-Bass, 1971)—especially Chapter Four, "The Technetronic Age," and Chapter Nine, "Formative Nature of Man"; also "Future Shock and the Technetronic Age," *Humanities in the South*, no. 33 (Spring 1971).

12. Herbert Russcol, "Music Since Hiroshima: The Electronic Age Begins," *American Scholar* 39, no. 2 (Spring 1970): 293. It is significant that John Cage, whose name is associated with the development of electronic music, is coauthor, with the assistance of C. J. Bashe, of *Theory and Application of Industrial Electronics* (New York: McGraw Hill, 1951). Convinced that reopening lines of communication with young people is crucial to the future of the performing arts, the gifted pianist, Lorin Hollander, has taken the music of Beethoven and Chopin to rock palaces and ghetto parties. In 1969 he gave the first classical concert at New York's Fillmore East rock theatre, where he introduced the Baldwin Electronic Concert Grand. In the summer of 1971, he performed a series of open-air street recitals with the Baldwin electronic instrument in New York City's Harlem and Flushing areas. Since his programs themselves have been entirely classical, his may be cited as efforts at creative mediation between the pretechnetronic and the technetronic in symbolization, idiom, and rhythm.

A program of May 1971, entitled "Dance-Montage," created and presented by students at The Pennsylvania State University shows how far we have moved into the Technetronic Age of Music. All of the music was furnished by taped recordings. Several of the numbers depicted automatous figures moving in the jerky, mechanized rhythms of the now traditional and obsolescent assembly line and so bitterly satirized by Charles Chaplin in his *Modern Times*. Yet one of the pieces, entitled "Designs," really projected us into the Technetronic Age. The explanatory footnote for this title tells why and how. "Designs" is a "geometric construction which seeks to illuminate the individual components of an angular matrix. This matrix is presented as an introduction to the main body of the piece. Individual angles are expressed musically in terms of diads, each note of which suggests a line by an increase or decrease in pitch or volume. The dancers place each of these angles in space. All of the sounds were generated electronically on R. A. Moog equipment."

13. Compare, in the nineteenth century, Thomas Carlyle's similarly extended and at least semimetaphoric use of *machine* in his "Signs of the Times"; and later, in the same century, Matthew Arnold's similar and often likewise satiric reiteration of the term *machinery* (as in his *Culture and Anarchy*).

14. *American Scholar* 39, no. 3 (Summer 1970): 428.

15. The mail has brought me the following: "Atlantic Richfield Company invites you to join the Electronic Age with the new Longene Symphonette *Digi-Light*." This is described as an "elegant new Electronic Center with rich-tones FM/AM Radio, tone Digital Clock (note the computer-related term *digital*) with 24-Hour Alarm, and 3-stage High-Intensity Lamp." This system includes a "built-in heavy duty transformer," a "total of *sixteen* transistors and diodes." We enter the Electronic Age on different levels and through varied means! I am sure the mailing was electronically processed and my name electronically retrieved from a cybernetic memory bank.

16. Norbert Wiener, *Cybernetics: Or Control and Communication in the Animal and the Machine*, 2d ed. (Cambridge, Mass.: The M.I.T. Press, 1961).

17. Cf. the text of *Jesus Christ Superstar* that accompanies the recording issued by Decca Records, New York (October 1970), p. 5.

18. *Life*, 28 May 1971, pp. 20B, 21, 24, 26. The front cover-page picture is that of Chris Brown, playing Christ, in what is captioned, on the same page, as this "Reverent Rock Opera." Referring to its choral version as a "secular cantata," Daniel Webster has described *Jesus Christ Superstar* as "the rock on which this decade of youth's rage for Jesus rests." He reports: "Hysteria was the reaction" to this cantata in Pittsburgh, Pa., in July, when arrangements for a film version, to be made in Israel, were already under way. One of the pictures accompanying Webster's article has this caption, taken from his text: *Jesus Christ Superstar* "does what the young demand of their world: show it all in their terms and language" (*The Philadelphia Inquirer*, 18 July 1971, section 5, pp. 1–2).

19. Cited in Tom Wolfe, *The Electric Kool-Aid Acid Test* (New York: Bantam Books, 1969) front matter. Compare the statement made in a television interview by the African author of *Bound to Violence*: "I used the French language but the African rhythms."

20. *The Greening of America* (New York: Random House, 1970). In thus citing Reich and his Consciousness III, I do not intend to imply that I accept his (to me) untenably deterministic and simplistic fantasy scheme of Consciousness I, II, III, IV. Henry Fairlie, "The Practice of Puffers: Reich's *Greening of America*," *Encounter* 37, no. 2 (August 1971): 3–13.

21. See, for example, William Braden, *The Age of Aquarius: Technology and the Cultural Revolution* (Chicago: Quadrangle Books, 1970); Orin E. Klapp, *Collective Search for Identity* (New York: Holt, Rinehart and Winston, 1969); Theodore Roszak, *The Making of a Counter Culture: Reflections on the Technocratic Society and Its Youthful Opposition* (Garden City, N. Y.: Doubleday, 1969). See also M. H. Goldberg, "The Humanities and the Alienated Adolescent," *School and Society* 95, no. 2292 (15 April 1967): 267–91; idem, "Continuing Liberal Studies and Self-Emergence," *Humanitas* (Journal of the Institute of Man) 5, no. 3 (Winter 1970), pp. 307–27; and in his *Design in Liberal Learning*, Chapter Four, "Self-Emergence"; Chapter Eight, "The Progressive Agency"; and Chapter Ten, "The Architectonic Mode."

22. Thompson "lines up the science fiction novels of C. S. Lewis, Arthur Clarke, and Doris Lessing; scholarly works like Shklovskii and Sagon's 'Intelligent Life in the Universe,' as well as his own *At the Edge of History*, and "potboilers like Erich von Daniken's *Chariots of the Gods*." He insists that in the evidence of each work, no matter what its literary or scholarly merit may be, "the *structure* of a new planetary consciousness is at work." "Beyond Contemporary Consciousness: II," *The New York Times*, 11 May 1971. Cf. Walter Abell, *The Collective Dream in Art: A Psycho-Historical Theory of Culture Based on Relations between the Arts, Psychology and the Social Sciences* (New York: Schocken Books, 1966).

23. *Soul on Ice* (New York: Dell, 1968), pp. 14–15.

24. See also pamphlet *Stony Man Nature Trail*, a pamphlet published by the Shenandoah National Park, Va.: "THREADS IN THE WEB OF LIFE. The anchor threads for the Web are the *Air, Sun, Soil*, and *Water*. Connecting threads consist of the *Producers*, green plants; *Consumers*, animals and man, and *Decomposers*, certain fungi and bacteria . . . All living things, including man, are dependent on every thread in the Web of Life."

25. Peter Marin, "Children of the Apocalypse," *Saturday Review* 53. no. 38 (19 September 1970): 71–72; Hart Crane, "Modern Poetry," reprinted in *The Collected Poems of Hart Crane*, ed. Waldo Frank (New York, 1946), p. 177; and Ralph Waldo Emerson, *Complete Writings* (New York: William H. Wise Co., 1929), "The Young American," p. 111 and "The Poet," p. 224.

26. See G. W. Brown, James G. Miller, Thomas A. Keenan, *EDUNET, Report of the Summer Study on Information Networks Conducted by the Interuniversity Communication Council (EDUCOM)* (New York, London, Sydney: John Wiley & Sons, Inc., 1967).

27. *Best Poems of 1961* (Palo Alto, Cal.: Pacific Books, 1962).

28. See Alan Trachtenberg, *Brooklyn Bridge: Fact and Symbol* (New York: Oxford University Press, 1965), picture section between pp. 86 and 87, and pp. 160–61. The "harp of death" passage appears in the concluding essay of Henry Miller's *The Cosmological Eye* (Norfolk, Conn.: New Directions, 1961).

29. *Look*, 4 May 1971. See also Karl R. Morrison, "Spindles, Spacers, and String," *Arts and Activities* 69, no. 5 (June 1971): 38. The illustrative pieces shown are all contributions to (or expressions of) fairly complex reticulum imaging, some drawing on traditional materials that predate our modern technological times: string, embroidery thread, wood, brass. One utilizes materials characteristic of the Technetronic era: plexiglass and monofilament. The traditional reticulum imagery is much in evidence: the net, the cage, the lattice. It is seen in a piece made up of a fish of mahogany, within a network of embroidery string and hoops; a double cone in a cage, made of plywood and kite string; and a fish of plywood and kite string that features the skeletal frame of the fish enclosed within a network. In this last piece, we have a parallel to those of the Emblems of Francis Quarles which utilize the skeleton as reticulum. See also George Gratzer, *Lattice Theory* (San Francisco: W. H. Freeman, 1971).

30. Prentice-Hall Freshman English Texts, 1971 (Englewood Cliffs, New Jersey, 07632); Jack Burnham, *Beyond Modern Sculpture: The Effects of Science and Technology on the Sculpture of This Century* (New York: George Braziller, 1968). On display in the window of one of the shops in the Bloor Arcade, Toronto, were suspended two electric "lamps" resembling mobiles in the form of golden-wired reticula. When a customer touched one of these, the shop-keeper immediately exclaimed, courteously but firmly, "please do not touch that, it is too delicate." The incident illustrates Professor Burnham's thesis, which he applies to other than conventionally designated works of

sculpture. In his opening chapter (p. 1), Professor Burnham cites Sir Herbert Read's characterization of the "tortuous dematerialization of post-World War II sculpture" as a reduction to a "scribble in the air."

31. This is seen also in the word *gin*, which, as in Whitney's *cotton gin*, is an abbreviation for *engine*. As such, along one of its lines of meaning, it suggests that which is constructive, creative, and hence liberating. On the other hand, at least through Shakespeare's time, it meant a *snare*—that which imprisons, confines, entraps. In *Macbeth*, Lady Macbeth speaks of the "pitfall and the gin." Gloating at the prospect of utterly discomfiting his would-be heirs, whom he has already "notoriously gulled," Volpone, in Ben Jonson's comedy of that name, declares that he shall work upon them "an engine of mine own design." Here we have the double semantic valence of a construction and of a contrivance that ensnares.

32. Paul Richard, *Washington Post*, 18 May 1971, pp. 1, 3, in a review of a centennial show of Marin's works, in Washington; and Walter Schott, "Doctor Williams, 'Beautiful Blond, Beautiful Brain,'" *American Scholar* 39, no. 2 (Spring 1970): p. 308.

33. M. McLuhan and Q. Fiore, *War and Peace in the Global Village* (New York: Bantam, 1968); R. B. Fuller, J. Angel, and Q. Fiore, *I Seem to Be a Verb: Environment and Man's Future—By the Visionary Genius of Our Time* (New York: Bantam, 1970). Quentin Fiore is likewise designer of Jerry Rubin's *Do It*.

34. *Media & Methods: Exploration in Education*, ed. Frank McLaughlin, (Philadelphia, Pa.).

35. Cited from *New English Dictionary*. As reported by Ralph Waldo Emerson, Goethe seems to have recognized how a reticulum image may be rendered explicit through dissolution of the intervening pieces of solid (that is, the intervening "lozenges"). In attempting to account for the origins of hieroglyphic inscriptions on obelisks, Goethe pointed out how "we may see in any stone wall, or a fragment of rock, the projecting veins of harder stone." These "have resisted the action of frost and water which has decomposed the rest" (Emerson, *Complete Writings*, vol. 1, pp. 637–38, lecture on "Art").

36. *The Poems of John Donne*, ed. Herbert J. C. Grierson (Oxford: The Clarendon Press, 1912), 1: 58. In the seventeenth century, John Donne and his fellow "metaphysicals" on both sides of the Atlantic sought to absorb the vocabulary and imagery of contemporary technologies into their poetry, and thus come to human, to personal and social terms with these technologies. Cf., too, the eighteenth-century clergyman-poet of Westfield, Mass., Edward Taylor. In the *Preface to the Lyrical Ballads*, Wordsworth ascribed to the poet a like creatively assimilative role; in the nineteenth century, declaring that "the future of poetry is immense," Matthew Arnold prescribed a similar office for the poet (in the generic sense of *Dichter*). In the twentieth century, English poets, such as C. Day Lewis and Stephen Spender, and American poets, such as William Carlos Williams, Hart Crane, and, more recently, May Swenson, have called for and demonstrated a similar role for the imaginative writer. See, for example, Jeremy Warburg, *The Industrial Muse* (London, etc.: Oxford University Press, 1958), pp. 117–18; Herbert L. Sussman, *The Victorians and the Machine: Literary Response to Technology* (Cambridge: Harvard University Press, 1968); Leo Marx, *The Machine in the Garden: Technology and the Pastoral Ideal in America* (London, Oxford, New York: Oxford University Press, 1964). In attempting to make good his own commitment to this function of personalizing, humanizing, and socialization of technological idioms, Hart Crane had recourse, often, to one of the reticulum-related words frequently seen and heard in the Tech-

netronic Age. This was the word *mesh*, as in "mesh the gears" when referring to an automobile. *Mesh* shows the dialectic ambivalence apparently so congenial to the technetronic temper. For while, as in the cited example, *mesh* carries strong positive connotations, it may likewise do just the opposite. When we mesh the gears, we are establishing meaningful connections, facilitating motion and momentum toward a practical destination or just for the sheer joy of it. Either way, the associations with mesh are positive. When, however, we speak of becoming enmeshed in some one's machinations, we are connoting that which is unendurable, annoying, painful. Thus, in the assimilation of the jargon term *mesh* into general and poetic usage, we have further illustration of the paradoxic ambivalence so often found in reticulum-related imagery (Hart Crane, *The Complete Poems and Selected Letters and Prose*, ed. Brown Weber [Garden City, New York: Doubleday and Company, Inc., Anchor Books, 1966], pp. 261–62). In other ways, Crane sought to carry out his own directive. Although Herbert A. Leibowitz sees it as a "minor motif, a snatch of melody in the overall symphonic form," he does note that, "though not to the extent that Crane called for it, Crane did make use of jazz rhythms and 'machine' rhythms—both 'jackhammer and ragtime'" (*Hart Crane: An Introduction to the Poetry* [New York and London: Columbia University Press, 1968], pp. 222–23). I deal elsewhere, in detail, with Hart Crane's use of reticulum imaging in his poetry.

37. *Look*, 6 October 1970, pp. 88, 90–94, 97. See also M. Pines, *McCall's*, June 1970, p. 48; and M. Eliade, *Patanjali and Yoga*, trans. Charles Lam Markman (New York: Funk & Wagnalls, 1969).

38. See James D. Watson, *The Double Helix: A Personal Account of the Discovery of the Structure of DNA* (New York: Atheneum, 1968). In his opera, *The Saga of the Super-Computer*—based on the highly pessimistic novel of the same title by the Swedish plasma physicist, Hannes Alven—Karl-Birger Blomdahl, director of the Swedish Broadcasting Company, included, in addition to mobiles used for mechanical ballets, a large chorus that plays "a collective starring role," singing words from the field of natural science and technology to music that often resembles "that of molecular diagrams" (Werner Wiskari, "Swede Is Writing Man's Last Song," *New York Times*, 12 November 1967).

39. In pretechnetronic biology, *reticulum* has a long history. In 1658 that philosopher-mystic and physician-scientist, Sir Thomas Browne wrote of the "Reticulum or Net-Like Ventricle of ruminating horned animals." From the early eighteenth century, likewise apropos ruminants, comes the reference to "the reticulum, which we call the honey comb." From the late eighteenth century comes the statement: "This reticular network in the seal is very coarse." From the early nineteenth century comes the statement that the "heart is always compacted together by a delicate reticular membrane." From 1835 comes a reference to "the fibrous sheaths at the base of the leaves of Palmes, called *reticulum* by some." From the previous decade we have reference to the neuropterous insects, or "those with 4 reticulate or network wings" (citations from the *New English Dictionary*).

40. *Human Values and Advancing Technology*, ed. Cameron P. Hall (New York: Friendship Press, 1967), p. 69.

41. *Through the Vanishing Point*, pp. xxiii, 15, 27, 28. Yet, for recent efforts toward the "spatialization of music" and hence toward its visualization as well as its audition, see Tadeusz Kowzan, "Music and the Plastic Arts in Conquest of Time and Space," *Diogenes* 73, (Spring 1971): 1–20.

42. James W. Carey and John J. Quirk, "The Mythos of the Electronic Revolution," *The American Scholar* 39, no. 2 (Spring 1970): 219–41 and vol.

39, no. 3 (Summer 1970): 395–424; S. Handel, *The Electronic Revolution* (Harmondsworth and Middlesex, England: Penguin Books, 1967). Yet compare Eugene S. Schwartz, *Overskill: The Decline of Technology in Modern Civilization* (Chicago, Ill.: Quadrangle Press, 1971). See also, Michael J. Apter, *The Computer Simulation of Behavior* (New York: Harper & Row, 1971), p. 9: "It is a commonplace of popular journalism that we are entering the computer age—the age of the 'electronic brain' . . . it comes as something of a shock to realize how recent this development is and how unforeseen it generally was before it happened, especially since there is hardly any aspect of our society which will not be influenced profoundly, if it has not already been. What this book *is* about is a technique which takes fairly seriously the 'electronic brain' epithet . . ."

43. I am reserving, for later presentation, my studies of the following: (1) an historic and comparative treatment of reticulum-related imagery, together with an elucidation of the absorption of such imagery into technetronic reticulum-related imaging in contemporary imaginative literature; (2) contemporary satiric and other humorous works in which technetronic reticulum imaging plays a significant, important, or central role; (3) the reticulum image as characteristic paradigm for the Technetronic Age. For further examples of reticulum imagery as characteristic of the technetronic age, see Marie Borroff, "Creativity, Poetic Language, and the Computer," *The Yale Review* 60, no. 4 (June 1971): 481–513. Regrettably, Prof. Borroff's article was not available to me until I had completed my own studies. Here, it must suffice to note that, as with the journalistic and fictive writing treated in my full study, so in Professor Borroff's essay in literary criticism. The traditional reticulum imagery—with the fresh nuances and twists distinctive of its creative absorption into the idiom of the Technetronic era—is much in evidence. Thus, reminding us of the "importance of cultural necessity as the mother of linguistic invention," and of the "need-filling processes . . . responsible for a vast array of metaphysical meanings," Dr. Borroff lists twelve "comparatively recent examples." Of these, eight are more or less directly related to technetronic reticulum imagery: cell, circuit, complex, dial, network, plug, primary tape, and transmission (pp. 489–90). Again, there is the reticulum image in the cited statement by Dwight Bollinger: "Our mental scanners seem to sweep vast networks of words and phrases with deep, invisible connections;" in the following quotation from Joost Meerloo: "The unconscious knows itself in contact and continual interaction with reality through thousands of threads of communication" (p. 49); and, in order to reinforce the notion that a "salient image in poetry at once startles and comes home to us, like a returning memory we did not know we had lost," there is a citation of Jacob Bronowski's statement that "the scientific fact," appears as not merely an item of descriptive content given form in words, but a "field—a criss-cross of implications" (p. 493). (Compare the lattice variation of the reticulum.) A recurrent reticulum-related image is seen in the following: "Additional strands of significance come together in *packed* . . ." (p. 493); ". . . an account of the strands of meaning convergent in it [Dickey's image of a great king packed in an acorn] reveals no arcane knowledge . . ." (p. 495). Related to this is the following, from molecular biology: ". . . the oak *is* in fact in the acorn in the form of what we are gradually coming to understand as the intertwined double ribbon, fantastic, in its submolecular intricacy, which bears the coded program for the full-grown tree" (p. 494). Later, Professor Borroff takes an "imaginative leap into the future . . . an excursion into the sort of science-fantasy that in process of time has so often come true." In this projective vision of an "electronic intelligence" capable of "enacting the sequence of memory,

convergence, recognition, and commitment" involved in the poetic process, Professor Borroff relies heavily on technetronic reticulum imagery. First, she concedes "the possibility that, in time to come, electronic circuitry may attain not only the same density, but also the same qualitative complexity, as the neural structure of the brain." She then specifies "the installation of multiple and interlinked associative networks, such as must somehow exist in the mind itself." One such network, she further specifies, "would be referential systems containing designations for things, acts, events, and ideas, linked in logical, analogical, and symbolic relationships and carrying 'charges' of varying intensity corresponding to positive or negative emotional cathexes." To this, moreover, "would be connected a linguistic system, including the vocabulary, *in toto*, of English or some other language." This would be "complete with phonetics, grammatical, and stylistic-information on particular words, as well as a complete grammatical system, a definitive version of the generative grammar of Noam Chomsky or the new stratificational grammar of Sydney Lamb (pp. 510–11). In *The Yale Review*, in Edward Pols' article "Consciousness-Makers and the Autonomy of Consciousness," which is bracketed with Professor Borroff's, the author shows that he has "passed over" from the "classical epoch of machine technology" to the technetronic epoch. "The word 'machine,'" he remarks, "is of course taken in a very wide sense, so that a piece of electronic apparatus can be considered a machine." He goes on to explain that, in particular, "we are interested in the machines usually called robots: machines that are under the control of a computer in much the same way in which a body is said to be under the control of a brain, and that also have appropriate sensory and effector, or motor organs" (p. 517). He associates this with the reticulum-related imagery of "system," for which the more overt reticulum image of "network" so often stands. He stresses the point "that is frequently made about computers, and indeed historically lies behind their development, namely, that the physical structure of a computer is an analogue of a formal logical system" (p. 521). Again he asks us to "suppose that brain physiology has been perfected sufficiently for us to be able to state with exactness the physical counterpart of any conscious state." He then observes: "On this supposition we can understand and plot the course of all electrochemical impulses in the central nervous system just as clearly as we can in principle chart the course of the electrical impulses in the computer." In this article, as well as that by Professor Borroff, Director of Graduate Studies in English at Yale (also her article "Computer as Poet," *Yale Alumni Magazine* 34, no. 4 [January 1971]: 22–26), we have substantial contributions to the mounting evidence of the seriousness with which scholars and critics are treating cybernational and related technetronic matters. "Computers, Creativity and Consciousness" alone occupies thirty-one pages in its issue of *The Yale Review*. The "Computer as Poet" was written up in *Time* 22 February 1971, p. 77. For earlier instances of the serious treatment of computer poetry, see John Morris, "How to Write Poems with a Computer," *Michigan Quarterly Review* 6, no. 1 (Winter 1967): 17–20. It is interesting to note that these serious treatments of the technetronic in art and literature are often given a touch of motley. The legend for the Morris article is "Syntax and Something of Wildness"; that for "Computer as Poet" is "IBM 7094–7040 DCS invokes its muse." Often such sallies of wit and humor are spells against the Cybernational or Technetronic Shudder and Future Shock.

Vytautas Kavolis

LITERATURE AND THE DIALECTICS
OF MODERNIZATION

IN STUDYING THE DIVERSE RELATIONSHIPS BETWEEN SOCIAL PROCESSES
and literature, a sociologist can concern himself with one, or both, of
two basic problems: first, what is the perception of a social process
implicit in a literary work? Second, what is the influence this social
process has actually had on the literary work?

The first problem is much easier to deal with. All one needs in
analyzing the social theories, explicit or implicit,[1] of a writer is an
ability to read signs and systematize the clues they suggest into a
coherent theory from which their meanings could be deduced. This
is not a mean task, but it requires no special theory telling us where
to look and what to look for. A cultivated intuition will do, by and
large.

The matter is somewhat different in dealing with the second issue.
By what indicators does one measure the influence one supposes a
social process to have had on a literary work, particularly if the latter
does not explicitly focus on this process and its consequences? One
needs theoretical models by which to comprehend the data before
one can make verifiable or falsifiable points about them. And the
sociology of literature is deficient in such models.

My main purpose here is to elaborate first a theory of the structure
of the literary (or, more precisely, dramatic) work, second a theory
of the effects which the social processes of modernization may be
expected to have on the imagination, and third some conception of

Delivered at the fourth national meeting of the American Association for the
Advancement of Slavic Studies on March 25-27, 1971, at Denver, Colorado.
Comments by Kostas Ostrauskas gratefully acknowledged.

the manner in which the raw material of the imagination is transformed into the structure of literary works. I am also interested in the light which this type of analysis might throw on the question of the aesthetic value of the literary product.

Since what I have in mind is a highly abstract theory which must nevertheless possess empirical utility for analyzing particular literary products, I have deemed it necessary to present fairly intensive analyses of only two literary creations. My choice of one "avant-garde" play from Soviet Lithuania, published in 1967, and one from Soviet Estonia, published in 1969, has the advantage of illuminating the ways in which writers from two distinctive traditions may respond, within an identical framework of social institutions, to very similar processes of modernization. In both cases, the most recent phases of modernization have presumably been refracted through the Soviet experience, but in both cases we might also inquire into the literary impact of the more universal aspects of modernization as well.

I shall offer first a "naive" inquiry, without methodological preconceptions, into the theory of social change implicit in the literary work itself. The second case will be analyzed on the basis of a specific methodological assumption, which has evolved in studying the work, and which will be suggested as a general paradigm for analyzing dramatic works.

The first case is *Love, Jazz, and the Devil*,[2] a play by the Soviet Lithuanian writer, Juozas Grušas (born in 1901). The play depicts a group of three young men and one girl who are amateur jazz musicians and who (except for the girl) search for intense experiences in ecstatic music, alcoholic intoxication, wild dancing, insulting language, and mutual fights. Their behavior is casual, impulsive, marked by sudden changes of mood and unmotivated actions. Their sense of boredom with life is consciously interpreted by them as a response to the lack of meaning and adventure in their lives. But their subconscious (given expression by a group of psychiatric patients) rather clearly reveals that this is a consequence of the loss of illusions and of hope.

One of the young men is a casual seducer without any evident passion, another is obsessed with the imagery of murder and rape, apparently without having actually committed any. His father is a former bourgeois philosophy professor, an expert on the conception of love in German idealism, who has nevertheless turned out of his home his son's seventeen-year-old mistress and her child. One of his companions, a rhetorician of violence, is the son of a Communist prosecuting judge who once tortured the philosophy professor. That the professor's son and the judge's son are great friends suggests the interpretation that their characters can be viewed as products of the historical clash between the idealist thesis and the materialist anti-thesis represented by their fathers. The synthesis, however, is not an integration of higher order in the grand Hegelian manner but an inner emptiness in search of shifting intensities. The source of this empti-ness seems to be the fact that both fathers have *betrayed* their own brand of humanism—the philosopher by his ineffectual bookishness, the withdrawal of love in the real-life situation in which it was called for—the prosecutor by his participation in the torture of helpless hu-man beings defined as "enemies of the people." The emptiness of the synthesis is the consequence of betrayal (and therefore invalidation) of two ideological goods.

Interestingly enough, both the seducer and the rhetorician come from "good" homes. Both of their mothers, now dead, seem to have been good parents, close to their husbands and their sons. The fathers, too, appear to have been concerned and basically decent parents. On the other hand, the two more attractive characters are products of broken homes. The innocent girl, who radiates the purity of love, was deserted by both parents; the third man, who keeps re-sisting the pull of evil represented by his friends, is a foundling. These two are immunized, in varying degrees, against the corruption of the soul by their dream of the return of the mother—the bad mother who has deserted her children. The two deserted children do not blame their mothers, because (they think) this betrayal has been motivated by the love their mothers had for someone else, while the betrayals of the ideological fathers of the other two boys have been impersonal, without love. Grušas finds residual goodness in whatever is done out of love, even a mother's desertion of her children, and ultimate evil in whatever is done without love—from writing books to building a presumably more just society.

This conclusion seems a little off-key psychologically and should probably be interpreted in metaphysical terms. At some level, I sus-pect, the deserting mother whose expected return inspires nobility is Grušas' image for religious faith. The mother—the faith of the church —has died altogether for the children of reason, but she has only de-serted those who still have illusions and hope—therefore, she might return after having repented her own selfishness. This dream of the return of the bad mother suggests a vision of the decontamination of religious faith from its complacency and its questionable alliances of the past. It is this vision which sustains "the temptation of goodness" which the girl is said to represent—until she is assaulted and unintentionally killed by the children of reason. The ultimate discovery for Grušas is the lovelessness of people shaped by the struggle between two different kinds of rationalism.

The analysis of *The Cinderella Game*[3] by the Soviet Estonian writer, Paul-Eerik Rummo (born in 1942), is based on the methodological assumption that the structure of a play consists of intelligible *systems* and that to understand it one has to identify, as economically as possible, *all* the distinguishable systems that are needed to account for whatever transpires in the play. A system can be conceived of as a set of events propelled by a single mechanism or a set of structures governed by a single principle. Each system must be internally consistent and autonomous from other identifiable systems.[4] An implication of this approach is that the structure of a play is understood not by asking what the actors do (or what they mean by their actions), but rather what identifiable systems they are participating in. A particular act is not by itself a component of a system, but its product and, as such, a clue to its nature. An act could be replaced by a different act providing it could be produced by the principle governing the operations of the system to which it is a clue. If structural analysis is to be comparative, the system of categories it elaborates must be sufficiently generalized to be applicable, in a consistent manner, to literary works widely differing in both style and content (but presumably within the same genre). The structure of *The Cinderella Game*, and perhaps of other dramatic works, can be seen as composed of systems of four types—systems of time, of roles, of struggle, and of power—that interpenetrate each other in a basic situation. The basic situation in the present case is as follows: nine years after his marriage to Cinderella, the Prince has become uncertain whether he has got the true Cinderella and begins a search for the truth.

The first type of system that structural analysis reveals in Rummo's handling of this situation consists of several systems of *time*. Three systems of time can be distinguished in the play: the first encompasses the various personal "shapes of time"—the distinctive ways in which the passage of time is experienced by individual actors. In the various personal systems, time is corrosive (for the powerful older generation—the King, the Master, the Mistress); or it brings about a transformation of happiness into consciousness (for the sensitive privileged young adult, the Prince); or it is experienced as a continuous stretch of baking beans and waiting (for the underprivileged adolescent, the ash girl). The second system of time is represented by the social ritual of annually repeated returns of the Prince and his Cinderella to the home in which he has found her. All aspects of these visits—each year the identical welcoming speech, and so on—are mechanically stereotyped and performed without engaging the personality. If personal times can have various shapes, social time is deadening in its repetitiveness. The third system of time is suggested at the end, when the Prince, still uncertain, has departed with his Cinderella, and the sleeping ash girl who has taken the Princess' place in the household is told that tomorrow she will have her turn, as Cinderella, to go to her ball—presumably at another castle, meeting another prince. This is an event that, if we can judge by comparing her with the Princess Cinderella who has already been through this experience, will transform a girl unsure of her identity into a self-conscious princess. But it will also transmute an attractive, if incompletely socialized human being into a machine-like performer of a social role. This is what the miraculous intrusions of mythological time into the social ritual seem to accomplish: they reenchant the world, confirm identities, but also impose masks that, when the mythological moment is over, provide merely a basis for the mechanical performance of a new social ritual—a Weberian process of the ritualization of charisma. In any case, while nature revives itself in the spring, society cannot. It needs myth to revive it.

The second type of system in the play is the system of *roles*. In *The Cinderella Game*, the system of roles is completely closed and frequently symmetrical. The basic repertoire of roles is divided into two subsystems: the household from which Cinderella originally came and the Prince's court. In the household, the roles are those of: Master, Mistress, two daughters and Cinderella the ash girl. The roles for the two daughters exist merely as roles: their occupants can be replaced, new incumbents indoctrinated by the "official version" of what their roles represent, they can even be acquainted with different intellectual interpretations of the history of their roles. But the basic structure for those "oversocialized" women of the younger generation is a mechanistic system of roles into which they must be impersonally fitted. Within this system, their "true" identities do not exist, only the roles they play. The family system is governed by the principle of an absolute division of functions.

The other completely mechanical system of roles is located in the court. The political system is an embodiment of the principle of a carbon-copy parallelism of structure. The King has a double indistinguishable from himself who is Regent for the Prince; the Prince has a double who is Regent for the King. This arrangement helps greatly to stabilize the system. So long as the Prince is well but not willing to participate he can be replaced by his facsimile—which, lacking a self of its own, cannot resist those manipulating it. It will therefore *always* behave as princes must. But if the Prince is incapacitated or disqualified, his Regent will presumably take over; and his Regent is the double of the old King. In this case, instead of the younger generation asserting itself, a "mechanical reproduction" of the old will take place. If the King is incapacitated, then his Regent, the Prince's double, will replace him. Whatever happens, the future in the political system seems to belong to the "mechanical reproductions."

Cinderella is the medium of exchange between the family system and the political system. In return for a kind of raw human material the family system has provided for the political system, the former has received "influence"—Cinderella serves as an agent of the Mistress at the court. Princess Cinderella is also purely a role: she performs her functions in a completely mechanized manner (for example, always using exactly the same sentences when praising the way she had been treated by her father and stepmother before she became a princess). But if Princess Cinderella is only a role without a person, her replacement in the family system, the current Cinderella, is a person without a role, undergoing anticipatory socialization for assuming it. She is responsive and spontaneous in a fragmented way, but to understand what she *is* she looks at nursery-type pictures depicting what Cinderella *does*. One of the two Cinderellas is the precise negative of the other: one has all that is most lacking in the other. The two apparently merge only in the moment of mythological time—when person and role become one vividly experienced whole— and never again.

The remaining actors—the Prince, the Master, and the Mistress— occupy positions in the role system, but they are more significant as participants in the systems of struggle and of power. The notion of struggle implies some degree of equality between the antagonists, making for a still open outcome. Power, on the other hand, suggests the possession by someone or something of a superior capacity to cause a particular kind of outcome. The system of struggle is dialectical, the system of power (or causation) is deterministic.

In the system of *struggle* of Rummo's play, there are two "true" subsystems in which the antagonists are challenging each other to combat, and one pseudostruggle in which the antagonists are merely exposing themselves to an active agent in the attempt to seduce him. One of the active struggles involves the Master and the Mistress of the household in which the original Cinderella had been found; the Mistress represents the insanity of life and the Master, perhaps, practical reason. The Master had been "collaborating" with his wife in the past, but nine years ago he had initiated a totally ineffective caricature of a policy of open resistance. The antagonists, however, fight against their own limitations more than against each other: life is crippled and moves around in a wheelchair, and practical reason is constantly threatened by the chaos, emptiness, and the morass of empty hopes lurking just under the surface of its ordering of objects, collecting of documents, and practical adjustments and deals. Experienced by an aging couple, the struggle of life versus practical reason may be seen as an "older" (bourgeois? parental?) kind of struggle.

The struggle in which the Prince engages is of a different kind. The Prince has discovered he does not know who his wife is (no wonder since she is merely a mythologically confirmed social role) and whether she is the true Cinderella or not (that is, whether he has lived with a valid or invalid myth). His awakening represents a challenge by "consciousness" to "reality"—a struggle at the tail-end of young manhood against *both* the no longer credible "official version" of reality *and* the multiple facets, models, and alternative versions that one discovers if one delves into the raw material of existence beyond the official version.

The Prince transcends the role system since he has developed a quest of his own: he knows himself to be the embodiment of *his own* uncertainty; and of his struggle against it. His struggle, moreover, is not for an authoritative conceptual mastery, the "firmness of mind" that the Master seeks to retain, but rather for an intuitive, or perceptual, comprehension of the larger whole: for a way to hold "everything" in his grasp for a moment and then to release it "unrecorded," unreified. By locating this kind of struggle in the experience of a young man, the play suggests that the dilemma of consciousness *versus* reality may be the characteristic struggle of the present—of the post-revolutionary generation, of the new intelligentsia, of postmodernity.

The pseudostruggle consists of the competition of the two daughters of the Master and Mistress—representing sensuality and intellectualism, respectively—to seduce the Prince by their particular charms. The Prince responds for a while (to both at once), but his essential search is not for the schematically segregated pleasures of the body and the mind, but for a grasp of the "true" reality. (Perhaps reality is dubious precisely because its elements have become segregated and do not merge on any level.)

The final system of the play is that of *power*. All the actors, except the current Cinderella, are preoccupied with power; the Prince with analyzing its "true" nature, everyone else with influencing people and placing agents to represent their interests in strategic places. But what emerges from the play is that no one has actual power—except the Mistress, the crippled representative of life. She has power on two levels: first, she acquires social power by placing Cinderellas in the various palaces of the land to represent her "interests" in perpetuating the game of life, *The Cinderella Game*, itself. Second, she has the mythological power of transforming the naive ash girl into the Cinderella of the golden slipper whom a prince will marry. It is "illiterate" life that has the power to bring forth the enchanting intrusions of mythological time into the deadeningly repetitive social rituals. For everyone else, it is only in the limits to their power that power becomes real to them.

For the Prince who is concerned only with the nature of reality, it is only limits to the power of consciousness to recognize reality that become real as a consequence of his search. He has tried to *force* reality to reveal itself by brutally mistreating the current Cinderella on the assumption that when Cinderella is mistreated the Good Fairy appears. The crippled Mistress does in fact come wheeling around, but the Prince is too disillusioned and angry with her to perceive the possibility of her being the Good Fairy. (And it is true: she is now appearing as the Good Fairy for *someone else's* Cinderella.) The Prince has had a surefire "experimental" test of the nature of reality, the original golden slipper, by means of which he has also tried to force reality to reveal itself. But the slipper does not fit the most likely candidate, the future Cinderella. Reality, particularly the reality-yet-to-be, will not be forced by self-conscious experiments.

The only approach to reality that seems to "succeed" is that of the ash girl: baking beans and waiting, a conjunction of being useful and having a dream. It is this dialectic that makes the Cinderella myth and the ash girl its embodiment. The Prince, the kind of young intellectual who is neither useful nor capable of waiting, who "does nothing" except trying to *understand* reality, to consume it with a sense of conviction that he is consuming the right product, cannot make the myth operate. Reality escapes him because he is only an appendix to it, but not the useful dreamer in whom its substance is generated.

What the Prince does not know, in addition, is that the slipper— the instrument he uses to identify the nature of reality—is one that has been mass-produced for traveling exhibitions, in a "slightly altered" form. The notion that he might have retained an exact measure of his moment of mythological enchantment provides the only occasion in the play for the old Mistress to feel threatened in her mastery. (This notion is, of course, also a challenge to the playwright, who is a producer of exact measures of reality; and whose plays may also be "slightly altered" for traveling shows.)

The system of power of *The Cinderella Game* is not a human system. It is a system in which a decrepit life uses human beings for the sole purpose of maintaining itself in power. The power of life rests on its ability to generate "mythological moments" that transcend social ritualism. The capacity of human beings to resist the tyranny of life rests on a potential ability to construct *exact measures* of the "mythological moments" of their experience and to retain those measures as basic definitions of the social reality binding to themselves. In this notion, Rummo reveals a sense of the possibility of a valid enchantment, even within the closed system of life, rather than insisting on the necessity of disillusionment, as Western "absurdist" playwrights do.[5]

I had read Grušas' play about a year before I read Rummo's, and the "naive" descriptive method of analysis seemed to me then to be adequate for bringing out the sociologically relevant content of a play. In trying to analyze *The Cinderella Game*, however, I was forced by the very nature of the play into the assumption that one needs an explicit conception of component systems to understand what is going on in the play. But when I tried to apply the approach developed in analyzing Rummo's play to *Love, Jazz, and the Devil*, I discovered that the component-systems method yielded rather trivial results in the latter case. I could not discover, by this method of analysis, much that was not immediately evident in the Lithuanian play. This suggests that the method of component-systems analysis, while perhaps universally applicable, may be particularly appropriate to a certain kind of dramatic work—perhaps one written by a highly sophisticated contemporary writer whose mind has been habituated to the scientific manner of thinking in terms of control systems, feedback mechanisms and so on even in dealing with humanistic subject matter. Rummo is apparently such a man, while Grušas is a more traditional type of humanist—a man whose work reveals a single "global vision" rather than the imagination of a variety of interacting systems. My approach may be most applicable to the dramas of advanced industrial society, to the plays yet to be produced.

The notion that advanced industrial societies may produce a distinctive type of dramatic literature, perhaps with its own distinctive standards of aesthetic value, underlines the more general issue: What is the influence of social processes—specifically, of the processes of modernization—on the structure of literary works? And how may these influences be transmuted, in the mind of the writer, into the symbolic and perceptual structures that he constructs?

I shall approach these questions once again with a theoretical model in mind, but this time with a model, not of the literary work but rather of the general psychological effects of social structural modernization. We will then be in a position to ask to what extent the structures we have found in the two plays can be accounted for by the theoretically postulated model of what happens to the human mind caught up in processes of modernization.

The basic assumption underlying my theory of psychological modernization is that when the human mind is affected by any social process it shapes itself *either* by affirming this process and identifying with it, adopting the process' characteristics as its own, or by rebelling against this process and forming itself in opposition to it, by embodying in itself and projecting outward that which the social process objectively is not. Thus, the mechanism of the imagination operates by the basic capacity of choosing between what is most striking in objective social reality and what one misses most in it.

> If, for example, the sociological trend is toward an increasingly rationalized and impersonal *bureaucracy*, its psychological resultant may be a more rationally organized and unemotionally performing type of personality, concerned only with the orderly application of rules rather than with the solution of immediate existential or ultimate metaphysical problems. . . . But, *as a reaction* to the sociological trend, an exaggeratedly irrational kind of personality might emerge— one inclined toward anarchic romanticism, expressionism, mysticism, and the politics and education of "ecstasy." . . . Increasing *com-*

plexity of sociocultural environments . . . should activate the psychocultural dilemma of becoming aware of the functional interdependence of everything with everything else vs. suffering a sense of incomprehensibility of the whole of social reality. . . . The active response to the sense of interdependence is an effort to explicate the ambiguities of complex relationships. The active response to the sense of incomprehensibility is a search for emotionally satisfying simplifications, credible models of the 'ultimate nature' of the objects and 'systems' presenting themselves to awareness. . . .[6]

I consider the process of psychological modernization to be characterized by an increasing awareness of these dilemmas (and others summarized in Table 1). A "modernistic" response to any one of the social trends of modernization is one which affirms and identifies with it. An "underground" response is one whereby the imagination exercises its capacity of negation and structures itself as the opposite of the "objectively given." I conceive of the "post-modern" man as one who is aware of these dilemmas within himself and is struggling to articulate "modernistic" with "underground" psychocultural materials, without repressing one of them in favor of the other.[7] It should be obvious that I am not using "underground" in a political sense and that my conception of the "post-modern" differs from that of Daniel Bell[8] and most other people who have used it, who tend to identify it with what I call "underground."

The raw material of the imagination can be seen as arising not only as responses to social *processes*, some of which may be shared by all societies undergoing modernization, but also as developing in response to the specific economic, kinship, political, communal, and stratification *structures* of particular societies. Indeed, to approach a complete sociological inventory of the raw material of the imagination potentially available in a society, its unique cultural traditions, maybe its physical environment and size, even leaders and events have to be taken into account—anything to which the imagination may respond by structuring itself in accordance with *or* as the opposite of.

The psychohistorical model of the workings of the imagination has three potential contributions to make to literary analysis. (1) It provides a potentially universal (that is, cross-cultural and transhistorical) framework for classifying those "raw materials of the imagination" of an artist or a period which have been provided, or could have been provided, by sociohistorical processes and the peculiarities of the organization of his society. (2) The psychohistorical model of imagination helps to conceptualize the element of "consciousness" in

TABLE 1
HYPOTHESIZED RELATIONSHIPS BETWEEN SOCIAL TRENDS AND THEIR REFLECTIONS IN PERSONALITY AND CULTURE

Social Trends	Reflections in Personality and Culture	
	The "Modernistic" Variant	The "Underground" Variant
Bureaucratization	Rationally organized and impersonally performing system Formalism (in language, standards of evaluation)	Pronouncedly irrational (romantic, expressionistic, mystic) individual Informality (casualness, improvisation)
Differentiation of functions	Separation, fragmentation Participation of "specialists"	Fusion or confusion Alienation of "innocents"
Centralization of social order	Hierarchy of control Internalization of restraints Focusing of personality (and culture)	Egalitarianism of control Rejection of restraints Defocusing of personality (and culture)
Mass society	Standardized repetitiveness	Need to reassert individual and group uniqueness
Affluence	Consumption orientation Sense that everything is in ample supply, therefore no "permanently treasurable" values	Inner void Need to produce objects in order to experience a sense of the "permanently treasurable"
Technological growth	Mastery	Impotence
Scientific advances	Knowledge of principles of operation of systems	Sensuous experience of concrete details
Acceleration of change	Immediate satisfaction Constant experimentation	Sense of not getting anywhere Recovery of the primeval
Increasing socio-cultural complexity	Interdependence of parts Explication of ambiguity	Incomprehensibility of the whole Dream of simplification
Electronic media	Vividness Passing, impermanent qualities; processes rather than standards	Numbness Need for unshakable points of reference

literary products. It permits us to identify a basic "alphabet" of psychocultural raw material that the evolution of a society and its current state and structural characteristics *should* have made available to the imagination and then to ask to what extent these raw materials have actually been used in the construction of the literary works of the period. Conversely, to what extent have such potential elements of the imagination been ignored or blurred over? (3) The psychohistorical model also helps to clarify the work done by an artist's imagination in constructing a distinctively *individual* work of art out of the raw materials, some of which are presumably supplied by his society and therefore generally available. The individuality of an artist is perhaps most precisely indicated in the way he handles generally available raw materials.

Indeed, I suspect that to deal with idiosyncratic raw materials (for instance, a childhood fear unusual in his society) successfully in a work of art, an artist is likely to use standardized models provided by society, since he could not otherwise make them intelligible to others. Consequently, it might be that an artist's *socialization* is most precisely revealed by his manner of handling idiosyncratic materials, and his *individuality* is indicated by his manner of dealing with socially provided materials. In a great work of art, one might expect a convergence of societally and individually provided materials in forms equally adequate to both. I can only touch upon some of these issues in my concluding comments on the two works I have previously analyzed in terms of their structures.

It seems to me that while the manifest content of the two dramatic works is quite different, much of the raw material of the imagination and many of the *psychocultural qualities* that have been given concrete articulation in these works are similar. A great deal of the raw material of both works can indeed be identified as various elements of the ten dilemmas of psychocultural modernization listed in Table 1. The different treatments given these materials by the two authors seem to go a fair distance in explaining the difference in aesthetic merit of the two works.

The basic difference is that Rummo responds to a larger number of the dilemmas of psychocultural modernization and deals with them on more levels and in a greater variety of ways than does Grušas. In Grušas, what I have conceived of as the psychological effects of *bureaucratization* all appear on one level, as a difference between the males of the older generation, who represent the "modernistic" response, and the young of both sexes, who represent two variants of the "underground" response—the loveless and the loving.

But in Rummo's play the register of the possible psychological effects of bureaucratization appears in various systems of the play in a variety of organically interpenetrating forms: (1) The time system of the annually repetitive social ritual is mechanically rationalized, the reenchanting intrusions of mythological time into this system seem to represent an "underground" element. (2) Since each of these intrusions initiates a new sequence of repetitive social ritual, the "irrational" mythological enchantments are the means of activating the "mechanized" system of the social ritual. (3) The symbol of the irrationality of life depends on rationalized mechanical propulsion of the wheelchair. (4) Two subsystems of the role system are mechanically rationalized, yet other actors do not fit into the roles provided for them in those systems and engage in "irrational" struggles as well —one, in the name of order, against life, the other, for the sake of his own consciousness, against the official version of reality and the ambiguities of flux behind it. (5) But even the individuals who do not entirely fit into the mechanical role system are occasionally sucked into a kind of symmetrical clockwork arrangement which makes them give identical performances in small, not particularly important details, such as assuming the physical positions and headaches of each other. (6) The condition for reenchanting life is a system of mechanically repetitive royal balls. Thus mechanized social ritual—the balls—provides the means for reenchanting life, and reenchanted life—the various Cinderellas—provides the means for operating mechanized social ritual (the annual return visits).

We have a complexly structured, but nevertheless, at its core, recognizably homeostatic model. In the construction of this model, the raw material provided by an intensified experience of the dilemma of "the mechanical, impersonally performing system" *versus* "the irrational individual" has been used to construct a variety of meaningful structures. These structures are essentially imaginings of how the dilemma might be experienced in particular situations. In each situation, one of its two elements is checked by, and dependent on, the other. Ultimately, at the center of these structures, we discover a hypothesis explaining how the "rational" and the "irrational" elements fit together, how their interaction makes and will continue to make the cosmic mechanism operate.

In addition to the more diversified treatment, there are also a larger number of the dilemmas of psychocultural modernization built into

Rummo's play. Thus, *Love, Jazz, and the Devil* does not contain any material dredged up by the experience of increasing sociocultural *complexity*. I have conceived of this material in terms of a sense of conflict between the ambiguities of complex relationships and a search of emotionally satisfying simplifications. If this dilemma exists in the substratum of Grušas' drama, it is blurred in its visible structure. Rummo, on the other hand, acknowledges it on two levels: both in the problematic and in the structure of his play. The problematic of the Prince's struggle is precisely the issue of how the simplicity of the myth he has been enchanted by in his youth relates to the complexity of the social reality he is now facing. The Prince does not resolve this issue in his substantive search, but Rummo does in the formal construction of his play: he overcomes the dilemma of incomprehensible complexity *versus* emotionally satisfying simplification artistically by incorporating his complex, multilevel *cognitive structures* into a simple overall *format of sequence* of a short and straightforward play without flashbacks, multiple scenes or any other "complicating" formal devices. His trick is having complex structural systems converge on simple visible forms and having those forms concurrently perform different functions for the various systems in which they participate. The result is a great structural complexity operating through simple forms—a graceful, even lighthearted game of interacting systems. Some "avant-garde" playwrights do just the opposite and provide more complex forms than the cognitive structures these forms are sustained by. The likely consequence is a "free-floating," unnecessary complexity.

My final point is that Rummo typically gives *equally* sharp attention to both sides of the dilemmas of psychocultural modernization that he touches upon, thus producing a more dynamically balanced, more "vital" play. Grušas tends to be more one-sided in his treatment of the same dilemmas: he concentrates on the "underground" side to provide the substance of his drama, and uses "modernistic" elements, for the most part as background variables, for explaining how the "underground culture" might have come into existence. But "modernistic" elements are not directly involved in propelling the current action of the play. This relative one-sidedness eliminates most of the stuff out of which internal variety could be constructed, leaving only the struggle between the "loving" and the "destructive" versions of the underground culture in the play.

I am left with the impression that whereas Rummo is an authentic post-modern imagination confronting post-modern materials, who therefore constructs a format both "fair" and "adequate" to the raw material of psychocultural qualities that he deals with, Grušas has a somewhat "archaic" personality in which the differentiation between the "modernistic" and the "underground" has not yet been fully experienced, thus he feels and acts "globally." Consequently, he perceives both "modernistic" and "underground" systems from a basically premodern point of view—and does not see very much in either. Rummo, on the other hand, has at his disposal an "underground" person's perception of the "modernistic" system which he knows fully in its own terms, since he has been shaped by it.

What is implicit in the previous section may now be explicated as a sociological model for analyzing a work of art. This model distinguishes three levels of analysis: (a) raw material of the imagination (the "psychocultural qualities"), (b) cognitive structure (the "meaningful systems" identifiable in an artistic work), (c) the perceptual structure (the "visible format" or sequence of events in a play). I would expect the dramatic works to which aesthetic value has been most consistently ascribed to be complex cognitive structures capturing a good deal of the raw material of the imagination of their times and comprehended in perceptual structures simpler than their cognitive content.

This approach seems to be most applicable to the "systematic" arts, in which the second level (cognitive structures) can be identified as present. This level is identifiable not only in drama, but also in much of epic literature, dance, and certain types of happenings. It is generally missing in lyric poetry, music, and nonrepresentational painting; and in those cases one might speak of the "impressionistic" arts, those in which the raw material of the imagination is immediately transmuted into a perceptual structure. In the "systematic" arts, on the other hand, a conceptualization of operating systems (which can be "read" as cognitive structures transmitting systematized information) occurs either before raw material can be transformed into a perceptual structure or during this operation, as an essential part of it. Such "conceptualization" is not necessarily a conscious process. The essential matter is that it *results* in what can be treated as cognitive structures and as systematized information. One coefficient of aesthetic value that may be common to both the system and the impression arts seems to be the effectiveness of *nonreductive* simplification (forms from which their original more complex or more ambiguous contents could be deduced or inferred without loss).

There are similarities between this approach to literature and that developed by Lucien Goldmann. But Goldmann assumes the objective existence "out there," in life, of global "world visions" (or, in his later work, of collective, unconceptualized feelings)[9] that writers can only become aware of, to varying degrees, and explicate in their writings. The quality of their awareness depends, among other things, on the degree of *completeness* to which they do, in an internally coherent manner, explicate such overall visions (or feeling states). I assume that, while there may be historical periods in which global visions exist, what is universally "out there," what is provided by any society for its artists, is a variety of psychocultural qualities ("raw materials of the imagination") on which the artist, using whatever documentary evidence or behavioral observations his "project" requires, imposes *his own* design.[10] These psychocultural qualities represent a more differentiated analysis of what Goldmann treats as collective states of feeling: what he perceives as overall qualities, I dissect into a fairly large number of distinguishable dimensions. And I would argue that to the extent that the writer is free to choose, he *constructs* a system (or a network of interacting systems), which may legitimately vary from one book to another and which, in any case, does not necessarily exist, even in outline, anywhere outside of the work of art.

The two perspectives are, in principle, not mutually exclusive, since Goldmann is concerned with very general characteristics shared by works of literature and philosophy or with a basic collective literary form such as the novel, whereas I am trying to analyze what is distinctive of individual works of literature. Perhaps related to this difference in the choice of the problem (or possibly giving rise to it), there is a difference in the intuition of the basic nature of the activity of the writer. In Goldmann's view, artists are revealers of the given. For me, they are constructors who, out of the given and their individual responses to it, make possible alternative symbolic orders.

It is, I would assume, the great cosmic or historical myths, not works of literature as such, that project—or perhaps help to shape—the global visions. Without denying that there may be "mythical" elements in some works of literature, one can still try to distinguish the specifically "literary" ones. It seems illegitimate to presume that the mythical element, in the sense of a socially provided global vision, is a necessary precondition of *literary* achievement.

Notes

1. "... it very frequently happens that his [the writer's] desire for aesthetic unity makes him write a work of which the overall structure, translated by the critic into conceptual language, constitutes a vision that is different from and even the opposite of his thought and his convictions and the intentions which prompted him when he composed the work" (Lucien Goldmann, "The Sociology of Literature: Status and Problems of Method," *International Social Science Journal* 19, no. 4 [1967]: 497).

2. Juozas Grušas, *Meilė, džiazas ir velnias*. Tragiška komedija (Vilnius: Vaga, 1967). My analysis here relies on my more extensive analysis in "Images of Young People in Soviet Lithuanian Literature," *Lituanus* 16, no. 2 (Summer 1970): 40–43.

3. Paul-Eerik Rummo, *Tuhkatriinumäng* (Tallinn, 1969). I am using the unpublished English translation, by Andres Männik and Mardi Valgemäe, by permission of Prof. Valgemäe. For a different (non-system) kind of interpretation, see Mardi Valgemäe, "The Ritual of the Absurd in P.-E. Rummo's *The Cinderella Game*," *Lituanus* 16, no. 1 (Spring 1970): 52–60.

4. Cf. Lucien Goldmann, *The Hidden God: A Study of Tragic Vision in the Pensées of Pascal and the Tragedies of Racine*, tr. by Philip Thody (London: Routledge and Kegan Paul, 1964), p. 12.

5. Cf. Benjamin Nelson, "*The Balcony* and Parisian Existentialism," *Tulane Drama Review* 7, no. 3 (March 1963): 60–79.

6. Vytautas Kavolis, "Post-modern Man: Psychocultural Responses to Social Trends," *Social Problems* 17, no. 4 (Spring 1970): 435–48. I am citing from an expanded manuscript version.

7. Spears has characterized the whole "classical" tradition of literary modernism by the presence of, and apparently some degree of balance between, these polar opposites, which he identified by the images of "the City" and "Dionysus." Monroe K. Spears, *Dionysus and the City: Modernism in Twentieth-Century Poetry* (New York: Oxford University Press, 1970).

8. See Daniel Bell, "The Cultural Contradictions of Capitalism," *The Public Interest*, no. 21 (Fall 1970), pp. 16–43; and the January-April (1972) issue of *The Journal of Aesthetic Education* devoted to critiques of his thesis.

9. Lucien Goldmann, "Zur Soziologie des Romans" in *Wege der Literatursoziologie*, ed. Hans Norbert Fügen (Neuwied am Rhein: Hermann Luchterhand Verlag GmbH, 1968), p. 205.

10. To be sure, an author's "system" is bound to the intrinsic requirements of the genre in which he wishes to construct it, and in this respect its design is not entirely "his own."

Harry Levin

"A MATTER OF NATIONAL CONCERN": THE REPORT OF THE COMMISSION ON OBSCENITY AND PORNOGRAPHY

THE ARGUMENT WAS ALREADY AN OLD ONE WHEN PLATO ADDRESSED HIM-self to it, and he chose to take the traditional side. He excluded most poetry and some music from his ideal republic, on the premise that they would weaken men's characters by appealing to the baser passions. Aristotle responded by formulating his theory of catharsis, arguing that men would be purged of their dangerous impulses through the fictitious experiences they vicariously underwent. The dialectical conflict between those two positions has never been fully resolved; indeed it has broadened and sharpened during the past two centuries, as the reading habit has been democratized. Books were often banned or censored in earlier periods, but mainly for religious or political reasons. Sexual offenses were dealt with by the law, which has mirrored the moral code of given times and places. The attempt to reduce or prevent such offenses through the censorship of suggestive literature does not seem to have taken much hold before the nineteenth century. Sex was, after all, the most private of private matters, and the freedom to read and publish has been one of the West's most hard-won liberties. Moreover, no one has conclusively demonstrated the ill effects of any kind of reading upon its readers. The question has been raised on many occasions, yet the most influential of all critical handbooks—Aristotle's—testified to the contrary. Jimmy Walker, mayor of New York in the nineteen-twenties, shrugged the problem off with the declaration that no nice girl was ever seduced by a book.

Well, Emma Bovary may not have been a very nice girl, although she certainly thought of herself as such. On the other hand, it could be said that Mayor Walker's skeptical generalization is lacking in due respect for the power of the printed word. Witness to this power was borne by Dante's Francesca, when she told of reading a romance with Paolo one day and of suddenly ceasing to read it by mutual agreement. The ambiguous name of that romance was *Galeotto*, which signifies not only Galahad but also "go-between." That books could act as pandars is the assumption that leads to blanket legislative controls, and consequently to legal actions which can be instigated by any reader who smells some potential offense in what he reads. The prudery of the Victorians was officially legislated by Lord Campbell's Act in 1857—the year in which France watched the trial and acquittal of *Madame Bovary*. The criterion that was long to prevail in Anglo-American courts is generally referred to as the Hicklin rule, though this is an injustice to the memory of Benjamin Hicklin, who had reversed a charge of obscenity in his intermediate court of appeals. When the prosecution appealed the case in 1868, Hicklin was overruled by Lord Chief Justice Alexander Cockburn, who proceeded to promulgate the test for which he merits the commemoration: "whether the tendency of the matter charged as obscenity is to deprave and corrupt those whose minds are open to such immoral influences and into whose hands a publication of this sort may fall."

This test was so readily accepted and applied, by American judges as well as British, that its wording is echoed almost *verbatim* by the Supreme Court of the United States, ruling on the Rosen case in 1896. The federal statute that had made it a crime to send obscene matter through the mails would be forever associated with Anthony Comstock, the self-appointed guardian of public morality. In cooperation with the Y.M.C.A., he had lobbied so successfully that both houses of Congress passed his bill in 1873 after less than a total hour of debate. Here, as in Great Britain, the avowed intention was to protect the morals of the young from being depraved and corrupted—albeit at the cost of keeping mature adults from access to such classics as *The Arabian Nights* or *The Decameron* and of inhibiting the publication of such important contemporaries as Dreiser or Shaw. The logical consequence, as phrased by Judge Curtis Bok in a Pennsylvania decision of 1949 legalizing the local sale of novels by Faulkner and others, was to "put the entire reading public at the mercy of the adolescent mind." Not only post offices and customs houses but libraries and school boards, not to mention publishers and booksellers, felt and relayed those puritanical pressures which Mencken liked to call Comstockery. The middle generation of our century, however, brought about a marked reversal of that tendency. Its turning point was the verdict of Judge John M. Woolsey in 1933, upheld on appeal by the opinion of Judge Augustus Hand, which allowed *Ulysses* to be published in the United States.

"Whilst in many places the effect of *Ulysses* on the reader undoubtedly is somewhat emetic," Judge Woolsey held, "nowhere does it tend to be an aphrodisiac." In a similar vein, Judge Hand described the notorious final chapter as "pitiful and tragic, rather than lustful." Had the net impression been more erotic, a judgment on that basis might well have been adverse. Both of these judges were willing to consider the novel as a whole, rather than excerpts taken out of context, and to apply a more sophisticated test for obscenity than the Hicklin rule: the novel's impact not upon a child but upon the *homme moyen sensuel.* Both were at considerable pains to distinguish serious fiction from pornography, as Joyce himself had been, and as D.H. Lawrence was in his turn. It has become increasingly difficult to maintain such a distinction in recent years. Mr. Justice Stewart has remarked that, while perhaps he could not define hard-core pornography, he knows it when he sees it; but, significantly, this remark supported his finding that the film in the Jacobellis case was not pornographic. How can the hard core be recognized, then, or has it altogether melted away? Justices Black and Douglas have consistently based their often dissenting opinions on the grounds that an unabridgable freedom of expression, as guaranteed by the First Amendment to the Constitution, should be absolute. The trend of Supreme Court cases has its landmark in the Roth decision of 1957, which found against the defendants. Mr. Justice Brennan, speaking for the majority, tried to draw a line which would indicate the limits of constitutional protection: "All ideas having even the slightest redeeming social importance—unorthodox ideas, controversial ideas, even ideas hateful to the prevailing climate of opinion—have the full protection of the guarantees, unless excludable because they encroach upon the limited area of more important interests. But implicit in the history of the First Amendment is the rejection of obscenity as utterly without redeeming social importance."

Sin may still be subject to condemnation here; but the loophole of redemption has been opened, since social value is determined by rapidly changing community standards. *Lady Chatterley's Lover* and *Tropic of Cancer*, though each is unquestionably obsessed with sex in its different way, could thus be redeemed during the early nineteen-sixties. *Lolita*, which a number of American firms had considered but not dared to publish, came out under a Parisian imprint in 1955; G.P. Putnam's sons was able to bring it out in New York by 1958; and it has never suffered from prosecution. In 1963 Putnam's resurrected from under the counter the *Memoirs of a Woman of Pleasure*, better known as *Fanny Hill*, which heretofore had never been regarded as anything other than pornographic, and indeed had occasioned the first obscenity trial in American history. When its extensive record of suppressions was reversed by the Supreme Court in 1966, Justice Brennan declared that it fell within the protective area he had pre-viously delimited: "a book cannot be proscribed unless it is found to be *utterly* without redeeming social value." How far short of utter its prurience falls is a nice speculation. At a time when monosyllabic taboos are so very casually violated, it may be that John Cleland's judicial readers were charmed by the euphemistic fastidiousness of his mock-heroic sexual metaphors. That literary qualities may be in themselves redemptive controverts the older notion that they enhance the seduction. Yet the very fact that a work of this sort has been handed down to us from the past lends it historical standing as a sociological document.

The term *pornography*, as literally derived from the Greek, means no more than writing about whores—a fair description of the shelf where Cleland may stand with Aretino and Restif de la Bretonne, all now redeemed by time and valued by society. (Recently Morse Peck-ham has devoted a rather muddled monograph to the esthetic status of this *genre*.)[1] As for *obscenity*, its etymology is as obscure as its interpretation is subjective. The original meaning of its Latin ad-jective was, not inappropriately, "ill-omened." Later usage, making *obscene* synonymous with "foul" or "filthy," illustrates how moralistic arguments utilize the imagery of purity and pollution. *Dirt* and *smut* seem frequently to function for the dirtier words they have pro-scribed. "A thing is obscene if, considered as a whole, its predominant appeal is to prurient interest . . ." So runs the definition of the Ameri-can Law Institute, as quoted by Justice Brennan in *Roth v. United States*. It is hard to see why this specification does not fit *Fanny Hill*, which must have been a harder book to defend than either *Lady Chatterley's Lover* or *Tropic of Cancer*. Since the same lawyer, Charles Rembar, was chiefly responsible for the successful defense of all three, it is valuable to have his personal account of that sequence of trials in a volume provocatively titled *The End of Obscenity*.[2] Mr.

Rembar claims and deserves a large share of the credit, assuming that credit will be accorded, for having widened Justice Brennan's loophole to the point where no publication whatsoever would seem altogether devoid of redeeming social value. The present situation is characterized, by Mr. Rembar himself, as a *seductio ad absurdum.*

The legislative point of view diverges from the judicial. The Comstock Act may be obsolete today, yet the Congress still votes unquestioningly for virtue as defined by those who profess it loudly. It was evidently a mood of reaction against the increasingly permissive drift of legal opinion which in October 1967 prompted the passage of Public Law 90–100, designating the problem as "a matter of national concern." The legislation, introduced by Senator John McClellan of Arkansas, called upon the president to appoint an advisory commission which would make appropriate recommendations, after a thorough investigation of the traffic in obscenity and pornography, including—and among the conventional verbiage, this would turn out to be an innovative proviso—"a study of the causal relationship of such materials to antisocial behavior." Four specific tasks were assigned to the commissioners: (1) to survey the state of the laws controlling and defining pornography, (2) to inquire into its operation and scope as a business, (3) to evaluate its effect on the public "and particularly minors," and (4) to recommend proposals for its regulation "without in any way interfering with constitutional rights." In January 1968, President Johnson appointed a panel of eighteen members, whose elected chairman would be William B. Lockhart, dean of the law school at the University of Minnesota and a leading authority on obscenity law. With one striking omission, the commission represented a fair sampling of the various other interests involved: public officials, professional women, the clergy, social scientists, educators (but not from the humanities). Literature and the arts had no direct representation, unless we count the presence of a librarian. This might be ascribed to philistinism, rather than illiberal intentions, on the part of the president and his advisers.

The controversy surrounding the commission, during and after its two-year deliberations, has been much better publicized than its 646-page report. Two of the commissioners—the Rev. Morton A. Hill, S.J., president of an organization entitled Morality in Media, and the Rev. Winfrey C. Link, administrator of the McKendree Manor Methodist Retirement Home—broke away from the procedures and policies of their colleagues at an early stage, and held public hearings all over the country to dramatize their belief in more rigorous controls. When

one of the commissioners—Senator Kenneth B. Keating of New York
—was compelled to resign on becoming ambassador to India, the in-
coming President Nixon was given his single chance to affect the
results. He appointed a namesake of the former incumbent, Cincin-
nati lawyer Charles M. Keating, Jr., who had qualified himself by his
energetic activities on behalf of censorship and had founded a pressure group known as Citizens for Decent Literature, Inc. Mr. Keating
was consistent in his campaign to obstruct and discredit the majority,
boycotting their executive sessions, abstaining from their final vote,
and filing suit to enjoin against publication until he had prepared his
own dissenting report. Meanwhile overwrought accounts of the majority report had been leaked to the press and to a Congressional
committee. Even before it was published, a White House spokesman
announced that the president was at variance with it. Just seventeen
days after the Government Printing Office had issued its small official edition, it was rejected by the Senate. Shepherded again by Senator McClellan, a condemnatory resolution was passed without debate by a vote of sixty to five.

The irony of the circumstance is twofold. On the one hand, obviously the Congress got something quite different from what it thought
it had bargained for; it had wanted dogma and was offered dubiety.
On the other, a new administration, whose watchwords were law and
order, had been embarrassed from the very first by this holdover
from a muddled if well-meaning liberalism, and was all too happy to
join in the general effort to sabotage it. Shortly before the elections
of 1970, President Nixon released a statement seething with indigna-
tion, declaring that he had "evaluated" the report—he does not say he
has read it—and that he both "categorically" and "totally" rejects "its
morally bankrupt conclusions."[3] As a defender of decency, which
one might almost be led to think the commission had attacked, he
repeatedly denounces "smut" and "poison" and—using a less old-
fashioned word—"pollution." Thus he begs the initial question that
the commission was established to study, the definition of obscenity:
when is it smut and by what canon? In the name of "an open society"
he reverts to the ideology of the Hicklin rule: "If the level of filth
rises in the adult community, the young people in our society cannot
help but be inundated by the flood." Heatedly, in language strongly
influenced by the rhetoric of Commissioner Keating's dissent, he calls
for more anti-smut laws and prosecutions in every state and at every
level. "American morality is not to be trifled with." The services of
Dean Lockhart and his hard-working fellow commissioners are final-

ly rewarded with the most thankless of discharges: "The Commission on Pornography and Obscenity has performed a disservice."

This "shabby political treatment" did not go unreproved by such monitors as the *New York Times*, which pleaded with legislators to "give the commission's report the belated benefit of a fair and rational hearing," since they had been too busy campaigning at the time they had voted for its repudiation.[4] Speaking more broadly, on behalf of twenty-five civic, educational, and literary organizations, the National Book Committee has appealed for a thoughtful reconsideration and a fuller public dialogue on the issues raised by the report—an appeal to which I, for one, am hereby venturing to set down a tentative response. Though the government did as little as possible to distribute the report, it is now available in commercial editions.[5] A spurious version of it, closely resembling the dissident reports, had come out in advance; an edition of the report itself, richly illustrated by pornographic exhibits, also kept curiosity stirred up. There has even been a documentary film, *Red, White, and Blue*, which inclines toward the latter shading. The actual text, while it is somewhat clogged by the competing jargons of law and the behavioral sciences, endeavors to come to grips with its peculiarly elusive and sometimes distasteful subject matter. But, in contrast to those question-begging adjectives which so often figure as accusations ("lewd," "lascivious," "lustful," and "licentious," to stay within the bounds of alliteration), the report consistently attempts to neutralize its material by such antiseptic phrases as "sexually oriented." The degree of consensus is roughly a little more than two-thirds. Twelve of the eighteen commissioners voted for it in its entirety, two dissented in part, three dissented completely, and Mr. Keating abstained.

Despite the absence of belles-lettres among the professional fields reflected in the membership of the commission, the report abounds in implications bearing on the complex interaction between society and literature. Hence there is particular need for these to be scrutinized and discussed from the vantage-point of literary criticism. In 1920 Mencken had complained that the courts would not admit critical opinion in evidence for prosecuted books. Latterly the defense has had more and more opportunity to call upon critics as expert witnesses, and Mr. Rembar attests the strategic role that they have played in a number of his cases. If the issue depends on whether a book has any literary merit, actually that is the very quality of which the critic is supposed to be the best judge. The book would not be on trial unless it stood at the borderline between literature and pornography, in the estimation of some, and he is presumably consulted to help the court draw that line. But how can literature and pornography be conceived as mutually exclusive categories? Objectively, the latter is merely a specialized branch of the former. If a work of pornography is legally identifiable as involving obscenity, then it may now be redeemed by the nonobscene elements it contains—if indeed it contains them—and Mr. Rembar, as I understand him, would find some ground for every book to meet this counter-test. Has he not rescued Cleland, as well as Lawrence and Miller, for American readers? Yet even his open-minded ingenuity might be hard put to discover the strain of mitigation in those works of Cleland's pseudonymous heirs which line the lurid counters of Forty-Second Street.

At all events, the pornographer's trade has come out from underground, and the commission's first panel has obtained a good deal of information about it to share with us. The mere fact that it operates in the open makes it look less sinister, though undeniably sordid, an agent of esthetic if not ethical degradation. The businesses that purvey it seem to be fly-by-night affairs, gathering tenuous profits from a limited volume of sales, even when individual prices are high. Sales for "adult only" magazines are estimated at between $25,000,000 and $35,000,000 in 1969, whereas during that same year the income of *Playboy* alone—which is considered mildly erotic but not pornographic—reached the total of $66,000,000. Cinema is the only medium that comes close to big business in this line, counting box-office receipts of somewhat less than half a billion dollars. But here the spectrum runs from downright "sexploitation" (skin-flicks or stag movies) through so-called art films (usually foreign imports) to standard Hollywood products rated X (no patron under seventeen admitted) or R (patrons under seventeen must be accompanied by a parent or guardian). The X rating is hesitantly attached, though flamboyantly advertised; it covers less than six percent of the motion pictures subject to the Production Code Administration. Pictorial representation differs considerably from verbal in some of the problems it presents; the source of its excitations is nearer the surface. Often the two media are combined, as in photographically illustrated marriage manuals or medical handbooks. These, like the classical texts once hidden away as *erotica* or *curiosa* and today universally procurable, assert a claim to legitimacy which cannot be vaunted by pornographic potboilers.

Facts and figures regarding the production and distribution of pornography are more accessible than an understanding in any depth about what goes on in the crucial process, consumption. There is still enough peep-show furtiveness in the atmosphere of pornographic bookshops for their customers to be wary of interviews. Field-observations report that the average consumer of this product tends to be a solitary white male, aged between twenty-one and fifty-five, married more often than not, dressed pretty much like any other man in the street—and not too much unlike him in sexual habits, insofar as these can be discerned. If women are seldom to be seen in such pur-lieus, it is because pornography, written for an exclusively masculine readership and focusing upon woman as a sex-object, has been sexist with a vengeance. But that inequity may be grounded in nature, for the researches of Dr. Kinsey and others indicate that women are less sexually responsive than men to visual and literary stimuli. This does not mean that women are less capable of arousal (*pace* Dr. Masters and Mrs. Johnson), but the evidence suggests that they feel more aroused by romantic subjects than by explicitly sexual ones. Since the moral and legal arguments for censoring books and pictures have always hinged on their presumptive influence over human character and conduct, and since so little has been understood as to precisely how this influence is effected and with what consequences, it is the report of the commission's second panel on "The Impact of Erotica" which should be its most interesting contribution, as it has already been its most controversial.

Many of this panel's findings are as predictable, or else as incon-clusive, as the usual tabulation of a sociological questionnaire. The inverse correlation between church attendance and pornographic indulgence will be no surprise to either moralists or libertarians. Nor can we dismiss the possible hazards of obscenity because, in a can-vass of current opinion, only two percent of those interviewed believe it is one of "the two or three major issues facing the country today." This simply proves that we are not so steeped in vice as the citizens of Sodom and Gomorrah. Given the national problems that have been ranked ahead of obscenity by the respondents (war, race, the econo-my, youth, law and order, drugs, pollution, poverty, moral break-down, government, foreign policy, education, overpopulation, as preferentially listed), it would take another Anthony Comstock to assign a higher priority to his peculiar obsession. The determination of community standards by door-to-door sampling makes for sim-plistic questions and inconsistent answers. For example, fifty-six per-cent of the people may believe that "sexual materials lead to a break-down of morals"; yet only one percent of them admit this in their own case; and few can think specifically of any instances. Exposure to pornography was linked with juvenile crime by fifty-eight percent of the police chiefs questioned. Large majorities in other groups—psychiatrists, social workers, and others versed in conditioning rather than crime—made little connection. Their negative conclusion is supported by further studies in the incidence of sex crimes by both juveniles and adults, which did not vary greatly during the nineteen-sixties, in spite of the manifold increase in sex-oriented materials.

Much of the commission's two-million–dollar appropriation has been employed to foster programs of research, which will be detailed in ten supplementary volumes of technical reports and summarized with graphs and tables in the body of the report. (Among the numerous teams of sociologists and psychologists working upon these projects, a sense of ironic propriety would single out the name of D.M. Amoroso.) The collective endeavor, unwittingly commissioned by the Senate's interest in causation, breaks new ground by bringing empirical data to bear upon the effects of pornography. Admittedly, it is hampered by limitations and obstacles. The time was rather short for a full-range study of after-effects. Children, the principal objects of concern, were decidedly *hors de combat* for such encounters as could be devised under such conditions. University students who volunteered would have their motives suspected, and would become a subject for Congressional reprehension. One might add that experiment with human guinea pigs, while never failing to outrage the obscurantists, likewise offers a standing invitation to Aristophanic burlesque or Swiftian satire. (Aristophanes would have been delighted to hear about the phalloplethysmograph.) The essence of Bergsonian absurdity is achieved when the superimposition of the mechanical on the living takes place within the sphere of sex itself. But, though some may be amused—while others are outraged—by the techniques so ingeniously developed for registering physical response to psychological stimulus, discovery can take no other course. That sexual arousal can be measured has with males been a comic byword, which may now be scientifically implemented for both sexes through the therapy of Masters and Johnson and the experimentation sponsored by the commission.

"Such direct measurements entail problems pertinent to the invasion of privacy," to quote the understatement of the commissioners. They are not unaware that "the instrumentation involved" may unduly excite or inhibit "the object which is measured." Objectivity so attained is all too narrowly limited, to say the very least, but it carries the will for exactitude and concreteness as far as they have yet ventured into this problematic zone. A central series of controlled experiments typically exposes groups of subjects to barrages of erotic photographs, slides, film, and reading matter, and—as the exposures are repeated or discontinued—charts the curve of reactions, both physiological and behavioral. The immediate reaction is the sort of intensification that might have been expected from so concentrated an incitement. But that priapic reflex soon gives way to an interval of satiation and a gradual falling-off in responsiveness. Shakespeare may have anticipated the pattern, when his Duke commands in *Twelfth Night*:

> Give me excess of it, that, surfeiting,
> The appetite may sicken, and so die.

Some of those subjects who were confined for electronic observation, as we learn from the report, had been provided with a surfeit of periodicals, most of them excitably pornographic, and were encouraged to browse as freely as they desired. Many of the browsers ended by turning to the *Reader's Digest*—an extreme gesture of practical criticism. We who have not submitted ourselves to so complete an immersion, but have sampled the stimulants when they have drifted our way, could reaffirm the sense of boredom induced by their repetitions and limitations. The report is disarming in its conclusion, based on its many avenues of inquiry, that it cannot demonstrate any causal relationship between pornography and delinquency. But this may be no more than a default in the face of uncertainty, a failure to develop methods for coming up with any conclusion at all.

"If a case is to be made against 'pornography' in 1970," the panel's negative induction concludes, "it will have to be made on grounds other than demonstrated effects of a damaging personal or social nature." This is not to deny that erotic themes are sexually stimulating, even as tragic or comic themes may elicit tears or laughter. Readers may not cry or laugh aloud when confronted with tragic or comic scenes, nor may they necessarily "achieve orgasm through nonintercourse means"—as the report, with heavy-handed delicacy, puts it—by responding to pornographic excitation. We shall never know to what extent consumers of pornography make deliberate use of it for such purposes, and accordingly the report does not pursue that opaque probability. Nevertheless the common assumption behind it offers a significant testimonial to the undeniable fact that erotic material provokes a sexual response. However, since masturbation is the least social of acts, and since hygienic counsel no longer preaches that it is personally damaging, it affords no grounds for any ban. The case against "pornography"—and note how the cited sentence neutralizes the word with quotation marks—must be made on the ever debatable grounds of morality. In the last analysis, the question is whether moral arguments should be fortified by legal sanctions, or whether a broader conception of legality should prevail. The commission's third panel concerned itself with positive approaches short of repression, such as codes for self-regulation in pertinent industries. Surveying ways and means for the improvement of sex education, it found an incidental usefulness in some of the controverted materials.

When district attorneys were queried as to the obscenity trade within their local jurisdictions, less than a third of them replied that it was a matter for serious concern. This reflects particularly the innocence of the less heavily populated counties, where pornographic enterprise would not be financially rewarding. The replies from the urban districts, where diversity works against conformity to an old-fashioned set of values, registered much greater apprehension. It is here that the Citizens' Action Groups have been organized, whose resolve to police the mores of the community implies an ultimate recourse to the law. Thence we are brought to the legal considerations of the fourth and last panel, which has struggled to clarify the confusion it has faced, reporting an "almost universal dissatisfaction with the present law." The historical background is sketched; the existing statutes and the federal agencies are canvassed; but the focus is on the sequence of judicial modifications that has unfolded with such bewildering rapidity during the thirteen years since the Roth decision. At the moment there are three accepted criteria, all of which must be met if a book is to be ruled obscene: (1) appeal to a prurient interest, (2) patent offensiveness by contemporary community standards, and (3) utter lack of redeeming social value. None of these definitions has any precision whatever, and each of them entails some degree of subjective judgment. The difficulty of deciding in their light on matters so inherently ambiguous has been pushing judges, juries, law enforcement officials, and the public—along with booksellers, publishers, and authors—toward an impasse of ambiguity. Furthermore: "A series of decisions of the Supreme Court, generally rendered without opinion, has given an exceedingly narrow scope of actual application to the constitutionally required three-part standard for adult legislation. These decisions leave it questionable whether any verbal or textual materials whatever may presently be deemed 'obscene' for adults under the constitutional standard and suggest that only the most graphic pictorial depictions of actual sexual activity may fall within it. Present law for adults is therefore largely ineffective."

The development of constitutional doctrine has been oriented, by Dean Lockhart and his colleagues, against the larger perspectives of changing public opinion. Cross-reference to the obscenity laws of fifteen other countries discloses inconsistencies and trends which are comparable to those of our own. The pace has been set by Denmark, the pornographers' Land of Cockaigne, where an increasingly permissive attitude during the nineteen-sixties culminated in the abolition of all legal restraints on commerce in pornography for adults. Statistics based on the records of the Copenhagen police for that period show a dramatic decline in the incidence of sexual offenses. This civilized model should be reassuring to those who fear the turbid inundation prophesied in President Nixon's jeremiad. Four factors, then, have pointed the report in a parallel direction: (1) the comparative insignificance of the pornographic market, (2) the dearth of psychosexual evidence demonstrating antisocial effect, (3) affirmative measures through sex education and more open discussion, which require no special legislation, and (4) cutting the Gordian knot of entangled laws and obfuscating precedents. Finding "no warrant for continued governmental interference with the full freedom of adults to read . . ." the commission recommends that "federal, state, and local legislation prohibiting the sale, exhibition, and distribution of sexual materials to consenting adults should be repealed." There are qualifying recommendations which would prohibit the sale or display of sexual materials to minors, and would impose restrictions on public exhibits and on the use of the mails for offensive advertising. (Bills designed to meet this last complaint have currently been introduced into Congress.)

After such knowledge, what forgiveness? Differences of viewpoint among the members of the commission, which must at times have rendered their sessions volcanic, come out in an appendix more than half as long as the report itself. Two behavioral scientists concur, but want to move farther toward total repeal. Two concurring physicians view the subject as "a nuisance rather than an evil." For a Methodist minister, the report is "a milestone in the history of human communications." A Jewish rabbi, not unsympathetic to its findings thus far, feels that more thorough investigation is needed. Commissioners Hill and Link have drawn up a lengthy counterstatement, whose strident pitch is struck in the opening sentence: "The Commission's report is a Magna Carta for the pornographer." Unshaken in their faith that pornography is the cause of vice and crime, they circularly proceed to roll back history since Roth. Obscenity should be redefined so that nothing could ever redeem it. Some of the experimental research is vulnerable, it must be conceded, to the methodological objections that they press. Tighter censorship, stricter legislation, and more frequent prosecutions are proposed *inter alia*, under the somewhat ominous byword of "vigilance." Not only films, but also rock lyrics and underground newspapers ought to be subjected to licensing boards and preliminary clearances. As for what Mr. Keating would call "the Danish solution," Messrs. Hill and Link explain that "we are a different culture with a greater commitment to the Judeo-Christian tradition." If this is not Pharisaism, it is crass ignorance, which should not put down the compatriots of Kierkegaard and Grundtvig.

Commissioner Keating, who concurred in the Hill-Link report, has gone on to write a minority report of his own at equal length. It is a fitting anticlimax to the volume—and to his own nonperformance on the commission, which he assails in volleys of mixed metaphor, calling for an investigation of the investigators (their "ivory-tower views" go "unhoned by the checks and balances of a competitive, active, real world"). The precision of his fuming prose can be gauged when he attacks the Supreme Court for "the flaunting of morality." What he apparently meant to say was "flouting," which has almost the opposite meaning; but those two words are frequently confused, especially in calorific moments. Like his clerical coadjutors, he is manifestly embarked upon a religious crusade: "For those who believe in God . . . no argument against pornography should be necessary." Nonetheless he is nothing if not argumentative, arming himself with quotations from such authorities as Marcel Proust, Arnold Toynbee, Whittaker Chambers, Spiro T. Agnew, John N. Mitchell, and J. Edgar Hoover. The documentation includes a list of addresses where pornography can be obtained, as well as a gloating series of sexual case histories, most of them hearsay. Mr. Keating has his own legislative program; he has prolific suggestions for running the country, the states, the cities, and above all private lives; he has a detailed plan for turning California into a kind of police state. And, of course, he has his Citizens for Decent Literature, which can boast the honorary membership of 124 Congressmen plus eleven Senators, notably the Hon. Barry Goldwater and the Hon. Strom Thurmond.

If this counter-report reads like a travesty, self-refuted by its overkill, we should note that it is wielding more influence in "the competitive, active, real world" than the Lockhart report. Mr. Keating, as a minority of one, is the only commissioner to whom the White House has been willing to listen. His diatribe sets a tone which reverberates through the president's discharge (a tone which might correctly be described as "the flaunting of morality"). In view of the Congress's treatment of the report, and of the hopes expressed for a narrower line from a reconstituted Supreme Court, it is more than conceivable that we may witness a widespread tightening of codes and bans. That should bring us one step nearer to Plato's republic— and to the official prudery and legislated morality that enter hand in hand with totalitarian regimes. Both of the dissenting reports look upon Dean Lockhart with a suspicious eye because of his association with the American Civil Liberties Union, as if he should be disqualified from his present assignment because of a prior commitment to free speech. A dialectic of permissiveness versus repressiveness emerges from the confrontation between a libertarian majority and a regulative minority. The commission's *donnée* was the ultraliberal turn that the courts had been taking. Surprisingly this seemed to be justified, rather than discredited, by the empirical studies of sexual materials. Finding no positive evidence of their harmful effects, the report had no warrant for recommending the abridgment of basic rights. "Surely," said Justice Frankfurter in a similar situation, "this [would be] to burn down the house to roast the pig."

The recommendation of the disregarded majority, as Clive Barnes points out in his preface to the reprint, turns the "matter of national concern" into a private matter. To leave it there, if possible, would be a happy ending. Critics of the report, though they mostly incline toward *laissez-faire economics*, are less inclined toward individualism in the field of morals. Messrs. Hill and Link, refusing to accept the negative conclusion with regard to harmfulness, insist that the burden of proof lies on the other side. If it has the slightest potential for harm, let the book show cause why it should not be banned. For the majority, it had seemed more dangerous to curtail freedom than to risk contamination. Though that choice seems clear to liberals, it must still be made with some embarrassment. Above and beyond our lingering uncertainties, pornography is without doubt a nuisance. The dissolution of the hard-core concept has brought some strange bedfellows together; cheap shockers jostle once-forbidden classics on the polychrome list of the Grove Press. It is true, as the report submits, that "dirty words" as such have lost their obscene force. This may be a loss both for colloquial speech and for literary style. It was their proscription from polite discourse that lent them their expletive vigor. When we think of what those dashes or initials used to portend, of the elegant circumlocutions of Cleland, of Hemingway's wry habit of substituting the word *obscenity* itself, or of Joyce's sparing, shocking, and self-conscious introduction of the familiar monosyllables into print, then Norman Mailer's casual scurrility seems much too easy, childish, and self-indulgent.

If everything is permissible at the level of publication, then at the level of criticism we must bear a new responsibility. If we shift our value judgments from ethics to esthetics, it is still our duty to discriminate art from trash. This is the critical consequence of the report; the other, perhaps the major consequence is scientific. The commission correctly claims, as one of its contributions, to have placed "the dimension of human sexual behavior on the agenda for further inquiry." It has shown how art, in its problematic relation to sex, can be a control for that inquiry. The deliberations of the Commission on Obscenity and Pornography were slightly overlapped by those of another national Commission on the Causes and Prevention of Violence, an overlapping which resulted in a curious contradiction. Though this other group did not undertake any research projects of its own, it did find certain television programs demoralizing for children, and concluded by proposing some curbs. It is worth noting that one commissioner—Otto N. Larsen—was a member of both groups, voting for causation and regulation in the one case and for nonregulation in the other. Are we to infer that violence is more contagious than sex, or merely that it is more dangerous and less desirable? As debate continues and enlarges, it appears that the censorship of pornography has its advocates in law and social science, as well as in the presidency and the Congress.[6] Whether we can turn back at so advanced a stage, without jeopardizing that individual freedom which the report puts highest among its mixed concerns, will be seen all too soon.

Notes

1. Morse Peckham, *Art and Pornography: An Experiment in Explanation* (New York, 1969).
2. Charles Rembar, *The End of Obscenity: The Trials of Lady Chatterley, Tropic of Cancer, and Fanny Hill* (New York, 1968).
3. See the *New York Times*, 25 October 1970, p. 71.
4. *New York Times*, 10 February 1971, p. 42.
5. *The Report of the Commission on Obscenity and Pornography* (New York, 1970).
6. See Walter Berns, "Pornography vs. Democracy: The Case for Censorship" and the ensuing discussion, *The Public Interest*, 22 (Winter 1971), pp. 3ff; Irving Kristol, "Pornography, Obscenity and the Case for Censorship," *The New York Times Sunday Magazine* (March 28, 1971), pp. 24ff; also Herbert L. Packer, "The Pornography Caper," *Commentary* (February 1971), LI, 2, 72–77.

Wilhelm Emil Mühlmann

TRADITION AND REVOLUTION
IN LITERATURE

Socioliterary Sketches in the Light
of German Writing

BORCHARDT'S THESIS OF "PSEUDOBALANCE"

IN A LECTURE DELIVERED IN 1931 IN GÖTTINGEN AND REPEATED IN Essen, Rudolf Borchardt attempted to define the concepts "revolution" and "tradition." The intellectual energy given to this attempt, and the close connection established between the work of literature on the one hand and the demands of advancing masses on the other lend a striking presence at this particular time to Borchardt's statement. The socioliterary point of view is brought out in this lecture, delivered forty years ago, in such a way as to allow us to list the most important problems contained in the topic. "The profound statement by Dante, to the effect that doubt begins at the roots of faith and error at those of truth, received its most serious confirmation in the centuries when the claims of newly advancing masses—on a share in the intellectual substance of the older minorities—split into a pseudo-balance" (Rudolf Borchardt, *Gesammelte Werke, Reden*, Stuttgart, 1955, p. 215). The concept of "pseudobalance" justifies the historical-philosophical doubts with which Borchardt views this process. For Borchardt is not one of those writers who in principle believe in the possibility of unlimited "democratization" of cultural contents; least of all when such a universal diffusion of the cultural contents forms the subject of a program represented by a "claim" based on the "social concept of emancipation." During the emancipatory movement of the nineteenth century the poles of revolution and tradition appeared in the contemporary disguise of "freedom" and "slavery." The flaw in the reasoning at the heart of this masquerade has become—in Borchardt's argument—the curse of European culture. In this connection he coined the phrase that the rule of freedmen brings, not freedom, but the end of freedom (Borchardt, p. 216). For the result was "the revolution in eternity, the permanent revolution, the proclamation of the emancipatory fundamental principle as the dominant universal law, and therefore for *Europe* the era of growing aggravation, atrophy, the impossibility of handing down its tradition" (Borchardt, p. 219).

This process he saw as reacting on literature. As long as even a remnant of inequality between classes remained, there were still new pockets of people to be emancipated. In this way a second, competing rhythm ("an abnormal second heart") would arise, as it were, alongside the organic rhythm of tradition, and it would serve to set free ever new masses of humanity. The outcome would be "political literature not as specialized literature, but as a politicizing literary literature and as a vassal to the primacy of politics."

Borchardt notes that this genre has existed only since the eighteenth century. Before that time it was unknown; there was only a form of literature—as found in the works of Dante, Petrarch, and Machiavelli—that gave content to politics. Beginning in the eighteenth century, however, politics became "a chain of rebellion leading to new rebellion, with ever diminishing pauses of passing calm, during which the expectant rebellion assumed an oppositional stance" (Borchardt, pp. 220–21). In this way, however, literature had created a new scale of values. The author, if he wished to achieve recognition, must become an agitator; in Germany this effect first came about in the "Young Germany" movement, and then again after the establishment of the Reich in 1880. After all the preceding emancipations, this rebellion found its fertile soil among the industrialists and the wide public. These groups no longer knew what to do with the handed-down tradition and even felt threatened by it; at the same time they were fascinated by the new as a value and felt free to somehow equate literature and rebellion. A literary "race of sycophants and parasites," which had sprung up out of the industrialists and the wider public, profited from quick returns and barely tolerated solid tradition wherever an attempt was made to affirm it. Whenever a "tradition" threatened to become too firmly entrenched, these cliques provided "all means for the acceleration of obsolescence and for removal." They smite "elitist culture in the flank and in the rear, sweep out the theaters, prevent the consolidation of a repertoire, undermine values that were on the way to becoming canonized, proclaim one new hero after another, and collect the quantity of heat produced by the destruction as carelessly as they pocket other by-products of the loss of real assets and quickened turnover." This permanent revolution does not lead to literature, however, but to its annihilation (Borchardt, p. 222).

In line with these premises, developed with great single-mindedness, Borchardt sets out on his crucial argument. In his opinion, this literary activity may assume a revolutionary mask but, in fact, it is not revolutionary. It is too willed, too deliberate, too undifferentiated, too programmatic. Whatever was *really* revolutionary in literature was not consciously revolutionary. Dante did not write the *Commedia* either to return Italy to its ancient traditions or to tear it loose from its history. What was "new" in the *Commedia* and what was faithful to tradition was not a matter that touched his soul. Petrarch was not conscious of the fact that his *rhyme* opened a new dimension for poetry. Goethe did not know what he was creating in the stroke of genius that was the *Urfaust*; only later generations understood that it served to destroy a decrepit convention. Novelty does not need to be programmed as such, it takes its place in the world "modestly and not sure of itself, half self-possessed and half heedless." It works through its nature, not through its program.

The genre concepts of "the revolutionary" and "the traditional" are therefore misleading. Their contents are changeable. Each new epoch sees something different in the "new," and all timebound interpretations are correct and incorrect at the same time, "for there is no great literature that by its conception and essence is only tradition or only revolution, only past or only future, and where it has aimed exclusively at one or the other, genius, with invisibly effacing fingers, has erased the signs of this calculating intention" (Borchardt, p. 224). Shelley's major poetry, for example, is "not to be found where it is in harmony with the emotional rhetorical clichés of his century." Further, the more fervent the advocates shaped by a contemporary trend out of the literary genius of an era, the more surely it degenerates into sophistry and jumps from the frying pan into the fire. Chateaubriand's *Le Génie du Christianisme*, Borchardt claims, is no less a Jacobin work, with signs reversed, than is the famous pamphlet by Abbé Sieyès, *Qu'est-ce que le Tiers État?* (Borchardt, p. 227).

Borchardt's lecture has outlined the set of problems involved in "tradition and revolution" to the extent that it can be used as the point of departure in considering the following clusters of problems:

1. The "democratization" of the cultural contents (Borchardt's "pseudobalance") by the claims of advancing masses.
2. The alteration of literary production by the representatives of the demands for emancipation (Borchardt's "sycophants," "parasites," and "agitators"); prevention of the establishment of tradition through literization.
3. The false revolutionary claim of *littérature engagée*, with its renunciation of "pure" literature, and the consequences of its distorted social criticism.
4. The genuine revolutionary traits in the pariah motif and in gnostic elements.
5. The discussion of these problems will conclude with a short section on "time-binding and incarnate history."

The problems will be adumbrated throughout in the light of literary works themselves, and almost exclusively German ones. (This restriction has its basis exclusively in the limits of my own familiarity with literature. Among foreign literatures, I am somewhat familiar with Italian works, I know French ones only slightly, English and American ones even less, Russian works only in translation. My observations are those of a dilettante—hopefully in an acceptable sense of the word.)

DEMOCRATIZATION OF CULTURE

In January 1808 Goethe remarked to Riemer: "The artistic genius works at all times in more or less malleable material—former ages responded to Homer, Aeschylus, Sophocles, Dante, Ariosto, and Calderon as well as to Shakespeare (the present generation to both Goethe and Schiller); thus the only change is *that now it is the turn also of mediocrity and of secondary figures* and of all the lesser artistic endeavors that are part of technology" (Goethe, *Werke*, Gedenk-Ausgabe, Zurich, 1950, 24: 214–15; italics added). Interestingly enough, Goethe does not regard this process in an entirely negative light, for he immediately adds: "Now the light shines even in the valley, whereas it used to be only the high mountains that were dressed in sunlight." In the 1820s Goethe returned to this topic in letters and conversations. As a result of modern transportation technology and the "easy means (*Fazilitäten*) of communication," he recognizes the tendency in the cultural world "to outdo itself, to overeducate, and thus to remain mired in mediocrity. And it surely is also the result of commonality *that mediocre art becomes common*" (Goethe to Zelter, Goethe, *Werke*, 21: 634). The concept of "mediocre culture" precisely designates the process with which we are dealing—Borchardt's "pseudobalance." Goethe also implicitly understood that the spread of this "mediocre culture" is carried out in the name of progress, for he continues: "As a matter of fact, it is the century for capable minds, for practical persons of quick comprehension, who, equipped with a certain agility, are conscious of their superiority over the masses, even though they themselves are not talented in the highest degree." In his conversations with Eckermann, Goethe repeatedly characterized the effects of this process on literature. More than once he expressed his opinion that since his youth standards had been raised (see Adolf Bartels, ed., *J.P. Eckermann: Gespräche mit Goethe inden letzten Jahren seines Lebens*, 2 vols., Jena, 1908. All citations in this paragraph are from vol. 1). "The high quality of German literature has stimulated productivity" (4 January 1827); what had once been high points now have become average performances. There is hardly anyone now who composes a bad stanza, hundreds of talents flourish and clamor for recognition, but they are essentially superfluous, "for the world can only be served by the extraordinary" (29 January 1826); the tablet of German literature is so scribbled over (18 February 1829) that an intelligent person has to look around for a place where he might still be able to perform useful work. In this endeavor, even a real knowledge of the tradition would rob the "hundred poetizing youths" of the courage to continue writing (20 April 1825). Further, the stimulus to production by the level achieved results in a situation in which political and philosophical ideas are abundantly scattered about; young people absorb them from the environment and reproduce them as their seeming intellectual property, while everything originates only in the atmosphere of that "middle culture." "In reality, they only return to time what they have received from it" (15 April 1829).

In this instance Goethe, with his acute insight, grasped that the connection between swelling production and the craving for originality is an inherent process. As a consequence of accumulation, communication, and diffusion, it becomes increasingly easier to absorb "ideas" from production and to reflect them, but also increasingly difficult to present something *truly* new; what was "new" today is "common" tomorrow, the standards for what is "original" steadily rise. If to this is now added the competition of business society, the determination to be original will inevitably take the place of originality itself. In this way, however, the person takes precedence over the work, the virtuosity of showing off comes before seriousness, *service*, and commitment to a subject (20 April 1825, Bartels, ed., *Eckermann*, vol. 1).

POLITICIZATION OF LITERATURE

Goethe's almost formally sociological observation hardly touched on the content of contemporary literature. The reason for this may lie in the fact that in the period of the restoration, "politicized" literature did not yet play the significant role it would play for "Young Germany" after the July revolution.

Recently it has become fashionable to inquire into the origins within the German-speaking areas of that "politicized literature" to which Borchardt addressed himself so negatively. In this endeavor it is only natural to fall back on the major experience of the French Revolution and to ask about the German "classicists'" position concerning the phenomenon and the ideas of this revolution. Let us pause a moment to examine this contracted phrasing of the question. It is understood, first of all, that the heirs of a historical upheaval have an entirely different retrospective and comprehensive grasp of it than do its contemporaries, who were surprised by the events and confronted with the daily occurrences (the storming of the Bastille, the execution of the king, the reign of terror by the Convention, and so forth).

In his *Historische Fragmente aus dem Nachlass* (Posthumous Historical Fragments) of 1867, Jacob Burckhardt wrote: "Most importantly, the revolution had consequences that already fully condition us and make up integral parts of our feeling of justice and our conscience—which we cannot, therefore, any longer separate from ourselves" (*Werke*, Gesamt-Ausgabe, 7: 420).

But if we are subject to "consequences that already fully condition us," we run the risk of unconsciously attributing these results and this conditioning to the contemporaries of the French Revolution. We then fall into the situation of the French Germanist, Pierre Bertaux (*Hölderlin und die Französische Revolution*, Frankfurt am Main, 1969), who discovered Hölderlin as a Jacobin poet. For Bertaux, the French Revolution is entirely a matter of course and therefore implicitly a positive achievement of history. When, therefore, he detects "Jacobin" tendencies in Hölderlin's poetry, he is inclined to credit these as positive traits in his work. In the process, Bertaux is quite unaware of the fact that he is already engaging in political evaluation. Extraliterary standards distort his judgment. It is claimed by Bertaux that Hölderlin, with his friend Sinclair, planned a "Swabian revolution," even a "tyrannicide." According to this reading, Hölderlin was not the quiet visionary depicted in traditional literary histories. (See Kirchner, Bertaux, and others for a discussion of these historical questions.) Bertaux himself notes that Hölderlin was a visionary, and he quite properly adds that it is precisely visionaries who instigate revolutions. If this is to the point, then the gap is closed between the traditional judgment of Hölderlin as an inner-directed "metaphysical adept" and Bertaux's Jacobin interpretation. For there is no absolute contrast between the two; it is even possible for both to coincide in the pure visionary's trait of incorrigibility by experience. In this respect comparing Hölderlin with his contemporaries is more instructive than subsuming him under our modern "relativity." While Hölderlin's contemporaries, influenced by the "Terror," turned against the French Revolution after 1793, he himself seems (always presuming that Bertaux is correct) to have remained loyal to it. Surely that can be explained only by assuming that Hölderlin did not perceive the facts of the revolution's course; he would thus have remained true to his inner motivation—incorrigible by conflicting facts. Many German writers who originally hailed the French Revolution as a torch of freedom became its antagonists when they saw how freedom turned into its opposite; this is true of Wieland, Herder, Novalis, and the Schlegel brothers, as well as the two honorary members of the Convention, Klopstock and Schiller—not to mention Goethe, who took a negative stance toward the revolution from the outset. After the execution of Louis XVI, Schiller wrote to Körner on 8 February 1873: "For the last two weeks I have been unable to read French newspapers, I am so sickened by these miserable loutish butchers" (Schiller, *Briefe*, ed. R. Buchwald, Leipzig, n.d., p. 318). Georg Forster, a Jacobin from Mainz, who had been convicted of contempt of the state in that city and condemned as a traitor—a genuine revolutionary, not merely a literary one—went to Paris in 1793 with the honest intention of putting himself at the service of the revolution. Several months later, forsaken and anguished, he perished in that city. His Parisian letters, written between April and December 1793, bear witness to his total disappointment (Forster, *Die Französische Revolution in Briefen*, ed. Gustav Landauer, Hamburg, 1961, pp. 341 ff.). "At no time has tyranny been so insolent, so unruly, at no time have all principles been trodden underfoot so carelessly, at no time has calumny reigned so wantonly" (26 June 1793, Forster, p. 47). Here we are confronted by the true revolutionary's turnabout, even if only in failure.

So much for the political aspect. As far as the poetic elements are concerned, it is difficult to understand how the artistic worth of Hölderlin's work can be augmented or diminished by possible evidence that one or another ode, or "Hyperion" or "Empedokles," embodies an echo of the French Revolution. In this instance we have no choice but to defend close reading of the texts. The debate concerning the "political" or "nonpolitical" Hölderlin demonstrates the flaws in a position which shifts the emphases too far from the poetic content to the possible "opinions," "views," "positions," or even the more or less cryptic "intentions" contained in a poetic work. This shift in emphasis is, of course, itself a consequence of the politicization of literary criticism.

Ever since public opinion emerged, "opinions" have flourished. In a democratized culture, they have abandoned princely councils and have gone over to the sovereign people. But they have retained their sovereignty. More power to anyone who can afford to despise "public opinion"—as it is put in Schiller's "Geisterseher." But the prince is a slave to public opinion, it is his wetnurse and tutor during childhood, law-giver and mistress during his adult life, a crutch in old age. "A prince who laughs at public opinion makes himself ineffectual, just like the priest who denies the existence of God" (Schiller, *Sämtliche Werke*, Munich: Hanser Verlag, 5: 124). This artificial, secondary, *mediatized existence*—that is, a life free from governmental control, making its possessor subject only to the king— which was most wittily stylized in Friedrich Rückert's poem "Im Parke" ("Geh'im Fürstenparke nicht spazieren . . ." or "Don't stroll through the prince's gardens . . .")[1] is by no means replaced in bourgeois society by a "free formation of opinion"; rather, it is transferred from the sovereign ruler to the sovereign people; thus, it does not remain "in the gardens" but roams through the open landscape, becomes universal, and serves as a medium for the universal growth of prejudice which has difficulty in even approaching facts and events.

In view of the foregoing, we should direct our primary attention to the literary shape given to general human problems emerging from the French Revolution, not to attitudes toward it, expressed in "opinions." German literature—or so it seems to me—can exhibit only *one* genuine revolutionary drama: Goethe's *Die Natürliche Tochter* (*The Natural Daughter*) of 1802. All controversies over the proper interpretation of this allegedly puzzling work seem superfluous to me, since one of the earliest reviewers of this tragedy, Johann Friedrich Ferdinand Delbrück, already fully grasped its critical attitude toward revolution. Delbrück characterized the tragedy's background as consisting of "a great powerful people, and so on," and he described it in such a way as to make it appear as a travesty of the society of the *ancien régime*:

> Religion, the law, public and domestic arrangements . . . relentlessly attacked and defamed by a countless host of conceited and garrulous sophists. Rather than seeking out and proclaiming the good that is hidden under much evil, their unprecedented impudence demeans everything that has been attested to in the course of centuries. Diligently they nurture man's natural tendency to discontent by exaggerating present grievances, by pretending to the existence of imaginary ones. Thus they arouse in the great mass an undefined longing for improvement and extol the overthrow of the existing order as the sole means for satisfying this longing. In the course of all this, we witness the growth of a thoroughly inimical relationship between the general mass and the individual, which lends a terrible reality to those frightful poems of gloating, malicious deities who arouse fierce cravings in man's breast in order to torture him by thwarting them.[2]

It is this society, then, that admits Eugenie, the tragedy's heroine and its only nonpolitical figure, and it is in this society that she must perish. The speeches between the active characters are permeated with false tones; in fact, at the court of the king everyone is in opposition to everyone else. Their actions, however, are steadfastly motivated by fear or hope of the approaching disruption of the existing order; all their decisions are determined by these feelings.

After the July revolution of 1830, the contemporaries understood that the Revolution of 1789 was not a passing episode, to be followed by restoration of the old order, but was the universal prologue to a *permanent revolution*. In his novel *Die Epigonen* (1836), Karl Immermann gave expression to this insight. Goethe's criticism of his literary contemporaries is enlarged by new, postrevolutionary perspectives; the mediatized existence of the grandiloquent men of letters who are not subject to the central authority is unmercifully castigated. No one any longer engages in action or defends a cause for its own sake; everyone deals in borrowed ideas. In former times only a few had any real understanding; now many believe themselves possessed of insight. "It takes only a minimal effort to find everywhere the most brilliant, most profound, most forceful expression of the flimsiest make-believe, the most hollow opinions, the emptiest heart. The old, plain 'conviction' has therefore fallen out of fashion, and it is popular to speak of opinions. But even that expression is almost wholly incorrect, for as a rule no attention has been paid to the matters about which one speaks and with which one pretends to be occupied" (Die Epigonen, part 1, chap. 10 in Immermanns Werke, Leipzig and Vienna, n.d., 3: 116–17, 134). "This so-called culture seems to me to be another barbarism which we are approaching or to which we have already, perhaps, fallen prey," a subsequent passage reads (Immermann, Werke, 3: 134). And again, with the most pronounced dialectical pithiness: "the refinement of our times begets a new barbarism" (Immermann, Werke, 4: 74). Finally the catchword "pessimism" is used, and it is defined as "striving among the factions artificially to create a condition of the utmost misery, so as to drive men into a rage which pushes them blindly toward the plans of the evil ones" (Immermann, Werke, 4: 111–12). This happens either by provoking the antagonist into taking rash steps or by artificially creating want, afflictions, and privation and increasing the hordes of the dissatisfied and the ruined.

A few years later (1838–1839) Immermann completed his criticism of his era by extending it to the utopianism of progress as exemplified by that "prince of liars," Baron Münchhausen: "This marvelous man constantly found the point of departure for his stories in something familiar and established, but he used this base to take off on his boldest and most adventurous flights, so that it could truly be said that in his own person he fairly represents the enormous progress of our day" (Immermann, Münchhausen, part 1, chap. 9 in Werke 1: 93).

Scientific research has long since proved that childhood fantasies, fairytales, and figures of speech are realities—according to Münchhausen. Let us therefore allow the teller of tales to lead us! "And so, the time-honored saying about castles in the air is given the dignity of actual existence by my corporation. From now on, airy buildings will no longer be meant metaphorically; rather, people will actually invest their money in them" (Immermann, *Werke*, 1:238–39). Thus Münchhausen is the forerunner of that utopian speculator in progress, August Weltumsegler, the creation of Knut Hamsun (in 1930); his projects also always teeter between a swindle and realized utopia: ". . . he sat in his chair, ill and mendacious, and was himself an expression of the times and of evolution" (Hamsun, *August Weltumsegler*, German trans., Munich, 1950, p. 269). This is how neatly epochs can be joined if their structural tendencies are kept in view!

In "Myself, Fragment and Developmental History" (Book 3, chap. 9), Münchhausen describes his change into a ruminant—again, a forerunner, as it were, of Kafka's Gregor Samsa or Ionesco's *Rhinoceros*: "Then I made the discovery in my inner self that was much worse than all external observations. . . . For I noticed, on examining myself closely, that in fact I rued the loss of my humanity only as a matter of form and honor, but that at heart I was very well pleased with the pelt covering my body and limbs, with my broad snout, with my nose stretching forward, with my eyes swerving sideways, with the slow growth of my nap and my spine. My soul, I could feel, was already hard at its work of oxifying" (Immermann, *Werke*, 1:270). But about his previous fellow creatures, "humans," the transmogrified narrator reports: "Only when they have pulled someone down to their level and have destroyed his best self, only then do they believe that he has become reasonable and deserves to be called one of themselves" (Immermann, *Werke*, 1:273). A comparison of Goethe's imperturbable remarks of the 1820s with Immermann's brutal irony makes clear the change that occurred within a bare two decades.

THE FALSE REVOLUTIONARY: *LITTÉRATURE ENGAGÉE*

Everyone knows that Marx is the author of the remark that it is not a matter of interpreting the world but of changing it.[3] In fact, however, the voluntarism manifest in this statement is much older; its roots lie—as does all of Marx's revolutionary thinking—in the Enlightenment philosophy of the eighteenth century. The desire to alter the world is not only expressed by the writers of that century, it is also an integral part of their professional ideology; this wish is even an aspect of their arrogance and their tendency toward smugness. These authors want to make a gift of happiness to mankind, that is their great reform. Robert Mauzi characterizes this literature as follows: "Too little has been said about the fact that these effusions and enthusiasms are used to express an enormous appetite for the absolute; no other means of satisfying it was available to the spirit of that age. Even the most high-flown rhetoric may contain a pitiful self-affirmation, an attempt to escape from nothingness" (*L'Idée du bonheur au xviii*^e *siècle*, 4th ed., Paris, 1969, p. 513). This then, is where the ancestors of Jean-Paul Sartre's *littérature engagée* can be found, even if Sartre considers himself a Marxist. The reverse side of social eudemonism is nihilism. True, this literature never escaped the vicious circle of the reciprocal relationship between "happiness" and "virtue" (to be happy is to be virtuous, to be virtuous is to sacrifice one's happiness for others); the French Revolution inherited this circle, as did modern socialism subsequently. In the meantime the new voluntarism served to unleash the battle against the authorities. The question is whether we can legitimately regard this literature as already revolutionary or even prerevolutionary. In the lecture cited at the outset of this essay, Borchardt attempted to claim Rousseau, for example, as being on the side of "tradition." But it is precisely in the case of Rousseau that Borchardt's own criterion of differentiating between "being revolutionary" and "wanting to be revolutionary" leads to a different judgment. Reinhart Koselleck has demonstrated that the omnipotence of criticism in the literature of the Enlightenment led to hypocrisy. When criticism becomes a weapon, it also becomes dishonest. Since its intention is to unmask, to reduce, to expose, it goes further and further in transcending its subject matter, it becomes the driving force of self-righteousness, it produces its own delusion. "Reciprocal criticism established the sovereignty of criticism and therefore for the critics themselves a shared, supraparty consciousness of mastery" (Koselleck, *Kritik und Krise. Ein Beitrag zur Pathogenese der bürgerlichen Welt*, 2d ed., Freiburg im Breisgau, 1969, pp. 98 ff., 195). Koselleck in this instance joins Merleau-Ponty's analysis of "metaphysical hypocrisy," as self-delusion through the means of universality. This condition inevitably sets in whenever an unconditional and exaggerated identification is made with any possible group or cause; it results in a neurotic disposition with hatred of everyone, of life and finally total loss of freedom. When this state of mind comes about, it must be more clearly expressed in the *style* of criticism and in the sociopsychological style of "criticism of criticism"—which has been, since the eighteenth century, the vital element of enlightened literature—than in direct statements, perhaps even in spite of itself (Maurice Merleau-Ponty, *Phänomenologie der Wahrnehmung*, German trans., Berlin, 1966, p. 195). At the end of Book Four, chapter eight (later omitted), of *Le Contrat social*, Rousseau writes: "All of them became enemies, reciprocally persecuted, one by all and all by one; man as seen by Hobbes is intolerant, and intolerance is humanity's warfare" (quoted in Koselleck, *Kritik und Krise*, p. 21). Unless I am much mistaken, this quotation already contains some of the sociopsychological atmosphere of false overtones which were later to have their expression in *The Natural Daughter*. I will here forego further bits of evidence from Rousseau, as I wish only to point out that the topic "nihilism" can boast of a longer family tree than is generally admitted.

In the present century, the thesis that literature is justified only when it is "engaged" and when it is intended to bring about changes in the world has been repeated in a number of variants. Hugo von Hofmannsthal's famous Chandos Letter (1902), which expressed the disgust with words, has become symbolic for skepticism about literature: "These abstract words—which by nature the tongue is forced to use to render any judgment at all—decayed in my mouth like moldering mushrooms" (Hofmannsthal, *Ausgewählte Werke*, Frankfurt am Main, 1957, 2:342). This is not the only time that Hofmannsthal used this uncanny metaphor of corruption. In the first version of *The Tower* (1925) a young lay brother reads from the work of the Spanish philosopher Antonio de Guevara: "Farewell, world, for there is no relying on you, one cannot trust in you; in your house the past rules only as a ghost, the present dissolves in our hands as does a rotting and poisonous mushroom, the brigand's fist of the future constantly knocks at the door at midnight, and in a hundred years you give us not one hour of genuine life" (Hofmannsthal, *Gesammelte Werke, Dramen*, vol. 4, Frankfurt am Main, 1958, p. 65).

Hermann Broch is therefore absolutely correct in taking up the Chandos motif specifically as the perennial problem of the "decay of values"; he considers it in his later works as well as in his essay "Hofmannsthal und seine Zeit" or "Hofmannsthal and his Times" (in Broch, *Gesammelte Werke*, vol. 6, Zurich, 1955, p. 155 and passim). After all, the theme of *The Death of Virgil* is the negation of literature, but stated paradoxically—it is given literary form. Broch was himself aware of this and even felt guilty about it. *Virgil* should not really have become a book (Broch, *Gesammelte Werke*, vol. 8, Zurich, 1957, p. 300). "... In our day, however, the practice of pure literature has become . . . an . . . illicit activity, almost an irresponsible one, both toward the world and toward one's own salvation, for we live like primitives . . . once more in the jungle—this time, it is true, in a cold jungle." Anyone who fails to contribute to clearing this jungle has become superfluous (Broch, *Gesammelte Werke*, 8:300). "The 'writer' as such no longer has a place of his own" (Broch, *Gesammelte Werke*, 8:267). This sounds like a resumption of that literary passage in Hofmannsthal's *Tower*, and it even evokes a reminiscence of an author so utterly different as Brecht:

> Was sind das für Zeiten, wo
> Ein Gespräch über Bäume fast ein Verbrechen ist,
> Weil es Schweigen über soviele Untaten einschliesst![4]

The consequences for Broch and Brecht are well known: during his final years, living in the United States, Broch turned away from literature and toward the positive sciences—with little success, for his mass-psychological depictions remained fragmentary and literary (see Broch, *Gesammelte Werke*, vol. 9, Zurich, 1959). Brecht opted for proletarian socialism and found himself on the side of totalitarian communist dictatorship.

The fate of writers who committed themselves to communism calls for a separate discussion. Whenever they struggled seriously with the problems, they could not escape the "Chandos question" in one or another form. Cesare Pavese, who committed suicide at the age of forty-two, left the following as his final diary entry (Pavese, *Das Handwerk des Lebens, Tagebuch, 1933–1950*, German trans., Hamburg, 1956, p. 414):

> All this is disgusting.
> Not words. A gesture. I will not write again.

Earlier, Pavese had criticized himself in his diaries: "I have simplified the world into a banal picture gallery with strong or graceful gestures. It is drama that is over there, not life itself" (Pavese, p. 43). The truly epic poet *believes* that what he depicts really happened (Pavese is thinking of Homer). The important books were not written, he notes, to make literature, nor is it worth bothering with anything but reality. We must believe that whatever we want to tell about has really happened (Pavese, pp. 134, 136). Therefore Pavese desperately strives to draw myth into life, to create the magical effect that it is happening (Pavese, p. 354). This is mythological theory, but what grows out of it is not myth but a highly sophisticated mythical

poetry, the *Dialoghi con Leucò* (1947). Pavese survives through this
work and through the novels of his maturity, whereas his final "gesture," though a humanly poignant act, cannot add any value to his
work—though it is surely useful for publicity.

Broch, a more inflexible man than Pavese, explains: "It is not a
matter of the world's readiness for myth—that is Nazi aesthetics—but
of the renunciation of the decorative function of artistic activity and
emphasis on its ethical obligation" (Broch, *Gesammelte Werke*,
6:65). But the question arises whether this postulate is tenable. Ana-
clitic mythology is not an invention of the Nazis. The eschatological
"political myth" was first proclaimed by Georges Sorel; it is therefore
the creation of revolutionary syndicalism—unless, that is, we wish to
espouse the thesis that the communist Manifesto already represented
one such political "myth." But Broch's attempt to ethicize literature
seems to me questionable under any circumstances. The rejection of
literature, the determination not to write again, is a personal motivation that cannot be judged. But aside from the question of the
ultimate sincerity of this attitude—Chandos-Hofmannsthal and Virgil-
Broch did, after all, have a kind of "relapse"—we must ask: if Broch
declares that "pure literature is "illegitimate" and only a literature
regulated by ethical standards may be tolerated (fortunately he
makes this claim only in letters), who then is to set the standards,
and where is the limit of the prohibition on writing, such as it was and
is practiced in totalitarian states? True, nothing was further from
Broch's mind than to appropriate the demands for "realism" of certain modern politicians of a totalitarian stamp; but the radical demand for "engagement" comes dangerously close to this area. But if
the satisfaction of the "required" ethos is left up to the individual
author's voluntary compliance, it cannot be predicted what the outcome will be; certainly it will not be unanimity. It might turn out
that the question is, after all, one of literary creation, whether or not
the author falls prey to "disgust with the word"; that, minimally affected by current events and surrounded by death and destruction, he
will create works which, according to the kangaroo court of his "engaged" contemporaries, have their origins in the ivory tower and
reveal their subtle connection with their present only to a subsequent
generation. One example might be furnished by the mature and late
works of Gerhart Hauptmann.

"Engaged" poetry is, as a rule, unpalatable. André Chenier was a
significant odist; as a revolutionary, he was put to the guillotine because his ethics made him "engage" himself in another direction than

the one expected of him at the time. The collection of allegedly suppressed German revolutionary poetry, published by two critics[5] in a magnificent edition, contains hardly one poetic line. As early as 1826 Platen in a sonnet openly ridiculed this sort of politically zealous production: "In an ocean of foolishness/ A few talented swimmers appear." Lenau also made fun of "all the dull fire-eating" (August von Platen, *Sämtliche Werke*, Cotta, vol. 2, p. 108; Nikolaus Lenau, *Werke und Briefe*, 1:347). A genuinely poetic work, such as Büchner's *Danton's Death*, at once transcends the politically leveling interpretation. Political ideology and literary quality stand in an inverse relationship to each other. As talented a dramatist as Brecht, who in his best works moved beyond the mold of Marxism, becomes untrustworthy just as soon as he attempts, in scenes intended to castigate Hitler's rule, to reduce this phenomenon to the cliché of the class war. Equivalent evaluations apply to Sartre.

Engaged literature is of particular interest when it promotes the theme of antibourgeois social criticism. Just as poets often take a position against poetry, so do the middle classes in this instance place themselves in opposition to middle-classness. This is a fad honored now and again even by such renowned literary historians as, for example, Walter Muschg, who, in his book, *Tragische Literaturgeschichte* (2d ed., Bern, 1953, p. 421 and passim) summons up the "dying bourgeoisie" so often that even the most inattentive reader understands at last: it isn't dead yet. Under these auspices, it is only natural that the misinterpretations of such writers as Gotthelf, Stifter, Storm, and Fontane mount up. Muschg succeeds in claiming with a straight face that no narrative writer of any worth was produced by German literature after Jean Paul (Muschg, *Studien zur tragischen Literaturgeschichte*, Bern, 1965, pp. 126–27). He bases this claim on a nationalistically narrow concept of German literature. Though it is quite impossible to maintain this argument logically, it allows him to eliminate Gotthelf, Stifter, and Keller from the concept of German literature; next he eliminates Storm as a "provincial" (even though the awakening of the Enlightenment as a "clarification" of consciousness after a long period of folly and moral darkness was nowhere rendered with so much genius—because it was free of ideology! —as in "Renate," 1878); he further eliminates Fontane by suddenly supplanting evaluation with critical history—and distorted at that— and claiming that Fontane had encountered resistance and lack of understanding. Perhaps so, but what does that signify? Among the deliberately antibourgeois writers he lists important figures, such

as Heinrich Mann, Döblin, and Brecht; but these men are important
as literary figures, not for their politics. Heinrich Mann, perhaps
the outstanding novelist in the German language during the first
half of this century, is the prototype of the bourgeois, even haut
bourgeois, with a strong Bohemian streak, which became exaggerated into hatred of bourgeois society. This is not to arrive at
any conclusion concerning the authenticity or inauthenticity of his
motivations. Mann is such a powerful literary figure that his artistically wrought work becomes a strong shield protecting his ideology.
But the social-critical purpose in his novels *Im Schlaraffenland* (1897),
Professor Unrat (*The Blue Angel*, 1905), and *Der Untertan* (1918)
remains ambiguous. Mann depicts ideal types, in Max Weber's sense
of the word—that is, by exaggerating to the point of utopianism and
by caricaturing tendencies of social behavior in the Wilhelminian
authoritarian state; these are surely very remarkable tendencies—but
everything becomes absurd if these tendencies are seen as *persons*
engaging in a form of behavior universally observed at the time. But
the reader is seduced into seeing the tendencies as people and the
novels themselves as "documentaries," and this is where the decep-
tion sets in.[6] This social-critical distortion does historical injustice
to countless honest, upright characters, none of them victims of the
"slave mentality," who, after all, also existed at that time. The novels
of Heinrich Mann furnish as little proof of the decay of bourgeois
society as do the social-critical literati of the latter day up to the
present moment. They themselves are the sickness which they claim
to diagnose in bourgeois society. "Apparently you do not know," an
artist in one of Mann's novels says to the woman, "that in a way we
artists are always using our work to avenge ourselves on everything
that has wounded our sensibilities, that has aroused longing in us:
the whole world" (*Die Göttinnen oder die drei Romane der Herzogin
von Assy*, Hamburg, 1969, p. 590). He is not, then, thinking of bourgeois society alone.

   Heinrich Mann's novel *Die kleine Stadt* (1907–1909) was intended
by the author to form a counterpart to his novel *Der Untertan*; it was
to be the "Song of Songs of democracy on the Latin pattern" (Klaus
Schröter, *Heinrich Mann in Selbstzeugnissen und Bilddokumenten*,
Reinbek, 1967, pp. 66 ff.). But surely this is idle infatuation. Heinrich Mann may not have spent enough time in the south to see
through the oligarchy of local dignitaries in these Italian hamlets;
and yet Mann's descriptions in this charming little novel suffice to
indirectly reveal the oligarchic conditions to the expert sociologist.

For Mann was a genuine poet, and he could therefore not avoid transcending his "tendencies." Furthermore, he was subject to the tragic error of the intellectual, who believes that he can be politically active by the critical means at a novelist's disposal. It is the paradigmatic case of the humane author who, because he rejects and attacks inhumane power, throws himself into the arms of the counterforce, which is not one whit better.

The upshot of this reflection is that we cannot possibly do politically engaged writers the favor of taking their political tendencies, intentions, self-interpretations, and manifestoes as seriously as they expect us to—unless, that is, we intend to compromise them. What will remain twenty years after the death of Heinrich Mann, Knut Hamsun, Sartre, Brecht, Ezra Pound, and others will not be their "political" partisanship and escapades, but solely the artistic value of their works. They are to be honored according to this criterion and no other.

We have stated that the creation transcends the creator. But even more importantly, the effect of the creation transcends the creator's intentions. "The view that the genuine poem is to be found in the intentions of an author is widespread . . . It justifies much historical research and is at the bottom of many arguments in favor of specific interpretations," write Wellek and Warren. But even if the authors themselves seem to encourage such interpretations, they need not be binding on the observer. Shakespeare would probably have voiced his intentions in writing *Hamlet* in a way we should find highly unsatisfactory (Wellek and Warren, *Theory of Literature*, p. 148; idem, *Theorie der Literatur*, p. 127). Further examples could be cited, such as Goethe's occasional utterances on *Die Wahlverwandtschaften* —which do, however, arouse suspicion of deliberate obfuscation. Joseph Strelka writes: "It is no accident that many of the most overwhelming literary creations even of sociological relevance came into being entirely without scientific or quasiscientific theory. The result is certainly not due to supernatural inspiration, but simply arises from the artists' refined sensibility for the internal and external conditions of the world of their time and their knowledgeable insight into the driving force of the heart beneath the props and superficialities" (*Die gelenkten Musen. Dichtung und Gesellschaft*, Vienna, 1971, p. 190).

Gerhart Hauptmann's *The Weavers* seemed rousing and revolutionary just *because* this drama was in no way intended to be "social" or "revolutionary." It grew out of the writer's humanity, it flourished in the soil of worldly experience. Having been an agricultural apprentice as a young man, Hauptmann experienced genuinely, at first hand, without any ideology whatsoever, the situation of labor that was dependent and exploited. In "Das Abenteuer meiner Jugend," he said, "That was—I felt it for the first time—true hard labor. It became visible, audible, and tangible to me, and I understood that until then I had known nothing of the foundations of our civilization" (see *Sämtliche Werke*, centennial ed., vol. 7, Frankfurt am Main, p. 709).

The counterpart to *The Weavers* is Brecht's *Life of Galileo*. In this work the author wanted to use Galileo's recantation before the Holy Office to present a crime against the universal solidarity of science and to show the inventor himself as a corrupt bourgeois manifestation. It was because of this "original sin" of science, the claim goes, that science had been robbed of its social meaning and had been reduced to a special interest of the middle classes; at the same time, it is admitted, science was relatively unhampered in continuing to develop its problematic "purity"—that is, its indifference toward the methods of production (Brecht, *Gesammelte Werke*, 7:1108–9). But as a dramatist Brecht failed with this typically Marxist didactic play. Aside from the untenable interpretation from the point of view of the history of science, Brecht's intention was completely misunderstood in both the West and the East; in the Soviet Union the protagonist was even hailed as a "hero of science," who had suffered for his convictions (Strelka, *Die gelenkten Musen*, p. 294).

AUTHENTICALLY REVOLUTIONARY TRAITS

The Pariah Motif

Authentically revolutionary elements in literature do not find their expression in the appeals, programs, and ideological interpretations of society and history. There are quite other aspects and motifs, both in the artist's situation and in his "expressive world" (Benn), where the genuinely new, fruitful, and supportive elements manifest themselves. But none of these are plain on the surface, they need not even be comprehensively verbalized; rather, they reveal themselves only to more deeply probing insight. We will here consider the pariah motif and the gnostic elements in a few selected works of German literature. Without claiming completeness, we will attempt to illustrate a few of these traits, which often overlap.

The position of pariah originally has a sociological or ethnological meaning. Derived from the Tamil word *paraiyan*, it designates the position of an oppressed caste—placed at the bottom end of the social hierarchy or, in theory, even standing outside the social order altogether; despised by all, shunned, not accepted, ostracized as "unclean" and associated with the lowliest and dirtiest jobs—such as removing animal cadavers and cleaning streets and latrines. Other occupations also carry this stamp of contempt; often it is the tinkers and smiths (gypsies are, after all, generically such a pariah class), but also strolling players, actors and jongleurs, fortune tellers, chicken farmers, and others. This social phenomenon extends from the Sudan by way of the Near East to India and Central Asia and can be found even in ancient Japan. But archaic Europe is not spared. As is well known, our own culture area admits of "dishonorable occupations." Among them are executioners, at times certain artisans such as millers or weavers, and always strolling players and actors, "vagrants" such as gypsies, although not necessarily identical with gypsies. In his time Max Weber strikingly labeled as "guest populations" (*Gastvölker*), those who have the position in society—or, more properly, on the edge of society—of a societal formation that was only partly or not at all accepted.[7] As a matter of cultural history, this odium of the pariah clings to the artist. According to the typology of artists developed by Walter Muschg in his *Tragische Literaturgeschichte*, the type of the juggler absolutely belongs in this pariah category. But surely anyone who entertains people with invented (that is, untrue) stories is a juggler? Naive members of the lower classes are to this day sometimes inclined to feel that way. The English expression *fiction* preserves an element of this attitude.

Along with the pariah situation goes the pariah ethic as it was described by Max Weber. This includes the ethos of patient endurance in the midst of a dominant ruling system or under the weight of foreign conquerors, together with cunning assimilation and the practice of slipping through, avoiding, and surviving, the ability to take the "underground route" wherever necessary, to render oneself unnoticed, perhaps to nourish secret resistance in the underground. In the negative sense—that is, judged "from above"—this is "toadyism" and "duplicity" toward the persons in power. In the positive sense, it represents intellectual introversion, an attempt to preserve one's inner dignity even while overtly cringing and stooping; and it also implies the weapon of the intellect (Nietzsche's "Chandala morality"): the ability to overcome one's enemies through goodness and love (subsequently practiced by Gandhi) and the positive transfiguration of a basically negative position, combined with a highly developed technique for showering the powerful rulers with feelings of guilt and remorse. Thus the "pariah ethic" has many shadings; it can neither be easily rejected nor simply applauded; it has practical potentials for the highest as well as the lowest forms of behavior. We need only fill in the details of this model to note the close connections between the pariah ethic and critical literature since the time of the Enlightenment. The pariah ethic constitutes criticism's emotional—and frequently its social—background or bedrock.

It is at this point that our examination begins. Without knowing anything at all about Max Weber, Hermann Broch, in his essay on Hofmannsthal, stressed the artist's marginal role. The artist, notes Broch, is not really a member of any specific social class. To become an artist means to be cut off from one's class and to become subject to a similar form of contempt as was earlier given to dishonorable professions, such as that of hangman. For "class" means dependence, subordination; whereas the most an artist can ask for is to be allowed to be a guest: the guest of a benevolent nobility, hardly of the bourgeoisie, certainly never of the "people" as such. As a rule, then, an artist is a guest of the nobility, perhaps even a very welcome guest. (Even Goethe's early years at the court of Weimar retain something of this marginal position, although Broch, of course, focused primarily on Austrian conditions.) But it is as a guest that the artist is and remains defined in his social role (Broch, *Gesammelte Werke*, 6:136). This situation does not in any way apply merely to representatives of the "low" arts—the jugglers, vagrants, and *poètes maudits* of the type of Rabelais, Grimmelshausen, Günther, Byron, Heine, Verlaine, and Rimbaud (Muschg, *Tragische Literaturgeschichte*, pp. 262 ff.); rather, it is the incarnate social history of a pariah profession, and isolated structural traits can be found in the situation of each of our important writers. Nor need it cause any surprise that, since the nineteenth century, Jewish writers have been particularly notable representatives of the pariah theme, for the topic has become vitally important for them since the emancipation.

In the one-act tragedy, *Der Paria* (1823) by the very talented young Michael Beer (1800–1830, a brother of the composer Meyerbeer), the eponymous hero stands for the Jew fighting for his emancipation. The pariah, Gadhi, appears as the prophet of a priestless enlightenment opposed to the prejudices and old-wives' tales of the Brahman priests. Thus, for example, a polemic against the Brahmans reads:

> Sie schmeicheln ihrem Hund und ihrem Rosse,
> Sie scheuen uns, als hätt'uns die Natur
> Zur Larve Menschenbildung nur gegeben.
> Stellt mich euch gleich und seht, ob ich euch gleiche![8]

But Gadhi also believes that he bears the *true* Brahman faith, not distorted by the Brahmans:

> Des eigenen Busens flammende Erkenntnis
> Macht seine Welt zum piegel seines Wesens.[9]

This passionate declaration clearly conveys to us a phenomenon frequent in the history and psychology of pariah groups; the reversal of the pariah's feeling of inferiority into the consciousness of constituting an elite entrusted with a particular message.

Goethe, who treated the pariah motif as early as 1797 in *Der Gott und die Bajadre*, took it up again in his pariah trilogy in the same year that saw the appearance and performance in Berlin of Beer's tragedy. He praised Beer's work, the manuscript of which the author had presented to him in Weimar in January 1824 (Goethe, *Gespräche*, Gedenk-Ausgabe, Zurich, 1950, p. 322). He discussed it the same year, in "Über Kunst und Altertum" ("On Art and Antiquity") and made it the occasion for interpreting his own trilogy: "Here we are faced with a pariah who does not consider his situation hopeless; he turns to the Lord in the Highest and asks for a sign—which, it is true is then given in a strange manner. Now, however, the caste that had heretofore been cut off from everything holy, from every sanctuary, is possessed of a divinity of its own, in which the Highest, injected into the lowest, represents a fearful third, though it has a beatific influence for mediation and balance."[10] "The Highest, injected into the lowest" and thus representing "a fearful third"—the motif of pariah as member of an elite could not be summed up more succinctly.

But it is impossible here to touch on the connections between the pariah motif and the hopes for emancipation in the time of Goethe without also calling attention to the destruction of these hopes in the pogroms of the nineteenth and twentieth centuries. In this light we can read the pariah transfiguration even in the act of being crushed, in the formulation left to us by the Jewish lyricist Gertrud Kolmar, who was killed in Auschwitz by Hitler's henchmen:

Du dunkle, zitternde Rasse! O Krone, die Unke trägt,
Wenn Narrheit vor ihr erschauert, wenn Bosheit nach ihr schlägt,
Der Sand Geheimnis bröckelt und Quelle Wunder rinnt,
Die allen Wesens Geschwister und Gottes älteres Kind . . .

Mag ich nur ekles Geziefer sein:
Ich bin die Kröte
Und trage den Edelstein.[11]

We will forego tracing the theme through the literature of the nineteenth and twentieth centuries. (It is not limited to Jewish writers; it can be discovered also in a Christian guise, for example in the work of Annette von Droste-Hülshoff.) I will cite only a few examples. In the process I must distinguish between two elements. (1) It is in the nature of the idea of emancipation to connect by preference with the *concept* (often only the *verbalization*) of "pariah" as soon as it becomes a matter of freeing and "redeeming" an oppressed caste, class, or other minority from a despised existence; in this endeavor, however, the emancipatory authority itself usually stands aside. (2) The feeling of a pariah, on the other hand, is expressed in a much more subtle form and is also more difficult to detect. Since only the substance is revealed, the word "pariah" need never be voiced; rather, it is enough to have an experiential identification with the oppressed, the humiliated, the injured (Hauptmann). A linking of the first and second elements occurs when the pariah sentiment leads from identification with to advocacy of the oppressed —therefore, when it becomes socially effective as an emancipatory postulate (Beer, Brecht). In the latter case the literary attitude can come very close to ideology and therefore to an inauthentic revolutionary stance. In *both* cases, however, the themes are removed from all sociological conditions. Feelings of pariahdom and identification with pariah groups need not be based on the author's social, racial, or ethnic origins, nor must advocacy of pariahs be directed at actual pariah groups in the sociological sense. The inner motivation is the decisive factor. But that circumstance seems to point to the fact that we can discover a dimension in the pariah motif that contains an anthropological (not sociological) quality. The pariah feeling is *discovered in* specific social conditions as its most visible manifestations, but it does not in itself *originate* in these social conditions; rather, it is a universal human potential of anxiety, of the feeling of being abandoned and estranged, of rejection and lack of acceptance in the world.

Advocacy of pariah groups as a political theme was first manifested in European literature wherever the revolutionary concept of emancipation was applied to despised, underprivileged groups of humanity—and that was long before the emancipation of the Jews. Thus, Abbé Raynal, one of the most diligent and notable ideological precursors of the French Revolution, as early as 1770, in his *Histoire philosophique et politique des établissements et du commerce européen* (*Philosophical and Political History of European Institutions and Trade*), writes of the oppressed "pariahs," and by this term he means not only the "savages" in the European colonial regions (the same group referred to later by Toynbee as the "external proletariat"), but also the bonded peasants and the impoverished urban manual workers in the European countries (quoted in Mauzi, *L'Idée du bonheur*, p. 171). It is not a new phenomenon that the social position of the populations of the "third world" (to use a modern term) is used to stand for an interpretation of European social history; the device was already applied two hundred years ago—though how justified it was must here remain unexplored. Among the writers of the next generation, if Robert Minder is to be believed, Hölderlin was an advocate of the pariahs, precisely on the basis of the frequently underrated fundamentals of Lutheran feeling for the last who shall be the first. Hölderlin, Minder claims, was familiar, not only with spiritual and mental anguish, but also with "the very real suffering of the deprived, the injured, and the humiliated" (Robert Minder, *Dichter in der Gesellschaft*, Frankfurt am Main, 1966, pp. 74–75). But to reopen the controversy concerning Hölderlin's Jacobinism is beyond the scope of this discussion, which will be limited to a few further examples.

I know of only one nineteenth-century example of the psychologically intuitive description of an applied "pariah ethic": Conrad Ferdinand Meyer's novella of 1879, *Der Heilige* (*The Saint*). The story deals with the methods whereby the chancellor of England, Thomas à Becket, himself the son of a Saxon and a Saracen woman—that is, a descendant of the population that had been conquered and violated by the Normans—subjugates his king "by his gentle determination": "I love thinking and art, and I like it when reason triumphs over the fist and when the weaker, aiming from a distance, strikes and overpowers the stronger" (Conrad Ferdinand Meyer, *Werke*, Dünndruck-Ausgabe, 4 vols., Leipzig, 1922, 4:52).

In this case the statement is made about a crossbow; nevertheless, the idea of striking from a distance is simultaneously intended in an intellectual sense, as a long-drawn design for destroying the opponent. But the crossbowman Hans speaks of the Saint as "the strangest man . . . that ever walked this earth, the model and the fashion of the century" (Meyer, p. 59). (It is impossible in this connection not to think of Gandhi and his apostle, Romain Rolland.) Sir Thomas was born pliable, submissive (Meyer, p. 61), he cannot help but obey. "Sir Thomas could shed no blood" (Meyer, p. 128). But slowly, step by step, with inexorable gentleness, he could corrupt his royal lord. The hired soldiers refuse obedience to their Norman lords and shrink back from Thomas, for he approaches them with arms widespread, blessing them (Meyer, p. 157).[12] The meaning of the pariah ethic for literary criticism becomes clear only when we recognize that it involves the problem of the "intellect as weapon"; in this connection Meyer's nouvella is paradigmatic.

A far more dramatic presentation, extending it additionally to the area of collective movements, is given to the pariah ethic in Alfred Döblin's masterpiece, *Die drei Sprünge des Wang-Lun* (*The Three Leaps of Wang-Lun*), written in 1912–1913. Significantly, in depicting his hero, Wang-Lun, the leader of a nonviolent popular movement in ancient China, Döblin attaches no positive value to the fact that Wang-Lun is the representative of a nonviolent ethic, any more than Meyer did with Becket. On the contrary. Döblin paints this folk hero as underhanded, cowardly, and brutal; it is only against the background of this paradox that the theme becomes imbued with meaning. The reversal of proclaimed nonviolence into violence (Sorel's "direct action"), discovered by modern sociology as a regular process in the course of "nonviolent" movements,[13] was already depicted sixty years ago by Döblin with deep insight into mass psychology. In front of the reader's eyes the thousand-armed Buddha is transformed into a raging crowd (Döblin, *Die drei Sprünge des Wang-Lun*, Olten, 1960, p. 489). The reality of the pariah existence is clearly shown: "They were outcasts, victims; they had an enemy and were ecstatic in their effervescent hatred" (Döblin, pp. 78, 81). But the theme of the pariah as member of an elite is also present: "We are outcasts, and we admit it freely. If we are weak, we are nevertheless stronger. Believe me, no one will slay us, we blunt every spike" (Döblin, pp. 78, 81). The final sentence was used almost verbatim by Gandhi—a positive ideology of the weak.

The theme of the pariahs as an elite is so clearly expressed in Döblin's novel that Walter Muschg (acting as editor of Döblin's works) holds the view that in *Wang-Lun* the Chinese collective of the weak is made to stand for the exodus of the chosen Jewish people (see afterword by Muschg in Döblin, p. 500). That may well be, but the significance of Döblin's work transcends this meaning by far.

It is, by the way, interesting to note that it is precisely the two socialist writers, Döblin and Brecht, who share a predilection for the East Asian Taoist symbolization of the pariah motif. In Brecht, the sense of uselessness and disappointment resulting from the identification with the underdog is stronger than forcible protest: "Wir stehen selbst enttäuscht und sehn betroffen/Den Vorhang zu und alle Fragen offen"—"We are ourselves disappointed and, stricken, see the curtain close while all questions remain open" (from the epilogue to *The Good Person of Szechwan* in Brecht, *Gesammelte Werke*, 2:1607). Döblin is aggressive, Brecht at heart melancholy. This is also revealed in his moving poem, "To Our Successors":

> . . . Ich wäre gerne auch weise.
> In den alten Büchern steht, was weise ist:
> Sich aus dem Streit der Welt halten und die kurze Zeit
> Ohne Furcht verbringen
> Auch ohne Gewalt auskommen
> Böses mit Gutem vergelten
> Seine Wünsche nicht erfüllen, sondern vergessen
> Gilt für weise.
> Alles das kann ich nicht:
> Wirklich, ich lebe in finsteren Zeiten![14]

Included among the "old books" is Brecht's beloved Tao Tê Ching of Lao-tzu. In another poem he describes its creation with its Taoist wisdom:

> . . . dass das weiche Wasser in Bewegung
> Mit der Zeit den mächtigen Stein besiegt.
> Du verstehst, das Harte unterliegt.[15]

One more element is held in common by Döblin and Brecht, and with them by the entire expressionist movement: the objection to traditional aesthetics, the rejection of the pursuit of classical beauty in literature. For the pariah perspective, which inevitably opens the view to so much ugliness, baseness, depravity, and misery, simply cannot be combined with traditional aesthetic norms. It is a provocation to all bourgeois concepts of beauty (to which the exotic chinoiserie of both poets' symbolization contributed). The beginning of the final saying in the Tao—"True words are not beautiful/ Beautiful words are not true"—throws more light than anything else on the rending of the traditional European ideal of the unity of "the true, the good, and the beautiful." The disenchantment with the world stemming from modern Western science put an end to this unity; the extremism of the struggle for deepened insight also arose from the pariah impulse and was reinforced by the energies of Near Eastern gnosticism. "The will to understand" is itself a pariah motif that has become revolutionary (Mühlmann, "Max Weber und die rationale Soziologie," pp. 11, 51). The same struggle, however, can also be seen in the art and literature of expressionism. "Understand the situation" was, as it were, Gottfried Benn's ultimate utterance. Between the radicalism of the striving for truth in expressionist art and literature—most purely expressed in the works of Kafka—and the radicalism of the emerging new psychology and sociology, especially value and ideology criticism, an undeniable parallel exists.

"Understand the situation." But this situation is not in any way a "class situation"; that would be too narrow a view. Of all the writers mentioned here, Döblin was the only one to come from a semiproletarian background of Eastern Jewish provenance. Heinrich Mann was descended from a Hanseatic bourgeois milieu; Benn was the son of a minister from Saxony, Brecht the son of a business executive in Augsburg; Kafka came from a well-to-do Czech-Jewish family in Prague. The case of Gerhart Hauptmann is unique. In his narrative of his early years he wrote that he had early on become conscious of being a "pariah"; he placed the blame for this feeling on the unbearable authoritarian conditions in his school in Breslau, where boys were whipped until they bled. Hauptmann writes of the "life of the pariah, which I led alongside things." These experiences early brought him to a natural identification with the "underdog," with the poor, the crushed, the deprived. At the same time the boy was aware of the absurdity of this identification from a social point of view, since he came from a "good bourgeois" home, with stable family relationships. It is well known that this attitude is most poignantly expressed in Hauptmann's early dramas and that his manner is particularly convincing because the dramas are "social," not in the ideological sense, but because of the writer's own humane sympathies and feeling of identity. In later years Hauptmann spoke of his youthful inner life as "the excessive reveries of a misunderstood, despised boy who was pushed around, who was a pariah child, a half-caste boy," who found himself seated in the back row even in confirmation class, farther back than the minister's look could ever reach (Hauptmann, "Das Abenteuer meiner Jugend," pp. 635, 695, 697). We cannot resist the impression that the depth of this painful existence is not exactly congruent with the external conditions; they must frequently have been harsh and mean, true, but they were never really "proletarian" or "pariahlike." It is more likely that the subjective experience far exceeded the actual situation and is felt as a symbol of a potentially universal human situation.

> I fell prey to . . . my feelings of inferiority. I had a low opinion of myself. . . . They would, I thought, despise a person like myself, one who bore on his forehead the sign of his depravity, in the sense of his inadequacy to the point of uselessness—that is, his wretchedness. My gloom spread . . . to everything everywhere. . . . To call it melancholy [Weltschmerz] would be to debase it by a fashionable term. Everywhere I saw suffering and death. I was gripped by a feeling, which I had sometimes had in childhood, as if I were marooned and alone [Hauptmann, pp. 733, 747, 770].

There is no doubt that the most important sources of Hauptmann's work lie in this pariah experience, as did his later gnostic interpretations of the world. On the biographical level, of course, a new layer of gradual success came to overlay this first layer: acceptance in "cultured" good society, with forms, manners, art, and science: the youth also "rises" inwardly but never loses sight of the pariah experience: "I felt that it was not necessary to lose the lower world if one possessed the higher one. But no one who does not know how to enjoy the lower world with caution will ever find the upper one open to him" (Hauptmann, p. 652). Hauptmann's adoption of the Don Quixote theme also seems entirely genuine; he surrounds Cervantes' fictional figure with the "nimbus of holiness" and deduces from it a motto suitable to the pariah ethic: "Take strength from your weakness"; in complete idolatrous identification with the "errant knight," he is prepared without further ado to join literature and life when, on a Mediterranean cruise in 1883, he is on the point of buying the freedom of a prostitute, a "Dulcinea," on Malaga (Hauptmann, pp. 921, 923).

We enter on quite another level in the work of Franz Kafka. There is no question here of pariah advocacy—any such tendency is quite foreign to Kafka. But even "pariah feeling" or "pariah identification" would be inadequate concepts. Kafka's work completely incarnates the pariah's existence at the same time that it transcends it, so that concrete designations remain insufficient. Accordingly, interpretations of Kafka are contested, they are far from the surface. But we can also say that in Kafka's work the pariah motif shines through in a highly ethicized manner. In each of his novels grace and desperation, acceptance and rejection are fundamental elements in the make-up of the leading characters—far beyond all sociological determinations of these relationships. Much of this can only be recognized by the trained eye; note, for example, in chapter nineteen of *The Castle* the reflection, from beginning to end saturated with brutal irony, that by his mere *existence* the surveyor K. causes suffering to the bureaucratic gentlemen with their exquisite tact (Kafka, *Das Schloss*, Frankfurt am Main, 1958, pp. 278 ff.). The mere fact of a pariah's *being* is, as it were, a tactlessness, a scandal in a well-ordered universe. To understand a passage such as this, it is necessary to have an idea of the relationships between "untouchables" and Brahmans in certain parts of India.

Gnostic Elements

Wherever the pariah situation becomes aware of itself, proceeds to coherent interpretations, and forms its own mythology, it becomes *gnosis*. We will here refer primarily to the first volume of *Gnosis und spätantiker Geist* (Göttingen, 1964) by Hans Jonas. But in a wider sense we will also take into account, not only various Near Eastern religious teachings of the first few centuries after Christ, but also, according to their spirit and their form, aspects of Jainist and Buddhist teachings. We cannot, however, go into the channels of religious history that combine gnosis with the West through medieval sects (Bogomiles, Kathars, and the like). As for the influence on Gerhart Hauptmann, we will merely refer to Jakob Böhme and Bohemian-Moravian mysticism and pietism. Originally conceived in the Near East during Hellenic occupation, gnosis gives the oppressed indigenous people an opportunity to express resistance and protest against the Hellenistic idea of the cosmos, not as a system, but as the mythological product of an existential situation. Because domination is rejected, the cosmos becomes damned. Gnostic writings convey to us "endless, multifariously resounding lamentations of the cosmically subjugated creature, hatred and contempt of the world, fear of its sinister coercion (the cosmic 'fate'), solitude in estrangement, aversion to their temptation, yearning for the light beyond, hope of deliverance, gratitude for the promise. . . . " (Jonas, p. 38). The godless world of the decayed cosmopolis takes on demonic—even satanic—elements, but the emerging gnostic movement is not simply a reaction to the "situation," but an active, highly aggressive response. "It is not life perishing under the pressure of the world, but life awaking in opposition to the pressure of this world that is capable of such an oppositional new formation, one that is already surpassing in opposition" (Jonas, p. 68). Here, therefore, there is not simply the amorphous state of mind of the pariah, but already a rationalization of the pariah situation *and* its translation into a mythologized "anti" world view and "anti" stance. Jonas therefore emphasizes the revolutionary character of the anticosmic resentment: the old order is rejected, and foundations for the new vision are established. The prevailing cosmos is transcended, as it were, by an incommensurable principle of otherworldliness. Gnosis flirts with the irritant of rebellion, sides with the mythical rebels—such as Prometheus and Cain (the "outlaw")—is addicted to the inquisitional methods of subversion, and utilizes the mythologems of the "reversed world." It is impossible to ignore the rebellious, defiant, and provocative tone; it "is part of the sense of the alienating, which is obviously congenial to this kind of allegorical interpretation" (Jonas, pp. 214 ff., 220–21). The values of antiquity were rejected with a raging hatred, anarchism and libertarianism took their place, it was only gradually that new, ascetic connections were entered into. The paradoxical, even blasphemous, element becomes the point of a new acosmic religion containing rebellious interpretations of traditional figures. Not only are there Cainites; Cain himself is made the allegorical figure for basically all outcasts. Gnostic adepts, however, the possessors of the new "pneuma," form a new spiritual nobility ("pariahs as an elite"). Pneumatic interpretation in gnosis is directed at a hidden sense which reverses the overt meaning and places a heretical tradition in opposition to the official one; all opposition (which subsequently was forced underground again) up to and through the satanism of the Middle Ages based itself on this gnostic faith (Jonas, p. 221). Thus gnosticism also became the stance of underground rebels; if they were caught, they used dialectical cunning to produce the overt sense, at the same time retaining the hidden meaning as a mental reservation.

In the gnostic existence great significance is embodied in the internalization of the "world"—that is, the demonic incarnation of the world sovereigns (called "Archonts" in early gnostic writings; the Western Middle Ages turned this into "Lord of the World" or, occasionally, gave the term literary feminization as "Dame World").

Existence means to be possessed (by strangeness). "Gnostic psychology is therefore demonology and demonopathy . . . and the . . . world's rulers [are] at the same time rulers of souls—even, in the final resort, internalized foreign powers" (Jonas, p. 194). This idea is at the root of the concept of "alienation" which, in the history of ideas, extends as far as the philosophy of German idealism (Hegel, followed by Marx).

Jonas also worked out the gnostic "movement forms," the most significant of which are "rising" and "sinking" (*anodos* and *kathodos*); these are stages in the movement of being that can assume crucial importance for "understanding the situation."

No attempt has as yet been made to systematically trace all these themes, structures, and allegories throughout European literature. Such an enterprise, though overwhelming, would seem to hold out great promise. We will here limit ourselves to a few sketchy examples. A distinction must, of course, be made between the adoption of gnostic elements for cultural reasons and acceptance because of genuine affinity. In Immermann's *Merlin*, a play that appeared in the year of Goethe's death, the literary echoes are quite pronounced, but they have been deliberately adopted to point out the dramatic thesis. "Merlin is the son of Satan and of the 'pure' virgin, the redeemer who considers himself a paraclete and who fails tragically" (Benno von Wiese, *Karl Immermann*, Hamburg, 1969, p. 104). We find in the play "the gnostic element that consists of a murky mixture of the sensuous and the purely spiritual" (von Wiese, p. 107), which Goethe only approached in his pariah poem but which at heart horrified him, as was shown by his outburst against Zacharias Werner.[16] It was probably that same gnostic element of violence and aggression that repelled Goethe in Kleist's work. On the other hand, Goethe is much too profound to have taken no part in the gnostic tradition; *Faust* embodies many of its elements, and the classical Walpurgis Night unleashes a pandemonium that can easily bear comparison with the gnostic mythologems. We must also remember Goethe's attitude toward the demonic in his numerous utterances on the subject,[17] especially his contention that, though the demonic was not part of his nature, he was nevertheless subject to it (to Eckermann, 2 March 1831). Surely that has the ring of demonopathy; possession by an outside force in the gnostic sense is *denied* in the statement, which only proves, however, that we are dealing, not with an objective explication, but with *resistance* to demons. The same holds true for Goethe's refutation, in the same conversation, of Eckermann's hesitant question whether Mephistopheles was not also imbued with some demonic traits; Goethe will not admit that there is any truth in that idea and replies with the argument that Mephistopheles is far too negative a being to be demonic. But surely that is not correct, Mephistopheles is by no means an unequivocally negative figure. Goethe feels himself unmasked by Eckermann's question just because there is a Mephistophelian element in his nature, *and along with it, very probably the demonic itself;* his answer is once more a form of resistance; it is formulaic, not objective. Goethe's cosmic faith is like a protective shield raised against the demons, and if his development (according to Muschg, "Goethes Glaube an das Dämonische," p. 41) represents "the transformation from a demonic poet into the poet of the demonic," we must add that it was only in the earlier role that Goethe was also a revolutionary poet. He would have liked to get the better of the demons through immortality, but finally they tripped up even him, as he had feared (to Eckermann, 11 March 1828), and a year after that other famous conversation with Eckermann about the demonic, he passed away. In his later years Goethe quite deliberately acted the part of the Olympian and the defender of cosmic harmony; it is the image held to this day by the educated classes—not without Goethe's own self-stylizing care; but this image is misleading. And if his cosmological position is debatable, it is precisely because in Goethe's case it appears flawed and therefore not convincing—just as the old gnostics of the East saw through the weaknesses of the late Hellenistic concept of the cosmos and therefore effectively undermined it.

In Gerhart Hauptmann's work gnostic traits are sprinkled throughout, already adumbrated in the Cain-and-Abel fragment of 1917, very noticeably in *Till Eulenspiegel,* in the "Dom" fragments, the plans for "Merlin" which were later absorbed into *Der neue Christophorus,* and massively in the magnificent intellectual epic, *Der grosse Traum (The Great Dream),* where Satanael appears as the brother of Christ and as a Dantesque guide through the underworld. The accomplishment here is unsurpassed, especially because the ostensible gnostic wisdom is finally unmasked as itself a delusion. The poem's tercets swarm with gnostic blasphemy. The Faustian "In the beginning was the deed" is perverted into the monstrous "In the beginning . . . was the criminal and the crime"; the inquisitorial court is held in the cathedral crypt, where Christ is squashed by a giant locust; copulation occurs in the realm of the dead, with a subsequent "ideological unmasking" by Hermes Trismegistus:

Was du hier phantasierest,
Nachtwandelnder, und wie du hier, mein Freund, purgierest
der alten Schlange meiner Muhme, Gift,
beglückt mich sehr; allein du korrigierest

damit die Gottessöhne und die Schrift.
Erwachst du einmal aus der Traumverwirrung,
so schaudert's dich vielleicht, wenn dich dein Stift

erinnern will an solche schwere Irrung.
Hier scheint dir alles bis ins tiefste klar,
und doch ist alles chthonischen Dunstes Flirrung.

Du glaubst, gestochen sei dir hier der Star;
allein, erwachst du eines Tages mit Gähnen,
ist weiss vielleicht von dieser Nacht dein Haar.

Und dann erkennst du: alles war nur Wähnen!
Nichts ist hier Stoff von allem, was du siehst:
Höchstens die Kiste hier mit Hobelspänen.[18]

Goethe would have been outraged again, but Goethe did not live to see the outrages of the present day.

Of course cultural elements are also involved here.[19] But as always when Hauptmann assimilates elements of "tradition"—*Faust*, Dante's *Inferno*, *Hamlet*, or themes from ancient tragedy—his intention, anchored in the depth of a powerful poetic genius, is not imitation, but a genuine desire to carry on the tradition. He never falls prey to an ideology, and even where he represents the rebellious element, it is seen more in humane terms than as a "social" event. In *The Red Rooster*, the sequel to *The Beaver Coat*, the central character of Mutter Wolff, now Frau Fielitz, takes on a tragic cast; it is only then that the central figure (who often seems problematic to critics) of the thieves' comedy becomes sensible. This effect is brought about by the final act, with its self-explication of the underdog who has once again become criminal (and much more severely so than in *The Beaver Coat*, for in this instance arson is committed for the sake of collecting the insurance). "Anybody who doesn't go along, anybody who does go along—he's bad. All you want is to get out of the muck. People like us, we've got to pick up all the muck. They keep telling us: be good. How do you go about doing that? Forget it—how could we

make the peace? Sure I flared up! And that's perfectly natural!"
(Hauptmann, *Der rote Hahn Sämtliche Werke*, vol. 2, Frankfurt am
Main, 1965, p. 70). The stage directions then indicate that the dying
woman "makes an odd motion, reaching high overhead with both
hands": "You reach . . . you reach . . . you keep on reaching like that
. . . you reach for something. . . ."[20]

This "anodic" gesture is the emblem of a lifelong protest and striving upward from the depths forever in vain, always at the edge of
criminality or even beyond the edge, and finally failing in the realization of the futility of crime. The "political" forms of this kind of revolt are far inferior to such heightening. The type of resigned inner
dignity of the pariah in surviving the changing ruling elites is expressed by the Chorus in Schiller's *Bride of Messina*:

> Die fremden Eroberer kommen und gehen,
> Wir gehorchen, aber wir bleiben stehen.[21]

Brecht, on the contrary, simply turns this idea upside down, convert-
ing it into the Marxist utopian negation of all rule:

> Ach, der Stiefel glich dem Stiefel immer,
> Und uns trat er. Ihr versteht, ich meine,
> Dass wir keine andern Herren brauchen, sondern keine![22]

Hauptmann's predilection for the type of the fallen angel, in the
"Dom" fragment and in other poems, demonstrates that his thought
was deeper, more subtle, and more sophisticated than he is given
credit for in literary criticism to date (with the exception of Joseph
Gregor, *Gerhart Hauptmann. Das Werk und unsere Zeit*, Vienna,
1952). The Luciferian theme of temptation appears in various guises
in the fragments dating from his later years, and there was no need
for German literature of the first half of the century to learn from
Kierkegaard that such a seduction is also an aesthetic one.[23] For one,
there is the fascinating figure of the "false messenger" in Borchardt's
mystery play, *Verkündigung* (*The Annunciation*), which was written in 1904–1906 and first published in 1920 (now available in Borchardt, *Gesammelte Werke*, vol. 8, Stuttgart, 1962). In this connection it must be remembered that Borchardt, like Hauptmann, is a
Christian gnostic, who struggles with the problem of evil even while
his concept of the world remains focused on redemption.[24] The motif
of religious temptation was presented by Hauptmann in "Emanuel
Quint," but the political relevance of eschatological temptation does
not break through until the "Anabaptist" fragments. The entire com-

plex—religious-eschatological foundations, temptation as aestheticism, its diagnostic signs in "kitsch" and the temptation to political
evil (the creator of kitsch is "criminal")—was understood by Hermann Broch; some of it, though by no means all, is contained in *Der
Versucher* (*The Tempter*), a novel about the fraudulent founder of
a religious sect (see Broch, *Der Versucher, Aus dem Nachlass*, ed.
Felix Stössinger, *Gesammelte Werke*, vol. 4, Zurich, 1953). The reference to contemporary dictatorship—Broch wrote this work in the
years following 1934—is clear without deviating into caricature or
satire. A conversation between the country doctor and the old village
sibyl, Mutter Gisson, contains the words: "Anybody who hates is a
poor devil, and he always needs a devil to hate. . . . But he calls that
righteousness." And further (p. 344):

> She looked at me. "But that's . . . " and she opened her empty hands,
> lightly spread her gnarled old woman's fingers, and it was as if she
> were letting naked nothingness flow down and through her fingers—
> "That's how it is," she said, crossing her arms again and hiding her
> hands under them. "And yet, Mother, you say that his time has come?"
> "Yes," she said, "because there's no longer any way out for hate, they
> have to run after the one who does the hating and the one who prom-
> ises them some knowledge that he hasn't even got himself."

Here the topic takes on a double meaning. For "the knowledge that
he [that is, the tempter] hasn't even got himself," but which he delu-
sionally dangles before the others' eyes, is itself gnostic knowledge.
The gnostic is objectified here but on the basis of a view from the
inside. I am inclined to believe that in this work Broch attained
his literary apex.

Let us not forget: Hauptmann, Borchardt, Hofmannsthal, Broch
and Kafka, even Karl Kraus—none of them was a "gnostic" writer.
They are Christian or Jewish writers, who express the gnostic-nihilist
themes of anxiety, despair, alienation, estrangement from God, evil,
and "dishonored mankind" because these themes are embodied in
the times and to that extent in themselves, in accordance with the
gnostic coincidence of demonic possession of other and self. Not one
of these writers completely omits any one of these themes. In Hofmannsthal's *The Tower* a physician speaks about the heir to the
throne, who is kept caged like an animal: "Only a quack could want
to heal the body by bodily means alone. More is at stake. This monstrous outrage has been committed against all mankind. . . . A whirl-
pool springs up at the place where this life has been uprooted, and
it sweeps us all away" (*Gesammelte Werke in Einzelausgaben, Dra-*

men, vol. 4, Frankfurt am Main, 1958, pp. 30–31).[25] Another passage in *The Tower* reads: "The prophecy contained matters that no one could have believed possible, and now they begin to appear possible! It contained horrors of which no one would have said that they could have been meant literally, and they begin to happen literally" (*Gesammelte Werke*, 4:62.)

When Hofmannsthal was writing the above, the First World War was already over, and Karl Kraus' apocalyptic drama, *Die letzten Tage der Menschheit* (*Mankind's Last Days*) of 1922 had already appeared; it presented similar insights with incomparably greater, more merciless force. In any case, the essential statements about man's capacity for atrocities had long since been made in *Hamlet*. They had been stated—but not understood. For that, modern times were needed.

> "The world is in the ice age. Incalculably there grows in us a murder, the glacier. . . ."

So wrote poet Rudolf Borchardt in 1935, in his farewell to Germany (*Jamben*, Stuttgart, 1967, p. 7). The theme had been developed even earlier by Gerhart Hauptmann in *Till Eulenspiegel*, when Till, who is at the ducal court, tells a horror story. One day the sun simply did not rise, so that the people, taken unaware at first, had to become accustomed to living in the dark. For the first forty-eight hours the metropolitan citizens are confused, but then the idea of a scapegoat arises among the masses, and everyone calls for the guilty ones. In the blink of an eye lampposts become gallows, and the executioner stands ready with his guillotine on the parapet of the cathedral, whose steeple has been toppled; he decapitates the emperor, the crown prince, the bishop, statesmen, generals and judges, but also simple people, whores, nuns, and the like, casting the naked bodies down from the parapet. Now a new theme emerges among the howling multitudes—the theme of "deprivation" (the same theme that has been coming to the surface again in the nativist movements of suppressed colonial peoples); the cry now is: "This did not begin yesterday, we have always been cheated of the sun"; but the butcher up on high is worshiped as the executor of the Last Judgment and as paraclete of the millenium:

> Und wer fühlte nun nicht, welch ein selig Jahrtausend jetzt anbrach!
> Plötzlich aber erscholl's in der Luft, wie von Vögeln gesprochen:
> "Alles Licht muss versinken in völliger Finstre der Gottheit!
> Schwarz, die Farbe Saturns, ist zugleich auch die Farbe der Allmacht,
> Betet, Menschen, zu schwarzen Madonnen und lest schwarze Messen!
> Das Reich Gottes hat heute begonnen!"[26]

A related topic turns up again in one of the "Dom" fragments. Here, too, the top of the cathedral has been dismounted, a cannon is placed on the platform; Satan serves as its gunmaster, ready to destroy the cities of man. This world, he says, is my work, God only tolerates it, he will also have to tolerate its destruction by the force of my hatred.

No works of literature are as permeated and affected by the gnostic schemata of distance, strangeness, imprisonment, and loss of mankind in this world as are the works of Franz Kafka. Without referring to Kafka, Jonas expresses this feeling: "Life is tossed into the world, light into darkness, the soul into the body. He expresses the violence done to me by which, without having been asked, I am where I am and what I am—the passivity of my existence in a world I never made and whose law is not my law" (Hans Jonas, *Zwischen Nichts und Ewigkeit. Drei Aufsätze zur Lehre vom Menschen*, Göttingen, 1963, p. 20).

This cuts off any possibility of a Marxist interpretation of "alienation." We must fall back on anthropological data, not merely on sociological, not to mention socioeconomic, determinants. Though the experience of strangeness can be evoked and strengthened through occupation by a different ethnic group, as significant historical examples attest,[27] it also arises spontaneously, without any such external impetus, perhaps by preference under conditions of authoritarian pressure, but it happens even when that element is absent. We recall the experience of alienation of the young Gerhart Hauptmann and the fantasy entertained by the six- or seven-year-old Rudolf Borchardt that he was not the true son of his parents but an adopted child "of unknown origin and unknown destiny" (Borchardt, *Kindheit und Jugend. Von ihm selbst erzählt*, Hamburg, 1966, pp. 64, 87).

At the age of almost eighty Gerhart Hauptmann once more immersed himself in the Goethean and Jean Paulian atmosphere of Lago Maggiore by his use of the mysterious figure of Mignon. The aging poet recapitulated the Mignon theme in the person of the mistreated orphan child Aga, who continues to act awkwardly with him, expressing a kind of love-hate, even in her fatal illness; her feelings contain the element of estrangement. "Over and over I was startled deep within myself when I would suddenly see darting from the sick girl's eyes a spark that seemed to enclose within itself everything mankind has ever kept concealed in the way of courage, stubbornness, hatred, rage, love, pleasure of the senses, despair, and death: horribly equipped . . . for eternal strangeness in this strange world" (Hauptmann, *Sämtliche Werke*, vol. 6, Frankfort am Main, 1963, p. 546).

If in Hauptmann this serves as self-release in the form of confessional writing, the impression arises for several of our most important writers that it is not—or not only—the characters they present who are subject to the Kierkegaardian despair in the form of the Sickness Unto Death[28] but that they present themselves, in an existential identification of person and work, logically corresponding to gnostic demonopathy. This impression invariably arises, for example, early in the nineteenth century in the work of Kleist, so that we must ask ourselves whether this writer was ever correctly read in his own century, if he was really taken seriously. "Fortunately, for most people books are only literature," wrote Nietzsche in *Der Antichrist* (Aphorism 44); we might better say, "unfortunately." The same impression prevails in the cases of Annette von Droste-Hülshoff and Giacomo Leopardi, and in the present century for Kafka and Pavese, surely also for Hofmannsthal and even for the late works of Benn. It is, in effect, a question of the degree to which a stance of absolute unworldliness and estrangement, if it is to be taken seriously and considered as more than "mere literature," can be maintained.[29] Benn in his later years asserted "that there is no such thing as mediation between productive and receptive humanity and that intellectual greatness is historically ineffectual."[30] This is surely to establish, not a socioliterary finding (as such, it would be false), but a personal attitude, and one not devoid of self-stylization. But this stance reflects Benn's genuine existential experience of life, and he was aware of its self-destructive consequences. It does not refer to society but to the world, just like the despairing outburst by the eighty-year-old Michelangelo in one of his last sonnets:

> Il mondo e cieco, e'l tristo esempio ancora
> Vince e sommerge ogni perfetta usanza.
> Spent'e la luce, e seco ogni baldanza,
> Trionfa il falso, e 'l ver non surge fora.[31]

"The light is spent"—"To work as best we can in the dark" was Benn's moral conclusion. While Michelangelo, with all his despair with theodicy, in the final stanza of this poem (not quoted here) nevertheless does not deny the Christian belief in salvation, Benn's nihilism rejected such a "solution." Benn is a modern gnostic disguised as a positivist physician.

Such a different literary personality as Rudolf Borchardt represents a harsh standpoint similar to Benn's, in reference to the writer's reception, and not only in his magnificent "Iamben" of 1935, written in reaction to Nazi rule, but also earlier. Borchardt even writes (1926) of the "writers' right to remain unknown" and in support quotes a verse by Theognis: "He who is gifted by the gods, honor him no matter what is done to him"; and he demands that the grounds for lack of appreciation and rejection of the decent spirit by universal indecency be made comprehensible and thereby turned into something "actually beautiful" (Borchardt, *Gesammelte Werke, Prosa*, vol. 1, Stuttgart, 1957, pp. 314 ff.). Yes, but if the world is still unable to grasp this "actual beauty," such a solipsistic aesthetics of failure does not advance matters. But to see lack of appreciation as the rule, as Borchardt does, is, of course, quite correct. "From Isaiah to Dante, to Milton, to Kleist and Hölderlin, almost all literary glories of world literature were products of renaissances." The despised writer represents a tautology. Borchardt might have cited many other names, and he should have added that there is no absolute expectation of such "renaissances," for future generations are no less unreliable than is the present one. Finally, what is meant by "honored" and "despised"? The writer's fame—about which Benn (in *Gesammelte Werke*, 4:281) quotes Balzac's saying that it has "no white wings"—often clings to only a few works, as a rule to the most accessible rather than to the most profound, if not only to the name. Borchardt notes in the lecture cited above that the late works of Rilke are fairly unknown, and as far as the extent of influence goes, the same holds true for George and Hofmannsthal (Borchardt, *Gesammelte Werke, Prosa*, 1:315–16). Fame itself can become a handicap for the work's influence whenever the renown of the famous name becomes the predominant criterion and knowledge of the work itself is submerged. But diffusion of the work itself, reflected in widespread literary "talk" *about* the work, can also have a deleterious effect on the spontaneity of the judgment concerning the work, which is why Goethe already thought that a book that had a great influence could not, in fact, be any longer evaluated (Goethe to Chancellor von Müller, 11 June 1882, in *Werke*, Gedenk-Ausgabe, 23:198). It is certain that Borchardt's "pseudobalance" has only served to widen the chasm between production and reception which Benn conjured up. At the end, then, the source of fame is "pure opinion, which deserves no kind of respect, since it is made up of lack of understanding, distortion, and hastiness and in reality is vain," as Henry de Montherlant admits in his diaries; the thirst for fame among Christians and pagans alike, he continues, is based on the "sinful weakness of wishing to endure," which brings us to the wisdom of the Preacher: "All is vanity and vexation of spirit" (see Montherlant, *Tagebücher 1930–1944*, trans. K. A. Horst, Munich, 1969, p. 43). What a difference from Schiller's "Das Siegesfest":

> Von des Lebens Gütern allen
> Ist der Ruhm das höchste doch!
> Wenn der Leib zu Staub zerfallen,
> Bleibt der grosse Name noch.[32]

The practitioners of modern skepticism believe that they have unmasked the "great names" as the result of a social process which involves numerous "interested" persons and institutions (authors, publishers, critics, commentators, and the like), "associated concepts," "a need for superlatives" (as demonstrated by blurbs if nothing else): "It surely must happen like that, that a lot of indeterminates are given shape and form in such a way that somebody becomes famous"; "the writer as a climbing pole for critics, historians, publishers, and so forth" (Robert Musil, *Tagebücher, Aphorismen, Essays und Reden, Gesammelte Werke*, vol. 2, ed. A. Frise, Hamburg, 1955, 2:422). Already the old Goethe—who knew his way around, for at times he himself manipulated favorable reviews of his works—spoke of the "comet's tail" of those who latch on to a work; he saw this process as the need of the work to make its own way more easily by "partiality."[33] This is an entirely correct observation, and today, in the age of literary mass production, one that is more than ever applicable. Today this is called the "totem value" of the famous name, and to the literary name are added the slogans of "concepts" (Strelka, *Die gelenkten Musen*, p. 287); naturalism, realism, symbolism, expressionism and the like are such "totems." The sociological dissolution of literary creations into a mere coordinate system of factors completes the nominalism which arises as a consequence of the "mediatized existence" of modern life as soon as gnostic mythology is clarified into abstract, pseudoscientific comprehensibility. Nothing remains in the shadow of this nominalism, and therefore there is no longer any tradition in literature, either.

TIME-BINDING AND INCARNATE HISTORY

The aging Goethe's strangely ambivalent attitude toward history is well known. History is both important and unimportant to him at one and the same time. In *Wilhelm Meisters Wanderjahre* ("Aus Makeriens Archiv") he writes: "Looked at more closely, it turns out that for the historian himself history does not easily become historical; for the author in each case always writes only as if he had been a participant in the past action, but he does not indicate what had gone before and what was agitating at the time." To which is added the reflection: "It is even unusual that a very aged person becomes historical to himself and that his contemporaries become historical for him, so that he neither wants to nor can any longer dispute with anyone" (Goethe, *Poetische Werke*, Cotta, vol. 7, 1953, p. 1241).

Just this, however, is the situation that befalls Goethe; as the most telling testimony, I choose a section from a letter of 6 December 1831 to Wilhelm von Humboldt: "If I may, most honored colleague, take advantage of our old intimacy, I would like to admit that in my old age everything becomes more and more historical for me: it is all one to me whether something happened in times gone by, in distant realms, or quite close to me at this very moment—indeed, I seem to myself more and more historical."[34] To this sense must now be added the time-binding element of a "worship of the present," the sum of which is given in a conversation with Chancellor von Müller: "In any case we value the present too little, carry out most of our tasks only under duress, to be rid of them. . . . We learn to honor the moment as soon as we turn it into history" (*Werke*, Gedenk-Ausgabe, 21:534, 22:232–33; *Gespräche*, Gedenk Ausgabe, 23:484–85). "The eternal present in every moment"—this phrase from a letter (17 April 1823) to the friend of his youth, Auguste Stolberg, is paraphrased in the same year (on 3 November 1823) in a conversation with Eckermann: "Every situation—indeed, every moment—is of unending value, for it is the representative of all eternity" (*Werke*, Gedenk-Ausgabe, 21:534, 22:67).

This *nunc stans* as the equivalent of a permanent flow, a permanent "present" (whereby, according to Husserl, the word "present" itself is inappropriate, since it already points to a time modality) is at the same time an absolute primal self—or, in Husserl's language, transcendental subjectivity (see *Husserliana*, vol. 10, The Hague, 1966). It is a vital question for modern man whether he can find his way back to this "reduction to the living present as the final absolute ground of all my values" (Husserl). The perfectionistic rejection of the entire present in favor of "progress," and the equally perfectionistic rejection of all tragedy, which was never diagnosed more acutely than by the poet-physician Benn, do not answer it affirmatively (Benn, "Nach dem Nihilismus," *Gesammelte Werke*, 1:156). In today's "mediatized existence," any sort of present is insufferable because further progress toward "something better" can always be dangled before our eyes; while every suffering has become a scandal. In Stifter's *Witiko* of 1867 (Munich, 1949) Frau Agnes says: "The sad things come to life again in my mind, they go on living there, and even if they're past and God has disposed of them, the past is still in me, and I am in it" (p. 156).

In this example, past and present melt into one. In this connection it is a matter (as Goethe's earlier statement already made clear), not actually of "memory," but (in Husserl's terms) of the "retentional modification" of old impressions: holding fast to a condition pertaining to me (no matter what its feeling tone)—one, therefore, in which the individual remains unchanged; that is, confirms himself as unchanged.

It becomes clear from the foregoing how little "memory" (or tradition in the common sense of the word) has to do with any reference to the tradition. Rather, the possibility for such reference depends to a great extent on that form of re-presentation which (to use Goethe's phrase) holds the eternal in every moment; and the genuinely revolutionary is also possible only as a "retentional modification." Indeed, in the adoption, vitalization, and re-presentation of tradition, the autonomy of the realized personality—in comparison with other realizations of past personalities—is already determined, so that, "flowing and resting" in itself, it need never fear to become an "epigone" or "slave to tradition." Among the liberated moderns, it is the absence of integration of the tradition into the "self"—in other words, the weakness of the personality—that drives them always to grasp at something new, supposedly revolutionary, that makes them susceptible to fads of every kind and allows them to revert to voluntaristic world views. What is truly revolutionary in literature *happens*, without the spasms of ambivalent strivings. On the contrary, something that is consciously programmed to be revolutionary immediately runs the risk of forfeiting both itself and the tradition. It is pure fear of nothingness. Only by using an externalized concept of revolution and an equally externalized concept of tradition was it possible until now to overlook the connections between the self and the world as the products of the retentionally modified tradition (always and per se).

Perhaps the phrase "the revolutionary happens" sounds too passive to many contemporaries who participate in the current mood of voluntarism. But it is in agreement, not only with the new psychology of action, but also with the phenomenological investigations of "passive synthesis" as well as with the reflected experiential world of the writer. The revolutionary who follows a program finds himself in the situation of the archer who misses his target again and again, just because he is so rigidly *determined* to hit a bull's eye, so that the Zen archery master must explain the situation to him: you harness yourself to failure from the outset. The Zen archer succeeds in hitting the target only when he has learned to relax and to let the arrow's flight from the bow happen (Eugen Herrigel, *Zen in der Kunst des Bogenschiesens*, 12th ed., Weilheim/Obb., 1965). For the rest, as far as historical considerations go, it is surely sufficient to point out that all historical revolutions since 1789 have missed their target in that the revolutionary actors were themselves forced to conclude that they had "intended something different": it was all too clear in their minds what they wanted to hit—and that is the reason their arrows went astray. Benn's radical disowning of "history," after all, is directed precisely at this external and planned history of revolts and wars, whose aftermaths resulted only in a feeling of enormous, Sysiphus-like futility and absurdity for the successors (see also Albert Camus, "Der Mythos von Sisyphos . . . ," in *Das Frühwerk*, German trans., Düsseldorf, 1967). But historical disowning includes not only the political revolutions, but also the literary "revolutions"; in every case there emerges, at least in the second generation, the consciousness of failure, with the most varied consequences: schism, disappointed turning aside (both occur, for example, in the Stefan George circle), or stubborn insistence on the wrong tack in search of the negativistic, aggressive device, "now more than ever." It is one of the points in Thomas Mann's favor that, in his early differences with his brother Heinrich, he attempted to make it clear to the latter that writers should not engage in politics, for when they do, they only engage in nonsense (as is also true, by the way, for academics). This is not to say that the politicians' politics are secure from this danger, nor does it exclude the possibility of our sympathizing, at least in part, with Heinrich Mann's political manifestoes and his political character; but this kind of sympathy appeals to the quixotic in us, since we see the writer acting as pure fool within the picaresque world of political scoundrels; and it includes the judgment that the high-minded person's road is marked by failure.

It is thus my thesis that revolutionary voluntarism is doomed to failure even in literature. The itch for self-involvement at short range —further coupled with the vanity of writers that leads them to believe that they must copy the political "man of action"—puts them on the wrong tack. Art, Hans Erich Nossack has emphasized, teaches us absolutely nothing about how to live; other professions exist for that sort of thing (*Die schwache Position der Literatur*, 2d ed., Frankfurt am Main, 1967, p. 78). Art can only present the problems and go on questioning. Writers do not transform the world. The attitude of resignation of many writers of the last few decades, especially in Italy,[35] rests on a consciousness of failure—an inevitable consequence of the Marxist cementing together of practice and theory, transferred to literature. Anyone who feels with Marx that he wishes to transform rather than grasp the world need not be surprised when he fails and, in the end, stands there with empty hands; that which he might have contributed he fails to contribute, and that which he wanted to give he was unable to bring about. By contrast, the phenomenology of literary creation shows not the least traces of the will to act but rather those of "passive synthesis" (Husserl) or (in the words of Nicolai Hartmann) the "emotional-receptive act": devotion, having something happen to one, being startled, shock, even "experience" in the most ordinary sense—none of these are "actions"; rather, as Gerhart Hauptmann realized, "writing is a great suffering." A strange sentence for a born dramatist! But it is an absolutely logical one if we remember the "universality of emotion" (Erwin Straus), as a result of which all forcible solutions to problems—and the programmatic writer desires "solutions"—miss precisely this dramatic element and remain mired in the dogmatic. To Broch, such dogmatism represented a horror as the direct source of "evil"; it was rejected also by Hauptmann as ossification and inhumaneness. For him, there was only sight and hearing, surrendering and devoting himself to people and objects. "In the process of my works' coming into being, I dare say I have done little besides watching silently, as it were, and I have, in a manner of speaking, served as mediator." For this reason, then, Hauptmann rejected all programmatic theories of art and all aesthetic "isms." The true writer, especially the dramatist, can see these only as "labels on a magazine," but they do not describe the contents. Logically, that is antinominalist in the sense of Husserl's Sixth Logical Investigation, the quintessence of which is, after all, the characteristic of "inauthentic thought" in nominalism.[36] Gerhart Hauptmann rejected the "predigested thoughts" quite in the sense of this Investigation (without being familiar with it). He distinguished between "thinking and predigested thoughts" and seldom or never wanted to see the latter formulated in drama (*Sämtliche Werke*, 6:1039). (As an aside, note that inadvertently he thereby also pointed out certain weaknesses in several of his own late works.) "Inauthentic" or "unfulfilled thought" ("the thinking of predigested thoughts"), however, exactly names the intellectual make-up of that form of literature that corresponds to the cultural formulas of mediatized existence. The accord between philosophical phenomenology and dramatic literature is determined by the common basis of worldly experience. For the "experiential world" supplies the sense basis for sociological experience. After all, the whole human drama is already present in the "experiential world," and exists there (if Nicolai Hartmann is correct) in a value-free aesthetic preformation "for each participant in life who can summon up enough distance and calm to see conflicts, struggle, sorrow, and defeat in their natural dramatic form. . . . It is very probable that there can be stage drama only because there is drama in life, which can be aesthetically experienced even as such" (Nicolai Hartmann, Ästhetik, 2d ed., Berlin, 1966, p. 20). This odd statement, which seems to impinge on aestheticism, is in reality its absolute opposite; it is not life that is being aestheticized; rather, the aesthetic is already contained within life, the aesthetic attitude (Kant's "disinterested contemplation"), which is akin to phenomenological reduction, is already glutted with the worldly experiences of the "universality of the emotional." Again, this sentence applies to no one more than to Hauptmann, in whose work almost all characters are drenched with living and suffering, so that the spectator loses all sense of confronting an "artistic product." Everything is experienced medially, as it were, always in the particular artistic form of retentional modification of the embodied emotional tradition; embodied to such an extent that the artist can at will "recall" moods, feelings, situations, and symbols experienced years and decades earlier and can re-present them in images and scenes.

This analysis has, it is true, taken us far from those external concepts of the "social" and the "historical" in which many critical investigations remain mired; far, too, from that well-meaning and illusionistic kind of anthropology of the old enlightenment which bluntly declared man to be "good." "The elements point to a being," Benn noted, "which is possessed of destructive traits, and these are always newly frightening traits of the depigmented Quaternary Period" (Gesammelte Werke, 4:283). It is the atmosphere of the Atridian tetralogy, where the "Tantalidans" stand as a synonym for human nature, for the atmosphere of Hofmannsthal's Tower, Kafka's Trial, Broch's Sleepwalkers, Camus' Plague, Döblin's Hamlet, oder die *lange Nacht hat ein Ende* (*Hamlet, or the Long Night is Ending*), Barlach's *Sündflut* (*The Flood*): everywhere, the glimpse of the abyss.

> Wes Seele blind ist, den besucht das Glück—
> Wes Seele auch nur blinzelt in die Welt,
> Besucht das Schaudern . . .[37]

The responsibility does not rest with particular "isms," eras, or social systems—they are only an alibi, decked out as pseudoscience, for those mediatized existences on the lookout for external determinants because they are no longer adequate to the concept of freedom (a recognition already achieved by Schiller, the dramatist) and therefore wish to renounce responsibility. "Do not say, apocalyptically, that the seven-headed monster of the deep and the two-horned one on earth have always existed," says one of "Three Old Men" in Gottfried Benn (*Gesammelte Werke*, 2:390). In his attempt at reviving myth, Pavese overlooked an important myth—the one about the chained (or caged) beast of prey which, set free, ravages mankind and the world. Gotthelf treated this motif in his novella *Die Schwarze Spinne* (*The Black Spider*). The raging of the plague can be a symbol for the devastation of man, even an intellectual devastation, as in Camus' *The Plague*. The monster is "always there," but in the normal course of events it is restrained; woe if it is released from chains. After all, to the present day psychopathologists can only speak of "psychic epidemics" but cannot give a realistic explanation for them, so that until now writers' encoded presentations have been more convincing. But we are surely referred back again and again to man's infirm nature. Guevara's grandiose farewell to the "world" can be echoed by Grimmelshausen (in chapter 24, Book V, of *Simplizissimus*) and by Hofmannsthal (in *The Tower*) only because their contemporary experiences (the Thirty Years' War, World War I and the postwar period) quite simply activate a transhistorical insight in both poets.

Such insights are, to be sure, not for the many. In response to the outrage produced among the critics by his dramatic sketch, of 1951, "Stimme hinter dem Vorhang" ("The Voice Behind the Curtain"), Benn allowed himself a comment on this work in an open letter to Alexander Lernet-Holenia (in *Gesammelte Werke*, 4:311):

> This voice behind the curtain expresses something that has pursued me all my life—a theme that recurs in my thoughts time and again. This voice teaches as its ultimate maxim and subterfuge: "Live in the dark, perform in the dark, whatever we can"—it is a sober voice, this is its Sermon on the Mount. The voice wants to say, stop your endless ideo-

logical chatter, your fuss about something "higher"; man is not a higher being, all we are is that species that strives out of the dark into the light—the exact goal of our striving, I have to admit it openly, is something I don't know, but what we have attained has largely been arrogance, atrocity, even stupidity—thus it would seem to me that a certain amount of dismantling of this arrogance of ours would be appropriate.

Modern viewpoints; civil wars in every part of the world under the pariah's slogan of "nonviolent resistance"; religious wars in the twentieth century (the "seven-headed monster" has, after all, always existed, it is not linked to a specific era); the impossibility of continuing to live in our physical environment; the population explosion with the expectation of mutual extermination, but exorcised only by "ideological chatter" and mutual fooling about "measures" which are not properly measures; the absurd torments of Sisyphus, whereby he rolls his stone day in and day out, but under such high-flying names as "development aid," "integration," "democratization," and the like; finally, the absolute perversion of language, which nominalistically functionalizes the old high concepts of freedom, of equality, so that today they are nothing more than *weapons*, designed to bring others low—this combination seems to us today, thirty years after the last world war, to be the outlook. The future, Benn thought even then, would confront us with a decision which we could not evade, not even avoid by "emigration." There would be two possible ways of reacting: one practiced by those who act and wish to rise, and the form chosen by those others who "silently await the transformation"; the delusionary tellers of tales and the criminals on one side, and on the other the deep ones and the monks, "and I cast my vote for the black habits" (Benn, *Gesammelte Werke*, 4:284). We are free to hope for a more convincing poetic voice if we believe that such a one must exist.

[Translated from the German by Ruth Hein]

Notes

1. Friedrich Rückert, *Gedichte*, new ed. (Frankfurt am Main, 1847), p. 352.
2. Published in 1804 in *Jan. Allg. Lit.*, quoted in Oscar Fambach, *Goethe und seine Kritiker* (Düsseldorf, 1953), pp. 72 ff.

3. Karl Marx, *Thesen über Feuerbach in Früschriften*, ed. Siegfried Landshut (Stuttgart, 1953), p. 341.

4. "What sort of times are these, when a conversation about trees is almost a crime because it means keeping silent about so many outrages!" Bertolt Brecht, "An die Nachgeborenen," written about 1938, in *Gesammelte Werke*, 8 vols. (Frankfurt am Main, 1967), 4: 722–23.

5. Walter Grab und Uwe Friesel, *Noch ist Deutschland nicht verloren. Eine historisch-politische Analyse unterdrückter Lyrik von der Französischen Revolution bis zur Reichsgründung* (Munich, 1970).

6. Another example might be English Restoration comedy, which, according to Wellek and Warren, must on no account be read as a true picture of its day; otherwise one would have to understand the England of that time as a fairyland of adulteries and mock marriages or as the Eldorado of a decadent and brutal aristocracy. Rejecting both views, it would be better to see what particular social group created this art and for what audience and to see further if it was a naturalistic or a stylized art. Possibly irony and self-ridicule, satire and fantasy might have been at work. The idea of any literature as "documentary," Wellek and Warren add, can be a trap. See René Wellek and Austin Warren, *Theory of Literature*, (New York, 1942), pp. 100–1; *Theorie der Literatur*, German trans. (Frankfurt am Main, 1963), p. 89. Similar considerations may be applied to the social-critical novels of Heinrich Mann. In the nineteenth century they probably apply also to Balzac, Zola, and other writers.

7. On this point and the following, compare W. E. Mühlmann, *Chiliasmus und Nativismus*, 2d ed. (Berlin, 1964), pp. 233–39, 335–44; Mühlmann, "Paria-kasten und -stämme," *Zeitschrift für Ethnologie* 89 (1964): 163–65; Mühl-mann, *Max Weber und die rationale Soziologie* (Tubingen, 1966), pp. 8–12.

8. "They flatter their dog and their steed, they shun us as if nature had given us man's shape only as a mask. Make me your equal, then see if I am not like you." Michael Beer, *Sämtliche Werke*, ed. Eduard von Schenk (Leipzig, 1835), p. 241.

9. "The understanding blazing in man's own breast turns His [God's] world into the mirror of His being." Beer, p. 281.

10. Goethe, *Schriften zur Literatur*, Gedenk-Ausgabe, vol. 14 (Zurich, 1950), p. 853; idem, *Schriften zu Literatur und Theater*, Gesamt-Ausgabe, Cotta, vol. 15 (Stuttgart, n.d.), pp. 938 ff.

11. "Oh dark trembling race! O crown worn by the toad, if folly shudders at its sight, if evil lashes out at it, the sand crumbles secrets and the well trickles miracles, the brother of all beings and God's first-born child."

    "Then let me be no more than loathsome vermin: I am the toad and wear the precious gem." Gertrud Kolmar, *Das lyrische Werke* (Munich, 1960), pp. 121, 160.

12. We will not go into the question here of the "historical accuracy" of the portrait of Thomas à Becket painted by Meyer. In his play, *Murder in the Cathedral*, T. S. Eliot gave a similar but much more favorable picture of Becket.

13. Compare Mühlmann, *Chiliasmus*, pp. 313 ff. as well as idem, *Rassen, Ethnien, Kulturen* (Neuwied, 1964), pp. 329 ff.

14. "I too would like to be wise. The old books tell us what wisdom is: to remain apart from the world's quarrels and to pass the short time without fear. Also to get along without violence, to repay evil with good, not to fulfill one's dreams but to forget—these are considered wise. I am capable of none of them: truly, I live in sinister times!" Brecht, *Gesammelte Werke*, 4: 723.

15. ". . . that the gentle, moving water in time conquers the mighty stone. You understand, hardness succumbs." Brecht, *Gesammelte Werke*, 4: 660 ff.

16. Goethe, *Gespräche*, pp. 530–31. Goethe on the occasion of Werner's comparing the moon to a consecrated wafer (cf. p. 484): Werner confused *agape* and *eros*.

17. These utterances are enumerated in Muschg's exhaustive study, *Studien zur tragischen Literaturgeschicte*; see the section "Goethes Glaube an das Dämonische" ("Goethe's Belief in the Demonic"), pp. 31 ff.

18. "What you imagine here, Nightwanderer, and how, my friend, you purge the poison of the old serpent, my kindred—all that pleases me mightily; you alone thus correct the sons of God and all their writings. Should you wake from your dreams' confusion, you will perhaps shudder if your pencil recalls to you such profound delusion. Here it seems to you that you can see clearly into the heart of all things, and yet all of it is but the flicker of chthonic mists. You think your eyes are opened here, and yet, should you one day awaken, yawning, perhaps your hair will have turned white from this one night. And then you will know: it all was but a fancy! Nothing is real here, especially not what you can see—at most this crate here, filled with sawdust." Hauptmann, *Sämtliche Werke*, vol. 4 (Frankfurt am Main, 1964) p. 1053.

19. Hauptmann had obviously read Ignaz von Döllinger's *Geschichte der gnostisch-manichäischen Sekten* (Munich, 1890), especially pp. 38 ff.

20. Hauptmann, 2: 73. In the supplementary material to *Der rote Hahn*, the dying Frau Fielitz says: "I always wanted to go ahead. I was always so scared. I don't know what I was scared of. I think maybe of my fellow men." Hauptmann, *Sämtliche Werke*, vol. 9 (Frankfurt am Main, 1969), p. 969. This, too, is effective, but the final "anodic" version is a stroke of genius. In the original the words are in Berlin dialect.

21. "The foreign conquerors come and leave; we submit, but we remain." Schiller, *Die Braut von Messina*, act 1, lines 253–54, *Sämtliche Werke*, 2: 832.

22. "Ah, the boot has always resembled a boot, and it was us it kicked. You understand, I think that what we need is not other rulers, but none!" Brecht, "Ballade vom Wasserrad," *Gesammelte Werke*, 2: 1007–8.

23. Sören Kierkegaard, *Entweder-Oder (Either/Or)*, German translation by V. E. Hirsch (Düsseldorf, 1964). I will quote only a single passage (p. 396): "The ethical is as boring in science as in life. What a difference: under the sky of the aesthetic, everything is easy, beautiful, skimming; when ethics is mixed in, everything becomes hard, angular, infinitely boring."

24. Werner Kraft, *Rudolf Borchardt. Welt aus Poesie und Geschichte* (Hamburg, 1961), p. 360. The same might be said of Hauptmann and also of Hofmannsthal.

25. This passage has an analogue in Hebbel. Mariamne says to Herod: "In me you have dishonored all mankind." Friedrich Hebbel, *Herodes und Mariamne*, act 3, lines 1684–85.

26. "And who, now, was not aware of the blessed thousand-year reign that was beginning! And now it resounded in the air, proclaimed as if by birds: 'All light must sink into the total darkness of the deity! Black, the color of Saturn, is also the color of the Almighty. Pray, O people, to black madonnas and hold black masses. The kingdom of God begins today!'" Hauptmann, *Sämtliche Werke*, 4: 726 ff., 8: 973 ff.

27. Compare W. E. Mühlmann, "Ethnische Entfremdung und Pseudologia," in *Homo Creator. Abhandlungen zur Soziologie, Anthropologie und Ethnologie* (Wiesbaden, 1962), pp. 311 ff.

28. Sören Kierkegaard, *Die Krankheit zum Tode und Anderes*, ed. Hermann Diem and Walter Rest, 2d ed. (Cologne, 1968).

29. What we mean here by the Sickness Unto Death is a nihilistic entelechy in the unity of person and work which does not actually *have* to have a connection with illness and early death. An example of the complete opposite to this is furnished by Schiller, with his unbelievable victorious energy in a sickly body that was early on destined for death—a logical analogy to his tragic idea of freedom. Schiller exhibits not one trace of nihilism—in the end he is simply defeated after a heroic struggle.

30. Gottfried Benn, *Gesammelte Werke* (Wiesbaden, 1959–1961), 4: 203. Compare an extract from a letter written in 1945: "I live in total solitude. An unwelcome situation at one time, and unwelcome now—really . . . absolutely unwelcome. This strikes me as proper and confirmation of my basic feeling, which I've often mentioned, that art stands outside the relationships of state and society and that its rejection by the world is part of it." Benn, *Dichter über ihre Dichtungen,* ed. Edgar Lohner (Munich, 1969), p. 267.

31. "The world is blind, and always the evil example triumphs and drowns perfect performance. The light is spent, and with it every glow. The false triumphs, and the true does not emerge." Michelangelo, "Di morte certo . . .," sonnet written in 1555 or later.

32. "Of life's many gifts and treasures/The most precious must be fame!/When the flesh to dust has crumbled/What remains is a great name. *Sämtliche Werke,* 1: 426.

33. Goethe to Riemer, January 1808, *Werke,* 9: 639; to Eckermann, *Werke,* 22: 481; *Italienische Reise,* Jubiläums-Ausgabe, 9: 639.

34. Goethe, *Werke,* Gedenk-Ausgabe, *Briefe,* 21: 1024. Similar utterances in letters: to Knebel, 17 March 1817; to S. Boisserè, 7 June 1821; to J. F. K. Hecker, 7 October 1829.

35. Consider, for instance, Ignazio Silone, Salvatore Quasimodo, Cesare Pavese, and Elio Vittorini.

36. Husserl, *Analysen zur passiven Synthesis* or *Husserliana,* vol. 11 (The Hague, 1966); Nicolai Hartmann, *Zur Grundlegung der Ontologie,* 4th ed. (Berlin, 1965), pp. 164 ff.; Erwin Straus, *Psychologie der menschlichen Welt,* Gesammelte Schriften (Berlin, 1960), p. 152; Kurt Lothar Tank, *Gerhart Hauptmann in Selbstzeugnissen und Bilddokumenten* (Hamburg, 1959), pp. 35, 43. To Husserl, *Logische Untersuchungen II/2,* 3d ed. (Halle, 1922), compare Marvin Farber, *The Foundations of Phenomenology: Edmund Husserl and the Quest for a Rigorous Science,* 2d ed. (New York, 1962), chapter 13: "Objectivating Intentions and Fulfillments." Husserl demonstrates that in thinking there are levels which proceed from mere intentions of meaning to clear, vital fulfillment.

37. "Those whose souls are blind are visited by fortune—those whose souls do no more than blink into the world are visited by horror." Hauptmann, "Iphigenie in Aulis," *Sämtliche Werke,* 3: 863.

Alphons Silbermann

ON THE EFFECTS OF LITERATURE
AS A MEANS
OF MASS COMMUNICATION

I

THE ENDLESS LIST OF BOOKS AND STUDIES CONCERNED WITH THE POSITION
of the writer and of literature usually culminates in despair. While
at the time of John Ruskin, validity was still attached to the thoroughly noncommittal statement "that the arts can never be right themselves, unless their motive is right,"[1] and while during the 1950s it
was held that "industrialization and commercialization of intellectual
production result in a certain proletarianization of the producers,"[2]
today the cry is heard: "In a self-generated atmosphere literature
loses touch with the observable world, wherein I consider the writer's
original sin to lie. Literature . . . believes that it acts and agitates,
whereas in fact it no longer does anything but react."[3] These remarks
alone call attention to the fact that the writer's position as such (with
or without regard to his creation) and his situation within society form
the primary interest of all efforts at literary scholarship; the point is
made even more clearly when we browse in anthologies intended to
interpret literary activity from a sociological viewpoint.

In a volume of this sort at hand, for example, *Wege der Literatursoziologie* edited by Hans Norbert Fügen (Neuweid and Berlin,
1968), there are twenty contributions on the topic of "author" and
only three articles on the topic of "audience." There are good reasons
why even the detailed *International Encyclopedia of the Social
Sciences*, under the heading "Literature," primarily concerns itself
with form, content, and lines of communication, and only marginally,

under the heading "The Sociology of Reading,"[4] appears audience-oriented.

The first reason can be found wherever the tradition of strongly history-oriented literary scholarship still fights against adopting sociological research methods in its investigations. While such scholarship correctly estimates the difficulties of audience research, it prefers to remain in the realm of one-sided, desk-bound contemplation of the meaning, form, and content of literary works; of signification and classification diagrams; as well as of esthetic-linguistic, occasionally sociological, problems. To view the writer and his creation in their interaction with the audience, to break through from this standpoint to modes of influence, is considered by traditional/literary scholarship as straining its bounds. Whenever this topic is *actually* considered, and not just paid lip service to with the rhetoric of "reflection," then we are faced with a jumble of statistics setting forth the amount of reading in one or another country, or the structure of the book-buying public, or current best sellers, or perhaps percentages of people who have read *Doctor Zhivago, Exodus,* or *The Brothers Karamazov* or, as the case may be, who plan to read them in the future. In short, literature and its readers (or nonreaders), as well as the proportional relationship between reading and leisure activities, sometimes even the meaning or value of reading, are all studied from time to time for particular countries and in intercultural comparisons, with the help of representatively coordinated statistical projections.[5] There is no reason to take particular pride in such studies. For, to the extent that they concern factors of influence, all these statistical compilations are nothing more than basic data. They do not have the slightest value as testimony concerning the power and extent of a book's effect. They are only significant if the discussion deals with the topics of literacy and illiteracy.

A further reason for such minimal concern with audiences is naturally based on the heterogeneity of consumer groups. But in addition to this, and closely connected with it, is the heterogeneity of the producing group on the one hand, as well as, on the other hand, the diversity of literary kinds, from escapist novels through comic strips to dramatic literature. This circumstance already makes it difficult to comprehend the consequences of the interaction between producer and consumer. To this must also be added the fact that the man of letters, considered as an artist, occupies an undefined position. Not that such definitions are lacking—quite the contrary. However, they have no relation to the social context, and surely this relationship is the first that must be clarified if we are to shed light on the implications in one or another direction—or, to put it differently, on the functional and dysfunctional aspects of the writer as artist or simply as author of literary works, whether these be intended for book, radio, film, television, or cassette production.

If the literature produced by one person—whether it is arbitrarily on a high, middle, or even low level—can or should exert any influence, then the role and status of the communicator assume the predominant position. From this angle the esthetic, stylistic, formal, or structural values of a literary work are without significance for the sociologist; they remain outside his concern. In fact, we insist on rejecting the blatant mixture of esthetics and sociology which suggests itself as a model for evaluation. Such declarations of esthetic ideology as, for example, "merits of cultural activity" ("Verdienste um das Kulturschaffen") or "an artist is someone who interprets the objects of the universe and gives them shape" must be put aside so that social reality can be clearly perceived. Only then will we be able to discern functions and spheres of influence. Only then will we be able to recognize that "the increasing reliance of the masses upon professional provision of recreational satisfactions"—that is, upon the arts—is peculiar to modern society.[6]

It would take us too far afield also to enter into the questions posed by economic and sociopsychological problems. Professional sociological elements, however, cannot and should not be overlooked in the indicated relationship of communicator and recipient, since the effect of the product depends so heavily on the recipient's vision of the writer, the producer of literature. It is, after all, generally known that the writer usually designates himself as a member of the "liberal professions," no matter whether he is a belletrist or writes for the theater, for newspapers, for the radio, for the movies, for television, or for other audiovisual media. This inclusion in the category of the "liberal professions" has always presented great difficulty, since the original meaning of the adjective "liberal," derived from "liberty" in the sense of freedom, has undergone such extensive changes that it simply cannot be sustained without specific clarification of the determining social-functional connections; neither is a definition tenable if it inclines so strongly to the ideological that determination as a value judgment becomes irrelevant.

Currently almost all empirically oriented considerations in the sociology of profession are based on implied social-functional connections. Theodor Geiger's book, *Aufgaben und Stellung der Intelligenz in der Gesellschaft* (Stuttgart, 1949) or *Tasks and Position of the Intelligentsia in Society,* can be considered basic to this attitude. Geiger distinguishes among three functional groups as cultural representatives: the intelligentsia, the cultured classes, and academicians. The functional representation of these groups—the presupposition for any and all spheres of influence—is roughly divided so that it is the intelligentsia's share to intellectualize existence, to create theoretical premises for rationalizing life, to recognize sociopolitical issues, and to exert criticism. It is the cultured classes' task to share in the cultural goods of an epoch with an eye to humanizing society. And academicians—to continue Geiger's premise—must "use" and "apply" cultural creations.

There can therefore be little doubt that, following Geiger's divisions, each member of the various professional groups, in view of his group's status, can and may also claim each of Geiger's functional representations. Therefore the determining factors producing impact must be more clearly elaborated, our perspective must be narrowed and directed purely on the profession. First is the profession of *intelligentsia,* determined by its exclusivity in intellectual activity; second the profession of *expert,* determined by its special knowledge of and competence in a discipline; third, the *liberal* profession, determined by its universally cultural mediating role.[7]

However we may view and categorize the practice of a liberal profession, somewhere and somehow the writer as "artist" is a "possible contender for leadership" and as such is to be seen "as category, not individual."[8] This "leadership role," whether it arises consciously or unconsciously, is naturally embedded in a sociocultural system, determining not only the writer's status and prestige within his environment, his culture, and his society, but also the impact of his production. This truism, of course, is frequently overlooked, especially when intercultural comparisons of literary influence are employed. It is therefore necessary to consider, not only function and functional representation, but also the social interactions arising from the cultural sphere. The following diagram can be derived from the cited attempts at categorization as well as others, not all of which can be detailed here.[9]

Functional representation:	Intelligentsia	Expert	Liberal profession
Function:	creative	practical	mediating
Social interaction:	exclusive	pragmatic	universal

This tripartite diagram reveals natural transitions and interactions in literary actuality that cannot be discussed here. However, it helps to show that the literary worker is neither priest nor slave to society, but one of its members, who possesses special qualities or functions essential to the society's existence. It is true that these qualities or functions are frequently and willingly stifled—not because literature is considered corrupting or the writer is seen as a Bohemian loafer,[10] but because within the framework of social interactions the writer is so closely related to the achievements of our advanced industrial society that the contempt for this type of society is vented on the literary man and his creations. The problem could fill whole volumes, but this discussion will be limited to illuminating the situation— which on the one hand has led to a distinction between "serious" and "frivolous" writers and on the other to such influence-conditioned catchwords as "stereotyping," "leveling," or "smattering of knowledge"—in a very specific context in keeping with our topic. In this effort we must not omit mention of the various media for which production is undertaken.

Any consideration of the relationships between the freedom of a profession and other facets of a socially conditioned life will sooner or later run up against institutions that have a functional relationship to freedom and liberty. By this we mean not only the "literary system," from which literary criticism gathers its strength,[11] but in our time all the technical means for the propagation of literary creations. Accusations of a social, pedagogic, and general nature are heaped at their feet. It is said that it is they and their contents that stultify, level out, and lead to passivity, whereby they prove themselves harmful not only to society but also to anyone who puts his creative power at their disposal: anyone who recasts *Wallensteins Lager* along sociocritical lines violates the "cultural heritage"; anyone who writes pop lyrics is considered a "fashionable exploiter." This situation clearly demonstrates the admixing of social and esthetic considerations; judgments as to what has utmost consequence according to the content may be distorted either by the defense of a no longer existing windmill or by the struggle against a windmill which has long since become a social datum, even as defense or attack are carried on. Mass communication and its means, for example, paperback books or popular nonfiction titles, have long since been raised to public facts by society—they have been institutionalized. If the relationship between literature and the litterateur on the one hand, and between literature and society on the other—or, more abstractly, the relationship between function and effect—is considered from that point, then we can recognize this interaction, its existence and its consequences, from two aspects; though in reality these two intermingle, they will be developed separately here for the sake of systematic presentation.

In the one case we are dealing with the viewpoint of mass culture, which is charged with negativism. Arbitrarily using such concepts as "the masses," "stereotyping," or "budgeting," observers from this vantage point have a predilection for making quantitative statements and in the same breath leveling qualitative criticisms. The goal is, on the one hand, to devalue the social fact of "mass communication" and its means in society's eyes. On the other hand, concepts such as *stereotyping* project an inferiority to society, in the naive belief that this or similar invective can make an individualized collective out of the collectivized individual.[12]

Closely related to this trend, though separate from it, a sociological attitude appears in the concept of popular culture—an expression disliked by those who consider that the word "culture" contains an element of exclusivity. If we say that sociology of popular culture is devoted to the cultural development of democratic and postdemocratic society, as well as with an emerging service society, we again underline the fact that cultural phenomena, their substance, their utilization, and their functions, are to be considered within the framework of society; that is, within the structural view of the existence of various levels, classes, and groups. The epistemological factor for the aspect that is of paramount interest here therefore resides in the totality of ideas, stances, and values that contribute to the development of personality through participation in cultural and social life.

This short comment on two points of departure that form the frame of reference is meant only to remove a certain amount of intellectual rubbish: first, the belief that literature is the privilege of an elite; and second, the related premise that the masses are culturally underdeveloped. If we want to look without prejudice at the mutual influence between writer and/or literature and society—that is, from the standpoint of an equal right for each member of society to a cultural form and to access to it through means of mass communication—then the cultural concept "popular culture" serves at least to diminish discrepancies and differences between the various social levels. For from the sociological point of view, any form of literature, working through its various spheres of influence, is one of the means used by the state to associate widespread levels of society with the processing of a cultural form common to all. But a fair and unprejudiced concept of popular culture has even wider usefulness. Among other purposes, it serves to facilitate the interchange between social status and cultural level within distinct social groups. Lastly we see popular culture and its utilization as one of the means for replacing the disappearing traditional, folkloristic element with a popular-cultural one. The spheres of influence therefore spread out in three directions: toward the reduction of social exclusivity, toward diminishing cultural conventionality, and toward preserving the culture. Thus, by way of literature and with the help of writers of every genre and with the help of the media of mass communication, statics and dynamics combine in the totality of a popular cultural system.

II

The above assessment already leads us quite far into the complex of problems concerning the effectiveness of literature as a means of mass communication. However, what we have established continues to be weighted heavily on the side of the producing component; the functional aspect still remains too far in the background. This imbalance has come about because we have personified the relationship between literature and society, yet we have left unspecified the relationship of the partner "society." Thus the function of literature as related to society must be elaborated more thoroughly. Here two conceptual worlds confront each other in the current critical views of culture: freedom and education work with fearful and unrelenting skepticism. Those people who have a mania about education, those who want with all their might to impose *their* ideas of proper education on society, detect some danger in a literature of mass communication, which they consider dangerous chiefly insofar as it impinges on their own function as cultural prophets, even though they themselves are only too eager to involve this medium in their educating activities. Elsewhere, a discussion of these persons and their hopeless starry-eyed lack of realism has shown that, from a sociological point of view, education *by way of* a medium of mass communication can only be considered "hoped-for" education.[13]

Rather, the forefront is occupied by functions that we may be able to classify by applying the terminology of leisure. The point of departure is the fact that a "discussion concerning leisure in industrial societies . . . is to be understood as concern with the symptoms of a complex process of the qualitative change of technologically developed societies."[14] Always considered from the point of interrelation between literature and means of mass communication and society or, respectively, leisure, these functions[15] can be briefly paraphrased as:

1. The function of relaxation. This is a matter of freeing people from the weariness caused by work and the responsibilities of everyday life.
2. The function of distraction. The monotony of everyday life is compensated for by an active or passive—or, better, by a real or only imaginary—series of activities, in order to preserve the balance of personality.
3. The function of development. Here there is a chance for the intellectual, moral, or artistic elements of the personality structure to develop; these serve, among other ends, to furnish a balance with industrialization and its traits of material and nonmaterial automatization.

If we combine these three basic functions, as they grow out of the concept of popular culture and exist and work interdependently with one another, we are able to recognize the essential elements of leisure activity through no matter what "major" or "minor" literary medium, conveyed by no matter which medium of communication. They serve: (1) as antithesis of work; (2) as psychological expression of freedom; (3) as satisfaction of the sense of play;[16] (4) as inadvertent satisfaction of sociocultural role fulfillment (education); (5) as connection with culture values; (6) as enjoyable anticipation; (7) as memory.

Such deliberately simplified classification is open to stringent attacks, especially since literature as an art form has been mentioned here in the same breath as the functions of literature as means of mass communication. But that is exactly as it should be. For, as Max Kaplan[17] says in reference to all sociocultural observations on the relationships among society, literature, and media, as well as to the effects of this relationship, it must be borne in mind that the functions of literature are to be viewed from two equivalent levels. On the one hand we have the *esthetic* functions and spheres of influence, which bring together producer and consumer by way of the literary material —form and content. On the other are the *social* functions and spheres of influence, which establish the connections among people, ideals, cultural norms, values, and behavior patterns; esthetic functions also play a part on this second level, but they are in no way crucial.

This discussion is chiefly concerned with those functions and spheres of influence relating to the social level. A systematic division, based on a general description designed by Max Kaplan, would result in the following influence-functional scheme:

1. Mass-media literature of a folkloristic sort, which unites individuals more closely with their groups (collective experience).
2. Mass-media literature that stimulates the imagination or brings distraction or makes a connection with groups and historical epochs to which the individual does not belong (individual experience).
3. Mass-media literature in which the content is presented as idea or social connection (symbolic experience).
4. Mass-media literature in which the content is manifested as good, decadent, inspirational, sensational, or cheap (moral-value experience).
5. Mass-media literature whose content does not arouse any esthetic sense (incidental experience).

The considerations discussed thus far—including the reduction of influence-functional areas to structures of artistic experience[18]—point in the last resort to a morphologically occurring change in the socio-cultural environment of society.

III

It becomes essential now to give examples of everything that has previously been stated in more or less theoretical terms. This will be done from two different standpoints, both of which are intended to illuminate separate facets of the spheres of influence of literature as means of mass communication in the framework of a developing turn toward popular culture. First let us look at the situation of the book trade in one European country, France, on the basis of new statistics that have been made available.

According to a statistical survey of the *Bibliographie de la France*, almost three billion francs' worth of books were sold in France in 1969. A third of this sum was spent on novels and essays. To this must be added the fact that French book production and consumption has risen by about ten percent per year. It has become evident that since 1966 a slight but noticeable drop in the production of novels has been compensated for by an increase in the number of history books, regional guides, and dictionaries. This means that readers' preferences have been directed more to nonfiction and reference books than to purely fictional literature. In this instance the exogenous influence of television may have played a role similar to the one taken by radio in the dissemination of music translated into records. After all, we are aware that all countries have television programs which, for example, popularize history in the form of actualizations, evoking in the audience an interest in verification and further information by way of nonfiction and reference books.

But the new statistical survey reveals a much more important point —one already made in 1965 by Robert Escarpit, in his study, *La Révolution du livre*:[19] the rise in the production of *livres de poche* or "pocketbooks." One half of the 9,464 titles published in France in 1969—about thirty new titles per day—appeared in the form of pocketbooks, which might lead to an imminent, quite unequivocal distinction between the "popular" and the "luxury" medium, both going under the name of "book." To this may be added that at that time in France there were 400 publishing firms of various sizes, among whom roughly twenty-five firms were responsible for sixty percent of total sales.

This development and the accompanying figures alone, however, are not sufficient to declare books and the literature they contain to be means of mass communication, as is unfortunately often claimed in superficial discussions. The primary systems of distribution must also be considered—anyone can print, but anyone cannot necessarily sell. First, there are the distribution groups known as "jobbers." They supply the retail outlets (bookstores, newsstands, and the like) and are paid with a percentage of the retail price. The second system is distribution by means of direct mail and circulars through book clubs, book societies, and the like, though at present this is a waning sales system. In contrast, distribution to the retail trade by salesmen and book fairs is becoming more and more widespread. While enumerating these three primary systems of distribution, we must not overlook those publishers who are less interested in sales than in production. They distribute their literary creations primarily by selling them to other publishers, to whom they leave the commercialization of their products. There are also the "vanity publisher," who takes on a manuscript and manufactures a book at the author's expense, and the "publisher" proper, who also carries on promotion and sales.

The diversity in the distribution system, and especially the wholesale trade connected with it, could in the long run render printed literature inaccessible from an economic point of view or could lead it back from its status as a means of mass communication or a mass commodity to an elitist status symbol. Only then would those predictions that speak of "the book without a future" or of the displacement of the Gutenberg Age by the Marconi Age come true. In any case, these overly intellectualized pseudosociological prognoses à la McLuhan are in error, if for no other reason than because they cram the term "literature"—and with it its effects—into a corset from a time long past and insist on recognizing as literature only and exclusively the printed word. But has this situation not changed? Is it not true that at the origin of any film, any television production, any audiovisual program (except for live performances) there is a written script, often suitable for publication—in other words, a literary product? Audiovisual culture, which is so much a topic of conversation, does not by a long shot mean the disappearance of either the literary form as such or of its elements as determined by writing and printing. For even an illustration accompanying a text—let us say the captions for a school television program—grows out of the literary context.

This remark brings us to the second example to clarify our theoretical statement. For this purpose we have chosen a literary genre that more often than not has drawn the scorn of cultural pessimists and literary scholars—comics. A number of studies and comprehensive presentations concern themselves with the typology, structure, function, and dysfunction of comics. It will have to suffice that we refer to them here.[20] To remain within the confines of our topic, we must concentrate our attention on the effects of the literary genre "comics" as a means of mass communication. Let us therefore first consider their effects on children and young people.

Relating to the researches of Wilbur Schramm on mass-media effects,[21] the following spheres of influence can be differentiated: physical effects, emotional effects, cognitive effects, and behavioral effects. Much research has already been done and a great deal has been written about each of these spheres as concerns children and young people, no matter what mass medium is under discussion. However—and this must be added at once—whatever has been or will be presented as research results is subject to a considerable limitation because of *situational elements*. These relate most strongly to what I attempted to stress as interaction in my theoretical discussion of the functional. For as far as effects are concerned, it is only very rarely that a child's behavior can be causally connected with his reading of comics or anything else.

Supposing a child or young person commits a crime and claims to have been incited by a comic strip, an adventure tale, a movie, or a television program; it is true that a stimulus to action may be found in such a source—but never the direct causality that self-styled guardians of public morals are so fond of claiming. It is situational elements—the social environment, the child's peer group, his school friends, his system of norms—it is the adaptive or defense mechanisms elicited through education that, interacting, lead a young person to deviant behavior, to theft or to prostitution, and not the single and sole cause named "mass medium." Quite other qualities play a role in this aspect of rousing dangers. Among them is primarily that element that can be designated as the *predominant trends* of a society.

These social trends, which influence the creative aspects of the comics or any other literary genre as well as their producers and their consumers or readers, do not remain static any more than does a society and its cultural manifestations. Producers as well as consumers —that is, each one of us—are subject to social change, subject to what might be called "overall societal change."[22] Insofar as sociology deals in an observing and analyzing capacity with the problems of social change, it is in a position to ascertain *typical trends* that go to make up the basis of any society-oriented judgment, including the position of comics as literature in present-day society. If only recently we spoke of the trend of "market orientation,"[23] then of "other-directedness"[24] and "identity diffusion"[25] we see in our present-day societal life the trend of "discontinuity," a trend that most often finds itself aphoristically designated with the catchphrase "permissive society." These social trends must be taken into account in any evaluation, especially since the determination of trends is impersonal and the concept has no inevitable moral implications. "Inevitability" in this context means that neither an individual, say a publisher of comics, nor an institution, let us say a television network, could succeed in changing the direction of a social trend by personal or institutional efforts. No one person, no group or institution, can arrest the particular trend toward the permissive society, including, for example, its manifest drift toward sexual freedom. As the American sociologist W. F. Ogburn wrote as early as 1957: "A knowledge of trends keeps us from believing in fairy tales."[26]

And now to offer a few extreme examples. If the heroine Phoebe in *The Adventure of Phoebe Zeit-Geist*[27] is in the habit of jumping com-

pletely naked onto her hi-fi motorcycle; if in Guy Peelaert's *Pravda*
(Bremen, 1968) art nouveau, eroticism, and esthetics intermingle; if
"scantily clad girls" gladden the sight of *Perry*, our man in the universe;[28] if Al Capp's *Li'l Abner* has become a Spiro Agnew in treating themes from actual life; if *Stars and Stripes*, the official newspaper
of the U. S. armed forces, has banned the publication of one comic
strip because one of its characters, a black soldier, wears an Afro
hairstyle and goatee and these are not permitted by military regulations—then all these are indices of a mass medium's adaptation to a
social trend, no matter whether it seems proper or depraved. True,
the examples I have cited here are nothing compared to the development of the new type of comics, that is, the science-fiction strip,
which may be structurally classified among the type of so-called adventure comics. An equally indicative example for our discussion of
the significance of social trends is the snob appeal exerted on adults
at the present time in the United States by a strip such as *Peanuts*.

And since we are now speaking of adults—and readership surveys
have shown that they make up a large proportion of all comics fans—
we should not simply dismiss their interests with cheap arguments
of semiliteracy, distraction, or escapism. I feel safe in saying that a
majority of adult readers of comics choose their favorite type of comic
according to identification with the hero of one or another type. If
this supposition is correct, it means that even the interpretation of the
content of the concept "hero" has changed in accordance with the
trends. Only superficially does the hero remain an active personality
who, guided by a vision of reality, dares to think and act independently. In short, the hero of yesterday as well as today contains the
heroic qualities forged in the ideal dream image which, though it
prevails always and everywhere, cannot be attained by the average
person, the man who enjoys comics in adult life; perhaps he is not
even aware of it.

These remarks are meant to stress the fact that in a dynamic society such as ours—that is, in contrast with a static society—conditions
often change so rapidly that the world of the adults is quite different
from that of children. In the prevailing permissive society, therefore,
fathers and sons, mothers and daughters, barely speak the same language any longer, because the young people, as a consequence of
their biological development, possess greater *daring*. Culture and
cultural norms, as well as morals and moral norms, are the products
of social conditions that for their part are subject to rapid change.
Connected with this intellectual change, of course, is technological

change—the very change that produced the easily accessible electronic media alongside printed mass media.

It is pretentiously said of the media that they disseminate a large amount of knowledge, by which is meant knowledge as the systematic organization of information and concepts. This statement, however, must be countered by the fact that the media communicate primarily *things*, and only in the last instance what people are and think. In other words, the electronic media, such as radio and television, create, as it were, a global shopping center. In contrast (in contrast also to the clever fantasy tissue of a McLuhan), the printed word as literature remains rooted in the specific, both by its substantive direction and its mode of acquisition or purchase, which is much more involved than that of the electronic medium. Nevertheless, a similarity exists between the printed and the electronic mass media when we reflect that for the world's masses both kind of media are not purely "entertainment," as they are for the well-to-do and elitist segments of our society, since these possess other means for learning about the world. For the great majority of children, young people, or adults, the mass media—and among them every kind of literature, from cheap paperback romances through pornography to the Bible—have nowadays become "the first access to a bigger world than that of peasant village or small-town slum."[29]

Do these circumstances, which we regard as the sociocultural background that must be considered in any evaluation, mean that this social context, which is reflected in the literary genre "comics," is simply dangerous, even immoral? Putting the question differently and focusing on practical considerations, is it not true that philosophers of ethics, and among them primarily educators, are all too easily seduced into generalizing the once-established principles that are at the base of *their* code of behavior to such an extent that they can be applied in any situation and with every mass medium? We are here addressing ourselves with rhetorical questions to situations of moral conflict that must be prevented for the good of society. At the point of departure are certain obligations of a moral and ethical sort which, it is assumed, must be certified to one social group. If that is true, this finding leads us to an *everyday morality*, which turns out to be a double standard to the extent that everyday morality—in our case that of a permissive social system—does not necessarily correspond to one's own moral principles, especially when these have grown out of a social system with an entirely different basis, one that *precedes* the permissive society. In this situation, therefore, it is less a matter of the threat of comics or literature in general than of combining and coordinating all relevant norms of yesterday and today in an equitable manner, that is, according to the premise of social responsibility.

IV

So much for our examples. They demonstrate those changes in the sociocultural environment that we spoke of above. We can observe these changes for ourselves within the contemporary social system without any reference to the future and without recourse to experimental methods. It is enough to note that social trends are reflected, not only in measurable entities, but also in literature, in the printed words and pictures of comics, as well as in the spoken words and pictures of the theater—both in a general and a specific sense. According to sociology of communication, it is of little point to design and publicize so-called influence models in the belief that the process of literary communication proceeds in a straight line from the transmitter of the message to its receiver. Anyone thinking in this way overlooks man's personality structure, since man has the gift of selective perception; with its aid, any line of communication—whether through a book or through the most perfect audiovisual means of communication—can be interrupted and diverted at any time.

Taking this into account, and on the basis of previous studies, certain fundamental assertions can be made regarding the effects of literature as means of mass communication in one or another form. First, the constantly ongoing change in the social trends of society—or, to put it differently and more specifically, the constantly ongoing change in the value concepts, behavioral norms, and problems of any society—will bring about considerable and ever more rapid changes in the content and form of presentation of products based on literature. Insofar as the literary work is able to do justice to this change, either by presage or by documentation, it will contribute toward influencing evaluations of life styles and needs as well as social, cultural, and economic wants.

Second, it must be said that the information-conditioned reinforcing effect that has always emanated from literature will increase to the extent that literature increasingly becomes an independent medium of mass communication by utilizing new communication techniques. In other words: consumers of literature will continue to prefer those presentations and utilization modalities and will continue primarily to notice and adopt those elements in them that correspond to their expectations. Thus even the newest means of communication that directly convey literary elements—as, for example, the "talking book" or the cassette magazine—are most likely to exert an influence if their content and purpose correspond to preexisting opinions and attitudes.

As a result of the change, already in full swing, from an elitist to a popularly determined element, and of the closely connected circumstance of an increasingly expanding and differentiated product, there will be an increase in reinforcement effect by the means of communication. In view of our increasingly more differentiated society,[30] the individual will feel a growing need to use the literary medium to inform himself more thoroughly than before about which opinions, attitudes, and positions are correct and which are wrong.

Third, it can be said that literature is best able to lead to the formation of opinions in matters of newly emerging problems, where opinions and attitudes are not yet defined.

V

Looking back on preliterate societies, we can, it is true, recognize forms of communication even among them that resemble the book. But the function of communication in less developed social groups was not sufficiently complicated to stimulate further concentration on those means. Therefore the functional nature of the book—and also, of course, its literary content—did not become distinctive until literature, precisely by using the medium of "book," became institutionalized. By way of explanation, this means: "An *institution* will be said to be a complex of institutionalized role integrates which is of strategic structural significance in the social system in question."[31] In other words, an institution is the method by which certain acts must be performed.[32] Thus the meaning of an institution is clarified by what it does, by the functions it performs or fulfills.[33] Accordingly, we define institutions according to the central functions they perform and according to the kind of social needs they satisfy. And since the medium (book and audiovisual means) as well as its content (literature of every genre) represent both cultural needs and a firm organization in social life, we will here speak of a sociocultural institution. If in this connection the term *needs* arises again and again, we must keep in mind the fact that in the process of the social growth of a society two opposing tendencies confront each other. On the moral plane, growth leads to a desire for greater equality, while on the functional level, social growth results in more complex division of labor. As a result of this dichotomy, the following functions and their respective influence on the sociocultural institution can be summarized.[34]

1. The increasing differentiation of a society necessitates the spread of at least fundamental learning, so as to make possible a basis for interpersonal relations among different social groups and to avoid extraordinary tensions.

2. Greater social mobility related to social growth necessitates each individual's further education to maintain his status. Discontent with the social status is often a strong motivation for change and thus for an increased need for knowledge.

3. Increasing differentiation in our society results in a greater desire for specialized knowledge, since this differentiation is related to increasing specialization.

4. Alongside the need for information as a result of differentiation there is the need for relaxation. Because of increasing division of labor (partitive work style) and work specialization, stronger tensions are aroused in the individual. The obligation continually to perform the identical tasks allows for the expression of only a small part of the individual's personality. As a result there is a heightened need for compensation, and means of mass communication of all kinds are used to satisfy it.

We may therefore say that on the one hand the complexity compels a more rational behavioral model and the need for knowledge and information moves further into the foreground; on the other hand, the emotional stresses closely related to the rapid changes in society evoke a need for compensatory literature.

As a result of this functional development of the sociocultural institution, it can be seen that the trend toward development and recognition of a popular culture must grow increasingly stronger, while adherence to an elitist culture decreases. As stated above, this must not be seen as the notorious "stereotyping" in a negative sense, but rather as the establishment of a new general concept of culture.

Almost unnoticed, from the most varied angles, the social-hierarchic concept of earlier times is crumbling. Whether the effective action manifests itself in hippiedom, in sexual liberation, in the churchs' attempts at reform, in women's emancipation—in short, in the establishment of powerful subcultures—this action overrides the control functions of the cultural-pessimistic ideologues of decline, for in its guise as dynamic action it opens paths that can no longer be closed off by thought and ideas. These are paths that have been barricaded for decades by elitist groups who had shut off access to knowledge of things on a higher or lower level. Now, with the new concept of culture, they are beginning to open up. The rejection, not to mention the suppression, of a popular culture until now was based less on contempt for human materials or the desire to exploit those materials than on a disparity between the disciplines and the values motivating the action. Now, in the course of development of a new concept of culture with a positive tendency, the days of gratuitous compromise are over. The slogan of the coming generations—those who will be alive when we are already strumming our harps in heaven—calls for courageous advancement in order to produce both balance and synthesis.

This confrontation, essential to the establishment of a universally accessible concept of culture, takes place first and last whenever the mental structures of the past (those that might pejoratively be called cryptomedieval) encounter modern technology. It is questionable whether in the course of this development, institutionalized literature in its entertaining, idea-shaping, or relaxing aspects can retain its foothold. For if the confrontation between traditional mental structures and modern technology results in the information revolution that already surrounds us, then this revolution will have a dramatic impact on education, teaching, and learning. In this way information becomes the energy center for the work of the mind. Therefore it was recently stated: "Young people, a few years hence, will use information systems as their normal tools much as they now use the typewriter or the telephone."[35] Whoever agrees with us in seeing literature as a mass medium—that is, as a sociocultural institution that has more to offer than a salable product—also recognizes it as an "information system" and, accordingly and beyond all possible dangers, a service that is consequently subject to social responsibility. If we combine these lines of reasoning, we see before us the birth of new literary media that—along with existing ones—will precisely do justice to those factors or social trends that are now developing.

The frequently deplored identification with "cheap" literature and the equally lamented gratification, both of which constitute the stimulus of literary experts, remain structurally active in literature as the expression of unconscious desires. However, they will have to adjust wherever these wishes are increasingly voiced in the field of learning. Surely no special mention need be made of the fact that, in the course of this development, the producers and distributors will have to use or deliver the newest audiovisual means for their products. This is especially true in view of the fact that it is already important today to prepare to plan for the structural change of literature into mass medium, so as to avoid a situation whereby literature no longer corresponds to the needs of society.

For this society of the future, which makes use of a multimedia system, will be what may be called a "multi-channel society,"[36] a supratechnological society with many conduits. This means that, as long as future society continues to be marked by abundance and affluence, both in material and nonmaterial directions, it will have to take care to guarantee the coexistence of pluralistic values and diverse concepts—in the present case ranging from popular culture to elitist culture. In this way, united in a new consolidated concept of culture, we proceed toward a social structure in which everything centers on receptivity, on acceptance—in other words, on a society that will have left the structure of the traditional industrial society far behind. For it has been properly noted: "The media have taught people what to *want;* they must now teach people how to *get.*"[37]

[*Translated from the German by Ruth Hein*]

Notes

1. J. Ruskin, *Selections and Essays*, ed. by F. W. Roe (New York, 1918), p. 399.
2. H. de Man, *Vermassung und Kulturverfall* (Berne, 1959), p. 63.
3. K.-A. Horst, "Der Schriftsteller und seine Öffentlichkeit," *Studium Generale* 23 (1970): 709.
4. D. L. Sills, ed., *International Encyclopedia of the Social Sciences* (New York, 1968), 9: 417 ff.
5. In this connection see, for example, *Schriften zur Buchmarktforschung*, ed. by P. Meyer-Dohm (Gütersloh), as well as the occasional surveys on this topic issued by UNESCO in *Annuaire statistique de l'Unesco*, most recently in 1965.

6. R. T. LaPiere, *Sociology* (New York, 1946), p. 323.
7. Compare H. Stieglitz, *Der soziale Auftrag der freien Berufe* (Cologne and Berlin, 1960), pp. 146–147.
8. T. Parsons, s.v. "Professions," *International Encyclopedia of the Social Sciences*, 12: p. 546.
9. See, for example, T. Caplow, *The Sociology of Work* (Minneapolis, 1954); J. F. V. Deneke, *Die freien Berufe* (Stuttgart, 1956); P. F. Lazarsfeld and W. Thielens, *The Academic Mind* (New York, 1958); R. König, *Soziologische Orientierungen* (Cologne and Berlin, 1965), pp. 179 ff.
10. Compare C. Graña, *Bohemian versus Bourgeois* (New York, 1964).
11. Compare K. E. Rosengren, *Sociological Aspects of the Literary System* (Stockholm, 1968).
12. Compare my study, *Vorteile und Nachteile des kommerziellen Fernsehens* (Düsseldorf and Vienna, 1968), part 1, "Über das Trauma von der Vermassung."
13. See my *Musik, Rundfunk und Hörer* (Cologne and Opladen, 1959), pp. 127 ff.
14. E. K. Scheuch, "Soziologie der Freizeit," in R. König, ed., *Handbuch der empirischen Sozialforschung*, vol. 2 (Stuttgart, 1969), p. 735.
15. The discussion of functions incorporates some of the arguments I proposed in "Soziologische Erwägungen zur Freizeit," *Kölner Zeitschrift für Soziologie und Sozialpsychologie*, vol. 14, no. 3 (1962): 504 ff.
16. On this topic, compare W. Stephenson, *The Play Theory of Mass Communication* (Chicago, 1967).
17. Max Kaplan, *Leisure in America. A Social Inquiry* (New York and London, 1960).
18. For artistic experience as a "fait social," see my remarks in *Wovon lebt die Musik? Die Prinzipien der Musiksoziologie* (Regensburg, 1957); or see the English edition, *The Sociology of Music* (London, 1963) or the revised French edition, *Les principes de la sociologie de la musique* (Geneva and Paris, 1968).
19. (Paris, 1965). For this topic, see also the latest publication by R. Escarpit et al., *Le littéraire et le social* (Paris, 1970).
20. See, among others, B. Hürlimann, *Europäische Kinderbücher in drei Jahrhunderten* (Zurich, 1959); G. Perry and A. Aldridge, *The Penguin Book of Comics* (Harmondsworth, England, 1967); K. M. Wolf and Marjorie Fiske, "The Children Talk About Comics," in P. F. Lazarsfeld and F. N. Stanton, eds., *Communications Research 1948–1949* (New York, 1949), pp. 3 ff.; D. M. White and R. H. Abel, ed., *The Funnies: An American Idiom* (New York, 1963).
21. *Television in the Lives of Our Children* (Stanford, California, 1961), pp. 146 ff.
22. See R. König, ed., *Soziologie* (Frankfurt, 1967), pp. 290 ff.
23. E. Fromm, *Man for Himself* (New York, 1947).
24. D. Riesman et al., *Die einsame Masse* (Hamburg, 1958), original edition, *The Lonely Crowd* (New Haven, Conn., 1950).
25. E. H. Erikson, "The Problem of Ego Identity," *Journal of the American Psychoanalytic Association* 4, no. 1 (1956): 58 ff.
26. William F. Ogburn, *On Culture and Social Change, Selected Papers*, ed. Otis D. Duncan (Chicago and London, 1964), p. 108.
27. M. O'Donoghue and F. Springer, *The Adventures of Phoebe Zeit-Geist* (New York, 1968).
28. Thus in the preview to *Perry*, No. 42.
29. P. F. Drucker, *The Age of Discontinuity* (London, 1969), p. 72.

30. On this topic, see remarks by A. Toffler, *Der Zukunftsschock* (Berne, Munich, and Vienna, 1970), original edition, *Future Shock*, New York, 1970).
31. T. Parsons, *The Social System* (Glencoe, Illinois, 1951), p. 39.
32. Compare R. König, ed., *Soziologie*, p. 143.
33. On this topic, see my *Ketzereien eines Soziologen* (Vienna and Düsseldorf, 1965), pp. 166 ff.
34. The following summary makes use of preliminary studies carried out by Dipl. Volkswirt R. Darius.
35. Drucker, *Age of Discontinuity*, p. 25.
36. In this connection, see J. Kishida, "Dynamic Balance in Political Innovation"; J. Hayashi and K. Yamada, "Methodological Approach to the Multi-Channel-Society." Mimeographed contributions to the International Future Research Conference, Kyoto, 1970.
37. D. Lerner, in D. Lerner and W. Schramm, eds., *Communication and Change in the Developing Countries* (Honolulu, 1967), p. 317.

Zdenko Škreb

LITTÉRATURE ENGAGÉE

RECENTLY YUGOSLAVIA HAS MADE TWO SUBSTANTIAL CONTRIBUTIONS toward the precise definition of the concept of "littérature engagée," a term used in both literary history and literary theory. From 9 to 12 October 1970, in Herceg Novi, the attractive spa on the southern Adriatic, the Beograd Institut za književnost i umetnost (Institute for Literature and Art) held a symposium on problems of Marxist literary criticism. On that occasion the Zagreb Romanist Predrag Matvejević read an exhaustive and very critical paper on the subject of Sartre's interpretation of "engagement." Though copies of the paper were distributed to the participants, it has not yet been published. But recently a large-scale study by Matvejević, published by Nizet in Paris, came off the presses. In *La poésie de circonstance*,[1] "littérature engagée" is subjected to a much more probing scrutiny.

The first stumbling block in the way of a more precise definition of the concept in question is correctly shown by Matvejević to be an insufficient limitation of the concept's content, a vagueness and ambiguity of usage[2]—"although in the course of the last few decades this concept turns up, as it were, at every step, as a technical term both in philosophy and in literary theory; in fact, it crops up even outside philosophy and literature in the narrow sense. . . ." Matvejević here refers to André Lalande's *Vocabulaire technique et critique de la philosophie* (Paris, numerous editions) which, under the definitions of *engagement* and *engagé*, declares the term to be a modish expression, the meaning of which has to be separately determined for each author who uses it.

The fashion seems to have spread from France even before the start of the Second World War, so that the expression was often taken over into other languages as a technical term in its original version. Matvejević refers to Adorno's essay "Engagement,"[3] where the German scholar unconditionally adopts the French expression. "The Italians," Matvejević further points out, "use vernacular technical terms—*impegno* and *letteratura impegnata*—alongside the French terms, while English-language usage often substitutes the expression *commitment*." He stresses the same problem in his book: "Le mot *engagement*, quoique fort courant dans la terminologie littéraire contemporaine, ne semble jusqu'à présent guère avoir été défini de façon satisfaisante" or "The word *engagement*, though extremely common in contemporary literary terminology, does not until now seem to have been adequately defined."[4]

The second stumbling block is the subordination of committed literature to a more comprehensive generic term; for Matvejević this generic term is *poésie de circonstance*, occasional poetry. In this, the Romanist Matvejević follows French usage, where *poésie engagée* is primarily "prise . . . pour une catégorie de la poésie de circonstance" or "seen . . . as a category of occasional poetry" (*PC*, p. 75). For it was the French Résistance and its writings which put the question of committed literature on the docket around 1945 (*PC*, pp. 75–79). There were those who responded by denouncing this poésie engagée as a betrayal of the meaning and nature of poetry. In an interview granted at the beginning of December 1945, André Breton grudgingly admitted it as "poésie de circonstance née de la guerre" or "occasional verse born of war," though he was in no way prepared to grant it "la vrai valeur poétique" or "genuine poetic worth" (*PC*, pp. 76, 77). The literary scholar Gaétan Picon, in his work *Panorama de la nouvelle littérature française* (Paris, 1960), renders a much more favorable verdict in that he absolutely equates *poésie de circonstance* and *poésie engagée* as synonymous. It is deeply significant that Paul Eluard, caught in this intramural French literary quarrel, which was contested with considerable vehemence, felt impelled to bolster his defense of *poésie de circonstance* by referring to Goethe, the great early promoter of occasional poetry.[5] But this reference introduces hopeless confusion into the definition of the term *occasional poetry*— a confusion not fully mastered by Matvejević. In his contribution to the encyclopedia (2d ed., vol. 1, Berlin, 1958, pp. 547–49), Rudolf Haller was aware of the confusion but did not have the courage to do away with it; rather, he promoted an additional confusion. "The concept *occasional poetry* encompasses poetic works," Haller instructs the reader, "which owe their existence to certain incidents from real life. In German literature the essential distinction is made by determining whether the work was created *for* a particular occasion or purpose—a wedding, an anniversary—or grew *out of* a particular personal occasion, out of the after effects of an 'experience' in the poet's creative imagination. . . . In the latter case—subjective occasional poetry in the Goethean sense—the connection between theme and object is less transparent and more complex, since an 'occasion' as a unique moment in his life has released in the poet inner feelings that become immortalized in his work. But in both cases we are dealing with a particularly close relationship between the poet and the given real-life situation." In the first instance, on the other hand, "we are dealing with functional and applied art; the particular objective occasion, then, directly gives rise to the choice of the poetic theme and subject matter. . . . In the narrower sense, the term *occasional poetry* refers only to poems meant in celebration of particular events, and dated whenever possible." But if Haller on the one hand includes in his definition occasional poetry in the Goethean sense and proves it by it, on the other hand, and without entering into the question more closely, he makes the assertion that, "as applied art," occasional poetry cannot be "distinguished from the equally functional poetry of a political, satirical-moral, or generally didactic nature." Thus the encyclopedia contains additional entries under headings for contemplative, instructive, political, patriotic, and tendentious poetry. Though the poetry of the French Résistance is designated as *poésie de circonstance* by French literary critics and, depending on the individual's orientation, is denounced or praised, it remains excluded from Haller's definition of occasional poetry. It would surely have to be assigned to political poetry, which, according to H. Heckel's argument,[6] includes "in its broader sense all poetic works which help in paving the way for bringing about any change in public conditions or which accompany such a change in a supportive or oppositional role." But faced with such a broad definition, Heckel finds the boundary with patriotic poetry too fluid, and he restricts political poetry to social poetry in a broader sense, to the "participation of poetry in the struggles of domestic political forces for a new order within the domestic balance of power . . . for the settlement of oppressive social differences, etc." Even so, he believes, "the boundary with patriotic poetry . . . frequently [remains] in flux." In his historical presentation of German political poetry, Heckel also uses the term "tendency"; but J. Wiegand[7] largely sees the term "tendentious poetry" as a negative value concept, to which clings the accusation of artistic inferiority. He too is forced to admit that "it is difficult to draw the boundaries."

Matvejević refuses to limit himself to a definition (*PC*, p. 85); not only do definitions of occasional poetry change from period to period and from one literature to another, he believes, but there are even contradictory definitions within the same period and the same literature. His aim is to characterize those literary works that fall within his concept of occasional poetry; three categories of occasional poetry may be roughly distinguished (*PC*, pp. 85–86):

1. occasional poetry (*poésie de circonstance*) concurring with varying ceremonies (generally of a *public* nature, but sometimes *private*)
2. occasional poetry that is called committed (most often referring to sociohistorical facts)
3. occasional poetry that celebrates private or subjective events (in the sense of Goethe's term *Gelegenheitgedicht*)

According to Matvejević, all occasional poetry can be most tellingly characterized by adding the phrase, "on the occasion of." But he is immediately forced to admit that as a rule, "on the occasion of" sets the limits much more firmly in his first category of occasional poetry, the *poésie de circonstance cérémonielle*, than in the third category—occasional poetry in the sense given it by Goethe (*PC*, p. 89). On the whole, he believes, it is almost impossible to set limits that would unequivocally justify designating certain works as occasional.

In his treatment of occasional poetry (*Aesthetics*, Part 1, chapter 3, B, II, 2c) Hegel takes his point of departure from the "particular situation which can be treated" by the poet "as a purely external, more or less particular incident" which furnishes the present occasion—"also in relation to external circumstances, festivities, victories, and the like." But Hegel saw very clearly that such a situation "encompasses the most profound contradictions. . . . In a lyrical situation of this kind, it is true that on the one hand any objective state, any activity related to the external world, can come to light, but on the other hand it can just as easily happen that the mind as such retreats into itself, into its internal mood removed from all other external relations, and that it can take its occasion from the inwardness of its states and perceptions." Thus in the same work (Part III, Section 3, chapter 3, A, 2b) Hegel is subsequently led to the sound conclusion that "in a broader sense of the word, most poetic works could be given this label." Hegel, however, separates from it the "narrower, specific meaning" that applies to "works which owe their origin in the present to some event to whose exaltation, embellishment, and commemoration they are explicitly dedicated." Hegel, too, refers to Goethe, who "took many lyrical situations of this sort for his material; indeed," he continues, "using the broader meaning, one could apply the name of occasional poem even to his *Werther*." After all, Goethe himself referred to "lyrical situations" as sources of his poetry; according to Eckermann, on 18 September 1823, he declared: "All my poems are occasional poems, they are stimulated by reality and are anchored in it." Goethe established the genesis of a poem out of a lyrical situation almost as a requirement: "They must," he stated on the same occasion, "all be occasional poems; that is to say, reality must furnish the instance and the material for them." Goethe's admission and demand, formulated as part of the struggle against philosophizing poetry, have been highly overrated in the theory of occasional poetry. On the one hand, Goethe himself was well aware of the discrepancy between the significance of the causative lyrical situation and the significance of the "occasional poem" that arose from it. He reported to Eckermann on 8 April 1829 that the king of Bavaria had wanted Goethe to tell him the basic "lyrical situations" underlying the *Roman Elegies*, but Goethe had replied: "It is seldom realized that the poet is generally able to make something good out of minimal occasions." On the other hand, he defined narrowly the poetry which, following his requirement, was occasioned by reality. This is shown both by his passionate diatribe before Eckermann at the beginning of March 1832—"Let us take care . . . lest we say that politics *is* poetry or that it is a suitable subject for the poet"—and by his efforts to justify his deep admiration for Béranger against his theoretical views. (For example, in the conversations with Eckermann of 2 April 1829, 4 May 1827, 14 March 1830, and 2 May 1831, "Béranger . . . never served a party.")

The blatantly obvious conclusion has never been drawn: occasional poetry in the "narrower, limited meaning" (Hegel), as "functional and applied art" (Haller), and occasional poetry "in the sense given to the expression by Goethe" are two concepts of a fundamentally different order and must not be joined under the same designation. Since they belong to two different areas of scholarship, they show no common traits and can be neither compared nor measured against each other. The first concept refers to poetic themes and belongs to the realm of poetics; the second belongs to the literary creative process and therefore has its roots in the psychology of literary creation. If we intend to take seriously Adolf Beiss' completely justified, precisely formulated statement—"Not the psychology of creativity but the poetics of the work itself is . . . the noblest aim of contemporary literary scholarship"[8]—then Goethe's concept of occasional poetry must be taken out of the area of literary theory, of poetics, and incorporated into the realm of literary history. In such a case, the relevant passage in Haller would also have to be deleted, and Matvejević's third category would have to be omitted. For Hegel saw, absolutely correctly, and clearly stated that in this sense—that is, in Goethe's sense—"most poetic works could be given this label"; applied in this way, the term ceases to be a characterizing criterion. Thus *one* stumbling block would be put aside.

The same fate can easily befall a second one if we are willing to work our way through to the insight that in a certain sense all literature is *engagé*, that engagement is part of the essence of all poetry. How could language raise itself to the summit of all its efforts, how could it create a literary work removed from immediate needs, rounded off and closed off in itself, if this literary work does not mean an enthusiastic witness for something, and therefore at the same time an equally crucial renunciation of something?[9] This approach may be clarified by the example of love poetry.

If a love poem had no purpose beyond announcing that some Jack is physically attracted to some Jill and strives for a more or less spiritualized union with her, it would contain about as much poetry as a rhymed weather report or safety regulation. But every love poem is, beyond that statement, a symbolic confession. Of what? Heine gave extremely convincing testimony on this point:

> Sag mir, wer einst die Uhren erfund,
> Die Zeitabteilung, Minuten und Stund?
> Das war ein frierend trauriger Mann.
> Er sass in der Winternacht und sann,
> Und zählte der Mäuschen heimliches Quicken
> Und des Holzwurms ebenmässiges Picken.
>
> Sag mir, wer einst das Küssen erfund?
> Das war ein glühend glücklicher Mund;
> Er küsste und dachte nichts dabei.
> Es war im schönen Monat Mai,
> Die Blumen sind aus der Erde gesprungen,
> Die Sonne lachte, die Vögel sungen.[10]

There are two worlds, says Heine's lyric: the world of cold, calculating reason and the world of loving devotion to something that transcends all personal interests. Every love poem, by virtue of its commonly comprehended symbolism of the sexual love relationship, is a rapturous confession of loving devotion to suprapersonal values. A paean to love in this sense is Hölderlin's *Hyperion*. "How powerless is man's most earnest effort against the omnipotence of unanimous enthusiasm," the poem reads—and continues: "Yes! Man is a sun, all-loving, all-transfiguring when he loves; and if he does not love, he is a dark habitation, where a smoking little lamp burns on."

All poetry, by virtue of the symbolic manner of organization and expression as its most profound essence, is in a certain sense *engagé*. But how are we to define *littérature engagée* in its "narrower, particular meaning"? Is it in fact "political poetry," poetry related to "socio-historical facts"? Here we must remove still another stumbling block: in a certain wider sense, all poetry is related to politics. No one has expressed this insight more magnificently, more powerfully, and more convincingly than Thomas Mann. In his *Lotte in Weimar*, toward the end of the sixth chapter, devoted to Goethe's son, he has young Goethe say: "Politics, for its part, is not something isolated; rather, it has a hundred references with which it shapes an inseparable whole. It is contained in and tied to everything else, the moral, the aesthetic, the seemingly purely intellectual and philosophical; happy the times when, all unconscious, it remains in a state of controlled innocence, when nothing and no one beyond its most familial adepts speaks its language. In such presumptively unpolitical periods—I would like to call them periods of political latency—it is possible to love and admire beauty freely and independently of politics, with which it stands in silent but inviolable equivalence. Unhappily it is not our lot to live in such a gentle time, which bestows tolerance. Our time has an acute eye, of inexorable clarity, and in each thing, each expression of human nature, each example of beauty it uncovers and reveals the politics inherent in it." Using Thomas Mann's wording, we might define the literary quarrel that broke out in France after 1945, mentioned above, as a struggle, carried on in the name of political latency made absolute, against a form of literature in which its inherent politics is discovered and revealed.

Thus it was precisely a struggle against literature's political latency that aroused and put on the agenda the whole complex of concepts of *engagement*. While the party of political latency hurled anathema at *littérature de circonstance* (or *engagée*), requirements had been set much earlier of how literature had to be—and that was *engagée*: commitment as a demand. This point of view has been insufficiently taken into account until now by scholars. On the one hand, the existing body of literature can be studied for its essential traits, and this study can lead to views about its artistic intentions and standards of value, along with, whenever possible, the establishment of technical terms to characterize the homogeneity of the existing works. On the other hand, without regard for the literary tradition, it is possible to postulate requirements along a normative literary or extraliterary standpoint that will establish regulations for future literature, according to which alone can the value of such rules be determined. This is, then, a resurrection of the archenemy of every originality in literary creativity—normative aesthetics. However it is interpreted, Lenin's concept of *partiynost* (partisanship) seems to have been the first resounding trumpet call in this direction; about 1930 it was succeeded by the official doctrine of social realism—indeed, by "realism" as the only style congruent with the present day, as the only style developed to the highest stage in the course of literary development. But Jean-Paul Sartre, who was free from all governmental or party coercion, also raised the demand for commitment in his broad study, *Qu'est-ce que la littérature,* now *Situations II* (Paris, 1948), as well as in the publication announcement of his magazine, *Les Temps modernes.* The announcement consists of a bitter accusation leveled at bourgeois literature, at its "political latency"; a shared social irresponsibility, Sartre claimed, unites pure science and art for art's sake (*Situations II,* p. 10). But the writer cannot escape his time, he remains compromised by it, "no matter how far he may withdraw in his flight from it. Each of his words, but also every silence, resonates widely. Since by our very existence we have an effect on our time, let us decide to exert this influence in reality" (*Situations II,* p. 13). But Sartre emphatically stresses one decisive restriction: "Pas politiquement . . . elle [la poésie] ne servira aucun parti"— "Not in the political sense . . . poetry will serve no party" (*Situations II,* p. 16). Thus today's most significant advocate of literary commitment emphasizes as forcibly as possible that *littérature engagée* must on no account be political literature.

What, then, are *littérature engagée* and *engagement?* Here Sartre expresses a profound insight, one that ought to become the common property of literary scholarship: it is important for a writer "que chaque . . . forme de sa vie psychique, manifeste sa position sociale"— "that each . . . expression of his intellectual life declare his stand on social matters" (*Situations II,* p. 22). Let us now try to arrive at a definition: the term *littérature engagée* may properly be applied to a form of literature which gives expression to the author's social stance, which is inherent in any literature. Of course this is a stance which is informed about all oppression and exploitation in the world, about all the misery and affliction of the deprived and disenfranchised, and which, by its mere stand, calls for crucial social change. For, as Sartre correctly points out, "la littérature est par essence prise de position"—"by its nature literature is commitment, the taking of a stand" (*Situations II*, p. 300).

We can agree without reservations to Sartre's theoretical observations—but even he, though without suggesting governmental enforcement or police coercion, claims engagement as a normative requirement. It cannot, therefore, be avoided that he become enmeshed in substantial contradictions in the course of his practical application of commitment. The question arises whether commitment contains all other values or whether it is one value among others, with which it might even clash at times. True, Sartre maintains "que dans la 'littérature engagée,' l'engagement ne doit, en aucun cas, faire oublier la littérature—"that in 'committed literature' the commitment must never let us forget the literature" (*Situations II*, p. 30). But on the preceding page it is given as a basic principle of the new magazine's planned reviewing policy that less was to be written about outstanding books, which tell us nothing new about our own time, and more about mediocre works, which by their very mediocrity present revelations. Commitment and literary worth are contrasted—but of what does the latter consist if commitment or *prise de position* is in the nature of all literature, but literary worth, on the other hand, is possible even without this particular commitment? The extent of this confusion in Sartre's thinking is shown by his own practical application of the concept of commitment. For anyone who makes demands on literature is led with logical inevitability to assigning the highest literary value to the literary traits he himself has called for: thus a literary descriptive concept is transformed into a literary value judgment. Thereupon any critic proceeding along these lines will presumably not hesitate to interpret this value judgment as an absolute and to apply it no longer to description but to evaluation. Thus, for example, Sartre talks of Mallarmé's "total commitment." But this robs the expression of its ability to act as a descriptive category for literary scholarship.

If we struggle through to the idea that genuine literary scholarship must ignore all requirements and be used only for understanding, we will logically deny any value to the concept *littérature engagée* and apply it only in the sense of the definition given above. But then the same logical consistency will lead us to simply sever the umbilical cord that seems to connect it with occasional poetry. Indeed, Sartre propagates a profound truth: every work of literature is commitment, *prise de position*; an author's every word and every silence proclaim it; we will have to introduce a new section into literary scholarship— the descriptive, (but by no means evaluative!) section dealing with literature's sociohistorical commitment—and this is where the concept *littérature engagée* in the sense outlined above will find its proper place. The concept of "stance and essential position," which Herbert Cysarz very happily introduced into his description of contemplative poetry,[11] is useful here. Accordingly, the concept *littérature engagée* may designate—but never as a value concept!—the stance and essential position of literature in the sociohistorical sense. We must also struggle through to the view that the historical significance of a literary work—which is of necessity written in a historically determined language and which at a given historical moment addresses an audience determined by language and by the historical moment— need not coincide, and for the most part does not coincide, with its universal literary significance, which can be measured against the highest creations of literature of all ages and people. Its literature did a great service for the French Résistance; at that historical moment, of course, Mallarmé could not hope to meet with a similar response; literary history will make careful note of this fact but will also be careful not to draw value judgments from it. That such judgments are on another plane is demonstrated by the contradictions in which Sartre becomes entangled when he contrasts excellent and mediocre books and grants the latter the priority of his interest, and again when he speaks of Mallarmé's total commitment. The same context leads to the most embarrassing overevaluations of literary creations in the literary historical scholarship of the smaller nations; unfortunately German literary historical scholarship is also not free from this error.

But what in the end remains of occasional poetry if Matvejević's three categories are demolished one by one? On this question Matvejević himself seems to have indicated the correct procedure by making a distinction which he calls a very important one: "An *occasional* work . . . may be written (a) *with regard to* an event which is familiar or fixed in advance by some convention; (b) *with reference to* deeds accomplished in some more or less distant past and having some relationship to the present time" (*PC*, p. 90). Following this distinction, Matvejević himself noted that the *"poésie de circonstance au sens strict du terme"* can, as a rule, be included in the first category. Thus he recommends that literary scholarship use the expression "occasional poetry" purely in this sense. Mallarmé's verse is instructive in this connection, as Matvejević points out (*PC*, p. 66): almost half his works are "vers de circonstance," and in the Pléiade critical edition they constitute a considerable section under this title; but they were not written for any outside commission, and the poet himself indignantly rejects any functional value of his poetry. But it would serve to muddle the issue if we equate this poetry with the historically fully attested genre, "ceremonial" occasional poetry as it is known in German literature "in the period from the baroque to the rococo."[12]

We should also bear in mind a further, older distinction, which today seems to have fallen into oblivion. In his *Geschichte der französischen Schriftsprache im Spiegel ihrer Entwicklung* (Heidelberg, 1913, p. 1), Karl Vossler differentiated between monumental and documentary literature: "The former works are *monumenta*, not *documenta*. The monument exists for its own sake, is its own document; it does not ask to be utilized but wishes to be honored, adored, viewed." Conversely, the oldest writings in the Romance vulgar languages can be described by the fact that "their nature is in no way monumental but explicitly documentary." Perhaps this distinction could introduce further clarification into the confusion that surrounds the term discussed in this essay; as soon as literature serves a purely documentary function, it may be called occasional literature; *littérature engagée* may take its place in either category. But even this distinction cannot be used to derive a value judgment: that strictly documentary literature can grow to universal monumentality is shown by the constant efforts of Pindar in this context.

[Translated from the German by Ruth Hein]

Notes

1. In the French book, the author's Croatian surname is transliterated quite inaccurately: Matvejevitch. In French spelling, *j* corresponds to the Croatian *ž*; but in this instance the Croatian *j* should have been transliterated by a *y*.

It is unfortunate that the author's name will now enter the literature of the field in this distorted form.

2. In his paper, pp. 3–4.
3. In *Noten zur Literatur III* (Frankfurt am Main, Suhrkamp, 1965), pp. 109 ff.
4. *La poésie de circonstance* (*PC*), p. 110.
5. Matvejević dealt at length and with great knowledgeability with the concept of occasional poetry in Goethe, in Hegel's *Aesthetics*, in Schiller, and among the Romantics. See *PC*, pp. 42–49.
6. *Reallexikon*, vol. 2 (Berlin, 1926), pp. 711–18.
7. In *Reallexikon*, vol. 3 (Berlin, 1928–1929), pp. 346–451.
8. In "Nexus und Motive," *Deutsche Vierteljahrsschrift für Literaturwissenschaft und Geistespeschichte* 36 (1962): 240.
9. Compare Adorno, "Engagement," p. 134: "Even in the most sublimated work of art there is a hidden 'It should be different.' But the moment of wishing is communicated by nothing but the form of the work, the crystallization of which becomes a trope for something else, which ought to be."
10. "Tell me who first invented clocks, time divisions, minutes, and hours. It was a chilly, grieving man. He sat through a winter's night and pondered, and counted the mice's secret squeaking and the woodworm's regular ticking. Tell me who first invented kissing. It was a radiant, happy mouth; it kissed and did not worry. It was in the merry month of May, the flowers sprang from the earth, the sun smiled down, the birds were singing."
11. In *Reallexikon*, 3d ed., vol. 1 (Berlin, 1958), p. 526.
12. Haller, *Reallexikon*, 1:546.

METACRITICAL SYNTHESIS

Peter Brang

SOCIOLOGICAL METHODS
IN TWENTIETH-CENTURY
RUSSIAN LITERARY CRITICISM

SINCE ITS BEGINNINGS UNDER PETER THE GREAT, CONTEMPORARY RUSSIAN literature has been engaged in an especially tense relationship with society. It seems natural, therefore, that in Russia literary criticism, both academic and popular, relatively early turned its attention to problems of the sociology of literature. Thus the work of Aleksandr Pushkin (1799–1837) reveals many sensitive utterances pertaining to the questions of the relationship of literature and society, in spite of the fact that for a number of generations this poet was a symbol of art for art's sake. But even older writers—such as Karamzin and Zhukovsky—and younger ones—such as Gogol, Turgenev, Dostoevsky, and Tolstoy—were always concerned with socioliterary problems, not to mention the "revolutionary" critics: Belinsky, Chernyshevsky, Dobroliubov, and Pisarev.[1]

An equally lively interest in the connections between literature and society characterizes Russian academic literary criticism of the late nineteenth century. After 1880 the so-called Cultural-Historical school reigned almost unchallenged in this area; its adherents held it to be the purpose of literary criticism "to illuminate the historical development of literature, as well as the spiritual and moral development of society, to which literature gave expression." They were convinced that the literature of any period can be truly understood only after one "has become familiar first of all with the social and national life of the country and with the socioeconomic system that underlies this system." This formulation of the views of this school was made by one of its outstanding exponents, D. N. Ovsianiko-Kulikovsky in the introduction to the five-volume *History of Russian Literature in the Nineteenth Century* (1908–1912). The compilers of this monumental work then went "from a historical sketch of the social and political setting to a description of the spiritual life of society in the respective period, and from there to a representation of the literary phenomena (directions, schools, problems, devices) in their historical development."[2] Besides the study of the respective "literary personalities that are most important or most characteristic of the period," the adherents of the Cultural-Historical school also called for research into popular literature. It is true, however, that now and then their interest was deflected rather too sharply into cultural and intellectual history, and in this effort they regarded literary works as immediate testimony of the latter in a way that today seems somewhat naive, even as they tended to overlook the specifically aesthetic nature of literature.

The Cultural-Historical school was strongly influenced by Taine's theory of milieu, as well as by Taine's student, E. Hennequin (1858–1888) and his aesthopsychological method, by which he wanted to investigate, not so much the influence of society on art, as the effect of art on society, because the nature of the reception of a work of art allows conclusions concerning the audience. A similar addition to and emendation of Taine's theory by way of studies in the history of audience reaction was written even before Hennequin by the Russian historian and sociologist N. I. Kareev.[3]

Hennequin's theories[4] stimulated the Russian bibliographer N. A. Rubakin (1862–1946) to undertake his numerous studies in audience psychology, with which he hoped to establish a "psychology of literary influence"[5] from 1895 onward. But Hennequin's postulates were especially congenial to the efforts of the Psychological school of Russian literary scholarship. Taking as its starting point certain theoretical literary contributions by the linguist and psychologist A. A. Potebnya (1835–1891), after the turn of the century this school took its place alongside the Cultural-Historical school, and displacing the latter to second place, it remained for several years the most important direction for research, until in its turn it was replaced by the Formalist school in 1916. In the series "Questions of the Theory and Psychology of Creativity"[6] and in monographs, Potebnya's followers (A. G. Gornfel'd, I. I. Glivenko, A. I. Beletsky, and others) investigated problems of reception and influence of the literary work. In his book *On the Interpretation of the Work of Art*[7] in 1912, A. G. Gornfel'd (1867–1941) suggested that, along with the genealogy of a work of art, its "biography" be studied as well; in 1922 A. I. Beletsky outlined the tasks of audience research,[8] and in 1927 he set up a "theory of audience response."[9]

It is characteristic of the Russian public's interest in socioliterary aspects that Frenchman M. Guyau (1854–1888) gained great influence in Russia, with his major work, *L'Art au point de vue sociologique*, which attempted to reconcile the concepts of Taine and Hennequin; the work influenced L. N. Tolstoy as well as M. Gorky and his friend, the populist critic L. E. Obolensky (1845–1906), who is today unjustly forgotten. The work was translated into Russian as early as 1891, two years after its original publication, just as Western European socioliterary classics generally found a Russian translator remarkably swiftly.[10]

Though the interest in socioliterary research was particularly lively in Russia from the beginning of the nineteenth century onward, the advent of Marxism in the one-time czarist empire and Marxism's subsequent rule were the chief causes of the unusually numerous discussions and applications of sociological methods in contemporary Russian literary scholarship.

True, the classics of "Marxism-Leninism" paid only scant attention to questions of art; nor did they ever seriously attempt to create a closed system of Marxist literary perspective.[11] They only formulated the "general methodological assumptions" of Marxist literary scholarship. Soviet literary scholarship was therefore faced with the difficult task of a "concrete application of the new methodology and the solution of a series of complicated theoretical problems."[12] The necessity for working out a methodology of literary scholarship imbued with specifically Marxist (and therefore in a certain sense sociological) principles was the result of the Marxist doctrine that every aspect of cultural life is to be seen as a phenomenon of the Marxist superstructure. A non-Marxist literary scholarship justifies a plurality of methods by the complexity of its subject matter and by its encapsulation in a highly diverse system of relationships and is aware of the fact that the various methods are not equally applicable to all works, that a particular method may prove fruitful for one work and be of no use to another,[13] in contrast to a Marxist literary interpretation, which may legitimize only one method: the Marxist one. Marxist interpretation is therefore unable to conceive of literary sociology as an auxiliary discipline of literary scholarship that arises more or less independently from reflection and observation of the relationships between literature and society. Logical Marxist thinking sees methodological pluralism as approaching agnosticism,[14] it appears "helpless";[15] the attempt to let the particularity of the subject matter determine the method in each case is open to the objection of "positivism."[16] The extent to which this dependence on "general methodological assumptions"—where even a working hypothetical isolation of particular phenomena and methods is suspect—complicates the work of socioliterary research is also made clear by the most recent efforts to revive a Soviet literary sociology. It is therefore the Soviet researchers seriously interested in socioliterary problems who in particular plead of late for methodological diversification. Thus only recently M. Bakhtin stated that literature was too complicated and too variously faceted a phenomenon and that literary scholarship was too new an area of research to allow mention of any "only true method" in literary scholarship.[17]

G. V. PLEKHANOV

The first attempt at creating a Marxist theory of art was undertaken by G. V. Plekhanov (1856–1918), the first significant Russian theorist of Marxism. Though today in the Soviet Union he is no longer considered "the founder of Marxist literary scholarship," a reputation he retained as late as the early 1930s, he is still held to be "one of the founders of the Marxist sociology of art."[18] In an analogy with Darwinism, Plekhanov sees it as a biological, naturally given fact that man "can have aesthetic feelings and concepts." The transition from possibility to actuality, however, is brought about, in his thinking, by environmental conditions; they explain why a particular social being (a particular society, a particular nation, a particular class) is possessed of just this aesthetic preference and not another. It is therefore the task of Marxist sociological literary criticism to establish the determination of aesthetic forms and of taste through the respective social conditions. The principles of such a form of criticism were enunciated most clearly by Plekhanov in the foreword to the third edition of the anthology *Twenty Years*. Like Belinsky in his day, Plekhanov, too, appropriates Hegel's thesis that the subject of art is identical with that of philosophy; just as the philosopher sees the truth in concepts, so the artist apprehends it in forms. While Belinsky asked that the literary critic translate the ideas expressed in the work from the language of art—which he defined as "thinking in images"—into that of philosophy, Plekhanov, as a follower of historical materialism, considered it the critic's first task to translate the idea of a particular work of art from the language of art into that of sociology "in order to find that which can be designated as the sociological equivalent of a particular literary phenomenon." Plekhanov, after all, saw art as "the expression of the strivings and the condition of a given society."

In fact, in his critical writings Plekhanov tried to establish the social determination of artistic development; in doing so, he referred —although with certain reservations—to non-Marxist "sociologists of literature" such as Madame de Staël, Guizot, Taine, and Brunetière. He gave an excellent example of his sort of conception of art in his treatise *French Dramatic Literature and French Painting of the Eighteenth Century from the Standpoint of Sociology* (1905), where he established the dependence of French drama and painting for their subject matter and theme on the social structure. In this work Plekhanov tried also to accomplish what he considered—again in connection with Belinsky—as the second task of "materialistic" critics: to trace the idea of the work of art to its concrete manifestation, that is, "letting an analysis of the artistic values of the work of art follow on the appreciation of the idea." True, Plekhanov had some difficulty in proving the necessity of such an aesthetic analysis; for him, it follows from his assumption of the dependence of even the forms of art on social conditions and on the conceptions reigning in the society. For Plekhanov, aesthetic analysis is in the nature of a corrective: "The establishment of the sociological equivalent of any literary work of art" would "remain incomplete and therefore also imprecise if the critic were to give up the appreciation of its artistic values." Plekhanov's sequence of sociological-ideological interpretation and subsequent examination of the " 'living garment' of ideology" by the critic was to play an important role again in the 1920s, during discussions concerning the usefulness of a Formalist approach to a Marxist understanding of literature. But it now seems that what Plekhanov was able to offer as concrete examples of sociological determination of artistic form was rather meager. He scarcely goes

beyond general allusions to "refinement of taste" among the aristocracy and even goes astray in considering the three dramatic unities
of French classicism as its expression. Missing is even the slightest
attempt at clarifying the essential question of *which* formal elements
of the literary work are actually or potentially subject to social determination; this problem was subsequently the subject of lively
discussions among postrevolutionary literary scholars.

Plekhanov, however, takes an unequivocal position on the question
of the extent to which literature is dependent on the "superstructure"
or the "basis" of the conditions of production. In his opinion, the
immediate influence of economics on art and other "ideologies" is
very rarely observable, especially in the more advanced forms of
society. With this opinion Plekhanov becomes the advocate of the
so-called Superstructure school in Marxist literary criticism, which
had to defend itself, especially during the 1920s, against those critics
who insisted on literature's direct dependence on the economic basis.
Plekhanov's utterances on the problems of tendentious art also have
a special claim on our attention. He criticized Chernyshevsky, Dobroliubov, and Pisarev for their call for an "auxiliary" form of art; he
condemned Gorky's novel *The Mother* (1907) because of its tenden-
tiousness; and he also refused to accept the Leninist principle of
"partisanship," which was later to become one of the pillars of "socialist realism." As early as 1897 Plekhanov also advocated the view
that under certain conditions, primarily in times of political reaction—Plekhanov was thinking of Russia in the time of Nicholas I and
Pushkin—an art for art's sake was to be evaluated as a positive phenomenon: if the muses had turned into establishment muses, they
would have "demonstrated the most pronounced traits of degeneracy
and sacrificed much of their truthfulness, their power, and their
charm." Here Plekhanov evinces a prophetic insight into the further
development of Russian literature, as he does also when he makes
the warning remark that sociological interpretation, like any method,
is unfortunately capable of improper application.

Plekhanov was unable to construct a closed system of sociological
literary research: "he directed his attention to only a few writers—
those who could most easily testify to his Marxist credo in his analysis of them";[19] he simply planned "a systematic work on art";[20] his
theses are fragmented and full of contradictions. The commitment of
his aesthetic theoretical views was further restricted for Russian
Marxists quite soon thereafter by the fact that Lenin sharply dis-
tanced himself from Plekhanov's "Menshevism."

LITERARY SOCIOLOGY IN THE 1920s

General Assumptions

The fragmentary nature of Plekhanov's theoretical structure of literary sociology was one of the causes for that altogether hectic search for a "sociological" or, as the case may be, "Marxist" method of literary scholarship, which set in in Russia after the Revolution of 1917. The second important reason can be found in the fact that at the time, nonsociological Russian literary research in the guise of the Formalist school for the first time disposed of a relatively closed system of literary studies and serviceable methodological tools. Books and treatises concerning a sociological method of literary scholarship—and aesthetic scholarship in general—appeared in such quantity during the 1920s that the general "methodomania" can actually be considered a pathological phenomenon.[21] In 1924, Formalist B. M. Eichenbaum feared that the amount of talk about methodology could lead to Russia's being taken for a "predominantly methodological" country, which was, of course, not at all the case.[22] In 1927 U. Fokht even named the 1920s as the "scientific methodological period" in the development of Marxist-sociological literary criticism.[23] This methodological fervor was also based in large part on an extensive backlog, for the Russian literary historians of the nineteenth century were much less interested in questions of poetics or in an exact methodology of literary scholarship in general than was literary scholarship in, say, Western Europe.[24]

One of the crucial questions was whether a deductive or an inductive procedure was to be preferred in creating a socioliterary methodology. As early as the nineteenth century, Russian criticism frequently pointed out the dangers of an excess of deduction, using as an example H. Taine's milieu theory.[25] In 1910 N. A. Rubakin, in establishing his "bibliographic psychology," had claimed that its practices must be inductive, "not medievally deductive."[26] Even now several researchers realized the necessity of shoring up the socioliterary studies with as much factual material as possible, and this might be gained by examining and restructuring known findings and by systematically collecting new socioliterary facts. Many literary critics and researchers—for the most part those who thought they were defending a Marxist standpoint—did, however, engage excessively in deduction. "Instead of applying new interpretations," complained B. M. Eichenbaum in 1927, "to previously gained insights concerning the specifics of literary evolution (which, after all, not only do not contradict a genuine sociological conception but rather tend to support it), our literary sociologists have occupied themselves with the metaphysical search for the source and ground of literary development and literary forms." Eichenbaum referred to Engels' letter to Conrad Schmidt of 5 August 1890, with its famous warning against any renunciation of the study of facts, and he went on to declare that it was hardly surprising that the most recent socio-literary attempts not only did not bring about any new results, but even amounted to a step backward into "Cultural-Historical impressionism."

In a similar vein in 1928, Germanist and comparatist V. Zhirmun-sky, in the preface to the Russian translation of L. Schücking's *Soziologie der literarischen Geschmacksbildung*, expressed the view that the works of this German Anglicist were valuable just because the author, taking his point of departure from the general assumption of a social conditionality of literary taste, is primarily concerned with determining the specific nature of these conditions for each respective period on the basis of careful study of all sources and of a strongly philological form of criticism. "He carefully avoids drawing hasty impressionistic conclusions from the author's intellectual physiognomy about the social setting which gives expression to the society's ideas: this sort of sociological intuitivism unconsciously continues the methodological tradition of philosophical-aesthetic intuitivism which prevailed at the time of impressionist criticism (in our country, *Aikhenval'd* and *Gershenzon*)."[27] One of the younger Formalists, T. Grits, noted in 1928 in his criticism of the school of V. F. Perever-zev that it was impossible to create Marxist literary scholarship without the study of the literary and economic facts, and in support he cited the same passage from Engels' writings that Eichenbaum had used earlier.[28] Finally, Viktor Shklovsky represented a quite unortho-dox view: "When the facts contradict the theory—so much the better. It is something that we have made and that was not given to us for preservation."[29]

But several Marxist scholars also expressly warned against excessive deduction and neglect of the socioliterary facts. Thus in 1925 P. N. Medvedev, in his review of Sakulin's *Sotsiologicheskii metod v literatutovedenii*, considered any attempts at synthetic constructions to be premature,[30] while A. Zeitlin stressed the fact that directions of scholarly research could not be generated on demand and that a synthetic method was only conceivable as the culmination of herculean analytic work which, however, had just begun.[31]

Independent of the question of a more inductive or deductive methodology, various trends may be discerned in Soviet research prior to 1930: the Basis school, which sought to derive literary phenomena directly from the respective economic conditions (this group included V. Pereverzev's "eidological" or "organic" school); the Superstructure school, exemplified by Plekhanov, toward which the majority of Marxist literary critics leaned; the Sociological school of P. N. Sakulin, N. I. Efimov, and N. K. Piksanov; the *forsotstvo* and the socioliterary studies of the Formalists' scholarly program.

The Basis School

The Basis school came into being even before the October Revolution. Its members included V. M. Shuliatikov (1872–1912), a critic who was subsequently considered one of the founders of this method.[32] He derived the ideology directly from the conditions of production and class interests and therefore sought "to illuminate the dark corners of the realm of artistic ideologies" and the author's class interests by means of a "social-genetic analysis." Although Shuliatikov's theories were already severely criticized by Plekhanov and Lenin, new editions of his essays in literary criticism appeared as late as 1929;[33] their methodological influence is clearly evident in the writings of V. Pereverzev.

Among the members of the Basis school we may also consider V. M. Friche (1870–1929), who concerned himself primarily with the literature of the modern period in Western Europe.[34] As early as 1906, in his book *Literature and Capitalism*, he undertook the attempt to establish a connection between, for instance, the subtle color sense in Impressionist art with the increasing differentiation of goods being offered by capitalism, which was compelled to create ever new incentives to buy by shading the basic forms of objects (p. 72). His *Sociology of Art* (*Sotsiologiya iskusstva*), published in 1926, attempted—following Wilhelm Hausenstein's works, *Die Kunst und die Gesellschaft* or *Art and Society* (1916) and *Versuch einer Soziologie der bildenden Kunst* or *Attempt at a Sociology of Pictorial Art* (1913)—to grasp sociology of art as a "nomothetic science of one of the phenomena of the ideological superstructure above the economic basis," to establish the normal connections between particular social formations and particular artistic types, and simultaneously to prove the potential recurrence of certain artistic types in the presence of analogous social formations.

Another, somewhat more moderate, representative of this school is P. S. Kogan (1872–1933), who also began in 1900 to base his numerous studies of Russian and Western European literature on the view that "the dominant forms of economic life" directly determine the work of art. In this effort Kogan, like the critic G. Lelevich, was interested only in studying content: "Formal researches do not appeal to me much. I am not interested in Mayakovsky's syntax or in discussions of composition, tropes, attributes, or the like. I have never been able to understand why these boring questions must be probed in public." (Mayakovsky took his revenge for this disrespect for poetry by exposing Kogan to the ridicule of future readers in his anniversary poem for Pushkin.)

In sharp contrast to Kogan, the chief representative of the Basis school, V. F. Pereverzev, focused precisely on the problems of artistic form.[35] Pereverzev (1882–1968) first developed his theory of "personality as a passive expression of class" in his book on Dostoevsky, *Tvorchestvo Dostoevskogo* (Moscow, 1912), later in his monograph on Gogol, *Tvorchestvo Gogolia* (Moscow, 1914, 3d ed. 1928), and in his essays on Goncharov (1923). This theory saw Dante, Pushkin, Goethe, and Tolstoy as "ideologues" who were incapable of rising above their "class existence." The predominating conditions of production, in Pereverzev's opinion, directly determine the author's social-psychological stance, which finds its expression in the stylistic attitude of the work of literature, in its imagery (obraznost'). Therefore the "economic substructure" in which the individual work is rooted can be discovered by a careful examination of all structural elements, of the laws of "formal reference." Thus Pereverzev in his book on Gogol attempted to derive all of the particularity of Gogol's art—the hyperbolic style, the composition, the descriptions of nature, the characters' intellectual and spiritual poverty—no longer, as in earlier scholarship, from the particularity of his talent and his psyche, but from the fact that the writer was descended from Ukrainian minor nobility, in contrast to such representatives of the landed gentry and the court circle as Pushkin and Lermontov. Pereverzev's theses represent a strange mixture of postulates of early Formalism (demand for an aesthetic attitude based on close reading of texts) and certain of Plekhanov's views (art as "thinking in images," style as the equivalent of a class situation). Though a number of Marxist critics—primarily A. Lunacharsky, A. Zeitlin, and U. Fokht—announced their serious reservations as concerned Pereverzev, they were nevertheless already prepared to award him the palm. For, first, his way of literary observation seemed to break with the long traditional enlightenment thinking—that is, with the tendency to see the literary work only as a reflection of social development and to overlook the problems of form, as Kogan and Lelevich were still doing; second, it seemed to them that Pereverzev's "idological" method offered the possibility of countering the Formalist school with a kind of literary attitude that was both form-oriented and sociological. However, the objections raised by such as Zeitlin and Fokht against Pereverzev's method were very much on the level of principle. Fokht, for example, himself a student of Pereverzev, objected in 1927 that Pereverzev did not yet possess any "in any way elaborated system of literary concepts" and that no theory appeared in his work that could mediate between general methodological ideas and literary historical practice. Instead, Fokht went on, at bottom there were only isolated thoughts, scattered from case to case: "The organic direction of Marxist literary scholarship is not able at the present time to counter the poetics of the Formalist school with anything."[36] A. Zeitlin noted that the social psychology of the various classes had been too little researched as yet to allow investigations of Pereverzev's sort; in the meantime he consoled himself with the thought that this was an overall difficulty of Marxism.[37] Formalist V. Shklovsky finally pointed out that in his book on Gogol, Pereverzev wrongly projected the social structure of Greater Russia onto the Ukraine, where a nobility in the Central Russian sense did not exist.[38]

In spite of these critical voices, Pereverzev, together with his students, the "Pereverziantsy"—G. Pospelov, V. Sovsun, I. Bespalov, and A. Zonin—in 1928 managed to achieve a monopoly position when he was able to declare his method to be the only Marxist literary sociology in the anthology, *Literary Scholarship* (*Literaturovedeniye*). The debates occasioned by this volume, however, led to Pereverzev's downfall as early as the end of 1929 and the condemnation of his method as a "popular sociological" aberration. He was particularly criticized, as he had been by Fokht, for his rejection of any influence whatever of superstructural elements (that is, of ideologies) on literature; for his neglect of literary tradition, which is part of the superstructure; for the value-free "objectivist" approach, and the view that the author is unable to rise above the principles prescribed for him by his class setting. This would mean, for example, that proletarian writers are incapable of adequately depicting characters from the bourgeoisie while, conversely, writers with a bourgeois background did not possess the ability to portray proletarians convincingly. Such a thesis could not be accepted, if for no other reason, because nascent Soviet literature was heavily dependent on the collaboration of the so-called fellow travelers (*poputchiki*) from the middle classes, who sympathized with the new order. Finally, Pereverzev was bound to provoke criticism by his theory of "parallel lines"—that is, the view that the various forms of expression of the ideology, in each case directly depending on the basis, had no causal connection with one another, as if literature could effect no change whatever in the political system. In Pereverzev's view, no reciprocal connection existed between the rising of the Decembrists and Pushkin's political poetry, no matter how much both grew from the same roots.[39] Pereverzev's system had no room for the educative function of literature, which was to become so important for Soviet literary criticism beginning with the first Five-Year Plan. In 1938 Pereverzev was "subjected to illegal repression," and he was not rehabilitated until 1956.

The Superstructure School

Following Plekhanov, the Superstructure school was inclined to accept the dependence of literary development on ideology but only rarely on economic or social factors; it included such critics as A. Voronsky, the talented editor of the periodical *Krasnaia Nov'*, who fell into disgrace in 1927, as well as the Nekrasov scholar, V. Evgen'ev-Maksimov; A. Zeitlin; G. Gorbachev; V. L'vov-Rogachevsky; M. S. Grigor'ev; and L. D. Trotsky. A. Lunacharsky (1875–1933), the first People's Commissar of Education, can also most properly be considered in this group. Its representatives were prepared, as was Lunacharsky as early as 1914 in his *Foundations of a Positive Aesthetics (Osnovy pozitivnoi estetiki)*, to attribute a certain amount of significance for the development of art to the immanent "naturally given" developmental tendencies of art—or at least to admit that certain factors of art history that were originally socially determined could possibly influence the further development of art as newly self-contained elements of the "superstructure." Of course, in the opinion of M. S. Grigor'ev, economic conditions did have an effect on the form of the individual work; but they did not in each instance re-create the "literary milieu." The "formal construction," no matter how much it was determined by economic conditions, conflicted with the literary milieu created previously that might deform the "formal construction."[40] Trotsky and Voronsky used this tendency toward autonomy of the elements of the superstructure to try to explain the fact—disturbing to Karl Marx—that great works of art were able to enthrall even people belonging to later and "more highly developed" forms of society: the creations of genius possessed "a drive transcending class boundaries and contradictions." Not *because* but *although* Dante was a Florentine petit bourgeois of the thirteenth century, he is meaningful to the proletariat as well. If a worker reads Pushkin, it is not in order to find out how an owner of serfs and a courtier at the beginning of the nineteenth century greets the spring and bids farewell to autumn, but because the expression given to his mood by Pushkin is saturated with the artistic and psychological experiences of millenia.[41]

The Sociological School

During the 1920s the appellation "Sociological school" was generally applied to a group of scholars whose concept of literary sociology could most closely be compared to the non-Marxist views of the tasks of socioliterary research because they divided their attention more or less evenly among the various societal relationships of literature (sociology of content, of the author and the reader, and the like). This method was indebted to the prerevolutionary Cultural-Historical school, but under the influence of the successes of the "Formalists," its adherents placed much greater weight on the problems of the social genesis of literary forms and simultaneously tried to meet the demands of historical materialism. The school's most important representative was P. N. Sakulin (1868–1930). It was characteristic of the enormous methodological efforts after 1917 that he planned a series of fifteen monographs under the overall title *Literary Scholarship. Its Findings and Perspectives;* of this series, however, only a few volumes were completed: volume 10, *Theory of Literary Style* (Moscow, 1927), with a chapter on "The Dynamics and Sociology of Style"; volume 14, *Sociological Method in Literary Studies* (Moscow, 1927), 240 pages, and volume 15, *The Synthetic Structure of Literary History* (Moscow, 1925). In his earlier work, *Russian Litera-*

ture and Socialism (Moscow, 1922), Sakulin gave a survey of the reception of the socialist intellectual tradition by Russian writers and the reflection of this process in their works. In his book *Sotsiologicheskii metod*, this scholar, who from the outset of his scholarly activity was "a pioneer of the sociological method" (N. I. Efimov), attempted to create a system of literary sociology. In contrast to V. M. Friche, for example, who considered literary sociology as a "component of a more comprehensive field of study—that is, social and economic history,"[42] Sakulin called for "a sociology for literature." He basically acknowledged the Marxist principle of sociological determinism, but he never tired of stressing the fact that such determinism was limited by creative individuality and the specific laws of the literary life.

Like various earlier representatives of the Cultural-Historical school (R. V. Ivanov-Razuminik, S. A. Vengerov, D. Ovsianiko-Kulikovsky), as well as some Marxists (especially Y. Solov'ev), Sakulin, basing his views primarily on examples from Russian intellectual history, advocated the thesis of the "classlessness of the intelligentsia." To be sure, in an attenuated form, the members of an intellectual stratum, especially writers, he declared, were able to raise themselves above the interests of their own class. The heavy stress, evidenced here, on the individual factor in Sakulin's thinking was polemically directed against the denial or trivialization of this element among orthodox Marxists. The same holds true of Sakulin's remarks on the significance of the "literary milieu," the literary tradition in all its manifestations (for example, literary language), which might in part originally have been sociologically determined (p. 141), and the literary groups and schools. On the other hand, social developments might influence not only the changes in major stylistic periods, but also the primacy of various genres, lexicology, even at times peculiarities of rhythm, for example, in Futurist poetry (*Sociology of Form*, pp. 149–60). In such cases, however, in evaluating "causality," the "evolutionary" factor must also be constantly taken into account. As proof of the possibility in principle of immanent developments, Sakulin quotes from Guyau's *L'Art au point de vue sociologique*, specifically the chapter concerning triviality and how to avoid it (compare Pushkin's ridicule of "trivialized rhymes"). Interestingly enough, he places it alongside the "defamiliarization theory" of the Russian Formalists! As a whole, Sakulin must be counted among those scholars who advocated a combination of the

Sociological and Formalist methods; for this reason some critics (among them Mashinsky) placed him among the *forsotsy*.

Sakulin devoted a special chapter to literature as a "social factor," in particular to the problems of the sociology of audiences and the laws of literary effect. These questions were extremely acute in the 1920s because at that time there were heated discussions over the posture to be assumed by the new proletarian society toward the cultural tradition of the prerevolutionary period and especially toward the works of the Russian classic writers, most of whom were members of the nobility.[43]

Sakulin's book was in part vehemently attacked for its tendency toward "desocialization" of literature;[44] nevertheless, and aside from an exaggerated tendency to Formalization, it compares favorably with other works because, in creating a sociology of literature, it seeks to take into account the necessity for a combination of deductive and inductive methods.

Closely connected with Sakulin's work is the principal work of the second important representative of the Sociological school, the Smolensk professor N. I. Efimov (born 1889), already mentioned (see n. 35). The specific value of his *Sociology of Literature*, subtitled *Sketches toward a Theory of the Literary-Historical Process and toward Literary-Historical Methodology* (Smolensk, 1927, 220 pages), lies less in the attempt to establish a system of his own as in a quite comprehensive survey of pre-Marxist and non-Marxist Russian socio-literary thought.

V. Keltuiala (1867–1942), a Soviet critic also considered a member of the Sociological school, based his views on the work of Marxist historian M. Pokrovsky, who was considered the authority during the 1920s but was outlawed after 1932 and not rehabilitated until 1956. In 1911 Keltuiala began his investigations of Russian literature on certain postulates of historical materialism. In opposition to the Romantic views of the Russian populists (to whom today's Soviet folkloristic studies are also heavily indebted), Keltuiala maintained that the Russian folk epics (the *byliny*) were ultimately of courtly origin; they could be traced back to the literature of the ruling and culture-carrying stratum of Old Russia.[45] This view, which could be traced back to the very similar opinions of the literary historian Vsevolod Miller (1848–1913), brought Keltuiala already very close to H. Naumann's theory of the "lost cultural heritage" or the "oral transmission" theory of modern folklore studies. After the Revolution, Keltuiala turned his attention to methodological problems. In two monographs he postulated, somewhat like Sakulin, a separation between the immanent-formal and the causal-sociological study of literary works.[46] Both works are characterized by a kind of abstraction and schematization (it is no accident that his second book is subtitled *Schemes of Literary-Historical Perception*) which are in no way inferior to those of the Pereverzian school,[47] and it is for this reason that we can absolutely agree to classifying the later writings of Keltuiala among the works of the Popular Sociologists.

With more justification than in the case of Keltuiala, the Sociological school counts as one of its members N. K. Piksanov (1878–1969), who began in the early 1920s to set pragmatic tasks for Russian literary sociology. Piksanov suggested collecting data concerning the significance of the provincial cultural centers for Russian literature; the relationship between Moscow and St. Petersburg; the literary circles; censorship; literature's relationship to music and the plastic arts; and the role of the social environment in the development of literature. He also called for a study of the social conditions underlying the "cult of friendship" in Russian literature during the first quarter of the nineteenth century. It seemed to him that the exact clarification of each individual writer's social situation, rather than the "icons" still prevalent, was a precondition for realistic evaluations.[48] True, various orthodox Marxist critics had no very high opinion of these efforts by an "epigone of the Cultural-Historical school," as Piksanov was called; U. Fokht believed, disparagingly, that in this work the Cultural-Historical school was becoming a "micrological method."[49]

The *Forsotstvo*

The effort to combine Marxist-sociological and Formalist methods is not characteristic of the eidological school of Pereverzev alone. It is also evident among a number of Marxist-oriented critics who considered it necessary for Marxist literary studies to take over certain Formalist research methods. Among the Formalists as well there were attempts to build bridges to the sociological view of literature. This attempt at a synthesis engaged critics of very different attitudes, ranging "from a predominantly intrinsic approach to literature, made 'respectable' by a protective cover of Marxist terminology, to a 'sociologism' tempered by awareness of aesthetic considerations."[50] The leading representatives of this school were A. Zeitlin,[51] M. Levidov,[52] and A. Voznesensky.[53] But their ideas were also enthusiastically adopted by several adherents of the *Lef* or Left Front (1922–1929), led by Mayakovsky, especially Boris Arvatov (1896–1940),[54] Sergei Tret'-iakov, and Osip Brik. B. Yakubos'ky,[55] P. Medvedev (1891–1938),[56] and L. Trotsky may be considered among the sympathizers of this school. In the view of the *forsotsy*, the assumption of the methodological gains of Russian Formalism was "the only possible way for the Marxist methods [of literary criticism] to become scientific."[57] In contrast to Plekhanov, the *forsotsy* believed that the critic should first of all investigate and describe the work of art itself as "literary fact"; only then were the immanent structural investigations and causal-sociological explanations to follow.

An early critical stand on the efforts of the Formalist-Sociological school was taken by U. Fokht, a follower of Pereverzev.[58] He considered the strict sequence of indigenous-immanent and exogenous-causal research to be inexpedient, and he felt that principles of sociological classification should be brought in in an auxiliary capacity at an early stage of research. It would be sensible very early on to consider those elements in the work that are most closely related to the socioeconomic facts, for since the formal elements could perform very diverse functions, a great danger exists of remaining mired in the statistics of artifice. S. Mashinsky's research report[59] also adopted a very hostile tone toward the *forsotsy*. On the other hand, a certain amount of recognition of Formalist research methods as preliminary to sociological criticism can be seen in the writings of N. Bukharin and A. Voronsky.

The Literary Sociology of the Russian Formalists

During the years of storm and stress, from 1916 to 1921, of Russian Formalism, the outstanding representatives of the Formalist school (V. Shklovsky, B. Eichenbaum, R. Jakobson, and Y. Tynyanov) vehemently rejected the study of social problems. Only such "semi-Formalist" scholars as V. Zhirmunsky early on pointed out the dangers of a one-sidedly Formalist orientation. Between 1924 and 1928, partly as a logical development of their own research method, partly as a defense against Marxist attacks,[60] even the strict Formalists began to accept and promulgate certain sociological research methods. Thus in 1927, in an essay characteristically entitled "In Defense of the

Sociological Method" and directed against Pereverzev's oversimplifications, V. Shklovsky gave a sample of sociological analysis of Pushkin's novel, *The Captain's Daughter*, where he demonstrated how Pushkin's class posture led to a more or less deliberate falsification and denaturing of the Pugachev uprising. However, he warned against purely sociological motivations on occasions when we are dealing more with literary matters (thus the description of Pugachev must be viewed in the literary tradition of "the noble robber"). Since literary technology often undergoes decisive changes within a very short period, it would be necessary, thought Shklovsky, to use a correspondingly differentiated manner to study the social basis as well, in order to illuminate its influence on literary method. Generalized statements—such as, "Gogol was a member of the nobility"—were of no use to an analysis of this process.

Convinced that a Marxist-sociological literary theory would first have to be created, and consulted only thereafter,[61] B. Eichenbaum drew up a plan for the study of what he called "the conditions of the literary life" or "literary mores." He called for research into the rise of professionalism in Russian literature, into the influence of periodicals on literary life, into the relationships between author and publisher and author and reader—that is, into the question of the relationship between the literary facts and literary living conditions.[62] Further, Eichenbaum called for a separation between those elements of artistic development that lie beyond sociological interpretation (Pushkin's use of a four-foot iambic line cannot easily be brought into juxtaposition with any socioeconomic conditions whatever of the era of Nicholas I) and those that do offer a socioeconomic motivation (for example, Pushkin's transition from verse to belletristic and polemic prose, which is connected with the expansion of the reading public beyond the limits of court and aristocratic circles, with the appearance of a new type of publisher, and with the transition from *de luxe* yearbooks to periodicals of a commercial nature). Eichenbaum suggested that the whole process of professionalization of Russian literature in the first half of the nineteenth century be thoroughly studied, and with it the rise of the "commercial tendency," which was evident after 1830, and its consequences for literary development.[63]

He considered these questions especially important because of their actuality in contemporary Soviet scholarship, where most writers—deprived of a whole set of supporting circumstances, such as a constant stratum of readers with high standards—had recourse to one of two situations. Either they took refuge in a dual professionalism, as suppliers of the daily press and as literary translators; or, in order to remain independent in their writing profession, they sought out a second career.[64] Y. Tynyanov finally called for studies of the development of the concepts of the essence and function of literature.

The Formalists shortly prevailed upon some of their students to produce samples of work of this preliminary kind. In this, pride of place must be given to *Literature and Commerce* by T. Grits, V. Trenin, and M. Nikitin; it was a study of the well-known publisher and bookseller, A. Smirdin, who during the second quarter of the nineteenth century crucially influenced the reading habits of the Russian public as well as literary development in Russia by mass printings and extensive price decreases. This study also contained a good deal of material on the Russian book market of the "pre-Smirdin" period, especially on the book trade of the eighteenth century, on authors' royalties, on the size of editions, and on the transition, under way since 1760, from dilettantism to professionalism in translating endeavors. The book's compilers were aware of the fact that literary mores are in no way the mainspring of literary development. However, they believed that any scholarly literary history must not bypass such questions as the social position of authors and translators, the connection between the prominence of certain genres on the one hand and the literary marketplace and the rise of new audiences on the other, or even the problem of "public relations"—the promotion of certain writers through periodicals with which they are allied.

Although a number of further works on the problem of literary mores—such as the essay by V. Bush on the social classification of the Russian reading public in the eighteenth century[65] or *The History of the Russian Book in the Nineteenth Century* by M. Kufaiev[66]—confirm the fruitfulness of such investigations, various "Marxist" critics showed themselves as only minimally impressed. U. Fokht declared that it was unnecessary to replace the study of literature with the study of its readers—in that way literary scholarship would lose sight of its proper subject and would go astray amid trivialities.[67] A. Zeitlin acidly observed that though the book by Grits, Trenin, and Nikitin contained commerce, it contained no literature, and that it replaced the sociology of Pushkin's style with a sociology of the printing presses that published his works.[68] Though the Formalists now wished to turn the "life" of the writer into the subject of a sociological study, the "work" continued to remain for them a simple system of devices.[69]

To be sure, Eichenbaum's concept of the study of "literary life" could properly be countered by the statement that it encompassed only a part of the sociological problems. Schücking's *Soziologie der literarischen Geschmacksbildung* or *Sociology of the Formation of Literary Taste* already gave much greater scope to sociological statements of the problem, as was noted by V. Zhirmunsky as early as 1928 in his preface to the book's Russian edition. Nevertheless, more could have been expected in the way of furthering Russian literary sociology from additional studies of the literary mores in Eichenbaum's sense than from those "intellectual short circuits from economics to poetics" (Erlich) which devalued many works of a Marxist cast. At least such procedures would have brought about the preconditions for meeting Sakulin's demands that socioliterary methodology be brought into close correspondence with the material to be studied.

SOVIET LITERARY SOCIOLOGY FROM 1930 TO 1965

At the beginning of the 1930s, fulfilling Eichenbaum's fear expressed in 1927, socioliterary studies were driven into the dead end of ideology, in spite of A. Lunacharsky's warning to the effect that in the area of aesthetics there was "as yet no Marxist orthodoxy, but only the danger of transforming Marxism into a rigid orthodoxy which has nothing in common with genuine scholarly thought or, of course, with Marxism either."[70]

The promotion of Socialist Realism to the official doctrine in 1934 was followed two years later by the discussions on Formalism and Popular Sociology. On 8 August 1936, *Pravda* published the essay "To Inoculate Students With Love of Classical Literature." This date may be seen as the official ending of Popular Sociology, that is, of most of the socioliterary paths and mazes of the 1920s. It is true that they continued to cast their shadow again and again, even to the present day, on Russian research, either through recurring symptoms of this "illness" or by the evasion of all questions of the connection between literature and society, for fear of renascence. During the mid-1930s, as a result of the slogan of "appropriation of the classical heritage," Russian literary scholarship replaced its efforts to demonstrate the author's class-consciousness in his literary work with the tendency to present the greatest possible number of significant writers of the prerevolutionary period in the guise of pioneers of the revolution. This movement emphasized the writers' sympathy with the revolutionary movement and their opposition to czarism as well as, in the spirit of the Slavophile and Populist tradition, their concern for the simple people, their "spirit of the people" (*narodnost'*), and their Russian nationalism. The book on Pushkin, written in the period 1946–1948 by the well-known literary scholar G. A. Gukovsky (1902–1950) was criticized by a subsequent critic because it "hastened history by tailoring Pushkin to the measure of Nekrasov."[71]

Insofar as literary criticism adapted itself to the official policy—a stance that was chalked up as "adaptive deviation" *prisposoblenchestvo* after 1956—it fell into new "errors," which later suffered the same fate as had befallen "Popular Sociology"; that is, they were labeled "harmful" theories. Thus, the view that a good writer from a "reactionary" milieu could as a rule rise above his class attitude *in spite of* (*vopreki*) it or *thanks to* special circumstances (*blagodariá*) was attacked as *Voprekism* or *Blagodarism*, respectively. Georg Lukács in particular was subjected to the criticism that he had stubbornly defended the teachings of "inspiters" as they apply to writers of realism,[72] while the tendency of "polishing" all significant writers into "people's authors" and of approaching their creations with the solemn sentimentality normally reserved for memorial occasions fell into disrepute, being stigmatized as the theory of the unified stream (*teoriia iedinogo potoka*). That is, it was pejoratively described as the thesis that Russian literature had developed without major leaps and inner contradictions and that the year 1917 did not signify any sharp break in literary history.

From the 1930s to the 1950s the focus of research remained restricted largely to a dogmatic (in the above sense) discussion of both ideological questions and the methods (realism, naturalism, romanticism, and so on) used by the various literary movements to depict reality. "The history of literature was at times more reminiscent of a history of social thought and aesthetic doctrine than a history of verbal art."[73] The high point of this development was reached in the so-called *Zhdanovshchina* (1946–1953), during which all modernistic writers were taboo and the comparative study of literature also succumbed to attacks on "cosmopolitanism." That period left hardly any room for any kind of socioliterary studies worthy of the name.

The Twentieth Party Congress (1956) brought with it the "surmounting of dogmatism in scholarly thought in the area of the humanities."[74] But long after this event, as *KLE* made clear in 1967, Soviet literary studies still gave evidence of a continuing "peculiar inertia of theoretical thinking."[75] This happened less "where problems of the specificity of art and literature are treated" (that is, in the area of Formalist studies) than "in the elaboration of another highly important theoretical problem—the sociohistorical determination of literary growth."[76] It was specifically in this area of sociology of literature that almost nothing had been done until this time to overcome the methodological clichés that had become established in previous periods.[77] In this connection the development of literary studies proceeded along obviously analogous lines with the fate of Soviet linguistic studies, where Structuralism prevailed as early as 1956 while sociolinguistic research was not revived until the 1960s.

According to A. S. Bushmin, it was possible as late as 1969 to detect a particularly skeptical attitude in Soviet literary scholarship "toward the study of literature from the sociological aspect." Sociological analysis of literature does not stand in very high repute with many literary scholars, propinquity with sociology is avoided;[78] in fact, it is even possible to speak of a renewed "lowering of the prestige of the sociological principle."[79] "It is symptomatic that for a long time no specialized study has appeared here that deals with the sociology of art. This topic is proving itself to be a dangerous area (*opasnaia zona*)."[80] Vladimir Kantorovich, who has vigorously advocated the reestablishment of a Soviet sociology of literature since 1967, was also forced to admit that the topic "Sociology and Literature" still often met with prejudice. The contemporary reader was afraid of an aesthetics that ignored the specific nature of art, as did the criticism of the 1920s and partially of the 1930s. "But the Popular Sociology of the 1920s is far from being an exact, scientific sociology of literature!"[81]

A reluctance to make any commitment to the "dangerous" area of sociology of literature, however, was evident in the *Literaturnaia Entsiklopediia*, originally scheduled to appear in twelve volumes (1928–1940). The article headed "Methods of Literary Scholarship" in volume 7 (1934) dealt only with "pre-Marxist literary scholarship," referring the reader to the final volume for "Marxist literary scholarship"; this volume, however, was never published.[82] The *Kratkaia Literaturnaia Entsiklopediia* (six volumes to date, 1962–1971) used the heading "Literary Scholarship" to list, among others, a characterization of the sociological methods of the 1920s and the "dogmatism" of the period from 1930 to 1955 (volume 4, pp. 376–378). A description of more recent sociology of literature was reserved for the article entitled "Sotsiologicheskii metod v literaturovedenii" (vol. 7, 1972).[83] This makes especially clear one of the chief weaknesses of

Soviet literary scholarship—the insufficient study of its own history. *"Until now we have had neither a Marxist history of literary studies,"* A. Bushmin commented in 1969, *"nor a history of Marxist literary studies; nor is there a history of Soviet literary studies. We further lack any more or less systematic critical survey of the methods of literary scholarship* and any attempt to evaluate it comparatively. For this reason, too, we do not possess any kind of firmer image of the stages and rules in the development of literary scholarship. . . . The schools that prevailed in turn in pre-Marxist literary studies are treated mainly as a history of aberrant thinking in terms of literary scholarship, as transitions from one error to another."[84] In 1967 Y. M. Lotman also spoke of that time in the future when "the history of Soviet literary scholarship will have been researched."[85]

Since 1966, however, a few works have appeared that have sketchily attempted to trace the history of Soviet sociology of literature, and in the course of this enterprise "many critics had their good names restored."[86] Shortly before the fiftieth anniversary of the October Revolution, S. Mashinsky published an exhaustive report on Soviet literary scholarship; the first part of it was devoted to the Formalist school, while the second dealt with questions of "how the sociological study of literature evolved within Soviet scholarship."[87] In this attempt, the author was fully aware that in the last analysis only a collective scholarly effort could clear up this problem in its entirety. Such an enterprise has not been undertaken to this day; the two anthologies, *Soviet Literary Studies During Fifty Years*, published in the anniversary year of 1967, deal only marginally with the history of socioliterary research.[88]

ATTEMPTS AT REVIVING SOCIOLITERARY RESEARCH
AFTER 1966

Against the hardly encouraging background of the general research situation, a series of varied and quite interesting attempts at reestablishing a Soviet sociology of literature have emerged in recent years. A not inconsiderable role in this effort is played by the journals *Voprosy literatury* (published since 1957) and *Russkaia literatura* (published since 1958), both established after the Twentieth Party Congress, and the liberal journal *Novy Mir.* Another significant event was the resumption of the tradition of scholarly symposia. The All-

Union debates on realism (April 1957) and on international literary relations (winter of 1960) were followed in February 1963 by a "Symposium on the Complex Study of Artistic Creation,"[89] where mention was first made of the efficacy of applying quantitative methods in "concrete-sociological" (that is, empirical) research.[90] In November 1966 a symposium on the problems of the sociology of art[91] was convened in Leningrad by the "Scholars' Council for World Culture" of the Academy, and in 1968 there was a symposium on problems of audience response,[92] also organized by the Academy.

In August 1965 the journal *Voprosy literatury* addressed an opinion poll concerning Soviet literature to its readers and received over a thousand replies; the report on these responses, published in the May 1966 issue (pp. 44–69), was revealing in spite of selective evaluation. The following were listed among topics that engage the reader: democratization of the state and of society, the struggle against philistinism, the structure of the New Man, the moral decay of a part of the intelligentsia and the reasons behind it, fatherless families, fathers and sons. Readers wanted books dealing with love and with the relations between young men and women as well and younger readers in particular wanted more books dealing with the meaning of life. The magazine established the fact, which had been no secret, that readers' opinions about individual books and about general problems of literary development are not as uniform as many editorial staffs are in the habit of making it seem when they publish correspondence from readers; the journal concluded that readers' opinions should be solicited, not sporadically, but constantly and thoroughly. Writers' congresses should also discuss the question of how readers' opinions could be ascertained. A special commission or an "Institute for Public Opinion" to deal exclusively with the problem should be established.

In 1968, writing in the same periodical, Y. El'sberg acquainted readers with the socioliterary and Marxist methods prevailing in "bourgeois" literary scholarship;[93] he explained its growing significance by the inadequacy of the "subjectivist" scholarly methods current in the West. In particular he discussed and criticized works by L. Goldman, G. Lukàcs, and H. N. Fügen. The "mechanical separation" of sociology and history of literature, recommended by several Western works, seemed to him unacceptable from the position of Soviet literary studies. It must be acknowledged that Soviet literary scholarship "still pays insufficient attention to concrete sociological research in the area of literature," although there are problems in

Soviet reality as well that could be solved with its help. It was, for example, characteristic of Soviet society that enormous masses of readers subscribed to a relatively uniform canon of reading matter (classics of world, Russian, and Soviet literature); nevertheless, we should also examine the relationship between artistically worthwhile and cheap reading matter. The latter exists in the form of whodunits, translated works of literature, and—insofar as one section of the audience reads certain classics, such as Maupassant—"substitutes for cheap writing." El'sberg also points to the lack of any "history of the Russian reader," preliminary studies toward which had been made in the 1920s by Kleinberg and others. In view of the great gaps in research, he thinks it advisable to work with the research results of Western "bourgeois" sociology of literature, especially where these deal with the press, the library system, and readers' cultural levels as well as authors' professional situations and general living conditions. For the same reason he considered it useful to hold joint symposia with Western sociologists of literature to discuss particular methodological problems.

Empirical ("Concrete-Sociological") Investigations

The recognition of the benefits of empirical investigations, which characterizes El'sberg's report, corresponds to a general tendency in more recent efforts in socioliterary research in Soviet literary scholarship. The authors of socioliterary works like to use the term "concrete" to stress that they are utilizing empirical-quantitative research methods. "Concrete-sociological" research has, after all, been neglected in the Soviet Union since the mid-1930s. In contrast, many sociological investigations that appeared in czarist Russia based themselves on rich statistical material—Lenin made extensive use of them. Soviet sociology of the "golden" 1920s "could, according to its origins, base itself on objective data, since the statistics were easily available and the researchers did not [as they do today] have to provide themselves with visas and permits to gain access to statistical materials, and even then only for official purposes."[94] On 22 August 1967, *Pravda* published a decision by the Central Committee "Concerning Measures for the Further Development of the Social Sciences ..."[95] that gave new impetus to the interest in "concrete-sociological" investigations. Since 1967 a number of essays of a pragmatic nature and various studies embodying research results have appeared in the field of empirical sociology of literature.[96]

Under the title "To Study the Entire Wealth of Facts" and acknowledging current descriptions of Soviet literature of the 1920s, Y. Andreev demanded in 1968 that an end be finally made of the method of selective analysis, so widespread in Soviet literary scholarship, which takes into account only those facts that support a given thesis.[97] In his tendentious essay, "Sotsiologiia i literatura,"[98] V. Kantorovich stressed the fact that sociology investigates not only classes, but also subgroups within them; that it studies not only objective processes, but also subjective ones. He felt that it was a non-Marxist attitude to overlook the secondary, mediating factors. "When the connection between superstructure and substructure is viewed too bluntly and directly and the possibility of a conversion process is denied, then the concept must arise that contradictions are foreign to socialist society —in literature, this resulted in the 'theory of absence of conflict.'"[99] The modern sociologist cannot content himself with generalized characterizations of the proletariat, the peasantry, the intelligentsia; he wants to know everything about them, wants to know the circumstances of their lives, their interests, the psychology of concrete population groups within the framework of a class. Caution is therefore also necessary to avoid the global demonization of foreign sociology, where it is a matter of the scientific methodology of concrete investigations (p. 151).

Sociology of Readership

"Even contemporary fashions in sociology" (*moda na sotsiologiiu*) were still unable—as Kantorovich noted in 1969—to bring the concepts "sociology" and "literature" into juxtaposition, with one exception: "it is generally recognized that the consumption of art can and must be investigated by sociology" with quantitative methods. In fact, most recently numerous inquiries and interviews have studied the artistic consumption of the different levels of readers, viewers, and listeners. Teams of sociologists in Sverdlovsk, Leningrad, and Perm are steadfastly working at a social analysis of cultural needs, in order to answer such questions as the uses of leisure time and the surviving differences in the cultural levels of the working population.[100]

The widely ramified network of Soviet libraries offers favorable conditions for investigations into the sociology of audiences, and in the last few years scholars have begun to take advantage of them, even though reluctantly. Thus in 1967, D. Sivokon,[101] in his article "Study the Needs and Preferences of Readers!" reported on investigations into readership sociology in the Ukraine (work teams at the Shevchenko Literary Institute of the Ukrainian Academy), in Moscow (at the Institute for World Literature), and in the Lithuanian SSR, where the librarians have begun on "the concrete study of rural readers." He called for the coordination of research into readers and into the social function of reading matter in an All-Union measure, because such coordination could facilitate the development of suitable methodological techniques. Research would have to focus on the perusal of literature among the various social strata; on the degree of popularity of the various writers and literary styles; on the reception of individual works and the demand for Soviet, classical, and foreign literature; on the readers' approval or disapproval of the size of an edition and the work's physical production, and so on. In this endeavor the experiments with methods of the 1920s were to be taken into consideration.[102] Such investigations would certainly bring to light more than readers' positive opinions. They would also illuminate and confirm the disaster of the second-hand book trade, and illustrate the fact that there are some Soviet books that "are considered bibliographic rarities even on their first appearance."[103]

In the view of A. Retivov,[104] examining readers' opinion would be extremely beneficial to writers also, since "at present they are only insufficiently informed about the fate of their books in one or another social stratum." An exact statistical survey of readers' requests and readers' opinion, as well as an investigation of role distribution between books and means of mass communication (radio, television) could furnish the material for a "fruitful theory of the functioning of literature within society." During the 1920s, at Upton Sinclair's request, an investigation was made of the reception accorded his work among Soviet readers, read against the social-demographic characteristics of 18,000 readers in Moscow; no corresponding research exists to this day concerning a single Soviet author. In his time Mayakovsky collected almost 20,000 letters from readers which promised to furnish extremely interesting materials toward the sociology of early Soviet readers and about which he planned to write a book (see "Ia sam" or "I Myself," 1928). Until now, it seems, this material has not been evaluated. How wonderful it would be if, by using empirical research on "the reception of works of art by mass readership," we could, for example, gain a view of the Soviet response to Kafka after the selected edition appeared in 1965.[105]

The publication in 1968 of the anthology *The Soviet Reader. Attempt at a Concrete-Sociological Investigation*[106] represented a study in audience sociology of greater scope. This book is the first result of a research project, undertaken by the Division for Library Science and Bibliography of the Lenin Library in Moscow, which proposes to investigate the reading habits of the leading social and professional groups in the country's economic and cultural life. The book vouchsafes an insight into the reading preferences of workers, engineers and technicians, kolkhoz peasants and agricultural specialists, university students, and high-school pupils and teachers from thirty-three areas of Russia and eight Soviet Republics. Although the book is disappointing in a number of respects, a precise analysis of the material it contains could furnish valuable insights. It shows, for example, the continued popularity of Esenin, who arouses much more interest than does Mayakovsky among high-school students—almost twice as much among university students (see pp. 230 and 260). Yevtushenko is considered significant by 48 percent of the specialized teachers of literature in the provincial cities, whereas Voznesensky gets this rating from only 13 percent; the ratio of 40 to 28 percent in Moscow and Leningrad is quite different (see page 201). Surely much could be learned from a comparison of the Soviet anthology with an analogous Polish work,[107] also published in 1968.

It seems clear that until now the revival of Russian research into audience sociology has too exclusively involved sociologists and librarians and engaged literary scholars insufficiently; it remains to be seen if the work will lead to substantial results. For the time being it seems that there is still a long way to go to reach the interesting research perspective unveiled in the 1920s by A. I. Beletsky.[108]

Cultural-Sociological Research

The notorious neglect of mediating factors led M. Bakhtín—a literary critic well known for his studies of Rabelais and Dostoevsky—to call for renewed close contact between literary studies and cultural history. Asked by the editors of the journal *Novy Mir* to pass judgment on the state of Soviet literary scholarship, Bakhtín pointed out the contradiction between its great traditions, its talented cadres, and its

technical research resources and its meager accomplishments. Bakhtín welcomed the temporary reduction, "necessary and useful at the
time," to questions concerning the particular nature of literature
(which was connected both with the rediscovery of Formalist problems after 1956 and with the rejection of vulgar sociology after
1930); but he was certain that the time had come to focus on literature in the context of the whole culture. "Our works of literary history
usually list the characteristics of the periods to which the works in
question belong, but these traits are for the most part only minimally
differentiated from those in general histories." They lack "a differen-
tial analysis of the cultural areas, their conflicts and interaction with
literature." Unfortunately the methodology for such analyses has
not been worked out to date.[109]

Pointing in the same direction as Bakhtín's demand is Pospelov's
remark to the effect that, though Soviet literary scholars must reject
the methodology of the Cultural-Historical school, they should nevertheless not forget "in the course of their researches to consult a
variety of facts of the ideological life of society, of its aspects that
are conditioned by the social milieu, and of the general cultural atmosphere." "The sharp condemnation of the study of literary phenomena which is abstractly class-connected" would not lead "to rejection of its concrete social-historical research" but, on the contrary,
must be followed "by a steadfast and deepened elaboration of the
principles" of such investigations.[110] It is quite proper, Pospelov believes, for the collective work *Theory of Literature*[111] to demand that
"the necessity for the birth of each form of the literary process, each
form of artistic thinking, be derived from the particular social conditions." But this expectation presupposes on the one hand an explanation of the total complexity of the connecting, intermediate links
that tie "social conditions" to "artistic thinking" and, on the other,
clarification of the nature of this thinking itself. Neither the one nor
the other, he noted, was examined in the book.[112] It was not by chance
that A. S. Bushmin also confronted those involved in interdisciplinary
research projects with the task of writing a "history of Russian culture."[113] Nor was it by chance that he hoped that literary scholarship
would not lock itself into its specifically verbal-descriptive ability
but would establish close mutual relations with the other sciences,
especially philosophy and sociology (p. 70). The core of the problem
is assuredly located "in the difficulty of realizing this complex connection of various aspects—in limits and proportions, where the particularity of literature does not lose its primary significance."[114]

Content Analysis: Type Studies of Heroes and Conflict

In his essay "Sociology and Literature," the Soviet literary sociologist V. Kantorovich[115] defined still other goals. He cited a series of
"concrete-sociological" research results which take specific aim at
certain stereotypes, cast doubt on the genuineness of the reflection
of reality in various works of recent Soviet literature, and give information about the effect of many of the examples set by literature.
Referring to sociological studies of population fluctuations, Kantorovich criticizes literary representations of the settlement policy in
Siberia; on this topic numerous writers, he claims, take "a thoughtless, irresponsible, if not hypocritical position" in that they arouse
romantic illusions instead of showing the reality. Further, he accused
literature of creating fashionable professions (electronics engineer,
pilot, radio technician) and of lowering other activities in the eyes of
society; thus, for example, the whole area of service trades, including
commerce, is almost held up to ridicule. True, this contempt for
trade is an old tradition in Russia: "the bookkeeper's fate has never
been a happy one in Russian literature."[116] Since, Kantorovich thinks,
almost all literary genres influence the development of young people,
the writer must be absolutely familiar with the complicated problems
of the educational process, unless "his pen is to produce only pastor-
als." He should, for example, know that the purpose of the program of
studies in the middle schools is preparation for higher learning, which
is why 80 percent of students in the middle schools want to continue
their studies; the higher schools, however, are able to admit only 25
percent of them. The "moralizing authors" do not seem to notice that
after having been qualified for higher studies, many graduates, just
because until this time they have lived only on scholarships or parental support, consider it humiliating to become workers. The present
middle schools are said to direct their education too much toward
the career of intellectual and too little toward a corresponding standard of life—though there is a crying need for intellectuals without
advanced degrees. Soviet writers ignore those workers who lead an
impoverished intellectual life (one-fifth of the young workers read
no books of any kind). For a long time "material" interests have
officially been held in low esteem in the Soviet Union. "Such hypocritical clichés are also cultivated in a particular area of literary
activity, where paper heroes had their being"—a sort of literature

which must of necessity establish in the reader's mind the idea that "ideology and practice" are "entirely different matters."

Kantorovich's remarks are of interest when he refers to the concurrence between the results of recent sociological preference polls inquiring about curriculum and character models and that "humanization of human relations" that can be observed in Soviet literature after 1956. The polls' results showed that the highest number of points went, not to the inconsiderate, "voluntaristic," successful characters, but to the "honest men." In this instance, the author believes, literature is obviously an expression of internal processes occurring in Soviet society (pp. 166–69).

But to what degree does the whole of contemporary literature reflect the problems and conflicts agitating the Soviet people? The answer to this question can best be found, according to Kantorovich, through "taking inventory of the themes and conflict situations" depicted in the literary works of the Soviet period, as well as through "taking a census of the literary population"—that is, through a compilation of literary figures as social types. Kantorovich could have pointed out that an inventory of literary types intended to serve both literary-historical and sociological generalizations had already been attempted in prerevolutionary Russia, by the *Dictionary of Literary Types*.[117] However, this encompassed only fifteen works by leading writers rather than, as Kantorovich suggested, including popular literature (in 1967 alone, more than 3,000 literary works were published in Russia) as well as periodicals intended to be read by the whole family (*Ogonek, Rabotnitsa, Niva*, and so on).

It took seventeen months from the publication of this proposal for *Novy Mir* to make a selection from the numerous readers' responses and to reprint "some supplementary statements and explanatory replies," most of which took a positive attitude toward research into literary consumption as well as into literature as an instrument of social consciousness. The idea of statistical surveys of types was received skeptically—further discussions were required.[118] At the end of 1969 Kantorovich spoke up once more. Saying that he did not wish "to talk about a new branch of the discipline of literary criticism or sociology," he addressed himself to an expanded interpretation of sociology of literature, which studies, not only the reception given to a work, but also its influence on writers and on the results of literary production. He pointed out that any intensified exploration of types of readers must also lead to the study of the internal structure of the work of art.[119] As an example of analysis of literary situations of conflict, he cited, as he had in 1967, an essay by Y. Kuz'menko, who had subjected the novels of O. Ziv, V. Ocheretin, and A. Bylinov to sociological analysis and had made it clear how little some writers know about the realities of life.[120] Since that time the debate concerning Kantorovich's proposals seems to have lain fallow. Yet, a study appearing fall 1972 investigates to what degree the social, cultural, psychological and ethical processes taking place in Soviet society at present are reflected in works of Soviet authors (*Sovremennaia sovetskaia literatura i novyie cherty deistvitel'nosti*, Moscow, 1972).

The Socioliterary Potential of Russian Structuralism

If the writings of Bakhtin, Pospelov, Bushmin, and Grigor'an unanimously deal with the necessity for and difficulty of understanding publications in literature in both in their aesthetic-literary and their historical context, the conqueror of this dichotomy appears in the form of Russian Structuralisms of the Lotman school, which has become increasingly influential since 1964. Y. Lotman also accuses all previous literary studies of actually employing two methodologies —studying a work of literature in the context of other monuments of social thought and studying a work with a view toward its formal traits (rhythmic patterns, verse forms, composition, style, and so on)—without establishing a convincing connection between these two research trends. It was true, Lotman conceded, that in the work of talented researchers the existing contradiction between the two was sometimes spontaneously bridged; the experiences of these scholars deserved serious study. It must also be possible, however, to resolve the contradiction in a systematic manner. It is possible when the scholar goes beyond the structure of the text to research the "structure of the ideas, the structure of the poetic representation of reality" and when he comprehends the individual aesthetic structures (particularly the work itself) as elements of more complex unities such as culture and history. In this respect Lotman can base his views on the later works of Russian Formalism. As early as 1928, Y. Tynyanov and R. Jakobson had called for an analysis of the correlation between literature and "the rest of the historical disciplines": "This reciprocal relationship (a system of systems) has its own structural laws, which are still to be discovered. It is fatal for methodology to study the correlation of the systems without regard for the laws immanent in each separate system."[121] Lotman follows Marxist re-flection theory in that for him literature is a particular, namely an aesthetic, form of social consciousness. It must not be dissolved in the history of social teachings, yet each element of an artistic struc-ture raises the question of its meaning—what signification does it embody? The significance is not revealed by descriptions of the iso-lated nature of the separate elements, but by the oppositions within which it is confined; these include extratextual—meaning "social" in the widest sense of the word—structures. The totality of the "basic oppositions" in a work reflects the understanding of reality by the author. In his essay "Literary Studies Must Become a Science" (1967), Lotman attempted to illustrate this principle by citing the example of two works by Pushkin—the ode "Vol'nost'" ("Freedom") and the poem "Tsygany" ("The Gypsies"). In the ode "Vol'nost'," the word *zakon* ("law") stands in opposition to the concept of "lawless-ness," which is realized in the variations "despotism" and "anarchy." In "Tsygany," on the other hand, the corresponding contrasting pair is *zakon* ("law") and *volia* ("freedom"); in this context *zakon* means any law, good or bad, while *volia* refers to the condition of "natural liberty." Lotman uses this example to make it clear at the same time that certain aspects of a structure become visible only when they are viewed through the lenses of another structure. "Here the way is paved for a more exact investigation of a wide area of problems: from the effect of reality on art to the problem of the influences, adapta-tions, and responses—the effect of certain types of consciousness, of culture, of art on others." Since the realization of the structure also depends on the understanding of reality of the recipient—on the structure of his artistic experiences as well as his life experiences[122]—Lotman finds a new approach from this starting point to the problem of the relationship between "author and reader." "How the author's work is transformed in the reader's mind and what shapes these trans-formations take—that is an entirely unexplored question." This verdict, though it fails to take sufficient account of the numerous audience-psychological studies in Russian literature of the first three decades of the twentieth century, is justified by Lotman's efforts to formulate and to formulize the study of the relationships between author and reader. He applies such concepts as "entropy of the aes-thetic languages of author and reader" and its contrasting "type study of texts and extratextual references."[123]

No matter how convincing the socioliterary results of Lotman's

structural interpretations of Pushkin's poems are, the question remains—as it did for numerous works by the Russian Formalists—
whether the examples were not chosen all too conveniently and
whether the effort needed for a similarly convincing structuralization
of other works does not jeopardize the fruitfulness of the method.
Without a doubt one would first of all have to carry out a good deal
of basic research in cultural history and cultural sociology (in this
area Lotman's concern borders on that of Bakhtín and other Soviet
literary scholars). This insight seems to have determined the choice
of topic for the Tartu Summer Institute of 1970, which was devoted
to discussions of the problem of the "unity of culture" or the varying
aspects of the "semiotics of culture."[124] In any case, Lotman's kind
of structuralism will first have to prove its socioliterary relevance
with a greater number of interpretations. Thus we may take literally
the editorial prefatory statement to Lotman's new book on the structure of artistic texts and extend it to non-Marxist literary sociology.
The preface claims validity, not only for the semiotic approach, but
also for other methods of (Marxist-Leninist) aesthetics "on the
epistemological, sociological, and axiologic level."

The Social Function of Art

Y. Davydov (born 1929) occupies a special place within the framework of the most recent aesthetic-sociological arguments. He first
announced his theses in November 1966 at the Leningrad symposium
on aesthetic sociology[125] and subsequently developed them in his
book *Art as Sociological Phenomenon. On the Characteristics of the
Aesthetic-Political Views of Plato and Aristotle*. In his view, aesthetic
sociology is not so much concerned with "artistic culture" or with
the work of art as the result of specific historical conditions; rather,
aesthetic sociology should regard the work of art as the cause of the
human actions resulting from it and should therefore study art primarily in its relation to its audience (that is, in the act of reception
by the various social levels, subgroups, and so on).[126] The particular
form of social behavior of the audience categories toward art calls
into being the corresponding art works and is "objectified" in them.
In that respect aesthetic sociology must also concern itself with the
structure of the individual work. Davydov—referring back to Kant
but obviously also basing his views on works by Russian Formalists—

sees the work's structure as determined by the two poles of "taste" and "genius." If the extremity of taste represents the element that unites artist and audience—the prevailing norms—genius incorporates the new, which destroys certain elements of the aesthetic and moral norms and determines the real value of the work of art (pp. 24–25). What are the possibilities of social-aesthetic behavior toward art? Davydov distinguishes among relationships based on epistemological function, educative function, ethical appeal, compensatory role, mere prestige thinking, and purely aesthetic traits. The body of the book locates these relationships in the aesthetic-sociological views of Plato (educative function in the name of establishing the ideal state) and Aristotle (social-manipulative function to direct popular sentiments with the aid of the intellectual pleasure and physiological enjoyment derived from art, the power of art to purify the emotions, and the like).

Davydov's theses met with serious criticism, not only because they aimed at limiting aesthetic sociology to a particular type of audience research, but also because, by emphasizing the pole of genius, they were too quick to grant art the dignity of autonomy.[127] Thus A. S. Bushmin, referring back to Belinsky, felt compelled to counter Davydov with the opinion that genius is not in opposition to society but is its highest expression in each case ("in [the work of] a major artist the personal element strengthens the social nature of his creation"). Bushmin's view ignored the fact that this relationship is also able to dialectically encompass the contradiction between genius and the contemporary social structure: if the great artist "knows more and sees more, and therefore has more ambition and is more capable" than the rest of society,[128] he must be allowed to criticize the Party.

Using another approach, G. Kunitsyn has recently attempted to define the specific function of art in Soviet society.[129] He argues against the view held by some writers that in socialist art there can be hardly any negative characters because the sphere of negativity is already too constricted (V. Novikov, 1969). Referring to N. G. Chernyshevsky, Kunitsyn also attributes the two basic functions of knowledge and education to Soviet art. Art must have the right, he claims, to pass moral judgment on the appearances of reality. Though in the present phase of artistic evolution the "principal appeal" of art consists in furthering communist ideals, this does not mean that art must "have mercy" on the prevailing conditions. When art genuinely reflects life, it fundamentally always consolidates some important communist position. Unfortunately, Kunitsyn notes, "for some reason or other" the thought of repercussions from art back to reality still evokes "the feeling of a certain theoretical risk."

Although during the last five years especially, socioliterary theses and themes can be found in many Soviet works of literary scholarship and criticism,[130] the process of forming new theories and new methodological considerations in the field of literary sociology has hardly begun. Today, as in 1966, when Mashinsky made this observation, Soviet literary studies still lack "breadth and depth in their social view of artistic creation."[131] Just because the "general methodological assumptions" of Marxist-sociological literary studies have been laid down for a long time, the "concrete application of the new methodology" proves especially difficult.[132] After all, the success of a scientific method depends not least on whether it is appropriate to the particular nature of its object—or, as the case may be, whether it can adapt to it. Further, the evolution of Soviet sociology of literature is hampered to this day by the continuing prohibition imposed on mention of salient problems and facts. And these taboos continue to prevent socioliterary research from becoming really aware of its own history—an unfortunate state of affairs that is thoroughly understood by a number of critics.[133] During the last few years a number of essays have been published that attempt to remedy this lack; but efforts in this direction will certainly have to be considerably intensified. A series of monographs dealing with the different tendencies of Russian and Soviet literary sociology, which was planned in 1930 by N. Efimov and which he launched with the study of the Pereverzev school,[134] is urgently needed, as are new editions of older books and essays of methodological interest—there is knowledge to be gained even from old errors! Yugoslavia, rather than Russia, has recently reprinted the works of P. Kogan (translated into Serbian); the Western countries have brought out editions of socioliterary works by L. Trotsky and B. M. Eichenbaum and the very important periodical, *Pechat' i revolutsiia*; Poland published a study of the critic A. K. Voronsky, known as having been "subjected to repression."[135] Only when Soviet literary studies "utilize the possibilities more boldly" (Bakhtín) and create new ones can there be any serious idea of structuring a modern sociology of literature. Nor can we long cling to the consolation that in Western literary studies the treatment of socioliterary problems is also still in its infancy,[136] in view of the increasingly evident strenuous efforts to achieve a methodology for sociology of literature.

According to a letter to the editor, published in *Novy Mir* in 1969, concerning the prospects for socioliterary studies, the Soviet intelligentsia is at present pinning its hopes on sociology and "expects from it truth in its ultimate form"—just as it expected truth from poetry and the young poets in the period 1960–1962.[137]

[Translated from the German by Ruth Hein]

Notes

1. See Peter Brang, "Der russische Beitrag zur literarsoziologischen Forschung. Versuch eines Überblicks," in *Jahrbuch für Asthetik und allgemeine Kunstwissenschaft*, vol. 9 (1964): 167–207, especially 167–75.
2. *Istoriia russkoi literatury XIX veka*, vol. 1 (Moscow, 1908), pp. 3–4.
3. See *Literaturnoie razvitiie na zapade* or *Literary Development in Western Europe* (Voronezh, 1886).
4. Neither Hennequin nor Kareev is mentioned in the Soviet *Istoriia russkoi kritiki*, vol. 2 (Moscow and Leningrad, 1958).
5. *Kratkaia literaturnaia entsiklopediia* (hereafter abbreviated as *KLE*), vol. 6 (1971), columns 409–10, bibliography.
6. *Voprosy teorii i psikhologii tvorchestva*, vols. 1–8 (Kharkov and Petrograd, 1907–1923; vol. 1, 2d ed., Kharkov, 1911).
7. *O tolkovanii khudozhestvennogo proizvedeniia* (Saint Petersburg, 1912).
8. "Ob odnoi iz ocherednykh zadach istoriko-literaturnoi nauki (izucheniie istorii chitatelia)" or "Concerning an Urgent Task for Literary-Historical Research (The Investigation of the History of the Reader)," in *Nauka na Ukraine*, no. 2 (1922). Reprinted in O. Biletsky, *Zibrannia prać u 5 tt.*, part 3 (Kiev, 1966), pp. 255–73.
9. *Teoriia chitatel'skogo vospriiatiia i russkii chitatel' konsta XIX-nachala XX veka.* See also A. I. Beletsky, N. L. Brodsky, and L. P. Grossman, *Noveishaia russkaia literatura* (Ivanovo-Vosnesensk, 1927), pp. 86–106.
10. On this subject, see P. Brang, "Der russische Beitrag," pp. 175–79.
11. Compare Peter Demetz, *Marx, Engels und die Dichter* (Stuttgart, 1959).
12. Compare S. Mashinsky, "Puti i pereput'ia. Iz istorii sovetskogo literaturovedeniia" or "Roads and Crossroads. From the History of Soviet Literary Scholarship," in *Voprosy literatury* (hereafter abbreviated as *VL*), no. 5 (1966), p. 73.
13. M. Rozanov, "Sovremennoie sostoianiie voprosa o metodakh izucheniia literaturnykh proizvedenii" or "The Current Status of Problems of Method-

ology in the Study of Literary Works," in *Russkaia Mysl'*, vol. 4 (1900), pp. 179–80.

14. I. Grossman-Roshchin in *Pechat' i revoliutsiia*, nos. 5–6 (1925), p. 85 (concerning B. M. Eichenbaum).

15. Iu. Ianel' in *Krasnaia Nov'*, no. 10 (1927), p. 254.

16. S. Mashinsky in 1966 criticized the fact that some Soviet studies gave evidence of the influence of one or another conception from "bourgeois positivist sociology." See *VL*, no. 8 (1966), p. 55.

17. M. Bakhtín in *Novy Mir* (hereafter abbreviated as *NM*), no. 11 (1970), p. 240.

18. Compare *Literaturnaia Entsiklopediia* (hereafter abbreviated as *LE*), vol. 8 (1934), columns 693–730, and *KLE*, vol. 5 (1968), columns 794–98.

19. A. Vetukhov, "Pervyie shagi po puti sozdaniia nauki o literature i ieie istorii" or "The First Steps on the Way to Establishing Literary Scholarship and its History," in *Rodnoi iazyk v shkole*, no. 8 (1925), p. 20; see also A. Umansky, "Marksizm v izuchenii literatury" or "Marxism in Literary Studies," ibid., p. 12.

20. P. N. Sakulin, "K problematike sovremennogo literaturovedeniia" or "On the Problems of Contemporary Literary Scholarship," in *Pechat' i revoliutsiia*, no. 8 (1926), p. 76.

21. S. Zolotarev, "Literaturnyie metody i gorizonty," in *Rodnoi iazyk v shkole*, no. 8 (1926), p. 29.

22. *Pechat' i revoliutsiia*, no. 6 (1924), p. 3.

23. *Pechat' i revoliutsiia*, no. 1 (1927), p. 62.

24. A. I. Beletsky, in the foreword to the Russian edition of Müller-Freienfels, *Poetik* (Kharkov, 1923).

25. Compare the compilation of corresponding judgments in A. M. Ievlakhov, *Vvedeniie v filosofiiu khudozhestvennogo tvorchestva* or *Introduction to the Philosophy of Aesthetic Creation*, vol. 3 (Rostov, 1917), pp. 144–57.

26. *Zhivaia zhizn'* (December 1910), columns 175–76.

27. L. Shiuking, *Sotsiologiia literaturnogo vkusa* (Leningrad, 1928).

28. "Po povodu prof. V. F. Pereverzeva," *Novy Lef*, no. 6 (1928), pp. 33–39.

29. V. Shklovsky, "V zashchitu sotsiologicheskogo metoda" or "In Defense of the Sociological Method," in *Novy Lef*, no. 3 (1927), p. 21.

30. "Sotsiologizm bez sotsiologii," *Zvezda*, no. 2 (1926), p. 267.

31. A. Zeitlin, "Problemy sovremennogo literaturovedeniia," in *Russky iazyk v shkole*, vol. 8, p. 10.

32. A bibliography of his works is given by R. Mandel'stam, *Khudozhestvennaia literatura v otsenke russkoi marksistskoi kritiki* or *Literature in the Judgment of Russian Marxist Criticism*, 4th ed. (Moscow and Leningrad, 1928), pp. 132–33 and 202–3.

33. V. Shuliatikov, *Izbrannyie literaturno-kriticheskiie stat'i*, "*Zemlia i fabrika*" (Moscow and Leningrad, 1929).

34. Compare R. Mandel'stam, pp. 128–29 and 192–202.

35. Compare N. Efimov, *Literaturovedeniie revoliutsionnoi epochi. Napravleniia i problemy*, vol. 1: *Eidologicheskoie napravleniie (shkola prof. V. F. Pereverzeva)* or *Literary Studies of the Revolutionary Period. Directions and Problems*, vol. 1: *The Eidological Directions (School of Prof. V. F. Pereverzev)* (Vladivostok, 1930), 52 pp.

36. "Problematika sovremennoi marksistskoi istorii literatury," in *Pechat' i revoliutsiia*, no. 2 (1927), p. 91.

37. *Iezhegodnik literatury i iskusstva na 1929 god* (Moscow, 1929), p. 165.

38. "V zashchitu sotsiologicheskogo metoda," in *Novy Lef*, no. 3 (1927), p. 20.

39. Compare Mashinsky in *VL*, no. 5 (1966), p. 65.

40. M. S. Grigor'ev, *Literatury i ideologiia* (Moscow, 1929), pp. 215–16.
41. A. Voronsky, *Literaturnyia tipy* (Leningrad, 1927), p. 213. M. S. Grigor'ev, who attempted to reconcile the literary views of the "Psychological school" with Marxist opinions, gave an explanation for this "continued life" of significant works of art which combined the doctrines of Potebnya and Plekhanov. In dealing with literary works, he made a distinction, as Potebnya had done, between the external form (sound, rhythm, and the like) and the internal form (structure) and content (message). The last of these he equated with Plekhanov's "sociological equivalent." The "internal form" is determined by the (ideological) content as well as by the literary tradition. The message could also be expressed in nonliterary form—for example, in promotional phrasing. The internal form is also capable of harboring other messages. This explains why *Don Quixote* and *Hamlet* can be understood in different ways. The "roominess," the depth of the "internal form" are the measure of artistic value (pp. 205–21).
42. *Ocherki po istorii zapadno-ievropeiskoi literatury* or *Sketches in the History of Western European Literature* (Moscow, 1908), p. 5.
43. Compare herewith the quarrel between V. Polonsky and L. Averbakh concerning the problem of immunity—the question whether the class-consciousness of working-class readers might be impaired by the ideologies contained in the works of writers born into the nobility. In *Novy Mir*, no. 9 (1927), pp. 169–76.
44. Compare, for example, P. N. Medvedev, p. 8, n. 30, as well as bibliographies in *Balukhaty*, nos. 273–76 and 291. For a highly critical, recent point of view, also V. Mashinsky in *VL* (1966), pp. 57–60.
45. *Kurs istorii russkoi literatury*, vol. 1, 2nd ed., (St. Petersburg, 1911), pp. iii–xii.
46. V. A. Keltuiala, *Istoriko-materialisticheskoie izucheniie literaturnogo proizvedeniia* (Leningrad, 1926), 63 pp.; *Metod istorii literatury* (Leningrad, 1928), 255 pp.
47. In his review of *The Method of Literary History*, I. Grossman-Roshchin justly labels the book an "organized muddle." See Grossman-Roshchin in *Na literaturnom postu*, nos. 7–8 (1928), pp. 17–20.
48. *Dva veka russkoi literatury* (Moscow, 1923, 2d ed., 1924; *Oblastnoi printsip v russkom kul'turovedenii* (1925); *Oblastnyie kul'turnyie gnezda. Istoriko-kraievednyi seminarii* (Moscow, 1928).
49. *Pechat' i revoliutsiia*, no. 1 (1927), p. 67.
50. V. Erlich, *Russian Formalism* (The Hague, 1955), p. 88; 3d ed. (1969), p. 110.
51. A. Zeitlin, "Marksisty i formal'nyi metod," in *Lef*, no. 3 (1923); idem, "Problemy sovremennogo literaturovedeniia," in *Rodnoi iazyk v shkole*, no. 8 (1925), pp. 3–11.
52. M. Levidov, "Samoubiistvo literatury," in *Proletariat i literatura* (Leningrad, 1925), pp. 160–69.
53. A. Voznesensky, "Poiski ob'iekta (K voprosu ob otnoshenii metoda sotsiologicheskogo k 'formal'nomu')," in *NM*, no. 6 (1926), pp. 116–28.
54. B. Arvatov, "O formal'no-sotsiologicheskom metode," in *Pechat' i revoliutsiia*, no. 3 (1927), pp. 54–64.
55. B. Yakubos'ky, *Sotsiolohychny metod u pysmentstvy* (Kiev, 1923), 63 pp.
56. P. N. Medvedev, *Formal'nyi metod v literaturovedenii* (Leningrad, 1928).
57. *Lef*, no. 3 (1923), p. 115.
58. "Problematika sovremennoi marksistskoi istorii literatury," in *Pechat' i revoliutsiia*, no. 2 (1927), pp. 78–92.
59. *VL*, no. 5 (1966), pp. 86–87.

60. Such attacks were first made by P. Kogan, S. Bobrov, A. Lunacharsky, and V. Poliansky in the context of a symposium on Formalism sponsored by the periodical *Pechat' i revoliutsiia* in 1924. See "K sporam o formal'nom metode," no. 5 (September–October), p. 1038. See also Erlich, pp. 83–87; 3d ed., pp. 105–8.

61. Compare the report on the public argument that took place on 3 June 1927, "between members of the *Opoiaz* and a group of Leningrad Marxists." B. Tomashevsky, B. Eichenbaum, V. Shklovsky, and Y. Tynyanov represented the Formalists. *Novy Lef*, no. 4 (1927), pp. 45–46, "Disput o formal'nom metode."

62. Eichenbaum's concept of literary mores included the material conditions of the literary life, while Sakulin's "literary milieu" referred to literary tradition. Sakulin paid far too little attention to the economic conditions of literary development. Nevertheless, see *Sotsiologicheskii metod v literaturovedenii* (Moscow, 1925), pp. 88–89.

63. One of the documents cited concerning this process is Shevyrev's polemic essay "Literature and Commerce" or "Slovesnost' i kommertsiia" in *Moskovskii nabliudatel'*, no. 1 (1935).

64. B. Eichenbaum, "Literatura i literaturnyi byt" or "Literature and the Conditions of its Existence" in *Na literaturnom postu*, no. 9 (1927), pp. 47–52. German translation in *Texte der russischen Formalisten*, ed. by J. Striedter, vol. 1 (Munich, 1969), pp. 463–81.

65. V. Bush, "Drevnerusskaia literaturnaia traditsiia v XVIII v. (K voprosu o sotsial'nom rassloienii chitatelia)," in *Uch. Zap. Sarat. Gosud. Univ.*, vol. 4 (Saratov, 1925), pp. 1–11.

66. M. N. Kufaiev, *Istoriia russkoi knigi v XIX v* (Leningrad, 1927).

67. *Pechat' i revoliutsiia*, no. 1 (1927), p. 70.

68. *Literatura i marksizm*, vol. 1 (Moscow, 1929), pp. 167–69.

69. *LE*, vol. 7 (Moscow, 1934), column 278.

70. *Pechat' i revoliutsiia*, no. 8 (1926), p. 79.

71. Pospelov "Metodologicheskoie razvitiie sovetskogo literaturovedeniia," *Sovetskoie literaturovedeniie za piat' desiat let* (Moscow, 1967), p. 96.

72. Mashinsky in *VL*, no. 8 (1966), pp. 73–74; *KLE*, vol. 4 (1967), column 378.

73. Mashinsky, *KLE*.

74. Compare Pospelov, pp. 108 and 100–1.

75. *KLE*, vol. 4 (1967), column 379 ("Literaturovedeniie").

76. Pospelov, p. 102.

77. Pospelov, p. 108.

78. Bushmin (1969), p. 61.

79. Bushmin, pp. 67–68.

80. Bushmin, p. 61. The same term, *opasnaia zona*, appears also in *KLE*, vol. 4, column 378, and in *VL*, no. 8 (1966), p. 75.

81. *VL*, no. 11 (1969), pp. 43–44.

82. Compare *LE*, vol. 7 (1934), column 241.

83. Compare *KLE*, vol. 4, p. 375, and vol. 5, p. 795.

84. Bushmin, p. 27. There is a connection between the lack of any Soviet critical survey of the methods of literary scholarship and the fact that Max Wehrli's *Allgemeine Literaturwissenschaft* (Berne, 1951) appeared in a Russian translation very quickly. M. Verli, *Obshcheie literaturovedeniie* (Moscow, 1957), 244 pp.

85. *VL*, no. 1 (1967), p. 94.

86. L. Kishchinskaia, "Literaturnaia diskussiia 1922–1925 gg." in *VL*, no. 4 (1966), pp. 35–56 (this quote, page 35). Compare Kishchinskaia, *Bor'ba*

za teoreticheskiie osnovy sovetskoi literaturnoi kritiki (1917–1932) (Sverdlovsk, 1967); N. Gei and V. Piksanov, "U istokov marksistsko marksistskoi literaturnoi kritiki," in *VL*, no. 8 (1967), pp. 131–52. During the period of the so-called personality cult, those literary critics interested especially in socioliterary questions were "subjected to repression." Among them were L. Averbakh, I. Bespalov, A. Efremin, G. Gorbachev, G. Gukovsky, V. Kantorovich, P. N. Medvedev, D. Mirsky, I. Nusinov, V. Pereverzev, and A. K. Voronsky (see also *KLE*).

87. *VL*, no. 5 (1966), pp. 70–90, and no. 8 (1967), pp. 54–77; see also above, n. 12.

88. *Sovetskoie literaturovedeniie za 50 let.* (Leningrad, IRLI, 1968), 530 pages; *Sovetskoie literaturovedeniie za piat'desiat let.*, ed. V. I. Kuleshov (Moscow, MGU, 1967), 550 pp.

89. Compare *Simpozium po kompleksnomu izucheniiu khudozhestvennogo tvorchestva. Tezisy i annotatsii* (Leningrad, 1963); B. Meilakh, "Sodruzhestvo naus-srebovaniie vremeni," in *VL*, no. 11 (1963), pp. 61–85. As early as 11 October 1962, the *Literaturnaia Gazeta* published an article by Meilakh entitled "The Totality of Scholarship and the Secrets of Creativity" or "Sodruzhestvo nauk i tainy tvorchestva"; this was the first time that collaboration between literary scholarship and sociology (as well as with psychology, cybernetics, and the like) was mentioned again. A report on the discussion occasioned by this essay appears in *VL*, no. 7, (1965), pp. 137–55.

90. Compare Bushmin, p. 73.

91. Compare N. N. Koziura, "Sympozium po sotsiologii iskusstva," in *Voprosy filosofii*, no. 7 (1967), pp. 140–51.

92. V. Kantorovich, *VL*, no. 11 (1969), p. 56.

93. "Sotsiologizm v sovremennom burzhuaznom literaturovedenii," in *VL*, no. 2 (1967) pp. 41–52.

94. V. Kantorovich, *NM*, no. 2 (1967), p. 149.

95. German translation in *Ostprobleme*, vol. 19 (1967), pp. 540–42.

96. Since the results of sociological research are generally issued only in small editions, they are almost inaccessible to writers as well as to the "mass readership." Not only their "availability," but also their representative nature is somewhat in doubt. On this, see *NM*, no. 12 (1967), p. 148, and no. 5 (1969), p. 275.

97. "Izuchat' fakty v ikh polnote," in *VL*, no. 3 (1968), pp. 121–37.

98. *NM*, no. 12 (1967), pp. 148–73. Writer Vladimir Kantorovich (born 1901) was Gorky's collaborator in the journal *Nashi dostizheniia* (*Our Achievements*) in the period 1935–1937; in 1937 he was subjected to "illegal repression" and only returned to literary work in 1956 (*KLE*, vol. 3, column 374).

99. On this theory, which greatly damaged Soviet literature (especially drama) and literary scholarship between 1935 and 1956, see *KLE*, vol. 1 (1962), columns 577–80.

100. *VL*, no. 11 (1969), pp. 43–44.

101. "Izuchat' zaprosy i vkusy chitatelia," in *VL*, no. 12 (1967), pp. 172–74.

102. In the year 1924 alone, more than 2,000 contributions to audience sociology were published in the Soviet Union (compare *Literaturnaia Gazeta*, 31 July 1968).

103. L. Kornilov, "Krupneishii izdatel' mira" or "The World's Biggest Publisher," *Nedelia*, no. 37 (Moscow, 1966); German translation in *Ostprobleme*, vol. 18 (1966), pp. 770–74; *Literaturnaia Gazeta*, 18 August and 22 October 1966; German translation in *Ostprobleme*, pp. 774–77.

104. "Vazhnaia zadacha sotsiologii" or "An Important Task of Sociology," in *VL*, no. 9 (1969), pp. 190–95.
105. Compare Bushmin, pp. 73–74.
106. *Sovetskii chitatel'. Opyt konkretnosotsiologicheskogo issledovaniia* (Moscow, 1968), 344 pp.
107. Józef Szocki, *Czytelnictwo i lektura ludzi dorotsych* (Wroctaw, 1968), 178 pp.
108. See above, nn. 8 and 99.
109. Compare "Smeleie pol'zovat'sia vozmozhnostiami" or "To Utilize the Possibilities Boldly" in *NM*, no. 11 (1970), pp. 237–40.
110. Pospelov (1967), p. 124. See also p. 123.
111. Vol. 1 (Moscow, 1963), p. 18.
112. Pospelov, p. 107.
113. Bushmin (1969), p. 71.
114. K. Grigor'ian, critical review of Bushmin (1969), in *Zvezda*, no. 11 (1970), pp. 221–22.
115. See above, n. 98.
116. *NM*, no. 5 (1969), p. 274; se also P. A. Berlin, "Burzhuaziia v russkoi khudozhestvennoi literature" or "The Bourgeoisie in Russian Literature," in *Novaia zhizn'*, no. 1 (1913), columns 169–96; E. Häusler, *Der Kaufmann in der russischen Literatur* (Königsberg, 1935), 127 pp.
117. *Slovar' literaturnykh tipov* (Moscow, 1907–1914), 24 numbers projected, 8 numbers issued. For the problem of Literary Types see Bernhard Küppers, *Die Theorie vom Typischen in der Literatur. Ihre Ausprägung in der russischen Literaturkritik und in der sowjetischen Literaturwissenschaft* (Munich, 1966).
118. *NM*, no. 5 (1969), pp. 273–81.
119. *VL*, no. 11 (1969), pp. 43–59.
120. Y. Kuz'menko, "K istokam problem, konfliktov, kharakterov," in *VL*, no. 11 (1965), pp. 17–36; see also Kuz'menko, "Chelovek tvoriashchii," in *NM*, no. 9 (1970), pp. 219–47, and no. 10, pp. 226–52 (concerning changes in the positive hero in Soviet literature, related to social changes).
121. "Probleme der Literatur- und Sprachforschung," German translation in *Kursbuch*, vol. 5 (Frankfurt, 1966), pp. 74–76. Lotman was also able to refer to Czech structuralism, which is very open to questions of the sociology of literature. See, for example, J. Mukařovský's 1935 work, "Estetická funkce, norma hodnota jako sociální fakty," German translation, "Ästhetische Funktion und ästhetische Norm als soziale Fakten" in *Kapitel aus der Ästhetik* (Frankfurt am Main, 1970), pp. 7–112; K. Chvatik, "Die strukturalistische Auffassung des Verhältnisses von Kunst und Gesellschaft" (1968) in *Strukturalismus und Avantgarde* (Munich, 1970), pp. 122–26.
122. Y. M. Lotman, *Struktura khudozhestvennogo teksta* or *The Structure of Artistic Texts* (Moscow, 1970), p. 349.
123. Ibid., see especially pp. 34–43, 345–49, 360–62.
124. See K. Eimermacher, ed., *Texte des sowjetischen literaturwissenschaftlichen Strukturalismus* (Munich, 1971), pp. 645–47.
125. See the (critical) report by N. N. Koziura in *Voprosy filosofii* 21, no. 7 (1967): 140–44.
126. *Iskusstvo kak sotsiologicheskii fenomen. K kharakteristike estetiko-politicheskikh vzgliadov Platona i Aristotelia* (Moscow, 1968), p. 18.
127. Besides Koziura (note 125), see also Bushmin, pp. 61–66. For a more positive view, see Stolovich, *VL*, no. 1 (1970), pp. 217–21.
128. Bushmin, p. 65.
129. "Spetsifika iskusstva," in *NM*, no. 11 (1970), pp. 240–66.

130. Thus, in the course of a discussion of the quality of contemporary poetry, the poet M. Isakovsky complained of the failure of criticism in selecting writers—he stated that the number of members of the writers' union was far too high (according to the union's statistics, there were 2,185 verse poets in the USSR in February 1967). See *VL*, no. 7 (1968), pp. 67–82. A. Tarkovsky proposed establishing a specialized publishing house to bring out small editions of poets' first books; this would relieve the editorial departments of the major publishers and would put an end to the egalitarian practices which lead to the publication of too many books. *VL*, no. 1 (1969), p. 40.

131. S. Mashinsky, *VL*, no. 8 (1966), p. 76.

132. See above, n. 12, and *VL*, no. 5 (1966), p. 73.

133. B. Belaia, "O sovremennom kritike. Spory i razmyshleniia," in *Zvezda*, no. 11 (1970), p. 217.

134. See above, n. 35.

135. G. Porębina, *Aleksander Woroński. Poglądy estetyczne i krytyczno-literackie (1921–1928)* (Kraków, 1964), 148 pages.

136. A. Retivov, *VL*, no. 9 (1969), p. 191; see also A. Iezuitov, "Sotsiologiia i iskusstvoznaniie," in *Sodruzhestvo nauk i tainy tvorchestva* (Moscow, 1968).

137. See "Sotsiologiia, literatura, zhizn'" or "Sociology, Literature, Life," in *NM*, no. 5 (1969), p. 276.

Hans Norbert Fügen

LITERARY CRITICISM AND SOCIOLOGY IN GERMANY

EMPHASES—ATTITUDES—TENDENCIES

ANYONE FACED WITH THE TASK OF COMPILING A MORE OR LESS SYSTEM-
atic survey of that aspect of scholarship in Germany that can properly be subsumed under the heading "Literary Criticism and Sociology" makes a depressing discovery. The more significant nineteenth-
century authors who contributed to this general topic (Hettner,
Gervinus, Bonald, Tocqueville, Guyau, and, in West German scholarship, even Marx and Engels) have been forgotten, so that they must
slowly and gradually be brought back into prominence. But more
recent writers as well often take no notice, or only superficial notice, of each other. To document this finding with the example of
a very few writers, who will be more adequately considered in the
subsequent survey: Adorno's strongly elitist and frequently anti-
empirical concept of scholarship allows him grandly to ignore recent works both in literary criticism and in empirical sociology of
literature. An essay by Paul Stöcklein, intended in his own words
to participate in the "present-day discussion," is written without
any awareness—or at least without any critical discussion—of the
essential contemporary writings in the sociology of literature. Lukács
is quoted at second hand.[1] The work of Hans Robert Jauss, discussed
in detail below, is intended to enlarge literary history with new sociological dimensions; but it takes no account of Arnold Hauser's *The
Social History of Art*, an exemplary work even in its familiarity with
literature. In the chapter discussing Marxist reflection theory, the
relevant passages from Marx are quoted only from the later 1970

edition and are for the most part squeezed into footnotes. Such examples could go on at considerable length, and the sluggish flow of communication precisely in the area here under discussion is almost worth a special branch of sociology. Especially since the demonstrated flaws can hardly be held against the various scholars. The branch of scholarship that could most easily integrate the two research fields—that is, sociology of literature—has begun to take firm hold only in the German Democratic Republic, but by no means in the scholarly activities of the Federal Republic. There is not a single professorship and only a few courses in sociology of literature. Naturally, highly qualified scholars can only occasionally direct major attention to a branch of scholarship that is not fully established; financial aid can only rarely be expected; the upcoming generation of scholarly talent has little desire to exile itself to marginality. Thus neither systematic documentation nor organized exchange of information is possible, not to mention fruitful, cooperative division of labor, which would have to bring together literary critics, folklorists, cultural anthropologists, social historians, and sociologists. As long as progress in this direction is not achieved, as long as mentions of society appear in literary-critical discussions in a "truly vague" sense, "supported by no methodology,"[2] even scholars who consider themselves sociologists of literature will have to submit to Günther K. Lehmann's accusation of "having only a nodding acquaintance with sociology."[3] But this charge could equally well be leveled against sociologists and their response to the findings of literary criticism, although they owe their most fruitful perceptions, if not to literary criticism, at least to literature—a circumstance that also deserves thorough study.

The consequences arising from this situation for a review of postwar German scholarship are easily stated: an area of research that is so minimally structured and that has often remained without connectives and consequences in its various forms of expression, since it lacks continuity, does not allow of any historical-progressive description. The only possibility is a critical examination of those endeavors that are the most significant for content and method. Nevertheless, an overall point of departure can be seen in the frequently noted idealistic orientation of German literary studies. Its causes as well as its effects have been characterized by Eberhard Lämmert as follows: "Given the confining conditions imposed on the German middle class by the continuing hierarchies of hereditary—and later of professional—restrictions, poetry and poetic life forms attained an almost mystical status; there was no other way for the younger generation as early as 1800, and subsequently for many further generations, to express an idealistic antithesis to a philistine or bourgeois pragmatism that suited the conditions only too well."[4] This describes the same process that was less tactfully characterized by Friedrich Engels as "the replacement of an insipid malaise with an effusive malaise" ("die Vertauschung der platten mit der überschwenglichen Misère").[5] At the same time the German literary scholar, whether his field was primarily literary history or literary criticism, was invested with the expectation of a moral-ideological role, which he often willingly assumed: "Thus, far into the twentieth century the Germanist—whether he was a schoolteacher or an interpreter of poetry from the university dais, or even a desk-bound scholar reverently engaged in reconstruction of texts—was imbued with the aura of a spritual adviser dressed in the robes of scholarship."[6]

The end of the Second World War brought no major changes in this situation. To this day neither the external definition nor the self-interpretation of literary scholarship allows for a position that admits any reflection on the social preconditions of their own scholarly activity, let alone of literature. Thus terse pronouncements by influential scholars for or against consideration of sociological findings are noncommittally arrayed. For example, as early as 1945, Karl Viëtor advocated a connection at least between literary history and sociology: "The less biased research of the sociologists has produced a series of important studies concerning the sociology of literary *life*, which we should consult more seriously. On the part of literary history . . . the problems of a sociology of the literary *work* would seem to have greatest priority: the question of the social conditioning of matter, content, and form of literature and of stylistics. The continuing power of the literary work is another subject that deserves more intensive and discriminating attention than heretofore."[7] This draft of a program, which has not been fully realized to this day, may be countered with a pronouncement by Walter Muschg from the same period (1948), which serves as an example of a widespread anti-sociological attitude: "The medical view of art, like the sociological view, sharpens the glance for second-order facts and blunts it to the focal issue."[8]

Thus the essays by Hugo Kuhn were the first to present a systematic attempt at confronting the core questions in which there might be a meeting of the epistemological interests of literature and sociology.[9] Kuhn does not question the validity of both aspects by which sociology has since included literature in its considerations. Of course literature has a differentiated reception among the different social groups and levels, and from these circumstances, sociology can draw well-founded conclusions concerning the literary interests and wishes of clearly distinguishable segments of the population.[10] As an example of research focused on this area, Kuhn cites L. L. Schücking's *Soziologie der literarischen Geschmacksbildung* (*Sociology of the Formation of Literary Taste*).[11] On the other hand, there is the sociology of writers, their social position, and their social consciousness—a line of research to which Kuhn reduces Georg Lukács. While fully admitting the justification of this line of questioning, Kuhn nevertheless believes that we must look elsewhere for the most important sociological nexus offered by literature. Using examples from medieval literature,[12] he demonstrates that literature transcends the social reality that affects it or that serves as its material. Starting from this correct assumption, Kuhn develops the fictional nature of literature—it is precisely in the fiction that he sees its "actuality." "The actuality of literature is fiction."[13] Obviously Kuhn wants to counter a false idea of literary reality that is sometimes articulated in the theory of image and reflection. What he achieves thereby is, for example, the recognition that the question concerning "the writer as social phenomenon" can be posed independently of direct class membership (but not of the structure of the society as a whole). His attempt is especially fruitful wherever it leads to the view of literature, not solely as function, but also as committing, intellectually structuring, interpretation of reality.[14] In this way literature is understood as concrete social action, which may lead beyond the difficulties posed by the concept of reflection as well as the autonomy theorem. True, this does not resolve the question concerning the ideological character of literature; rather, only now can it be posed in a sense commensurate with the peculiarity of literary articulation. In this endeavor, however, both disciplines touched by these problems would have to achieve a level that has not so far been reached: "If the literary historian succeeds in his discipline in exactly determining the form or extent by which social or human behavior appears as actuality in literature—then the sociologist should be able to step in at this point. It remains questionable whether such points interest him. But that is also a basic question of sociology. Its subjects, its concepts, and its methods are in part determined by the way it chooses or is able to encompass such questions."[15]

It is no accident that Kuhn develops his thesis in respect to medieval literature. For even when the cited literary documents are not
a faithful expression of social reality, if they take a critical stance
precisely toward this reality and if they are even able to express it
in a new perspective, they can only be comprehended with specific
historical—that is, sociological—facts as a relatively closed, though
changeable, continuum. This is possible only when economic conditions guarantee the existence of a relatively homogeneous ruling
class and when, as was the case with the culture of feudal nobility,
literature is an additional privilege of this ruling class, which allows
it to verbalize its problems and thus assigns a positively cooperative
function to literature. The difficulties confronting sociology in the
case of a discontinuous or less unambiguous ruling situation are
shown in Arnold Hauser's *Social History of Art*.[16] What is not and
cannot be observed by a scrutiny directed at a relatively stable culture with a largely homogeneous ruling class is now revealed as the
prevailing problem: "The more developed the level of culture is
whose art we are examining, the more complicated is the network of
relationship and the more obscure the social background with which
they are related. The greater the age of an art, of a style, of a genre,
the longer are the periods of time during which the development
proceeds according to immanent, autonomous laws of its own, unaf-
fected by disturbances from outside, and the longer these more or
less autonomous episodes are, the more difficult it is sociologically to
interpret the individual elements of the form-complex in question."[17]
To justify this conception, Hauser in another work recalls Engels and
his essay, "Ludwig Feuerbach and the Death of Classical German
Philosophy." In this work Engels comments on "those ideologies that
depart further from the material, economic basis" (though he does
not, in fact, list literature among them on this occasion, referring only
to philosophy and religion). "Here the connection of ideas with their
material conditions of existence becomes ever more complicated, ever
more obscured by intermediary links."[18] The difficulties resulting
from the described situation are to be overcome by deliberately re-
nouncing the representation of the "full contents" of the cultural
structure and "the entire multiplicity of its relations." According to
Hauser, the "essential traits" are to be resolved into a "common
denominator" under this limiting condition, for "cultural structures
are social structures, vehicles of the self-preservation of society and
the mutual understanding of its members; and as such they remain
forever comparable, forever to be interpreted in the same sense. In

the course of their development they may take on traits not grounded in their social origin and not accessible from this source, but they preserve ... their character as symptoms of the same societal existence, as expressions of the same interests, and as the answer—now positive, now negative—to the same question, the same challenge" (Hauser, *Kunstbetrachtung*, pp. 293–94).

This attitude still leaves enough room for consideration of the changes in style and form that are not only socially determined. "Among the conditions determining their moment in time, social conditions surely occupy first place; but it would be insane to assume that social existence itself generates the forms by which the change expresses itself" (*Kunstbetrachtung*, p. 14). Hauser rejects the current sociological typologic concepts—such as "courtly," "bourgeois," "capitalistic"—as inadequately differentiated to allow for relevant comprehension of the "variety of artistic conceptions and objectives" (*Kunstbetrachtung*, p. 15). Instead he prefers a kind of detailed descriptive analysis that still allows him to demonstrate the influence of social and ruling conditions in the very different but contemporaneous forms without denying "the individuality and complexity of the work of art" (*Kunstbetrachtung*, p. 15). What is evidenced in most chapters of Hauser's *Social History* as a very useful connector between literary works and social conditions are the empirically comprehensible structures of the "literary system"—that is, the producers' forms of interaction and organization, as well as those of the recipients and brokers (criticism and the book trade).

The tension between ideal and reality pointed out by Kuhn in medieval literature was presented by Erich Köhler in a very detailed historical-sociological study.[19] Here, as in his later analyses, Köhler starts from the premises that "courtly poetry is social poetry" and that the use of "a decidedly sociohistorical method" of research concerned with this poetry is a matter of course.[20] When he applied the same method to later French literature,[21] in which social determination is harder to recognize, he could not avoid reflecting on his own theoretical presuppositions. This reflection he undertook in an essay intended to present "certain possibilities of historical and dialectical literary sociology," but at the same time to take into account the "esthetic autonomy of art." "The greatest danger for literary sociology lies in a kind of sociologism that denies this autonomy."[22] Köhler combines, as it were, the premises of Kuhn on the one hand and of Hauser on the other by referring to "the inertia" of literary forms and "the center of gravity of its ideals" ("Historisch-soziol-

ogische Interpretation," p. 86). He has no doubt that "literary sociology represents a particular, independent method of literary criticism"
(p. 83) even though recognition is still far from being given it. He
explains the widespread rejection of this line of research by pointing
to the social consciousness of literary scholars, who experience the
alienation of individual and society under capitalism and therefore
mistakenly understand creativity and freedom only as absolute freedom *from* society. Köhler instead counterposes his conception of
genius, which he sees as "the sum of the possibilities of its time"
(p. 84).

Two complexes important for sociologically oriented literary criticism and already treated by Hauser were theoretically established by
Köhler more clearly than before and brought to a convincing resolution: how can style changes be explained sociologically, and how
are we to interpret the coexistence of divergent stylistic trends within
the same period? Hauser insisted that changes in taste and style were
regularly caused by "the emergence of a new public" (*Kunstbetrachtung*, p. 25). Köhler also recognizes the connection between the
"differentiation of the literary audience" and change in literary style
("Historisch-soziologische Interpretation," p. 86). He does not, however, stop at this observation; rather, he breaks through to changes
in the socioeconomic base. He clearly states the theoretical assumptions justifying such a procedure: "At such turning points of history
the impulses of the substructure break into view through the traditionally and ideologically consolidated forms, styles, and value concepts of literature. Their almost immediate effect is especially clear
and tangible when they are reflected in new literary styles and genres
and when a new view of the world and man is born with them. Such
cases give evidence to show how objectively ascertainable circumstances of the socioeconomic substructure, of concrete historical reality, are transformed into structural elements of art and displace the
traditional forms" (p. 86).

Köhler gives a concrete illustration of such a drastic literary upheaval of social conditions in the displacement of the *chanson de
geste* by courtly romance. The new prevailing structural principle of
the *Aventure* can only be explained through the new form of life
of the courtly knight. The unpropertied knight of low rank, who in
traveling from court to court was forced to offer his military services,
used the *Aventure* to idealize what he was compelled to do by social
conditions. The knightly order *as a whole* accepted the idealization
embodied in the courtly romance because the upper feudal class, in

its conflict with the central royal power, needed the help of the lower nobility as it was symbolized by the knight errant ("Historisch-soziologische Interpretation," p. 87).

Here Köhler indicates that the focus of sociohistorical research must be directed not only at the level of producers, but also at those who are the recipients for demonstrable social reasons. A similar situation is illustrated in another example subsequently cited by Köhler: the middle class of the medieval city, having achieved wealth, adopts "the aristocratic concept of love" and its lyrical form "because for the time being its social claim to recognition can only assert itself in assimilation to the life and cultural forms of the ruling class" ("Historisch-soziologische Interpretation," p. 89). With this statement Köhler comes close to the theory of referent groups, which has been formulated and utilized with good results by sociology and whose uses for socioliterary investigations has been emphasized by various researchers.[23]

Under certain conditions, however, themes and literary forms can survive an aggravating social change. According to Köhler's formulation, this is the case when "they are suited to esthetic mediation between existence and consciousness even under altered circumstances" ("Historisch-soziologische Interpretation," p. 89). On the other hand, the forms do not remain static during periods of relative social stability; rather, they are subjected to an "almost imperceptible functional change," which can be detected even with a "presumed distance from reality of literary fiction" (pp. 91–94). Köhler, however, does not intend to stop at a sociological *explanation* of literary forms but wants to grant to historical-socioliterary criticism the opportunity and "the right to a compulsory esthetic judgment." For this purpose he adopts the categories of totality and the exceptional as developed by Georg Lukács. A work can be considered esthetically successful when it encompasses the "hidden elements of the essence of reality" through correct choice and artistic exaggeration and when it encompasses in one constellation, forced into being by "inner necessity," the characters and individual situations personifying the typical. Only by poetic alienation of reality can the "extensive totality" be changed "into the intensive totality of the self-contained complex of meaning of the literary work" (pp. 95–97).

As indicated, Erich Köhler used a theoretical essay to state the basic assumptions in which his separate studies are grounded. Only in this way does the developed theory become didactically available, and only in this way can it be tested for contradictions. The fact that such a theoretical statement is lacking for Theodor W. Adorno's socioliterary investigations can be explained by Adorno's own conception of scholarship, which sees the courage "to say something that cannot arbitrarily be tested by repetition" as resistance to "collective control."[24] Thus the methodology, essentially represented and considered as a critical theory by Horkheimer and Adorno, achieves what it exalts as the merit of art in the late bourgeois period: to serve human emancipation by "detaching itself from the directed and leveling relationships of a consumability."[25] In this way those art forms that are often disregarded by sociology of literature as "less penetrable for events of historical reality"[26] become, not perhaps the only object, but definitely an important one and therefore a revealing one for this branch of scholarship. This refers to lyric poetry since Goethe and—of course from quite different aspects—to twentieth-century art which is estranged from society. Quite soon after the end of the Second World War, in 1948, Max Horkheimer named "poems like those of Trakl, *Guernica* by Picasso, a composition by Schönberg" as those works "in which the rift between it [the subject] and the barbaric environment seems most emphatic." In these works, which "renounce the illusion of existing community . . . faith is kept with the individual against the infamy of prevailing conditions."[27] This position is exactly the opposite of Georg Lukács'; though using other examples (e.g. Anouilh, Gide, Malraux, D. H. Lawrence), he refers to the same phenomenon, but he sees in this kind of art "a false position of the artist toward society," which must fill him with disgust and hatred. "But at the same time the isolation of the individual means a psychomoral perversion." This literature stands "in opposition to the representation of actual and total—that is, social—man" and gradually turns him "into a shapeless bundle or a boundless flow of loose, uncontrolled associations, until it finally robs him of every determination, every direction, every psychological and moral stability."[28] What Lukács denounces as "sterile revolt" has value for Theodor W. Adorno as well as Horkheimer as "exact, wordless polemic representation of dawning absurdity."[29] Adorno has been charged with holding the view that this very effect corresponds "to the nihilistic intentions of an existentializing bourgeoisie."[30] Adorno, however, believes that the representation must not be blamed for what it represents, that social reality comes alive only in autonomously structured works of art, and that "this autonomous organism expresses that which is only veiled by the empiric form of actuality." Only "structure can hope immanently to master the accidental nature of the purely individual."[31]

A similar set of problems arises for the sociological interpretation of traditional poetry—that is, poetry of the bourgeois period—not because of its content, which is to be compared with avant-garde art, but because the intention not to recognize "the power of socialization" or to "surmount" it is the "sentimentality of distancing."[32] How is it possible, Adorno asks, to join "what is most delicate and fragile . . . with just this commotion," since "the traditional sense of poetry lies, at least ideally, in its remaining untouched by it" ("Lyrik und Gesellschaft," pp. 73–74). In no case should "the social interpretation of poetry—as of all works of art . . . aim directly at the so-called social attitude or societal sphere of interest of the work or even of the author" (p. 76). Rather, it must try to understand "how the *totality* of a society, as a unity filled with self-contradictions, appears in the work of art" (p. 76). But this is the locus of the problem inherent in Adorno's method and the reason why it cannot be imitated except epigonally: as long as the *totality* cannot be represented somewhat systematically on an empirical basis, the social significance of literature within the *totality* cannot be determined. Thus interpretation must erect the bridge between it and literary detail—a kind of interpretation that often demands more of detail than it can deliver.

Adorno very resolutely rejects a sociology that limits its interests to "the social effect of works of art"[33] without taking its point of departure from the work itself. He has expressed the fear that empirical sociological research abstracted from the work itself serves less to promote social understanding than to supply data for potential users. There is some basis for these misgivings, as is shown by those empirical studies that are undertaken from purely commercial aspects and look for nothing more than previously neglected market opportunities.[34] In this form, says Adorno, sociology of art is indeed a "mere technique benefiting the agencies that want to calculate which methods will succeed in winning customers and which will not." The ideal method, he continues, "would be to coordinate objective analyses (that is, analyses of works themselves), analyses of structural and specific mechanisms of effectiveness, and analyses of the recordable subjective findings. They would surely be mutually illuminating."[35]

Adorno's attitude, vacillating between skepticism and rejection, toward empirical sociology can be explained in considerable part by the specific situation of scholarly history and practice. It can be understood as rejection of a naive empiricism that was widespread within West German sociology after the Second World War, when the discipline was fascinated by the methods of practical social studies. In this situation, reflection concerning the conditions that would make empirical investigation possible did indeed tend to get lost, and a real threat existed of an imprudent turn in the direction of instrumental reason—to use a term from critical theory, which fought against the trend. Developments in the German Democratic Republic proceeded in an opposite direction. Hans Koch verbalized his understanding "that the concrete problems of the insoluble mutual relations between economic and cultural development, the concrete questions of the role of culture as a condition for development of the material-technical progress in the GDR have been investigated hardly at all."[36] This led to the question concerning the possible application of empirical methods even in connection with literary researches. The first steps in this direction were taken very uncertainly and carefully.[37] At the same time, the need arose to consider the problems associated with the "Marxist sociology of literature" that was thus inaugurated.[38] It was chiefly a question of the relation of sociology of literature to literary theory and literary history within the overall field of Marxist literary scholarship. Marxist sociology of literature has no intention of separating "the connections between the esthetic characteristics of the literary work of art and social reality; these connections are dialectical and complex, but in the last resort they are essential to interpretation of the work and its effects" (Höhle, "Marxistische Literatursoziologie," p. 482). Though literature is a *particular*—that is, esthetic—form of reflection of actuality, this admitted specificity must not be carried so far as to lead to the assumption of an "esoteric autonomy of literature outside social life" (Höhle, p. 482). In this connection a specific accusation is leveled against bourgeois sociology of literature, of which Hans Norbert Fügen's *Hauptrichtungen der Literatursoziologie (Principal Trends in Sociology of Literature)* is considered representative.[39] The claim is made that works such as Fügen's promote an abrupt division between literary scholarship and sociology of literature because they consider the literary work only as a social phenomenon and do not appraise it according to its literary characteristics. The fact is that this critique does identify an erroneous point of departure for a sociology of literature that claims to be empiric.[40] Since Marxist sociology of literature treats literature "as a specific artistic and social phenomenon simultaneously . . . literary scholarship and sociology of literature" come into "closer juxtaposition than is the case for bourgeois theoreticians." Literary history and literary theory would be incomplete areas of scholarship without sociology of literature, just "as a sociology of literature would not be a truly Marxist sociology of literature if it did not join with literary history and literary theory in a larger unity" (Höhle, "Marxistische Literatursoziologie," p. 483). Nevertheless, literary theory, literary history, and sociology of literature are not identical in either their methods or their object. Marxist sociology of literature concerns itself chiefly with the origin, distribution, and effect of the literary work of art (Höhle, pp. 478–79). It is precisely in investigating the effect of the literary work of art that Marxist sociology of literature wants to utilize the methods of empiric sociology (Höhle, p. 483).

Finally extensive attention must be given to a new attempt that promises to open up literary criticism and especially literary history in the direction of sociological investigation by way of the effects of the literary work. In his sketch toward a "reception esthetic,"[41] Hans Robert Jauss begins by taking a position against positivist history of literature, against the Marxist reflection theory, and commits himself to the literary theory of the Russian Formalists, though with certain critical reservations. As Jauss correctly notes, positivism, by applying the principle of purely causal explanations to the history of literature, has brought to light only externally determining factors. By considering the series of literary facts as a piece of history of literature, it confused the essential character of a work of art with that of a historical actuality. This "objective" description of a series of events kept it from grasping both the artistic nature and the specific historicity of literature (Jauss, *Literaturgeschichte*, pp. 153, 171, 172, 216–17). The "orthodox reflection theory"—Georg Lukács and Lucien Goldmann serving as its representatives for Jauss—is charged with reducing the work of art to its illustrative function, where literary production is seen only as reproduction of the economic process (Jauss, pp. 157, 161). In this way an opportunity is squandered for recognizing "the revolutionary nature of art," which, in Jauss' view, consists in "its ability to lead mankind beyond the established conceptions and prejudices of his historical situation to a new perception of the world or of anticipated reality" (p. 162). Aside from the fact that Jauss, who is still very close to the idealist conception, views revolutionary processes as changes of consciousness rather than alterations in social reality, the critical objections remain valid. These are that so far the reflection theory has furnished no explanation for the simultaneous existence of very diverse literary phenomena, that nonmimetic genres have received almost no consideration, and that for this reason alone, if for no other, "until now no major literary history is on record" (pp. 155, 158, 159).

Jauss hopes to alleviate these shortcomings by a theory that takes its point of departure from the insights of the school of "Russian Formalism." The superiority of this approach over all socioliterary efforts—though these are unjustifiably reduced by Jauss to Lukács' and Goldmann's theories—is considered by him to lie primarily in the fact that Formalist theory treats literature as an independent object of study and, in a sort of functionalism imbued with literature, evaluates the literary work as the sum of all the artistic means employed in it. By extending this theoretical-systematic point of departure beyond the individual work, Formalism necessarily became persuaded of an isolated, purely literarily determined historicity of literature. True, it extended its historical consideration from diachronic description—proceeding from work to work or from genre to genre—to synchrony, which allowed a view of the pluralistic coincidence of varying schools of literature. Jauss also adopted this intention of the Formalist school in that he urged the view that "the diachronic view, which until now was the only usual one," could be "overcome" by synchronic cross-sections that "reveal the heterogeneous multiplicity of concurrent works by equivalent contrasting, and hierarchic structures" (Jauss, *Literaturgeschichte*, p. 194). But "revealing" is not "interpreting." Therefore the criticism must be noted here that neither Formalism nor Jauss' projected "reception esthetic" extends beyond defining description. This circumstance surely raises the suspicion that the structuring of the literary system of one particular epoch cannot be sufficiently understood without recourse to extra-literary factors. Precisely in evaluating this problem Jauss seems to retreat from the Formalists' standpoint, since he takes no notice of the following programmatic statement by Yury Tynyanov: "The dominant significance of the most important social factors is not disputed thereby: rather, they are to be clarified to their full extent, but precisely as an inquiry into the evolution of literature."[42]

Thus Jauss unreservedly adopts the assumption of the Formalist school that literary history is an autonomous progression, independent of nonliterary developments. On one essential point, however, he goes beyond this assumption. While the epistemological interests of the Formalist school focus exclusively on the succession of literary production, Jauss is not content with seeing the historicalness of the work of art merely in its representational or expressive function. Rather, he hopes to include effect in the topical realm of literary history: "Literature and art become procedural history only when the succession of works is brought about, not only by the producing subject, but also by the consuming one—by the interaction of author and reading public" (Jauss, *Literaturgeschichte*, pp. 163–64). Thus the reader's horizon of expectation becomes a fundamental category of literary history (pp. 175–89). If we examine Jauss' attempt at reception theory for its sociological relevance, the following two problems primarily emerge: (1) How is this horizon of expectation formed? (2) Which section of the population—more or less clearly definable in sociological terms—is concealed behind the abstract idea of "reader"?

(1) The horizon of expectation disclosed in a literary work essentially includes two components: the familiar and the new. The difference between the two—the "esthetic distance"—results in the criterion for determining the esthetic value of a work of art. The new can be recognized only against the background of the familiar. Thus the author presumes on a specific disposition among his audience. This disposition can be objectified with the help of literary data given by the work. These are especially the well-known esthetic norms or the immanent poetics of the genre and, further, the "implicit relationships with known works of the literary-historical surroundings" (Jauss, *Literaturgeschichte*, pp. 174, 177).

(2) Having followed Jauss' presentation almost literally to this point, we must now ask: who are these people among whom it is possible to postulate this disposition formed by familiarity with the immanent poetics of the genre and knowledge of the literary-historical surroundings? Since, as Jauss notes, it is not a matter of fortuitous disposition, dependent on subjective factors, but rather of a "trans-subjective horizon of understanding" (p. 176), this presumption can only be satisfied by a small cadre of people professionally trained in related areas, who can at most be joined by a group of connoisseurs privileged by extensive freedom from other work to prepare themselves accordingly. In fact, those passages in which Jauss has to contextually specify—that is, personalize—the initially empty concept of "reader" speak only of critics, new producers, literary historians, whose "position . . . becomes the vanishing point of the process" of literary evolution (pp. 191–92). Obviously contrary to his own intention—certainly without pondering on this circumstance—Jauss points to a fact that has not heretofore been sufficiently considered

in sociological discussions of the position within the literary system of academic or journalistic literary criticism. Obviously the canon of works considered worthy of preservation is regulated by that small section of the public that has an opportunity, for its part, to express itself in writing and that possesses opportunities for opinion-molding influence in books and journals. Jauss focuses only on this segment of the readership, which is privileged by its opportunities for both reception and verbalization, though empirical sociology of literature has already designed more useful, far more comprehensive concepts of audience analysis.[43]

Certain passages clearly demonstrate that Jauss is aware of the necessary limitations of a reception-esthetic approach if the only recognized guidelines of literary history are to be the evolution of forms and the disposition—determined only by literary experience— of the recipients. He therefore introduces a third factor into objective determination of the horizon of expectation alongside the previously named ones of immanent genre poetics and familiarity with the literary surroundings. This factor includes the possibility "that the reader can perceive a new work both within the narrower horizon of his literary expectation and within the wider horizon of his life experiences" (Jauss, *Literaturgeschichte*, p. 177). Reference to extraliterary life experiences absorbed in the literary work inevitably leads to the question of moral problems incorporated in one way or another in literature. Here Jauss has reached the point where, in his opinion, the nexus is established between the particular history of literature and "general history." He sees this connection in the "society-shaping function of literature" (pp. 189, 200, 207). By this he means the fact —surely disputed by no sociologist—that not only do experiences of actual life enter into literature, but that it also anticipates previously unrealized possibilities. This statement nevertheless suffers from an extraordinary lack of differentiation. Certain questions are not posed, much less answered; these concern the problem of whether the presented problems are given in social reality and only articulated by literature, so that they are raised to new consciousness, or whether it is a matter of general-historical or, more probable, of class-specific problems. This would mean that there is almost always a sifting of the problems that are dealt with by literature, that problems concerning wide segments of the population can be suppressed by literature and in fact have been suppressed, that this circumstance reveals an ideologically retarding function of literature—surely also a society-shaping factor which, for its part, again selectively affects the audience. Thus the provocation of Jauss' design seems to lie chiefly in the fact that—perhaps contrary to his intention—he poses these questions and that he demands from literary criticism a reflection of its own disposition of experience and consciousness.

[Translated from the German by Ruth Hein]

Notes

1. Paul Stöcklein, "Literatursoziologie. Gesichtspunkte zur augenblicklichen Diskussion," in *Literatur und Geistesgeschichte, Festgabe für H. O. Burger,* ed. R. Grimm and C. Wiedemann (Berlin, 1968), pp. 406–21. The quotation from Lukács, cited by M. Wehrli, is on p. 409.
2. Alfons Silbermann, "Literaturphilosophie, soziologische Literaturästhetik oder Literatursoziologie," *Kölner Zeitschrift für Soziologie und Sozialpsychologie* 18 (1966): 140.
3. In *Deutsche Zeitschrift für Philosophie* 17 (1969): 1148.
4. Eberhard Lämmert, "Das Ende der Germanistik und ihre Zukunft," in *Ansichten einer künftigen Germanistik,* ed. by Jürgen Kolbe, Reihe Hanser 29 (Munich, 1969), p. 80.
5. Karl Marx and Friedrich Engels, *Über Kunst und Literatur,* 2 vols. (Frankfurt and Vienna, 1968), 1: 468.
6. Lämmert, "Ende der Germanistik," p. 81.
7. Karl Viëtor, "Deutsche Literaturgeschichte als Geistesgeschichte," in *Methoden der deutschen Literaturwissenschaft. Eine Dokumentation,* ed. by Viktor Zmegac (Frankfurt, 1971), pp. 191–92.
8. Walter Muschg, *Tragische Literaturgeschichte* (Berne, 1948), p. 272.
9. Hugo Kuhn, "Dichtungswissenschaft und Soziologie," *Studium Generale* 3, no. 11 (1950): 622–26; "Soziale Realität und dichterische Fiktion," in *Soziologie und Leben. Die soziologische Dimension der Fachwissenschaften,* ed. by Carl Brinkmann (Tübingen, 1952), pp. 195–219.
10. Kuhn, "Dichtungswissenschaft," p. 622.
11. Levin L. Schücking, *Soziologie der literarischen Geschmacksbildung,* Dalp-Taschenbücher, 3d ed., vol. 354 (Berne, 1961). The study originated in 1921.
12. Kuhn, "Dichtungswissenschaft," pp. 623–25; "Soziale Realität," pp. 201–14.
13. Kuhn, "Soziale Realität," p. 215.
14. Kuhn, "Dichtungswissenschaft, p. 626.
15. Kuhn, "Soziale Realität," pp. 218–19.
16. Arnold Hauser, *The Social History of Art,* 4 vols. (New York, 1957); German ed., *Sozialgeschichte der Kunst und Literatur,* 2 vols. (Munich, 1953).
17. Hauser, *Social History,* 1: 25; *Sozialgeschichte,* 1: 23.

18. Hauser, *Methoden moderner Kunstbetrachtung* (Munich, 1970), p. 22. The quotation, incompletely cited by Hauser, can be found in full in Karl Marx and Friedrich Engels, *Werke* (Berlin, 1956), 21: 303.
19. Erich Köhler, *Ideal und Wirklichkeit in der höfischen Epik. Studien zur Form der frühen Artus- und Graldichtung*, Beihefte zur Zeitschrift für romanische Philologie, vol. 97 (Tübingen, 1956).
20. Erich Köhler, *Trobadorlyrik und höfischer Roman. Aufsätze zur französischen und provenzalischen Literatur des Mittelalters*, Neue Beiträge zur Literaturwissenschaft, vol. 15 (Berlin, 1962), p. 5.
21. Erich Köhler, *Esprit und arkadische Freiheit. Aufsätze aus der Welt der Romania* (Frankfurt and Bonn, 1966).
22. Köhler, "Über die Möglichkeit historisch-soziologische Interpretation," in *Esprit und arkadische Freiheit*, p. 102. This essay is the German version of a lecture, composed in French, given at a colloquium in Brussels. The lecture was followed by a discussion that included a number of the leading European sociologists of literature (Robert Escarpit, Alfons Silbermann, Lucien Goldmann, Roland Barthes, Edoardo Sanguinetti): *Littérature et société. Problèmes de méthodologie en sociologie de la littérature*. Etudes de sociologie de la littérature (Brussels, 1967), pp. 47–71.
23. Robert K. Merton, *Social Theory and Social Structure* (New York, 1957), pp. 225–386; Hans Norbert Fügen, *Wege der Literatursoziologie*, Soziologische Texte, no. 46, 2d ed. (Neuwied and Berlin, 1971), p. 34; Fügen, "Triviallyrik—Küchenlieder," *Kölner Zeitschrift für Soziologie und Sozialpsychologie* 21 (1969): 107; Hilmar Kallweit and Wolf Lepenies, "Literarische Hermeneutik und Soziologie" *Ansichten einer künftigen Germanistik*, p. 136.
24. Institut für Sozialforschung, "Kunst- und Musiksoziologie," in *Soziologische Exkurse* (Frankfurt, 1956), p. 94.
25. Institut für Sozialforschung, "Kunst- und Musiksoziologie," p. 97.
26. Hans Robert Jauss, *Literaturgeschichte als Provokation*, edition Suhrkamp (Frankfurt, 1970), p. 158.
27. Max Horkheimer, "Kunst und Massenkultur," *Die Umschau. Internationale Revue* 3 (1948): 455.
28. Georg Lukács, "Gesunde oder kranke Kunst," in *Schicksalswende. Beiträge zu einer neuen deutschen Ideologie*, 2d ed. (Berlin, 1956), p. 157.
29. Lukács, "Gesunde oder kranke Kunst," p. 159; Theodor W. Adorno, "Erpresste Versöhnung," in *Noten zur Literatur II*, Bibliothek Surkamp, vol. 47 (Frankfurt, 1969), p. 166.
30. Leo Kofler, *Zur Theorie der modernen Literatur. Der Avantgardismus in soziologischer Sicht* (Neuwied, 1962), p. 168.
31. Adorno, "Erpresste Versöhnung," pp. 166, 169, 168, 167.
32. Adorno, "Rede über Lyrik und Gesellschaft," in *Noten zur Literatur I*, Bibliothek Suhrkamp, vol. 71 (Frankfurt, 1961), p. 74.
33. Adorno, "Thesen zur Kunstsoziologie," *Kölner Zeitschrift für Soziologie und Sozialpsychologie* 19 (1967): 87.
34. *Buch und Leser in Deutschland*, Schriften zur Buchmarkt-Forschung, no. 4 (Gütersloh, 1965); Gerhard Schmidtchen, "Lesekultur in Deutschland. Ergebnisse repräsentativer Buchmarktstudien für den Börsenverein des Deutschen Buchhandels." Archiv für Soziologie und Wirtschaftsfragen des Buchhandels, vol. 5 (1968), pp. 1977–2152.
35. Adorno, "Kunstsoziologie," p. 89.
36. Hans Koch, *Unsere Literaturgesellschaft. Kritik und Polemik* (Berlin, 1965), p. 395.

37. Cäcilia Friedrich, "Einige Überlegungen zur literatursoziologischen Frage-technik"; Isolde Walter and Achim Walter, "Bericht über die Arbeit eines wissenschaftlichen Studentenzirkels am Germanistischen Institut zu litera-tursoziologischen Problemen"; Ernst-Ludwig Zacharias, "Zwischenbilanz eines Versuches zur Wirkungsforschung," *Wissenschaftliche Zeitschrift der Martin-Luther-Universität Halle-Wittenberg*, Gesellschafts und sprachwis-senschaftliche Reihe, no. 15 (1966), pp. 499–502, 503–10, 511–17.

38. Thomas Höhle, "Probleme einer marxistischen Literatursoziologie," *Wissen-schaftliche Zeitschrift der Martin-Luther-Universität Halle-Wittenberg*, pp. 477–88.

39. Hans Norbert Fügen, *Die Hauptrichtungen der Literatursoziologie und ihre Methoden. Ein Beitrag zur literatursoziologischen Theorie.* Abhandlungen zur Kunst-, Musik- und Literaturwissenschaft, vol. 21 (Bonn, 1964),

40. Fügen, *Hauptrichtungen*, preface to the 5th ed. (1971), p. viii.

41. Hans Robert Jauss, *Literaturgeschichte als Provokation der Literaturwissen-schaft*, Konstanzer Universitätsreden (Constance, 1967). This essay, in much expanded form, was included with other essays and published in Jauss, *Literaturgeschichte als Provokation*, pp. 144–207.

42. Yury Tynyanov, "Über die literarische Evolution," in *Texte der russischen Formalisten*, ed. by Yury Stridter, Theorie und Geschichte der Literatur und der schönen Künste, vol. 6, no. 1 (Munich, 1969), p. 461.

43. Robert Escarpit, *Sociologie de la littérature*, Que sais-je, no. 777 (Paris, 1958); Fügen, *Hauptrichtungen*, pp. 169–76; Harald Weinrich, "Für eine Literaturgeschichte des Lesers," *Methoden der deutschen Literaturwissen-schaft*, ed. Viktor Zmegac, pp. 325–39.

Hans H. Rudnick

RECENT BRITISH AND AMERICAN STUDIES CONCERNING THEORIES OF A SOCIOLOGY OF LITERATURE

IF LITERATURE IS TO BE UNDERSTOOD AS ONE OF THE FUNDAMENTAL manifestations of human knowledge and experience, literature has to be granted the independent status of an art. It also, then, should be granted that any work which deserves to be called art tries to establish a totality of meaning within the coordinates of human existence. This totality of meaning represents one of the touchstones for the validity and the value of art.

British and American criticism of the sociological and sociocultural bent has restricted itself in the past largely to studies concerning economical and social aspects. This strong concentration on economical questions can only cover small aspects of the entire work of art, and sensitive critics like Christopher Caudwell[1] have tried to further the understanding of the literary work of art by pointing out that purely economic and social approaches can only touch a small segment of the spectrum to be investigated by a serious critic who attempts to do justice to an artwork. Even the most radical partisan of strict materialism will have to concede that ideas, which may have been conceived initially through asking economically orientated questions, have an existence in themselves, an existence beyond the range of economic conditions. As long as the socioeconomic critic is aware that his method will only cover certain aspects of the work of art and not its entirety, this kind of critic will know the limits of his method with regard to literary judgment.

These limitations as well as the possibilities of the use of sociological methods within literary criticism have been recently shown most convincingly in a critical overall view of a real handbook of literary sociology written by Joseph Strelka, an American critic, who came originally from the field of Germanic studies to comparative literature and literary theory.[2]

The work of art contains and reflects a multitude of experiences and insights which stem, among others, from socioeconomic sources. Hippolyte Taine's influence reaches into the present in the writings of T. K. Whipple, Joseph Wood Krutch, Granville Hicks, Newton Arvin, and others.[3] From Barrett Wendell's statement that "literature is the expression of national temper," it does not take much to write a primarily sociologically orientated literary history like Parrington's and further along, via Van Wyck Brooks and Arthur Hobson Quinn, to compile a sociocultural literary history like Spiller's.[4] Even F. O. Matthiessen's *American Renaissance* (London, New York, Toronto, 1941), written in reaction to Parrington, has difficulties in finding a truly workable formula for the purpose of developing aesthetic and economic perspectives; a general restraint from more than vaguely subsuming individual authors and their works to prevailing literary trends begins to manifest itself in American criticism since Matthiessen. The specific literary artwork becomes an isolated reflector of the social situation in general. More comprehensive statements on the relation between art and society are generally shunned in unhistorically inclined critical presentations, apparently indicating an insecurity on the critic's side as to how far a relation between art and society really exists. Howard Mumford Jones[5] explains that the history of the American society has fascinated the American sensibility. It is, therefore, no wonder that the American sociocultural critic would have a very strong tendency toward sociological interpretation.

However, there are several serious attempts to free literature from the subjugation of mere socioeconomic or sociocultural criticism. The emancipation of literature from the submission to mere academic sociological interpretation becomes evident in studies by Bernard de Voto[6] where literature is understood as the manifestation of social experiences in which the myths, ideals, and goals of a society crystallize. Joseph Wood Krutch[7] and David Daiches are using the term "civilization" in such a manner that it does not rob literature of its dignity. According to Krutch, poetry and civilization are parallel phenomena which owe the form of their existence to the prevailing spirit of the time. Both poetry and civilization are closely interrelated in their content; while poetry reflects the realm of thought, civilization reflects the same content on the level of action. Daiches holds similar views which, however, have the advantage of being more clearly developed and more concisely stated in several of his works reflecting the theory of sociology of literature.[8] Daiches states that the primary influence on the general development of literature stems from the entire civilization which man has created for himself. Civilizations are understood to be a macrocosm of human nature while those individuals living within the civilization represent the microcosm of the particular civilization. Thus, the creation of a literary work of art by an individual as well as the reception of this work of art by the audience depends in two ways on the present constitution of the environment that has been created by the civilization. On the one hand, the experience and understanding of myths and archetypal forms within a civilization is facilitated through their continuous recurrence in literature; on the other hand, great literature of that particular civilization will generally reflect, in a natural and comprehensive manner, all those essential characteristics typical of the existing culture.

Other important problems of a sociology of literature are illuminated by Harry Levin in his important article on "Literature as an Institution." He not only sees literature as a result generated by social cause, but also grants it a creative role in relation to society, namely in being able to effect social consequences.[9] In a similar vein James T. Farrell points out, above all, how damaging a purely sociological approach to literature can be.[10] In spite of these warnings, most of the recent theories of a sociology of literature have been written by sociologists and not by sociologically orientated literary critics. Adolph S. Tomars, for example, is primarily interested in making the social sciences into a comprehensive science with strong emphasis on interdisciplinary studies and comparisons. This sensitive effort by an open-minded sociologist has been exceptionally successful in its findings; not only has it resulted in a study on the possible usefulness of anthropological methods for the sociologist's purposes,[11] but it has also led to a formulation of a useful sociological theory of literature and art. Tomars demonstrates the influence of social classes on objects and forms within a society, following Robert M. MacIver's pattern of at times united and at times warring classes.[12] In a manner similar to Tomars', general problems of a sociology of literature are touched upon by Paul Honigsheim, a German-American scholar of sociology, in his theory of a sociology of art.[13]

One of the most comprehensive recent theories of a sociology of literature has been developed by the late Hugh Dalziel Duncan.[14] It is Duncan's merit to have responsibly recognized the enormous influence of the sociocultural environment on the creation of a literary work of art. He places his consideration of the author, of the critic, and of the author's audience into the larger context of an all-encompassing social environment. Following Kenneth Burke's rather broad view of what constitutes literary form, Duncan develops an equally comprehensive and systematic theory of a literary sociology. In this theory, literature has a clearly defined place within society; it is divided into the categories of "magical art," "great art," "make-believe," and "a social institution." Literature is clearly defined as an independent utterance stated by an individual, but reflecting the prevailing social condition within that society. An extensive bibliography which comprises one third of the study proves to be extremely helpful in further illuminating Duncan's arguments.

Another important step toward a more genuine analysis of the relation between literature and society was undertaken by Alexander C. Kern when he wrote, conscious of the possibilities and drawbacks of his method, on the sociology of literary knowledge.[15] Beginning his argument with a reference to Karl Mannheim's *Ideology and Utopia*,[16] Kern stresses that he is striving to achieve greater objectivity than Mannheim since Mannheim's doctrine of a "total ideology" has invited a radical relativism for the sake of a complete and systematic theory. Without lessening the importance of economic and social forces, Kern, in a way similar to the American pragmatists, recognizes the power of "theory"—that is, the creative power of mental and immanent forces—as an innovative element within the social context. Kern's study contains fundamental implications for the method of establishing a theory of literary knowledge. Kern proceeds to develop his method by taking a number of steps which are flexible enough not to be applied in all cases but only in those where a response to the step taken is possible. He proposes that the first step be taken by choosing a certain literary theme that can be defined within specific temporal limits and within a circle of problems related to that specific area. The next step would demand that all works falling into the time period in question be analyzed in order to isolate the common denominator and the actual type which expresses the ideology. The next step should be to investigate how far the representation of the ideology differs in the works examined. This process will reveal mixtures and interrelations of views within the particular works and it will then become necessary to deduce from these insights the emergence or the history of a way of thought. Having arrived at this point, Kern proposes that the sociological background of the ideology be analyzed (in sociological terms), thus enabling the critic to relate the structures and tendencies of the ideology to certain groups, classes, generations, professions, religious sects, parties, geographic regions, cliques, or schools of thought that have expressed this ideology in any way. Finally, the development of this thinking is to be explained from the background of the general social structure and from the changes to which it is subjected, as well as from those continually changing problems which result from the constantly fluctuating social structure.

Kern's method makes it possible to arrive at more than merely sociological results. He has shown in the case of the New England transcendentalists that his method can be profitably applied to literary studies.

Another important theory concerning the influence of the social environment on the artist's style of creativity has been developed by Vytautas Kavolis.[17] Style is understood as an artistic manifestation of the existing relationship between society and artist. Kavolis separates direct social influences from indirect, cultural influences. Within these two categories of style, there are several subdivisions. Direct social influences on style stem from economic or political forces; style may appear as a result of the general structure of a particular society or as an expression of particular factions within that society. Style may also represent general artistic attitudes among certain social classes before or after the emergence of urbanization. Concerning indirect influences on style by the weight of a culture, Kavolis understands style as reflecting religious characteristics and other varying cosmologies and value systems. A mixture of the above categories of style appears to be prevalent in the phenomenon of the abstract style, which is explained by Kavolis as an expression of secularized puritanism. After discussing some more "modern styles" from the perspective of how they reflect social development, Kavolis offers a conclusive "sociology of imagination."

Even though Kavolis' tables and charts do not escape the flaws of rigorous abstraction, it appears that his thoughts and syntheses provide useful insights into the problem of literary style and into the possibilities which such sensitive sociological studies are able to provide for literary scholarship. It is obvious that any syntheses of this type cannot represent at this point perfect laws but rather general tendencies with an ample number of exceptions. These exceptions themselves will not only be of an accidental or individual nature but also of a more comprehensive character within the coordinates of space and time. But in spite of these shortcomings, such a theory of the sociology of style and imagination can illuminate many problems of style. No reasonable scholar of stylistics will deny that style is influenced in some way or another by social forces, even if he must reject a total reduction of questions of style to mere sociological interpretation. A careful approach to questions of style from sociological aspects should be considered as one of the many equally important and mutually supporting approaches to literature, especially if it is remembered that entire stylistic eras have been named in the past after predominant technical and formal elements, which as such are rather unrelated to literature. While literary critics of the formalist bent tend to overemphasize the immanent stylistic characteristics of a literary work of art, other critics interested in questions of "realism" may overemphasize transcendental problems and overstress sociological conditions.

Still another attempt to develop a universal typology of a sociology of literary style deserves to be mentioned here. Even though Paul Ramsay's contribution does not reach the depth and scope of Pitrim A. Sorokin's study, Ramsay lays some basic groundwork for a typology of a sociology of style.[18] He begins with the sociological description of different social forms and refers from this angle to the very complex and sometimes paradoxical relation between independent individual freedom on one hand, and the subordination of the individual to the rules of society on the other. Ramsay has recognized four basic types of social forms which recur in history and support certain forms of life and style. His first social form is the one of a harmonious society which may manifest itself, for example, by people standing united behind a common goal. This society does not have to be a closed society in spite of being united by a common interest. The second social form is the divided society which reveals itself most clearly in times of civil war. The third social form is the endangered society in which man is confronting situations which he is extremely afraid of. The fourth and last social form is the fragmented society in which the loss of common values is caused by a strife between pluralistic and individualistic forces within the society. Every one of these social forms prompts tendencies which, as reactions and answers to impending problems, are reflected in the general structure of the literature of the times. In this sense literature reflects the essential and constant artistic struggle between the forces of social bonds and the innovative creativity of the artist who contributes to breaking these bonds because they are felt to be confining.

If the term literature has been used up to now as a comprehensive term including all literary genres, it must be mentioned that Cecil M. Bowra has shown convincingly that the form of poetry in particular relates to the political environment during the first half of the twentieth century.[19] Political ideas, according to Bowra, seem to influence the formal structure of poetry. For the English comedy from Congreve to Fielding, John Loftis has shown that a similar correspondence between the form of the comedy and the sociopolitical environment exists.[20] The form of the comedy is seen as an expression of the social situation and its changes. Besides this sociopolitical approach, Loftis also does justice to the comedy as an aesthetic literary form. His study shows clearly that the English comedy of those times gained as much sociopolitical importance as it lost aesthetic qualities. The general decline of comedy is attributed to the loss of its audience to other competing literary forms like the opera or the mixture of artistic expression called "entertainment" in those days. Other causes for the decline of comedy in England stem from the financial structure of the theater, which for financial reasons avoided the performance of plays by living authors, and from Walpole's Licensing Act of 1737 which dealt the final politically motivated blow to the English theater.

Regarding the birth and the development of the novel, Arno Schirokauer finds that the changing attitude toward oral presentation during the Renaissance caused the emergence of the novel as a new literary form.[21] When the individual separates itself from the congregation, a demand arises for a literary form which supports the increasing emergence and isolation of the individual. This fundamentally sociological process finds its closest ally in the invention of printing so that Schirokauer can claim that the novel was born when the printing press was invented. Schirokauer's arguments about the emergence of the novel have not necessarily contradicted the historically more narrowly defined opinion, especially among scholars of English, that the novel is a more recent literary form that emerged in the eighteenth century and which is held to be fundamentally different from preceding prose forms of some length. This view was held by Madame de Staël, Hegel, Taine, and Leslie Stephen; other critics of the nineteenth century followed their example with the result that most modern critics from Ian Watt to Maurice Z. Shroder are also convinced that the emergence of the novel should be interpreted in this historically more limited sense.

Following this narrowed perspective, the novel has frequently been understood as a typical literary expression of the bourgeois and middle classes.[22] But such an interpretation appears to be too vague, especially if it is kept in mind that the Baroque novel slowly develops bourgeois traits,[23] and that feudal elements reach into the novel of the eighteenth century. Even Harry Levin, whose insights are usually enlightened by a well-balanced critical approach to literature, supports the view that at present no literary form is more representative of sociological developments than the novel.[24] But this observation should not lead to the conclusion that the history of the novel reflects in general the social predominance of the bourgeois middle class. Levin trusts that most novelists are better sociologists than those scholars who claim sociology as their profession.[25] This opinion seems symptomatic of the general distrust between literary and sociological scholarship.

One further reason for the broadly held view that the novel is a typical sociologically orientated literary form may find its unconscious support in the fact that most of the modern novels are set within these sociological limits.[26] It therefore is not surprising that many modern critics emphasize sociological elements within the novel. Philip Rahv stresses that the novel should not be recognized as a literary genre by means of its form but by its performance as a vehicle for the description of a social environment.[27] W. J. Harvey proposes similarly that the novelist's technique is determined by the author's view of life, which itself is considered to be a result of the prevailing spirit of the time.[28] Alan Friedman and John Henry Raleigh share Harvey's view that the novel depicts a developmental process combined with a mimetic reproduction of the reality of experience as it is generated by the particular environment.[29] Steven Marcus, a follower of Lionel Trilling, also states that the form of the novel is determined by its environment and, going one step further than Friedman and Raleigh, he attributes to the novel a role of social responsibility with ethical and informational purposes.[30] David Daiches considers the English novel a "public instrument" which deals with events and situations that have emerged from the social environment shared by author and reader alike. For this reason the content of the novel is of common interest to both.

The limits of a mere sociological interpretation of novels are demonstrated in Diana Spearman's study of the forms of the novel.[31] A comparison between the Japanese and the European novel leads to the conclusion that both novelistic forms have developed in completely contrary directions even though no sociological reasons for this development have been detected. The otherwise implied assumption that identical sociological circumstances could lead to nearly identical literary forms would have introduced the notion of determinism into literature which up to this point must be considered completely alien to literary thought. In part two of her book, Diana Spearman comes to the conclusion that even in the case of the eighteenth-century English novel no proof can be found for a conclusive theory of the reflection of social forces within the novel.

Even if some of the above-mentioned, largely sociological studies of literature have held views to which some purists among literary scholars would not be willing to subscribe, it must be granted that sociologically orientated studies of literature have the same right of existence as formalistic, historical, psychological, and mythopoeic ones. As long as literary works of art are approached by a critic with sensitivity, insight, and comparative capability, there is no reason why such a critic should be rejected by fellow critics from a less tolerant camp. Only when criticism degenerates into a game of numbers and a doctrine with positivist implications, must a clear rejection be expressed for the sake of self-preservation of literature and, above all for the sake of all art. Sociological approaches to literature and the arts in general do have a great potential for valid insights into the genesis and meaning of literature as long as these approaches do not confine themselves to the limits of mere sociological insight. Scholars like David Daiches, Harry Levin, and Hugh Dalziel Duncan have contributed immensely toward opening literary studies to sociological approaches. Daiches has divided the literary work of art into two very workable constituents. The first component is the general spectrum of the macrocosm of human nature as such. The second component is the particular spectrum of the microcosm of each creative individual. The conserving forces of history and the innovative power of the individual are represented in an adequate way which allows an enlightened approach to the sociology of literature and art in general. In this system, literature is allowed to play a creative role in that it is permitted to cause social change.

Harry Levin still carries some of the burden which a stronger feeling for history has loaded on his shoulders. But his potential danger of being crushed by this burden is checked by his interdisciplinary and comparative mind. The late Hugh Dalziel Duncan came as a sociologist to literature, but his close friendship with his teacher Kenneth Burke enabled him to become aware of the true place of literature in society. Literature is clearly considered to be an independent utterance which contains within its independence significant traces of its social and cultural environment. Alexander Kern acknowledges the power of theory as a creative force within a sociology of literature, and Vytautas Kavolis analyzes the relation between artist and society as manifested within literary style. The interaction between pluralistic and individualistic forces, between history and constructive revolutionary creativity has to be reflected in any meaningful theory of a sociology of literature. It is not enough to say like Philip Rahv that the novel describes the social environment. It is not enough to say like W. J. Harvey that the novel reflects the spirit of the times. The ingredient of artistic creativity has not achieved full recognition in these statements. It becomes clear from Diana Spearman's study that the historical approach to literature has its limits. It is very effective in analysis, description, and comparison of the preestablished; but as proven in the comparison between the European and Japanese novel, there are no common traits in the development of the novel that can be traced to corresponding sociological reasons in both cultures.

It is evident that modern studies toward a sociology of literature have come a long way. In 1946 Richard T. LaPierre was still convinced that "the arts, in sum, are the least important and the most variable of the elements that ever enter into a social structure."[32] Today this statement no longer holds, since important studies that abstain from interpreting literature from the limiting point of view of ideological preoccupation have been published. Instead, literature is being taken seriously as an independent utterance that contains reflections of the general social situation of the creative individual and also of man.

Notes

1. Christopher Caudwell, *Illusion and Reality* (London, 1939; 5th ed., 1950).
2. The book has appeared so far only in German: Joseph Strelka, *Die gelenkten Musen* (Wien, Frankfurt, Zurich, 1971).
3. T. K. Whipple, *Spokesmen* (New York, London, 1928), especially chap. 1: "The Poetic Temper"; Joseph Wood Krutch, *The Modern Temper* (New York, 1929); Granville Hicks, *The Great Tradition: An Interpretation of*

American Literature since the Civil War (New York, 1933; rev. ed., 1935); Newton Arvin, *Whitman* (New York, 1938).

4. Barrett Wendell, *A Literary History of America* (New York, 1900; latest ed., 1928); Vernon L. Parrington, *Main Currents in American Thought* (New York, 1930); Van Wyck Brooks, *The Wine of the Puritans* (New York, 1909), *The World of H. G. Wells* (New York, 1915), *Three Essays on America* (New York, 1934), *The Flowering of New England 1815–1915* (New York, 1952), *The Writer in America* (New York, 1955); Arthur Hobson Quinn, ed. *The Literature of the American People: An Historical and Critical Survey* (New York, 1951); Robert E. Spiller et al., *Literary History of the United States*, 2 vols., 3d rev. ed. (New York, 1963) and also *The Cycle of American Literature* (New York, 1955).

5. Howard Mumford Jones, *The Theory of American Literature* (Ithaca, 1948), p. 176.

6. Bernard de Voto, "Interrelations of History and Literature," *Approaches to American Social History*, ed. William E. Lingelbach (New York, London, 1937).

7. Joseph Wood Krutch, "The Drama and Society," *Comedy and Conscience after the Restoration* (New York, 1924), pp. 24–47; and *Experience and Art* (New York, 1932), p. 193–222.

8. David Daiches, *Literature and Society* (London, 1938); "Fiction and Civilization," *The Novel and the Modern World* (Chicago, 1939); "The Scope of Sociological Criticism," *Epoch* 3 (Summer 1950): 57–64.

9. *Accent* 6 (Spring 1946): 159–68.

10. James T. Farrell, "Some Observations on Literature and Sociology," *Reflections at Fifty and Other Essays* (New York, 1954), pp. 180–87.

11. Adolph S. Tomars, "Some Problems in the Sociologist's Use of Anthropology," *American Sociological Review* 8 (December 1943): 625–34; and "Sociology and Interdisciplinary Developments," *Modern Sociological Theory*, ed. H. Becker and A. Boskoff (New York, 1957), pp. 501–27.

12. Adolph S. Tomars, *Introduction to the Sociology of Art* (Mexico City, 1940).

13. Paul Honigsheim, "Soziologie der Kunst, Musik und Literatur," *Die Lehre von der Gesellschaft*, ed. Gottfried Eisermann (Stuttgart, 1958), pp. 338–73.

14. Hugh Dalziel Duncan, *Language and Literature in Society* (New York, 1961).

15. Alexander C. Kern, "The Sociology of Knowledge in the Study of Literature," *Sewanee Review* 50 (1942): 505–14.

16. Karl Mannheim, *Ideology and Utopia: An Introduction to the Sociology of Knowledge* (New York, 1936).

17. Vytautas Kavolis, *Artistic Expression: A Sociological Analysis* (Ithaca, 1968).

18. Paul Ramsay, "Society and Poetry" in *Encyclopedia of Poetry and Poetics*, ed. Alex Preminger (Princeton, 1965), pp. 775–79. See also Pitrim A. Sorokin, *Social and Cultural Dynamics*, vol. 1: *Fluctuation of Forms and Art* (New York, 1937), pp. 3–54.

19. Cecil M. Bowra, *Poetry and Politics 1900–1960* (Cambridge, Mass., 1966), esp. p. 95.

20. John Loftis, *Comedy and Society from Congreve to Fielding* (Stanford, 1959).

21. Arno Schirokauer, *Germanistische Studien*, ausgewählt und eingeleitet von Fritz Strich (Hamburg, 1957), pp. 150–68.

22. Cf. the general tenor of selections in *The Theory of the Novel*, ed. Philip Stevick (New York, 1967). For a summary of this approach see Diana Spearman, *The Novel and Society* (New York, 1966), pp. 17–60.

23. Cf. Arnold Hirsch, *Bürgertum und Barock im deutschen Roman* (Cologne, Graz, 1957).
24. Harry Levin, "Toward a Sociology of the Novel," *Journal of the History of Ideas* 26 (1965): 153.
25. Ibid., p. 152.
26. Geoffrey Wagner, "Sociology and Fiction," *The Twentieth Century* 167, no. 996 (February 1960): 108.
27. Philip Rahv, "Fiction and the Criticism of Fiction," *The Myth and the Powerhouse* (New York, 1956).
28. W. J. Harvey, *Character and the Novel* (Ithaca, 1965).
29. Alan Friedman, "The Stream of Conscience as a Form in Fiction," *Hudson Review* 17 (1965): 537–46; John Henry Raleigh, "The English Novel and the Three Kinds of Time," *Sewanee Review* 62 (1954): 428–40.
30. Steven Marcus, "The Novel Again," *Partisan Review*, 29 (1962), 171–95.
31. Diana Spearman, *The Novel and Society* (New York, 1966).
32. Richard T. LaPierre: *Sociology* (New York and London, 1946), p. 333.

LIST OF CONTRIBUTORS

BRANG, PETER

Born: May 23, 1924, in Frankfurt-am-Main.

Education: University of Frankfurt a. M., Marburg. Ph.D., 1952.

Present Position: Professor of Slavonic philology, University of Zürich.

Books: *Puskin und Krjukov. Zur Entstehungsgeschichte der "Kapitanskaja docka"; Studien zu Theorie und Praxis der russischen Erzählung (1770–1881).* Wiesbaden, 1960.

Editor: *Festschrift für Margaret Woltner zum 70. Geburtstag am 4. Dez. 1967.* Heidelberg, 1967.

BRUFORD, WALTER H.

Born: 1894 in Manchester, England.

Educated: St. John's College, Cambridge, England. University of Zurich. B.A. Cambridge, 1915. M.A. Cambridge. Hon. LL.D. Aberdeen, 1958. Hon. D. Litt. Newcastle, 1969.

Present Position: Professor Emeritus of German, St. John's College, Cambridge.

Books: Coauthor with Joseph H. Findlay. *Sound and Symbol: A scheme of instruction, introductory to school courses in modern languages and shorthand.* Manchester, 1917; *Germany in the Eighteenth Century. The social background of the literary revival.* London, 1935; *Die gesellschaftlichen Grundlagen der Goethezeit.* Trans. Fritz Woltken. Weimar, 1936; *Chekov and his Russia. A Sociological Study.* London, 1948; *Theatre, Drama and Audience in Goethe's Germany.* London, 1950; *Literary Interpretation in Germany.* London, 1952; *Anton Chekov.* New Haven, Conn., 1957; *Culture and Society in Classical Weimar 1775–1806.* London, 1962; *Deutsche Kultur der Goethezeit.* Konstanz, 1965.

Editor: *Faust Parts I and II.* In the Sir Theodore Martin translation. Introduced, revised and annotated by W. H. Bruford. London, New York, 1954.

FÜGEN, HANS NORBERT

Born: Mainz, 1925.

Education: University of Mainz, Ph.D. 1962.

Present Position: Privatdozent at the Institut für Soziologie und Ethnologie at the University of Heidelberg.

Books: *Die Hauptrichtungen der Literatursoziologie und ihre Methoden. Ein Beitrag zur literatursoziologischen Theorie.* Bonn, 1964. *Wege der Literatursoziologie,* hrsg. von Hans Norbert Fügen. Darmstadt und Neuwied, 1968; *Dichtung in der bürgerlichen Gesellschaft.* Bonn, 1972.

GOLDBERG, MAXWELL H.

Born: Malden, Mass., October 22, 1907.

Education: B.S. University of Massachusetts, 1928. A.M. Yale, 1932. Ph.D. Yale, 1933.

Present Position: A.J.R. Helmus Distinguished Professor of Humanties and Literatures, Converse College, Spartanburg, South Carolina.

Books: *Meaning and Metaphor.* Brookline, Mass., 1965; *Magnanimity in Motley.* Washington, D.C., 1966; *Design in Liberal Learning.* San Francisco, Washington, and London, 1971; *Thomas Carlyle's Relationships to the "Edinburgh Review."* Ann Arbor, Michigan, University Microfilms, 1972; *Cybernation, Systems and the Teaching of English: The Dilemma of Control.* Urbana, Ill., 1972.

Editor: *Blindness Research, the Expanding Frontiers: A Liberal Studies Perspective.* University Park, Pa., 1969; *Needles, Burrs and Bibliographies.* University Park, Pa., 1969.

KAVOLIS, VYTAUTAS

Born: September 8, 1930.

Education: B.A. Wisconsin, 1952. M.A. Harvard, 1956. Ph.D. Harvard, 1960.

Present Position: Chairman, Department of Sociology and Anthropology, Dickinson College.

Books: *Žmogaus genezé: Psichologiné Vinco Kudirkos studija.* Chicago, 1963; *Artistic Expression—A Sociological Analysis.* Ithaca, N.Y., 1968. Swedish translation: *Vad konsten speglart: En konstsociologisk analys.* Stockholm, 1970. Spanish translation forthcoming; *Nužemintuju generacija: Egzilio pasaulejautos eskizai.* Chicago, 1968; *History on Art's Side: Social Dynamics in Artistic Effloresceces.* Ithaca, N.Y., 1972.

Editor: *Lietuviškasis liberalizmas.* Chicago, 1959. *Comparative Perspectives on Social Problems.* Boston, 1969.

LEVIN, HARRY

Born: July 18, 1912 in Minneapolis.

Education: A.B. Harvard, 1933. University of Paris, 1934. Litt. D. Syracuse University, 1954. LL.D. (hon.) St. Andrews, 1962. L.H.D. (hon.) Union College, 1968. L.H.D. (hon) Clarkson College, 1970.

Present Position: Chairman, Department of Comparative Literature, Harvard University.

Books: *The Broken Column. A Study in Romantic Hellenism.* Cambridge, Mass., 1931; *James Joyce. A critical introduction.* Norfolk, Conn., 1941; *Toward Stendhal; an essay: to which is appended an open letter by George Mayberry to the publisher of the Modern Library.* (Pharos No. 3) Norfolk, Conn., 1945; *The Overreacher. A study of Christopher Marlowe.* London, 1954; *Symbolism and Fiction.* Charlottesville, Va., 1956; *The Power of Blackness; Hawthorne, Poe, Melville.* New York & London, 1958; *The Question of Hamlet.* London & New York, 1959; *Irving Babbit and the Teaching of Literature.* Cambridge, Mass., 1961; *The gates of horn; a study of 5 French realists.* London & New York, 1963; *Countercurrents in the study of English.* Vancouver, 1966; *Refractions; essays in Comparative Literature.* London & New York, 1968; *Why literary criticism is not an exact science.* Cambridge, Mass., 1968; *The Myth of the Golden Age in Renaissance France.* Bloomington, Ind., 1969; *Grounds for Comparison.* Cambridge, Mass., 1972; *Veins of Humor.* Cambridge, Mass., 1972.

Editor: *Selected Works of Ben Jonson.* With an introduction. New York, 1938, London, 1939; *A Satire against Mankind and other Poems by John Wilmot, Earl of Rochester.* Norfolk, Conn., 1942; *The Portable James Joyce.* With an introduction and notes by Harry Levin. New York, 1945; *The Essential James Joyce.* With an introduction and notes by Harry Levin. London, 1948; *Perspectives of Criticism* by Walter Jackson Bate et al. Cambridge, Mass., 1950; *Shakespeare's "Coriolanus."* London, 1950; *Nathaniel Hawthorne's "Scarlet Letter."* With an introduction and notes. Boston, 1960; *Shakespeare's "Comedy of Errors."* New York, 1965; Daniel, Aaron, and Levin. *Edward Bellamy, Novelist and Reformer.* Schenectady, N.Y., 1968; Harry Levin and Joanna P. Williams. *Basic Studies on Reading.* New York, 1971.

MÜHLMANN, WILHELM EMIL

Born: Düsseldorf, October 1, 1904.

Education: University studies in anthropology, ethnology and sociology, Ph.D.

Present Position: Professor and Director of Institut für Sozioloige und Ethnologie at the University of Heidelberg.

Books: *Staatsbildung u. Amphiktyonien in Polynesien. Studie zur Ethnol. u. polit. Soziol.* Stuttgart, 1938; *Methodik d. Völkerkunde.* Stuttgart, 1938; *Krieg u. Frieden. Leitf. der pol. Ethnol. mit Berücks. völkerkundl. u. geschichtlichen*

Stoffes. Heidelberg, 1940; Coauthor with Karl Christian v. Loesch. *Die Völker und Rassen Südosteuropas*. m. e. Reisebericht v. Gust. Adolf Küppers. Berlin, Amsterdam, Prag, Vienna, 1943; *Der heutige Bestand der Naturvölker*. Heidelberg, Berlin, Magdeburg, 1943; *Assimilation, Umvolkung, Volkwerdg. Ein globaler, Uberblick u. e. Programm*. Stuttgart, Prag, 1943; *Geschichte der Anthropologie*. Bonn, 1948; *Mahatma Gandhi. Der Mann, sein Werk u. seine Wirkung. Eine Untersuchung zur Religionsoziologie u. polit. Ethik*. Tübingen, 1950; *Arioi und Mamaia. Eine ethnolog. religionsoziolog. u. histor. Studie über polynesische Kultbünde*. Wiesbaden, 1955; *Chiliasmus und Nativismus; Studien zur Psychologie, Soziologie und historischen Kasuistik der Umsturzbewungen*. Berlin, 1961; *Homo creator. Abhandlungen zur Soziologie, Anthropologie und Ethnologie*. Wiesbaden, 1962; *Rassen, Ethnien, Kulturen, Moderne Ethnologie*. Darmstadt und Neuwied, 1964; *Max Weber und die rationale Soziologie*. Tübingen, 1966; Coauthor with R. J. Llaryora, *Klientschaft, Klientel und Klientelsystem in einer sizilianischen Agro-Stadt*. Tübingen, 1968.

Editor: Coeditor with Ernst W. Muller, *Kultur anthropologie*. Köln, Berlin, 1966.

RAMSEY, PAUL

Born: November 26, 1924 in Atlanta, Georgia.

Education: Universities of Chattanooga, North Carolina and Minnesota. Ph.D. University of Minnesota, 1956.

Present Position: Poet-in-Residence, Alumni Distinguished Service Professor, University of Tennessee, Chattanooga.

Books: *The Lively and the Just: An Argument for Propriety*. Tuscaloosa, 1965; *Triptych*, Stockton, 1964; *In an Ordinary Place*. Raleigh, 1965; *A Window for New York*. San Francisco, 1968; *The Doors*. Tennessee, 1968; *The Art of John Dryden*. Lexington, 1969.

RUDNICK, HANS H.

Born: November 1, 1935 in Belgard, Germany.

Education: B.A. Kaiser-Karl-Schule, 1957. Ph.D. University of Freiburg, Germany, 1966.

Present Position: Assistant Professor of English, Southern Illinois University, Carbondale.

Books: *Das Verhältnis von logischer und aesthetischer Sprachform bei den "New Critics" und das Problem der literarischen Wertung*. Freiburg, 1966; *Two Planets*, by Kurd Lasswitz, translated from the German into English by Hans H. Rudnick, epilog by Wernher von Braun, afterword by Mark Hillegas, Carbondale, 1971.

Editor: *Erläuterungen und Dokumente zu Shakespeares Hamlet*, critical commentary of the text, with a history of the sources, and critical voices from Goethe to Jan Kott, Stuttgart, 1972.

SAMMONS, JEFFREY L.

Born: Cleveland, November 9, 1936.

Education: B.A. Yale, 1958. Ph.D. Yale, 1962.

Present Position: Chairman, Department of Germanic Languages and Literatures, Yale.

Books: *The Nachtwachen von Bonaventura. A Structural Interpretation.* The Hague, 1965; *Angelus Silesius.* New York, 1967; *Heinrich Heine, the Elusive Poet.* (YGS 3). New Haven, 1969.

Editor: With Ernst Schürer, *Lebendige Form. Interpretationen zur deutschen Literatur. Festschrift für H. E. K. Henel.* Munich, 1970.

SILBERMANN, ALPHONS

Born: August 11, 1909, in Köln.

Education: University of Köln, Freiburg/Br., Grenoble. Musikhochschule Köln.

Present Position: Professor and Director of the Forschungsinstitut für Massenkommunikation, University of Köln.

Books: . . . *of Musical Things.* Sydney, 1949; *La musique, la radio et l'auditeur. Étude sociologique.* Paris, 1954; *Wovon lebt die Musik? Die Prinzipien der Musiksoziologie.* Regensburg, 1957; *Musik, Rundfunk und Hörer, (La musique, la radio et l'auditeur).* Die soziolog. Askpekte der Musik am Rundfunk. Köln u. Opladen, 1959; *Das imaginäre Tagebuch des Herrn Jacques Offenbach.* Berlin, Wiesbaden, 1960; *The Sociology of Music.* Trans. from the German by Corbet Stewart. London, 1963; *Vom Wohnen der Deutschen. Eine soziolog. Studie uber d. Wohnerlebnis.* Köln u. Opladen Düsseldorf, 1963. (Fischer Bucherei, 1966); Coauthor with René König, *Der unversorgte selbständige Künstler. Über d. wirtschaftl. u. soziale Lage d. selbstständigen Künstler in der Bundesrepublik.* Hrsg. von d. Stiftung z. Förderung d. wissenschaftl. Forschung uber Wesen u. Bedeutung d. Freien Bühne. Köln, Berlin, 1964; *Ketzereien eines Soziologen. Kritische Äusserungen zu Fragen unserer Zeit,* Düsseldorf, 1965; *Bildschirm und Wirklichkeit. Über Presse und Fernsehen in Gegenwart und Zukunft.* (Mitw. v. Abraham Moles, Gerold Ungeheuer.) Frankfurt am Main, 1966; *Vorteile und Nachteile des kommerziellen Fernsehens. Eine soziologische Studie.* Düsseldorf, 1968. Coauthor with Ernest Zahn, *Die Konzentration der Massen-medien und ihre Wirkungen. Wirtschafts- und kommunikations-soziologische Studien.* Düsseldorf, 1969.

Editor: *Militanter Humanismus. Von den Aufgaben der modernen Soziologie.* Frankfurt aM., 1966.

ŠKREB, ZDENKO

Born: September 21, 1904.

Education: University of Zagreb

Present Position: Chairman of Department of German, University of Zagreb, Yugoslavia.

Books: *Znacenje igre rejecima (Die Bedeutung des Wortspiels)*. Zagreb, 1949. Coauthor with Aleksandar Flaker: *Stile und Epochen*. Zagreb, 1964.

Editor: *Uvod u književnost (Einführung in die Literaturwissenschaft)*. Zagreb, 1961; *The Art of the Word*. Zagreb, 1969.

Translator: Walzel, *Die deutsche Romantik*, 1944; Keller, *Die Leute von Seldwyla*, 1949; Eckermann, *Gespräche mit Goethe, Auswahl*, 1949; Goethe, *Dichtung und Wahrheit*, 1950.

TOBER, KARL

Born: 1928 at Desselbrunn, Austria.

Education: University of Innsbruck, Ph.D. 1952.

Present Position: Head of the Department of Germanic Studies, University of Witwatersrand, South Africa.

Books: *The meaning and purpose of literary criticism*. Johannesburg, 1965; *Urteile und Vorurteile über Literatur*. Stuttgart, Munich, 1970.

INDEX OF NAMES

Vigée, Claude, 54
Vittorini, Elio, 173
Voronsky, 221, 225, 244, 246, 247, 249
Vossler, Karl, 205
Voto, Bernhard de, 271, 280
Voznesensky, A., 225, 236, 247

Waddington, C. H., 60, 80
Wagner, Geoffrey, 281
Walker, Jimmy, 107, 108
Wallenstein, 47
Walpole, Sir Robert, 276
Walther von der Vogelweide, 46, 49, 52
Warburg, Jeremy, 85
Ward, Jack, 73
Warren, Austin, ix, 8, 141, 171
Watson, George, 7, 19
Watson, James D., 86
Watt, Ian, 276
Webber, Andrew Lloyd, 64
Weber, Brown, 86
Weber, Max, 140, 143, 144, 171
Weber, Ronald, 54
Webster, Daniel, 83
Weckherlin, Georg Rudolf, 43
Wehrli, Max, 248
Weidlé, Wladimir, 48
Weinheber, Josef, 47, 54
Weinrich, Harald, 269
Wellek, René, vii, ix, 8, 31, 141, 171
Wendell, Barrett, 271, 280
Werner, Zacharias, 154
Weyle, Heline, 81

Whipple, T. K., 271, 279
Whitman, Walt, 67
Wiedemann, C., 267
Wiegand, Julius, 197
Wieland, Christoph Martin, 130
Wiener, Norbert, 64, 83
White, D. M., 193
Wiese, Benno Von, 154
Wilhelm II, emperor of Germany, 50
Williams, William Carlos, 67, 74, 85
Wilson, Edmund, 7
Wiskari, Werner, 86
Wolf, K. M., 193
Wolfe, Tom, 65, 83
Wolkenstein, Oswald von, 52
Woolsey, John M., 109
Wordsworth, William, 35, 85

Yakubos'ky, B., 225, 247
Yamada, K., 194
Yeaton, Kelly, 68

Zäch, Alfred, 54
Zacharias, Ernst-Ludwig, 19, 269
Zeitlin, A., 216, 219, 225, 227, 246, 247
Zeller, Hans, 54
Zelter, Karl Friedrich, 128
Zhirmunsky, Victor, 216, 225, 228
Ziv, O., 240
Žmegač, Viktor, 269
Zola, Emile, 171
Zolotarev, S., 246
Zonin, A., 219